ETHNOGRAPHY

A Way of Seeing

A way of seeing is always a way of not seeing.

—Kenneth Burke
Permanence and Change, p. 70

ETHNOGRAPHY

A Way of Seeing

Harry F. Wolcott

ALTAMIRA
P R E S S

A Division of
ROWMAN & LITTLEFIELD PUBLISHERS, INC.
Lanham • New York • Toronto • Oxford

ALTAMIRA PRESS
A division of Rowman & Littlefield Publishers, Inc.
4501 Forbes Boulevard, Suite 200
Lanham, MD 20706

PO Box 317
Oxford
OX2 9RU, UK

British Library Cataloguing in Publication Information Available

Library of Congress Cataloging-in-Publication Data

Wolcott, Harry F., 1929–
    Ethnography : a way of seeing / Harry F. Wolcott.
        p. cm.
    Includes bibliographical references and index
    ISBN 0-7619-9090-9 (alk. paper)
    ISBN 0-7619-9091-7 (alk. paper)
    1. Ethnology—Methodology. 2. Ethnology—Fieldwork. I. Title.
GN345.W62 1999
301'.01—dc21   99-6260
                                                                                CIP

Printed in the United States of America

⊖™ The paper used in this publication meets the minimum requirements of American
National Standard for Information Sciences—Permanence of Paper for Printed Library
Materials, ANSI/NISO Z39.48–1992.

Cover Design by Joanna Ebenstein

Contents

PART ONE: INTRODUCTION

CHAPTER ONE

Ethnography in the Good Old Days

A meeting of teachers from Oxford, Cambridge and London was held to discuss the terminology of our subject. We agreed to use "ethnography" as the term for descriptive accounts of non-literate peoples. . . . The comparative study of the institutions of primitive societies was accepted as the task of social anthropology, and this name was preferred to "sociology."

—A. R. Radcliffe-Brown
"Letters to the Editor," *American Anthropologist,* 1952

Imagine a group of ethnographers meeting today and agreeing on *anything,* let alone a definition limiting ethnography to "descriptive accounts of non-literate peoples." Surely that must have been in the "good old days" so often mentioned, so selectively recalled. Even at that, Radcliffe-Brown's recollection in 1952 of an event that had transpired some 43 years earlier makes no mention of whether the agreed-upon definition of ethnography as "the term for descriptive accounts of non-literate peoples" was all that acceptable, even among his British colleagues.

On this side of the Atlantic, the "tasks" of ethnography and social anthropology were not regarded as separate facets for anthropological pursuit. The wide-ranging interests of scholars in the U.S. were adequately accommodated under the rubric of a "cultural anthropology" that invited attention both to the ethnographies of particular groups and to a concern for universal laws governing human behavior. As far as the Americans were concerned, the preoccupation with social anthropology in general, and kinship and social structure in particular, raised nagging questions as to whether British anthropologists were concerned with "culture" at all.

That accusation, that British social anthropologists were not concerned with "culture," was what had prompted Radcliffe-Brown to write his letter published in *American Anthropologist* under the heading "Historical Note on British Social Anthropology" (Radcliffe-Brown 1952). The letter also afforded him the opportunity to remind an essentially American readership that "British Social Anthropology" reflected a distinction that Franz Boas—often referred to as the father of American anthropology—had made as early as 1888 between the two major tasks of anthropology. The British system distinguished between a first task, reconstructing the history of particular peoples (which the British customarily refer to as "ethnology"), and a second one, discerning laws of general applicability derived from comparative studies. "In America," Radcliffe-Brown observed, "this distinction between two branches of anthropology was not recognized, with the result that American anthropologists find the British system puzzling" (p. 276). Such puzzlement notwithstanding, he suggested that "when American anthropologists write about British anthropology, they should recognize the fact that this is the British system" (p. 276). To insist that British social anthropologists do not concern themselves with culture, he pointed out, "sounds more than a little strange as applied to Malinowski, who defined his own theories as entirely concerned with culture" (p. 277).

Through the years, differences as to the proper definitions of terms within their discipline, as well as to the purposes of anthropology itself, have been the subject of endless debate among anthropologists on both sides of the Atlantic. And while anthropologists concerned themselves with defining it, ethnography found its way into the public domain to become a matter of general interest in many fields formerly dominated by methodologists preoccupied with rigorous research design and carefully meted treatments.

Recent concerns generated by the postmodern critique as to the future of anthropology, including prospects for ethnography, need to be viewed in a context of insider argumentation about virtually every aspect of the discipline. What is anthropology's proper place among the social sciences? Or should that read "among the humanities" instead? Are its subfields really compatible; do primatologists, archaeologists, and anthropological linguists have that much to say to each other? Or have they been thrown together in American universities (both figuratively and literally) for the sake of argument, to keep department members at odds divvying up diminishing resources allocated for dwindling enrollments? Perhaps anthropology is indeed the "science of leftovers," as some have posited. If so, is ethnography of importance to each of its subfields, or is it essentially the field arm of only one?

Looking more internationally, how many "anthropologies" are there, and how are differences reflected in ethnographic practice? American, British, French, yes, but what of the anthropologies of other nations: Brazil, Indonesia, Japan? How many subfields are there within anthropology; could we ever reach international agreement on that? How removed should anthropologists be from the peoples or projects that engage them? For example, should Japanese anthropologists conduct their studies in Japan, or should they be working in Brazil conducting the inquiries that Brazilian anthropologists are doing? Closer to home, should educators interested in pursuing ethnographic inquiries in schools be encouraged to study something called "school culture" or should they first conduct studies in settings less familiar, while aspiring medical anthropologists make their initial forays into elementary schools? Finally, is anthropology essentially a "reformer's science" as some insist, or should anthropologists accept that their mission and contribution is in trying to understand things as they are? How amazing to think that once upon a time in the good old days some good old boys from Oxford, Cambridge, and London could sit down and seemingly resolve a question once and for all.

My concern in this writing is with ethnography. The emphasis is on contemporary practice, its core traditions, and some of its many adaptations. Although the focus is on the present, looking more at how things are than how they got that way, no ethnographer dares ignore the past. I will note some important names and moments along the way, with particular attention to the recent past, the decades of my own experience. I draw heavily on that experience; I have not hesitated to write anecdotally, and I ask your indulgence, especially at the beginning of the next chapter and at the conclusion of the final one. But the account is not intended as a personal history. My primary purpose is to explain how ethnography "works" and, particularly, whether and how it might work for you. If you are especially interested in historical developments and the relationship between ethnography and the discipline of anthropology, you might want to consult the several engaging volumes in the History of Anthropology (HOA) series under the general editorship of George W. Stocking, Jr.

The definition agreed upon in 1909 and later recapitulated by Radcliffe-Brown, that ethnography henceforth shall refer to "descriptive accounts of non-literate peoples," can serve as our starting place. So, too, do the circumstances that saw British anthropologists continuing a tradition that distinguished between the ethnographer reporting about a specific group and the social anthropologist pondering the same material in search of broad cultural universals. That division was virtually inevitable in the British setting, given Radcliffe-Brown's important observation that "the early social anthropologists did not themselves carry out ethnographic studies" (p. 276). Today we refer somewhat deprecatingly to those early social anthropologists as "armchair anthropologists," oblivious to the fact that ethnographic accounts arise not from the facts accumulated during fieldwork but from ruminating about the meanings to be derived from the experience. It is only the armchairs themselves that have been surrendered—they keep us too far away from the computer keyboard.

The big shift for British anthropology came with the recognition (which Radcliffe-Brown attributes to A. C. Haddon in his letter) that social anthropology should be "based on systematic field studies carried out by trained anthropologists using scientific methods of observation" (pp. 276–277). Such thinking not only marked the end of an era for the armchair types, it signaled in England what Radcliffe-Brown called "a new kind of ethnography, in which the field worker did not confine himself to simple description but sought to include in his account some sort of theoretical analysis" (p. 277).

That shift may have marked the first of the "new ethnographies." It was certainly not the last. Scholars around the world have been busy inventing and reinventing anthropology—and ethnography—ever since. I suspect that Radcliffe-Brown was already engaging in a bit of revisionist history in employing the term "non-literate" in reference to the subjects of early ethnographic investigation. By 1952 not only had the scope of ethnographic inquiry expanded, but terms like "primitive" and "savage," or phrases like "lower culture" and "rude culture" that once dramatized anthropological concern with The Other, were no longer in vogue. Anthropologists, American anthropologists in particular, certainly did not confine their studies to non-literate populations, although they had not yet become accustomed to the idea that the people they were writing about might be both able and interested to read what was said of them.

Ethnographers today pop up everywhere, studying not only all kinds of people but all kinds of topics. Nevertheless, that original preoccupation with The Other has played an important role in defining what ethnography is about, or at least fanning the embers of internal arguments as to what it *should* be about. That central question will be explored here in terms of what has become a pressing issue that would have been unthinkable in an earlier day: Can one do ethnography among one's own people, among a group in which one already plays other roles, and perhaps even do ethnography "on" oneself? I offer what insight I can on such issues. I trust that you will be able to distinguish fact from opinion.

I have not been any more hesitant about offering advice than I have been about proffering opinion. I assume that anyone drawn to a book with ethnography in its title is in some way already engaged with the topic intellectually, and perhaps planning or considering an ethnographic inquiry. If, as a result of your reading, you gain a firmer basis for making a decision, we have both made a good investment, even if you decide that ethnography is not for you. Should you decide to proceed, and my warnings and advice seem helpful, so much the better. On important points or issues, I have endeavored to include references to the work of others, by no means restricting citations to those who agree with me. There are numerous citations to my own writing as well, both to substantive pieces from my ethnographic studies and to discussions of method. (References to my work are abbreviated "HFW." Too late in my career did I realize the advantages of the hyphenated surname: how much more impressive my pronouncements might appear had I arranged to become H. Fletcher-Wolcott. As I explain later, I did become a hyphenated anthropologist, but it was my academic specialization, rather than my patronym, that took the hyphen.)

In contrast to earlier writing in which I have addressed broader interests in qualitative research (HFW 1990, 1994, 1995), I focus almost exclusively on ethnography here. However, I have not written with only anthropologists in mind. As a matter of fact, there is a lingering tradition among them that holds that the neophyte is supposed to intuit all this during fieldwork rather than become concerned prematurely with how one actually goes about it. Nor do I imagine that I have said much that is new or startling to experienced ethnographers, except on points with which we differ. I have written for anyone interested in learning about ethnography, regardless of academic allegiance, previous training, the arena in which it might be applied, or whether there is necessarily going to be any application at all.

The perspective is that of a researcher admittedly enthusiastic about ethnography and concerned with maintaining its integrity as a clearly identifiable research approach. Ethnography will *not* be treated here as a synonym for several other closely related approaches that also assume the presence of a researcher. A critical distinction will be observed between employing a set of research procedures that ethnographers share in common with many other fieldworkers—with an emphasis on data-gathering techniques—and employing those approaches with the intent of producing a full-blown ethnography. In practice, however, such a distinction is a matter of degree; the boundaries are not well defined.

If you have a researchable topic in mind and ethnography might be a reasonable way to approach it, this may be *a* right book for you, but it is not necessarily *the* right book. There is a fast-growing literature dealing with every aspect of qualitative research. Some contributors treat ethnography as a clearly identifiable genre within qualitative inquiry, others offer a qualitative broadside that includes mention of many fieldwork techniques without making any big deal out of ethnography per se. Here I do make a big deal out of ethnography. Even when I note some of the alternative outcomes that spring forth from closely related approaches, I present them in comparison with "traditional" ethnography. So brace yourself; this discussion might tell you more about ethnography than you ever wanted to know!

However, it may also tell you less, particularly if you have been following the postmodern critique and its "crisis of representation" that has sought to upbraid ethnographic authority and make literary form a central preoccupation in ethnographic discourse. To whatever extent that preoccupation has helped ethnographers become more sensitive to their roles as fieldworkers and more attentive to their writing, the consequences have no doubt been salutary. For many, however, postmodernism came to be regarded as something of a diversion that made the ethnographer so central that "I-witnessing" seemed about to dislodge "eye-witnessing." That wave has flattened out, and I make no attempt here to anticipate the next one. By its very nature as the study of ourselves (but, as I will argue, not of *ourself*), ethnography generates fascinating philosophical, ethical, and methodological dilemmas. It always has, and always will, provoke discussion and debate. There are those interested primarily in the *doing* of ethnography and others who seem to devote their energies worrying it to death. I have written with the former in mind, with an emphasis on how to go about it rather than addressing all the cautions as to why one should not. I have yet to be convinced that the extended rhetoric exerts a profound influence on what a lone researcher can accomplish through a research strategy characterized by one anthropologist simply as "deep hanging out" (Renato Rosaldo, quoted in Clifford 1997:188).

As you will discover, I lean heavily on the integrity of the ethnographer to figure out what he or she is up to, rather than admonishing everyone to work at devising grand theories or themes. That is the "other" task as Radcliffe-Brown and his colleagues defined it, the one they left to social anthropologists. Finally, after all these years, I understand the rationale for what had heretofore seemed the strange way the British originally divided up the work. I still prefer the American idea of an all-embracing cultural anthropology, but ethnography is the focus, and if the way I present it warrants the label of "old-fashioned" ethnography, I hope you will be satisfied to read about how things were, rather than how others feel they ought to be. Going back in my reading for this project, I was also reminded how much of what I felt was unique to my generation of ethnographers had already been worked out quite satisfactorily by those who were there before us, Radcliffe-Brown's narrow conception of ethnography notwithstanding. Anthropology is just young enough as a discipline, the aggregate number of anthropologists just manageable enough, that it is still possible to trace ideas through individuals, and our forebears were a formidable lot indeed. The same seems to be true for anthropologists who have ventured into other fields to introduce ethnography or to researchers in other fields who have embraced ethnography in order to enrich their own vision and the work of their colleagues.

You will surely come to the realization that you cannot learn enough about ethnography as *method* simply by reading. The problem is no longer with a dearth of materials, as was the case when I began pursuing formal doctoral studies. This book joins what has become a wide shelf of sources devoted specifically to ethnography. The impressive compendium edited by R. F. Ellen (1984) not only delivers on its title, *Ethnographic Research: A Guide to General Conduct,* but includes a 58-page bibliography of relevant materials published to 1983. Noteworthy recent additions are Michael Agar's *The Professional Stranger: An Informal Introduction to Ethnography* (now in a second edition, 1996), H. Russell Bernard's substantial contributions (1988, 1994b, 1998), and Roger Sanjek's *Fieldnotes: The Makings of Anthropology* (1990). Mine is not the first word, and most assuredly will not be the last, on an approach that currently enjoys broad scrutiny and constant reinterpretation and adaptation to new problems and settings.

What I have to offer is an understanding of how ethnography works as filtered through my own experience with it. If you are or are about to be involved in *doing* this kind of research, I encourage you to get on with it, to get some experience of your own. Not only will your involvement make a better reader of you, it will lead you to the inescapable conclusion that the making of an ethnographer is in the doing, not in reading about it. On the other hand, if you have done ethnographic research, you may begin to wonder whether you should have written a book like this yourself. If (or when) you do, I think that whatever problems you find with my way of going about it will become your problems. Anyone engaged in qualitative research develops an idiosyncratic style. We are drawn to certain kinds of settings and certain kinds of people in them, are guided by certain prior experiences and suppositions, work in specific historical time frames, and recognize different problems. Regardless of what anyone has experienced, nobody can anticipate for someone else exactly what advice and counsel to offer beyond a litany of clichés such as to "act natural," to remain inwardly skeptical, to maintain a tolerance for ambiguity, and never to confuse our limited human opportunities for and powers of observation with our infinite human capacity for inference.

The promise of ethnography is compromised by its ambition. There is no way we can totally capture the lifeway of another person or group of people, any more than we could ever satisfactorily convey to another all that constitutes our own persona. "Partial and incomplete" are marching orders of the day. One might think we would find comfort in such phrases—and to some extent perhaps we do—but they belie our efforts to be recognized as thorough researchers whose time-consuming, depth-probing approach should virtually guarantee that when we get around to reporting, we *do* know what we are talking about. Pretty much.

The role of ethnographer is equally elusive. There is no full-time role, there are no degrees offered in ethnography as an academic specialization, no licenses are granted for engaging in it, and there are no qualifying exams to pass in order to become board certified. Seminars, formal courses, or summer fieldwork training programs offer instruction and guided practice, but they cannot guarantee success. There is no substitute for "being there" and "doing it." Yet simply being there is not enough to guarantee results; if it were, we would all be doing ethnography all the time.

Neither do I intend to make a mystery of ethnography. All humans do what ethnographers do, only on a more modest scale and for personal rather than professional reasons. That idea can be turned around to state correctly that ethnographers *as ethnographers* do what everyone else does all the time. How is it, then, that their efforts result in ethnography? What do ethnographers do, or add, that is so special? My goal in initiating this writing was to track down ethnography's "essence." You must judge for yourself whether my search has proven satisfactory. Your assessment will have to take into account your own inclination as to whether ethnography needs to be defined more rigorously or made even more accessible to researchers of different persuasions. If you intend to pursue ethnography, you have a role of your own to play in determining the extent to which tomorrow's ethnography will resemble yesterday's.

Collectively, the chapters offer a kind of map of alternative routes and destinations, along with some advice about the journey, noting points of interest and side trips along the way. Chapter 2 does that quite literally, calling attention to the importance of "place" in recognizing that the purposes that guide ethnographic research have a context of their own. There is a remarkable correspondence between what ethnographers choose to study and where they happen to find themselves. That correspondence needs to be acknowledged rather than buried in high-sounding purposes put forward after the fact.

An analogy that I follow in organizing subsequent chapters is the familiar one of "ripples on a pond." At the epicenter I put ethnography in its most traditional form, as revealed in a few much-revered texts, classics that, as Adam Kuper points out, have gradually come to be taught *as classics* rather than as exemplars (1996:176). The figurative ripples radiate outward from the epicenter of traditional ethnography until hardly a trace of their ethnographic origins remains and they yield to the force of other traditions (biography, history, traditional sociology) or dwindle to less neatly categorized approaches such as participant observation research, observer studies, or case study research. There is no clear line to be drawn, but the emphasis here is on what makes a study discernibly ethnographic, with a bias toward its development in anthropology.

Method is part of it. Chapter 3 reviews some of the ways of doing research associated most closely with ethnography. However, a major presupposition here is that ethnography is more than method: it is a way of conceptualizing as well as a way of looking. That "way of seeing" is the focus of Chapter 4, and the chapters that follow are grounded in that supposition. Chapters 5, 6, and 7 examine some of the many forms that ethnography has taken as it has been adapted for circumstances markedly different from what once could be described so succinctly as "descriptive accounts of non-literate peoples." The chapters of Part Four examine ethnography in the bigger picture, beginning with problems inherent in a time-consuming research strategy for an impatient world.

Recognizing that not everyone shares my concern about maintaining ethnography as a separate and distinct form of inquiry, I devote a chapter (Chapter 9) to exploring the question, "Does it matter whether or not it's ethnography?" The purpose of that chapter is not to resolve the issue as if in formal debate, but to suggest how attending to those aspects of human social action to which ethnographers ordinarily attend has the potential to enhance the work of researchers of other orientations. I have endeavored to communicate that same message about employing research techniques. In short, a little ethnography is not a dangerous thing.

Although it appears as the next to last chapter rather than as the final one, Chapter 10 is the culminating chapter on ethnographic process, so if you are the type of reader who likes to do a bit of reconnaissance before you get started, you might want to look at that chapter first. Chapter 11, the final chapter, reviews some changes we are witnessing and examines ethnography from its personal dimensions. If you can be patient with a sometimes meandering style, then let me develop the ideas in the sequence set before you. If you are going to pursue ethnography, you may as well put yourself in a proper frame of mind; it need not drag on and on, but neither is it something to be done by anyone in a hurry.

CHAPTER TWO

Where in the World
Do You Think You Are Going?

First Ethnographer: Where are you going to do your fieldwork?
Second Ethnographer: I don't know yet.
First Ethnographer: What are you going to study?
Second Ethnographer: That depends on where I go.

At some point during the conversation between a group of anthropology students and their distinguished guest from overseas at a Berkeley restaurant in 1926, Radcliffe-Brown is reported to have leaned across the table and said to Lloyd Warner, "I say, Warner, how would you like to come to Australia with me?" He had to reassure the student that he was not joking: "No, no, I'm serious. If you are interested, let's get together and talk." They did and he did, and an anthropological career was born. From 1926 to 1929, Warner conducted the fieldwork that led to publication in 1937 of *A Black Civilization: A Social Study of an Australian Tribe* (the anecdote is reported in Mildred Warner 1988:1).

We are accustomed to hearing about research framed in terms of purposes, goals, objectives, theories, issues to be investigated, or problems to be addressed. Ethnographic research is often spoken of that way, but it is not necessarily *practiced* that way. As Clifford Geertz observes in *After the Fact* (1995), the usual question one addresses to an ethnographer is *"Where* are you going to do your fieldwork?" The answer is likely to be a location (e.g., "I'm working in Brazil") even if you happen to (mis)phrase your question to ask instead, "What are you going to study?" Reflecting on an earlier day when he was being inducted into the discipline, Geertz recalls that the neophyte anthropologist has always

had one thing going for him in keeping himself reasonably on course: the realization, immediately instilled in him (or—there were a few women—in her) and continuously reinforced, that he was going to have to do fieldwork. . . . The problem was where, and it filled our consciousness—at least it filled mine—almost all the time. [Geertz 1995:101]

There was a time when the problem of "where" filled my consciousness, too. Allow me to illustrate the impact of "place" in defining a career by recapping my own journey from that perspective rather than the more customary ones of time or purpose.

The Problem of *Where?*: A Personal Account

It is relatively easy toward the end of one's career to create a logic and flow to demonstrate how one thing led to another, how circumstances at one place set the stage for a seamless move to the next. With the wisdom of hindsight, it is tempting now to argue that my initial fieldwork among the Kwakiutl Indians of British Columbia, Canada, was not only a natural and obvious outcome of joining a commitment to education with my newly acquired perspective in cultural anthropology but also set in motion the logical chain of studies that followed: a school administrator in the Pacific Northwest, drawing upon the earlier cross-cultural experience with a village chief; African beer gardens in Bulawayo, Zimbabwe, to gain further cross-cultural experience by studying an urban institution quite different from schools; next, an educational innovation designed and implemented by a federally sponsored R & D (Research and Development) Center, drawing on experience overseas to provide a cross-cultural perspective for looking at a case closer to home; then a study of change efforts at the level of community development on the outskirts of Kuala Lumpur; and so on.

Yes, looking back, it all seems to make good sense. Or, putting it more candidly, the major pieces now firmly in place, I can make good sense of it: education across cultures, the culture of the school, the transmission (eventually refocused on the acquisition) of culture, processes of innovation and change. With a backward look at the topics investigated, I can construct the career history of a once-young man who always seemed to know exactly where he was headed, what he ought to study next.

I had rather conveniently forgotten that I, too, once faced the cold, hard fact that in order to validate my claim to anthropology, I was going to have to do fieldwork. Matter of fact, as a hyphenated anthropologist, an "educational" one who joined anthropology to a budding career as an educator (although the category educational-anthropologist did not exist at the time), it was as important for me to go to some dramatically different place as it was for my fellow students in "pure" anthropology. As Gupta and Ferguson suggest in their introduction to *Anthropological Locations,* there is a subtle "hierarchy of purity" of field sites; in short, "some places are much more 'anthropological' than others" (1997:13). As a former classroom teacher, simply stepping into someone else's classroom would never have been adequate to validate a claim to ethnography. My problem, like Clifford Geertz's a decade earlier, was not *whether* but *where?*

I had forgotten about the long period of worry that ensued after my mentor George Spindler first asked for my thoughts as to where I would do fieldwork or what general issue I might address. I had few leads and nothing that held promise for a study that would join my new interest in cultural anthropology, my formal Ph.D. minor at Stanford University, with my work as an educator. Then an unexpected opportunity manifested itself, matching the need for field sites among Spindler's new cohort of doctoral students with a critical need for experienced teachers at schools on Indian reserves in western Canada.

That link was provided by another of Spindler's students, Lyman Jampolsky, a Canadian educator who at the time was Director of Indian Education for the Indian Affairs Branch in Alberta. Jampolsky had taken a summer off in 1961 to study at Stanford. Later that year I motored north to visit a likely post and fieldwork site on an Indian reserve between Calgary and Edmonton, not too far from where the Spindlers had been conducting research among the Blood Indians for several summers. "What was our Trobriands, our Nuerland, our Tepoztlán to be?" asks Geertz (1995:101). Finally I had my answer: the Hobbema Reserve in Alberta. I was set.

Set, that is, until word arrived that Jampolsky had been transferred to British Columbia. The Hobbema school was now under someone else's jurisdiction. But all was not lost. Jampolsky relayed an encouraging message. He saw even greater opportunities for research in his new assignment, which included Indian schools in both BC and the Yukon Territory. And just-like-that, not only one but three career trajectories were set in motion. Because Lyman Jampolsky happened to attend Stanford in the summer of 1961, and happened to be transferred to Vancouver a few months later, three of Spindler's doctoral students at Stanford—Richard King, Ronald Rohner, and Harry Wolcott—found themselves heading north to begin fieldwork. That was in the late summer of 1962.

Accompanied by his wife, Lee, Richard King was assigned to the Indian Residential School at Carcross, Yukon Territory. His dissertation was subsequently revised for publication (King 1967) in the then-new Case Studies in Education and Culture series edited by George and Louise Spindler. From that time forward, King maintained a strong interest in Canadian Indian education, residential schools (toward which he developed a strong aversion) in particular. Eventually he relocated in Canada and taught at the University of Victoria, where he remained throughout his academic career, working especially with teachers interested in Indian education.

Ron Rohner coauthored a case study with his wife, Evelyn, based on ethnographic research conducted at Gilford Island, a Kwakiutl Reserve (see Rohner 1964; Rohner and Rohner 1970). His interest in culture change subsequently drew him back to Boas's earlier work among the Kwakiutl. He discovered that almost 700 pages of letters and diaries remained untranslated from their original German in the vast archive of Boas material held by the American Philosophical Society. Evelyn's mother, Dr. Hedy Parker, offered to do the translating, and Ron was off on a second ambitious project, one that resulted in a major historical contribution to Kwakiutl ethnography (Rohner 1969).

Separated from the Rohners by only four miles, but across what we felt at times was surely the widest, roughest river mouth in the world (Knight Inlet), I taught at "my" village school and pondered how one transformed the personal experience of being the teacher and only non-Indian resident of a tiny (13 households) isolated village into an ethnographic study. Under Spindler's influence and Ron's tutelage I gradually became an ethnographer; under Evelyn's influence Ron and I both became better writers; and under my influence (and somewhat to my dismay) Ron's first article dealt with the education of Indian children in "his" village.

I did not become a Northwest Coast specialist. Nevertheless, my fieldwork there validated my claim as ethnographer. I was offered a post-Ph.D. position on the basis of that claim, and I remained at one institution, the University of Oregon, for the balance of my academic career. Oregon's newly funded unit for educational R & D, the Center for the Advanced Study of Educational Administration, had recruited me in order to bring anthropology within its interdisciplinary mission and vision. On arrival, however, I was seconded to a senior sociologist investigating (through a paper-and-pencil questionnaire) community normative structures. It was two years before I could extricate myself from that project and propose something more anthropological. At that, my work had to be related to school administration, a field in which I held a master's degree and had intended to pursue a career, but not an academic specialization that held great intellectual appeal. I would have preferred to conduct an in-depth ethnography of schooling, perhaps making the teacher and pupils of one classroom my focus, but the Center's charter necessitated studies more immediately related to school administration. I translated my broader interest into a study focused around the day-to-day life of a school principal.

My first opportunity for a sabbatical leave some years later found me heading off to Zimbabwe (Rhodesia, at the time) where a former doctoral student from the university headed a missionary organization. He extended an invitation for me to spend the year in exchange for offering instruction in applied anthropology. I was intent on studying in what I assumed would be a perfect "laboratory" for looking at education cross-culturally. As it developed, the Ministry of Education was not at all anxious to turn an American social scientist loose in that setting. Repeated requests for permission to become anything more than a one-time visitor went unanswered. A chance tour through the local African townships, coupled with the sympathetic support of an administrator who originally had been trained as an anthropologist (Hugh Ashton), opened the way to a study of the municipally operated beer gardens that catered to the urban African (i.e., Black) population in Rhodesia's second city.

When I returned from sabbatical leave, I was out of sync with ongoing projects. I was assigned to contribute a descriptive account of an ambitious project attempting to adapt PPBS (a program planning and budgeting system) for use in schools. Both ethnography and PPBS were "in" at the time, although they made a strange pair. Capitalizing on the ethnographic tradition for long-term, intensive fieldwork, I turned a short-time assignment into an extended one. I was able to stick around long enough to watch the three-year demise of an educational innovation after a major three-year effort had been put forth at the R & D Center to build it up (HFW 1977).

I spent my next sabbatical leave in Kuala Lumpur, Malaysia, at the urging of a close friend who headed the international school there. His contacts included a Peace Corps official who put me in touch with a community development project that I was able to track for several months. It was fortuitous in both senses of the word to be able to compare the community development project with the development project at the R & D Center that I had been observing for the previous three years, but it was strictly chance that found me there. Whatever insights I gained had no immediate application in R & D, and the Center's federal funding appeared to be drying up. I turned to full-time teaching, rather than divide my time between teaching and research. There was little point to remain where the money wasn't, and I did not care to pursue research topics simply on the basis of what federal bureaucrats felt would be "interesting."

Six more years and another sabbatical. With planning and good luck I received a Fulbright award to spend a year in Thailand, which I was able to renew again a few years later. This award was designed to bring resource people to assist faculties at Thai universities in learning more about ethnography and other qualitative approaches in social research. I devoted my time to that goal. I did a bit of writing, but lacking fluency in Thai, I did not undertake any systematic effort beyond the experience of living in Thailand and finding my way about. That proved time- and energy-consuming enough, and it did provide another unexpected and much valued opportunity to "live" cultural differences.

"What if?" one can ask, looking back. What if Jampolsky had not been reassigned to British Columbia or had not happened to spend a summer at Stanford? What if Ron Rohner had gone elsewhere than among the people where Franz Boas conducted so much of his research? It seems far less likely that Ron would have become intrigued with Boas's research conducted more than half a century earlier had he not found himself doing fieldwork among the same people. And what if his mother-in-law had not been fluent in German and willing to engage in the huge task of translating handwritten correspondence?

What if I had not taken the position at the University of Oregon, a position that (eventually) allowed me to pursue interdisciplinary interests, drawing on an anthropological perspective by employing an ethnographic approach virtually unknown in educational research at the time? It is hardly surprising that anthropologists credit so much to serendipity. I wonder the extent to which they recognize "place" as a major player in what serendipity is all about.

My graduate student colleagues and I were fortunate indeed to have a mentor able to connect us with such ideal placements, for, like most ethnographically oriented doctoral students, we were in need of settings in which to conduct our initial fieldwork investigations. Although those were pre-funding days, and we were entirely self-supporting through our teaching assignments (Evelyn was the teacher at Gilford village, freeing that lucky Ron to devote all his time to research), those placements were dramatic interventions in our professional lives. Not until later did I realize how lucky I had been.

In Place of Place

I think it essential to recognize not only the importance of place in the evolution of ethnography but to recognize as well that until recently it did not matter where the place was *as long as it was dramatically different from one's own*. Such difference, rife with implicit contrast and the courageously anticipated strangeness and challenge to cope, was built into the choice of place without anyone having to ask. As Geertz notes, *where* became "a much more important question, actually, than what we would do (one could always think of something, so much was unstudied) when we got there" (1995:102).

Over time, that reputation for openness to inquiry, to set one's problem focus in the course of coming to know a field site, has remained one of the unique characteristics of ethnography. It is still OK to make a decision on the basis of *where* one will study, rather than having to specify exactly *what* one intends to study. But the expectation that the inquiry will be conducted among others exhibiting behaviors dramatically different from the researcher's has not been so rigorously observed, especially as researchers from other fields have taken ethnography unto themselves to conduct studies of their own colleagues and communities.

In place of place, the emphasis has been shifting to problem focus, theoretical links, and, most recently, to meeting the needs of clients who in earlier times might have been the subjects of study. The once-fashionable idea of the ethnographic broadside, scurrying to document fast-disappearing societies in what was known as salvage anthropology, has been replaced by smaller, more tightly focused, and seemingly more purposive studies easier to complete in a short time and far easier to defend before an institutional review board ritually "protecting" human subjects or a funding agency trying to get the biggest bang for its research buck.

During this long, slow, but apparently inevitable process of "coming home," ethnography lost its single most defining feature as the study of *others*, or at least of others who differed dramatically from the ethnographer. Such differences are implicated with a single term, but one confounded by its double meaning: *culture*. Culture refers to the various ways different groups go about their lives and to the belief systems associated with that behavior. But it has also been taken to suggest, and continues to do so more subtly today, a relative measure of how far any particular group had yet to climb to attain the cultural achievement (*Kultur*) characteristic of an advanced civilization (like our own) or people of refinement (i.e., the European bourgeoisie).

Adventurers and world travelers could make sojourns to Athens or Rome or Mayan ruins, along with the odd archaeologist or art historian, but the ethnographer traveled remote byways in search of "primitives" who might never before have seen a "civilized" person. These were more or less idealized objectives, of course. Not everyone sought such remoteness, but even today there is a certain appeal in finding a group that has had little contact with "the outside," and there is probably no better way to validate how deeply one has penetrated into a remote region than to be able to report that among a people visited no one (or at least no children) had ever before seen a person of another skin color.

In the absence of such high adventure, the extent of previous contact (missionaries, traders, explorers) was sometimes simply overlooked, so that, through the ethnographer's eyes, readers *felt* they were privy to a special occasion. Roger Sanjek faults Boas for reporting "a past from which one hundred years of Western contact was filtered out" (1990:196). Those old habits die hard. By selecting the word "resident" in referring earlier in this chapter to "my" village and my status in it, I suspect I am guilty of attempting to make the Kwakiutl village appear a tad more remote than it was. Such temptation probably grows out of an effort to emphasize the psychological remoteness I sometimes experienced, thereby adding to the inventory of hardships I endured. In fact, there were not only official White visitors to the school but occasional White visitors to village households. One of the village chief's daughters who frequently visited her parents had married a "White guy." Under Canadian law, her children were, therefore, legally "White," since Canada does not reckon Indian and non-Indian status in fractions as we do in the U.S. At the village, their grandfather, Henry Bell, found it amusing that the government could make a distinction among his grandchildren that categorized some of them as Indian, some White.

Of course, one did not absolutely have to undergo the hardship of life in the bush or on the ice. There were acceptable village studies and "little communities," with emphasis on *little* to denote a population no larger than what a lone ethnographer might come to know in the course of a year or so. I recall surprise the first time I saw the word "urban" in the title of a book about Africa purported to be anthropological; the idea of an "urban anthropology" struck me as an oxymoron. I wanted the communities and cultures that today's ethnographers study to exhibit the same neat boundaries that earlier ethnographers seemed able to discern. I failed to recognize that the boundaries were to a great extent put there by, and for the convenience of, the ethnographer.

None of this is to say that social scientists, including anthropologists, had no interest in problems at home. There were exceptions, but they were few enough that they could be taken to prove the rule, as with Lloyd Warner's multi-volume Yankee City series published in the 1940s, or Hortense Powdermaker's pioneering work in the Deep South initiated in 1932 (see Powdermaker 1939). In general, home turf belonged to others, sociologists in particular, and most work was done under the broad banner of "social research." What came to be known as Chicago School sociology evolved using essentially the same "live your way into a group" techniques at home that anthropologists followed in doing participant observation abroad, with the difference that in working at home and in one's own language, one can usually "go home" when the day's observations and interviews are completed.[1]

Furthermore, the anthropology/sociology distinction to which we have become accustomed has not always been important. At their home institutions, anthropologists and sociologists often were members of the same department (the latter typically in the majority), frequently taught each other's courses, and were sometimes joined by political scientists or historians as well. Working the local scene made a sociologist of everyone, and sociologists who conducted studies abroad could play their allegiance to anthropology up or down.

In some places, neither Americans nor anthropologists had (or have) distinguished themselves, and I discovered that in some parts of the world that to be *both* American and an anthropologist can put one at a decided disadvantage. I recall an instance in Rhodesia when, during the course of a seminar, I kept insisting that my American-born host, Professor Marshall Murphree, was speaking as an anthropologist, hardly a stretch for someone with an M.A. in cultural anthropology taken under Melville Herskovits and William Bascom at Northwestern and a Ph.D. in social anthropology taken under Isaac Schapera and Raymond Firth at the University of London. I thought he would be pleased, but he resisted my effort to assimilate him, explaining to those present, "Professor Wolcott calls himself an anthropologist, but he will soon be returning to his home in the States. I plan to continue my work here, and in this setting it is far preferable to be recognized as a sociologist." Until that moment, I had always been buoyed by an old joke that the difference between an anthropologist and a sociologist was that sociologists never go anywhere. I was reminded once again of the importance of attending to local meanings.

The mobility of ethnographers is by no means as random as it may seem, even to ethnographers themselves. The regions of the world in which the preponderance of their studies have been conducted have had their influence on the development of anthropology. British "social" anthropologists tended to go where the British Empire exerted its power and influence. That drew them largely to their own colonies, especially to British-dominated regions in sub-Saharan Africa and to India and Nepal. A central theme observed and reported in British anthropology is the attention devoted to social relationships, social systems, and social processes in those areas.

Beginning with Boas's own studies, American cultural anthropology evolved primarily through studies among native North American Indian (and Eskimo) groups, with an emphasis on cultural inventory, the diffusion of cultural traits, culture contact, and culture change. Similarly, other "national" anthropologies (what Fredrik Barth has referred to as the "smaller traditions" of anthropology in, for example, Scandinavia, France, India, or Latin America) have their preferred frameworks and customary places for carrying out research. The results of such efforts have, in turn, been influenced both by the groups where the research was conducted and by local expectations as to the contribution the anthropologist can make. Thus, where the anthropologist comes *from* has been an important factor both in selecting where the research will be conducted and what will be identified as appropriate for study once there.

I do not want to set this shift in emphasis from place to problem too far back in time, to make it appear as a fait accompli, or to treat it as unilateral. Historically, it was Margaret Mead on her first fieldwork expedition in 1925 who set out to do problem-focused ethnography, although, as was standard practice at the time, she went to the field with doctorate in hand, her dissertation completed as a "library study." Her purpose was to study whether or not adolescence invariably had to be the period of *Sturm und Drang* that it appeared to have become in American society. She concluded from her study *Coming of Age in Samoa* (Mead 1928) that it did not. It is "ironic," as Roger Sanjek writes, that Mead, "who so valued and indeed pioneered problem-oriented ethnography early in her career . . . turned against it in later years" (Sanjek 1990:225). As Sanjek notes, Mead came eventually to denigrate the very kind of testing and systematic data-gathering that defined her own work in Samoa (under the direction of Boas) and subsequently in Manus.

One can find a comparable shift in the career trajectories of others who continued to conduct ethnographic research throughout their professional lives. It is my impression that, if we take at their word everyone who labels their work as ethnographic, most people who do ethnography do one major study, based on one *major* period of extended fieldwork. Among those who continue to pursue ethnographic research I suspect one also would find instances of researchers who either went from broad ethnographic description to problem-oriented work or who began their careers studying a well-defined problem but gradually shifted their focus in pursuit of what Mead enthusiastically endorsed as "grasping as much of the whole as possible" (1970:250 ff., quoted in Sanjek 1990:225). In word if not in deed, Malinowski saw it no other way, for although later critics have commented on the narrow scope of his work—reporting essentially on only a single institution, the Kula exchange, as engaged in by one particular group among the Trobrianders—he clearly pictured himself as the Compleat Ethnographer:

> The whole area of tribal culture *in all its aspects* has to be gone over in research. The consistency, the law and order which obtain within each aspect make also for joining them into one coherent whole. An Ethnographer who sets out to study only religion, or only technology, or only social organisation cuts out an artificial field for inquiry, and he will be seriously handicapped in his work. [Malinowski 1922:11]

Malinowski was offering his fieldwork antidote to the armchair anthropology of the day when one could pick and choose from partial inventories of the world's more exotic societies to illustrate the strangeness of others.

The firm skeleton of the tribal life has to be first ascertained. This ideal imposes in the first place the fundamental obligation of giving a complete survey of the phenomena, and not of picking out the sensational, the singular, still less the funny and quaint. The time when we could tolerate accounts presenting us the native as a distorted, childish caricature of a human being are gone. [P. 11]

To study some group "in all its aspects" is not helpful advice. Both Malinowski and Mead have been criticized for their haphazard descriptiveness, and perhaps that is just as well, for they have taken the heat for the rest of us. There is no way any ethnographer can escape such an accusation, at least without risking the even more onerous one, that not enough detail has been provided. What Malinowski was urging on his followers was to study and report *in context*. No ethnographer wants or can ever be expected to take responsibility for providing the full and complete account of some group of people. Such a goal is unattainable. We do well to capture some of the relevant detail, and do even better when we can capture some of the more elusive spirit of those among whom we study. Most fieldworkers try to capture and to convey as much of the relevant scene as possible, but the wisest among them keep their public claims modest.

It seems doubtful that Malinowski ever imagined that ethnographers might someday turn from studying the tribal cultures of distant groups of "natives" to studying tribes whose natives are quite like ourselves. If it had occurred to him, he might have placed "tribal culture" in italics rather than emphasizing tribal culture *in all its aspects*. By mid-century, anthropologists frequently found themselves in more familiar settings. Sometimes this was a consequence of following "their people" as they moved from rural to urban centers, as with Oscar Lewis, whose original study in Tepoztlán (1951) evolved into *The Children of Sanchez* (1961) as he tracked the lives of a cohort studied initially in a rural Mexican village.

In spite of the gradual urbanization of ethnographic work, a preference lingered for conducting research in distant places and requiring both a lengthy time commitment and the ability to converse in the local language. Geertz notes two phrases heard in an earlier day suggestive of the pressure he and his fellow students felt to conduct their inquiries under circumstances that satisfied implicit norms as to where ethnography was properly accomplished:

Those days anyway, the ideal of alone among the unknown, what has been called the "my people" syndrome, was still very much alive, and there were depreciative murmurs to be heard about "gas station anthropology" and "meadow work rather than fieldwork." [Geertz 1995:102]

By accepting assignments to do their initial fieldwork in Indonesia, the Geertzes (Clifford and Hildred) embarked on dual careers without risk of being faulted for engaging in gas station anthropology. In other ways, however, they believed themselves to be at the vanguard of a new era in the evolution of anthropological study, bringing it into modern times by joining "a well-financed, multidisciplinary, long-term, team field project directed toward the study not of an isolated tribal culture but of a two-thousand-year-old civilization fully in the throes of revolutionary change" (1995:103). The project was to be a turning point:

> There was the idea that the time had come for anthropology to turn away from its nearly exclusive focus on "primitives" and begin to investigate large-scale societies directly in the stream of contemporary history. There was the idea that it should also turn away from intellectual isolation, cultural particularism, mindless empiricism, and the lone ranger approach to research and begin to work together with other, more conceptualized disciplines . . . in a big-push effort to construct a unified, generalizing science of society. [1995:103]

"That, of course," Geertz summarizes, "never happened, has still not happened, and in my opinion anyway, is no nearer to happening now than it was then" (p. 104). Today, almost half a century after the Geertzes were about to embark on their first fieldwork, I don't think we hold such high hopes for the social sciences or insist that anthropology join or spearhead an effort to construct a "unified, generalizing science of society." Certainly that is not the aim of this volume; for all that I will draw here *from* anthropology, I do not propose to point new directions for the discipline. Even in that, there is something to be learned about ethnography, for it is not well suited either to predict or to help determine the future.

Keeping Ethnography in Perspective

For the cultural anthropologist, ethnography has served as the bedrock of the discipline, at once the foundation upon which the rest of it has developed and a ballast so heavy as to keep anthropology from seeming to get anywhere. Those very elements that the "new" project was designed to overcome, a project the Geertzes were joining in the 1950s, remain today as shortcomings manifested in ethnography itself. Ethnography is ideally suited for studying small-scale, isolated, tribal cultures, and ethnographers have been known to go to great lengths to demonstrate the match between those criteria and the group they have chosen to study. Of necessity, the emphasis in ethnography is always on cultural particularism; as Geertz himself has observed, "The important thing about the anthropologist's findings is their complex specificness, their circumstantiality" (1973b:23). Mindless empiricism is only an overzealous effort at "thick description," the phrase Geertz borrowed from Gilbert Ryle and enshrined in his essay by that title. In that same essay he commended the Lone Ranger approach to research—known more euphemistically by the phrase "self-as-instrument"—for "the power of the scientific imagination to bring us into touch with the lives of strangers" (1973b:16).

This sometimes helter-skelter, place-dependent approach to problem finding creates problems of its own. For the development of their discipline and the future of cultural anthropology, anthropologists need to pay closer attention to assessing the contribution ethnography can make toward understanding the broad issues some of them now appear eager to tackle. Ethnography is no longer the only answer, the best answer, or necessarily any answer at all for addressing some of these issues. To illustrate, let me draw on a publisher's announcement that happened to cross my desk as I was first drafting this chapter. The announcement described publication of *The Anthropology of a Hydraulic Kingdom: Irrigation and State Formation in Hunza* (Sidky 1996). The flyer summarizes the study as "the evolution of political complexity and centralization in Hunza, a remote high-mountain kingdom in the western Karakoram mountains." It briefly outlines the author's argument linking the rise of the Hunza state in Pakistan and the earlier construction of a large-scale irrigation works, noting that he draws upon Wittfogel's "hydraulic hypothesis" in examining linkages among ecological conditions, hydraulic agriculture, and the emergent pattern of socioeconomic and political organization. The flyer calls the book to the attention of as broad a range of social scientists as the social scientists from whom it has drawn: "historians, anthropologists, cultural geographers and South Asian specialists."

To the budding researcher who does not know how to frame an ethnographic question, or lacks an adequate grasp of what ethnography can and *cannot* accomplish, initiating a full-scale ethnographic inquiry can be as serious a misstep as failing to do any ethnographic reconnaissance at all.[2] Without further knowledge of either the Hunza study or its author, one should reasonably be able to assume from the title and the conscious inclusion of "anthropology" within it that the author is familiar with the relevant ethnographic research and has spent time getting to know the territory as part of his preparation for this ambitious work. But I am willing to bet my bottom dollar that he did not set out to research so encompassing and esoteric a topic by searching for a household in which he could become a participant observer. There are important distinctions between ethnographic studies and "ethnographically informed" ones.

Given that some anthropologists today are drawn exclusively to macrocultural issues at state or national levels, at the time when researchers of other persuasions are now conducting small-scale ethnographic inquiries, my sense is that anthropologists are probably conducting less and less of all the research purported to be ethnographic.[3] Anthropologists might, of course, draw a hard line, to insist that only graduates trained in anthropology conduct "real" ethnography—thus excluding everyone else by definition. But they have never been that protective about reserving the label "ethnography" for their exclusive use. Further, not all anthropologists, not even all cultural anthropologists, are concerned with ethnography. There are many facets of anthropology worthy of full-time attention, including the development of theory and the secondary analyses of research reported by others. Collectively, anthropologists regard ethnography as *one* among many of the things they do and potential contributions they have to make. A senior anthropologist encapsulated this view when he reflected, "I've done ethnography, but it is not the defining experience in my life."

I think that as they have done in the past, anthropologists will continue to support and encourage the efforts of others in the ethnographic endeavor, provided that it conforms to ethical standards of the day and does not jeopardize opportunities for further research. On the other hand, the tradition is firmly established; firsthand ethnographic experience will undoubtedly continue to be regarded as the sine qua non for neophyte cultural anthropologists, although it will be redefined in ever-broadening ways that would surely astound our forebears.

Fully 15 years ago, while I was editor of the *Anthropology and Education Quarterly,* one of my fellow hyphenated anthropologists upbraided me when I rejected as not being sufficiently "anthropological" a manuscript describing "ethnographic" telephone interviewing. Today that person's students may be monitoring computer bulletin-board systems and conducting interviews by e-mail, making due without voice or face contact (see, for example, Correll 1995; Markham 1998). Although I feel some relief that a technological age so effectively isolating us from face-to-face—and even voice-to-voice—communication is now putting us in communication once again (although hardly "in touch," as the ads claim), I am of too old a generation to look fondly on these times and all the ethnographic adaptations they are likely to foster. But I must concede that as long as there is human interaction, there will be opportunity for ethnographic inquiry, and proponents for electronic forms of communication raise a good question by asking why certain forms of communication should be privileged over others. Well into several drafts of this book I was not fully aware how often I was using e-mail to check facts and impressions among colleagues, including people I have never met in person.

At the same time that the status and future of ethnography within anthropology may be somewhat endangered, the advantages that accrue to the individual ethnographer are becoming more widely shared as ethnography finds its way among the research approaches recognized in other arenas. Under ideal circumstances, ethnographers are relatively free to find the places where they would like to conduct their studies and then tease out the problem(s) they would like to investigate in those settings. That is why I have given special attention here to "place" as opposed to "problem."

Place, in the sense of venturing someplace else, was important to the early ethnographers because it virtually assured studying among those different from oneself. Locating an exotic research site is no longer critical for guaranteeing difference because difference itself is no longer universally regarded as a defining attribute of ethnographic inquiry. Nevertheless, the precedent lingers and the attractions of place deserve recognition. If there is a place, a setting, of genuine interest to you, I hope you can find a way to get there under circumstances that allow you to identify your focus *in the course of your fieldwork*. That seems preferable to conducting a study in a setting that holds no interest but has lots of convenient problems to address.

Do keep in mind when reading those early accounts that ethnographers always and only had *dramatic* differences in mind as they related what they had done and offered advice and counsel to students anticipating fieldwork of their own. Malinowski also felt it necessary to remind prospective researchers not to remain too aloof from "the natives," commending his own Polish background as an added asset in that regard:

> It is good for the Ethnographer sometimes to put aside camera, note book and pencil, and to join in himself in what is going on. He can take part in the natives' games, he can follow them on their visits and walks, sit down and listen and share in their conversations. I am not certain if this is equally easy for everyone—perhaps the Slavonic nature is more plastic and more naturally savage than that of Western Europeans—but though the degree of success varies, the attempt is possible for everyone. [Malinowski 1922:21]

Similarly, advice as to what one might need in the field (Kroeber's "Take a big skillet") or how one should proceed (Radcliffe-Brown's "Get a large notebook and start in the middle because you never know which way things will develop" was based on the assumption that virtually everything in the setting was likely to be unfamiliar and unpredictable.[4]

I suspect that most proto-ethnographers entertain romantic hopes of situating themselves in strange circumstances, if not necessarily exotic ones. The sense of adventure has not diminished, and there is always the chance one might have something unique to contribute to fieldwork lore. During the one opportunity I had in Rhodesia when I was able to spend some time "in the bush" (i.e., in a remote rural area among African, rather than White, farmers), a goat was butchered in my honor. I appreciated the symbolic meaning but experienced a growing dismay as I realized that goat was to be the main course for every meal that followed, whether breakfast, lunch, or dinner. I also discovered that at my departure I was expected to take whatever had not been consumed, since the goat had been presented to me. I savor recounting the story more than I savored the goat (even the *first* time). But the story is part of building the image "With Harry in Africa," for in all I was able to spend only four days in the bush. The experience provided a brief respite from my urban research about beer gardens, all the while enjoying the genteel surroundings in one of the last vestiges of colonial life and residing in a comfortable downtown apartment within walking distance of every amenity.

Today's ethnographers, anthropologically trained or not, are likely to be found conducting inquiries in those totally familiar settings once left to the sociologist: schools, hospitals, churches, factories, research organizations—yes, even gas stations, although I don't recall any published title on that subject.

A Watershed: Spradley and McCurdy's *The Cultural Experience*

In 1972, James Spradley and David McCurdy collected 12 of their undergraduate students' essays in a little volume that has remained in print ever since. Titled *The Cultural Experience,* the book came to mark for me, and perhaps for others as well, a watershed. Although I failed to recognize it at the time, I think the authors paved the way for generations of students to conduct modest studies in their own communities by giving them examples of inquiries into cultural scenes easy either to access directly (schools, stores, a senior citizen's apartment complex, a fire station) or to learn about through interviews (hitchhiking, the work world of the airline stewardess, even a car theft ring).

In classes on ethnographic research that I offered, students conducted studies in such nearby settings or among such approachable groups as pool players, skateboarders, a topless bar, a trailer park, a bicycle repair shop, a recycling center, a Buddhist meditation center, a store selling used clothing, a bingo parlor, regular players of duplicate bridge, and a senior employee's impending retirement. Too few of these self-selected topics put students in quite the "dramatically different" circumstances I hoped they could find, but the settings or topics alone do not tell the entire story. The student who chose the used-clothing store (she volunteered as a helper in return for being able to be a participant observer in the store and to interview its owners) was from Taiwan, and she was fascinated—if also a bit horrified—by the idea that anyone would purchase and wear clothes previously worn by an unidentified stranger. Another foreign student once reported being struck by seeing a bold sign that read VISA guarding the door of a shop where he proposed to do a study. He could not resist making a joke that most of us would never think to make: "VISA? Now what is so special about this store that I must bring my visa and passport in order to enter it?"

I was not all that taken with the Spradley and McCurdy book when it was first published. The full title, *The Cultural Experience: Ethnography in Complex Society,* seemed to offer far more than the book (make that any book, this one included) could deliver. The 12 examples—inquiries conducted by undergraduate students who surely could not have had much background in anthropology—were of uneven quality. Granted, they were adequate, even exceptional, as undergraduate student papers, but they hardly seemed worthy to be paraded as models for other students to emulate. Further, the 77-page introductory essay by editors Spradley and McCurdy described one very explicit way to conduct ethnography. The approach incorporates an elicitation technique designed to probe for culture by discovering specific categories and terms through which people in that scene "categorize" their world. The approach was becoming widely known at the time and was variously heralded as ethnoscience, ethnosemantics, or the New Ethnography.

Discounting what seemed the questionable value of the 12 examples, I was reluctant to have students purchase a text just to read a 77-page essay, although I did like the logical sequence and emphasis the authors give to cultural scenes, cultural informants, and cultural meanings. The idea of the cultural scene, which the authors defined as "the information shared by two or more people that defines some aspect of their experience" and closely linked with "recurrent social situations" (Spradley and McCurdy 1972:24), may have been inspired by Charles Frake's earlier paper, "A Structural Description of Subanun 'Religious Behavior' " (Frake 1964). Spradley and McCurdy drew a cogent quote from Frake's paper. I was glad to see his definition of ethnography brought to the attention of a wider audience. I quote it here as it appeared in the original:

A description of a culture, an *ethnography,* is produced from an *ethnographic record* of the events of a society within a given period of time. . . . To describe a culture . . . is not to recount the events of a society but to specify what one must know to make those events maximally probable. The problem is not to state what someone did but to specify the conditions under which it is culturally appropriate to anticipate that he, or persons occupying his role, will render an equivalent performance. This conception of a cultural description implies that an ethnography should be a theory of cultural behavior in a particular society. . . . [Frake 1964:111–112]

I had no trouble with ethnography defined as "a theory of cultural behavior in a particular society." But I was uncomfortable with the way Spradley and McCurdy presented their highly systematic way of inquiring into categories of cultural knowledge. Their approach seemed so structured that I felt it was more likely to keep beginning ethnographers busy pursuing questions of the order "A _____ is a kind of _____" than to help them become better informed. I joined the ranks of skeptics concerned that ethnography itself might be swallowed up in the apparent rigor of the New Ethnography. I personally chided Jim Spradley for creating what I dubbed "ethno-Spradley."

The approach did herald a call among anthropologists concerned with making ethnography more systematic, but it ran its course as even fervent advocates came to realize the rather low yield of insight for the effort involved, an effort that required extensive interviewing and remarkably patient informants. With that threat safely passed, I rediscovered the Spradley and McCurdy text. I have used it with students new to ethnography ever since (graduates and undergraduates alike) and I continue to recommend it to other instructors and to anyone seeking to grasp ethnography on his or her own. For the newcomer, even the book's weaknesses can be a strength. After reading several of these modest accounts, it would be difficult not to insist, "Hey, I can do that!"[5]

What Spradley and McCurdy had managed to accomplish in *The Cultural Experience* was to offer a solution to the newly emerging problem of *how to do ethnography in one's own society*. Anthropologists had given some attention to conducting fieldwork in familiar settings, but those doing so had validated their fieldwork credentials through the essential prerequisite of cross-cultural work conducted among strangers. Jules Henry, Margaret Mead, Hortense Powdermaker, Lloyd Warner, and others turning to "American culture" had met that prerequisite. Nevertheless, they encountered some resistance as to whether they were still "doing anthropology" when they began looking at such familiar institutions as American schools (Henry 1963; Spindler 1955), American families (Henry 1965), Hollywood (Powdermaker 1950), or American life in general (Gorer 1948; Mead 1942; Vidich and Bensman 1958; Warner 1953; West 1945).

Because I was still a relative newcomer to ethnography, was somewhat marginal as a hyphenated "educational" anthropologist, and was given to the fervor often demonstrated by recent converts, I may have been more concerned than some about this sweeping embrace of a "new" ethnography in which virtually anyone could engage. After all, Spradley and McCurdy's undergraduate students weren't necessarily even majoring in anthropology. It seemed that a cultural scene was all one needed; one might do ethnography anywhere!

Gas station ethnography? Absolutely, and without apology. Spradley and McCurdy specifically include the automobile service station among 66 cultural scenes they list as possible and relatively accessible sites for study, such as traffic court, pawn shop, Boy Scout troop, or musical group (Spradley and McCurdy 1972:32–34). As well, they remind the student ethnographer that even his or her own place of work has special advantages as a research site (efficient use of available time, ease of finding informants, value of how much you already know), cautioning only against taking anything for granted: "It takes a very skilled person with a high degree of self-awareness to study a cultural scene he has already acquired" (p. 34).

Meadow work instead of fieldwork? Well, the authors didn't specifically include meadows among their suggested sites, although they did mention cemeteries and ski resorts. I can't imagine they would have objected to studies of bird watchers or picnickers, and American bar behavior had already been subjected to ethnographic scrutiny (Cavan 1966).

Spradley himself, although one of a new breed of anthropologists whose locus remained close to home, followed the earlier tradition in his first fieldwork. His graduate requirements for both his master's thesis and doctoral dissertation were met through the extended life history he collected from James Sewid, a Kwakiutl leader who resided at the time in Alert Bay, British Columbia (Spradley 1967). That explains how I personally came to know Jim Spradley as a young doctoral student who had been conducting research with the nephew of Henry Bell, one of the major figures in my own study. I admit to feeling a certain smugness in comparing Spradley's fieldwork with my own, for I had spent an entire year in a "relatively remote" Kwakiutl village, while Jim could pop in and out of Alert Bay via scheduled flights linking Seattle, Vancouver, and Port Hardy and then chartering a plane for the short hop to Alert Bay. From the outset he was leaning toward the oral tradition that he subsequently helped to develop as ethnosemantics (see, for example, Spradley 1979).

In their early teaching assignments prior to joining forces at Macalester College in 1970, both Jim Spradley and David McCurdy discovered that their students had no way to grasp whatever might be described as "culture" in the too-familiar settings that students typically selected for their fieldwork projects. Instead, they directed their students to pay particular attention to the labels and categories shared within any group of people who customarily interact together.

Of course, such a line of inquiry could also lead one astray inventorying technical jargon unlikely to reveal much about someone's world view. For example, the student who chose a local fire station for her research site uncovered what struck me as a major concern among firemen: their public image. Rather than pursue that topic—one ideally suited to ethnographic inquiry— she directed attention along lines better suited to domain analysis, which is at the heart of the ethnosemantic approach. That tack kept her and her informants preoccupied with technical aspects of the work, rather than drawing her into an exploration of the underlying ethos of what it is like to be one of the men (this is the late 1960s) who do it. Instead, she addressed two questions that seem to me to sidestep rather than realize the ethnographic potential: "What kinds of fire runs are there?" and "What is done at a fire?"

The systematic approach of the New Ethnography was so seductive that many failed to recognize how very narrow it was, not only for students learning it as a technique (as long as they recognized it as such) but for ethnographers in the field caught up in finding out too much about too little (as reflected, for example, in the title of a 1977 paper by Frake, "Plying Frames Can Be Dangerous"). In the absence of continuing support for what was no longer the latest in fieldwork techniques, its shortcomings became more apparent, but the orderly approach of Spradley's Developmental Research Sequence (Spradley 1979, 1980) is still a boon to students who cannot seem to find their "way in" to an ethnographic assignment.

We do a better job of examining ethnography for what it has been than for what it will become; a genuine ethnography of ethnography could have it no other way. That is what I have done here, taking the Spradley and McCurdy book to represent what was for me the watershed when ethnography in North America broke free from the esoteric realm of the professional anthropologist. One might associate other authors or texts as instrumental in this regard—no single book produced the change—but the net effect was that ethnography became a more widely recognized approach to the study of everyday social life, something *anyone* interested might engage in, more self-consciously, *anywhere, any time.*

Where Do You Think You Are Going?

So, where in the world might you do your ethnographic research? In the chapters that follow, don't lose track of the importance of *place* as I turn attention to a number of other issues: fieldwork techniques, problem statement, use of theory, organizing and writing the account. Forget notions of randomness— if you are already so indoctrinated that selecting *randomly* is your overriding methodological concern, you are ready for frequencies and distributions, and those are not accomplished through "deep hanging out." Keep *culture* clearly in mind, for even in the turnabout we have witnessed from the study of the dramatically different "them" to the agonizingly familiar "us," from exotic *tribal culture* to everyday *cultural scene*, ethnography is still about groups of people engaging in customary forms of social interaction. That *explicit* cultural emphasis is peculiarly American—ethnography as practiced elsewhere is guided by different orienting concepts—but the overriding concern of ethnographers everywhere is for the description of collective human behavior, accompanied by the kind and extent of analysis and interpretation deemed appropriate by one's colleagues and patrons.

How you go about selecting a site (or how a site goes about selecting you) should reveal a great deal about the direction your fieldwork will take. Were problem and site assigned? Did you have a question to pursue that required a certain kind of setting in order to be researched, or were you at liberty to "go anywhere and study anything"? Don't be fooled into thinking that the latter option is necessarily best. I have known anthropologists so overwhelmed by the possibilities of all that might be of possible interest that they never actually got around to studying anything in depth. During the years when my primary appointment was in a college of education, an anthropologist once said to me, "You people in education are lucky—you always know what you should be studying." I thought he surely must be joking, for at that point I felt severely restrained by an implicit obligation to restrict my work to study in schools. (This was before I took the broad sweep of culture acquisition as the locus of my interests.) It seemed to me that the world was his oyster: he could address any problem he wanted. Like a number of anthropologists I have known, he was overwhelmed by opportunity and never did manage to find a suitable niche or focus.

Maybe I was luckier than I realized. It was the narrowness of my formal *research* assignment as an ethnographer of education (I was able to define my *teaching* assignment more broadly) that gave impetus to my deliberate search for calculatedly different experiences for travel and sabbatical leave. I needed to experience those other places in order to maintain or "recharge" my cultural perspective. The places that I visited opened up the possibilities; the ethnographic questions followed.

Place and purpose have to intersect. For the ethnographer, I think there is no necessary order as to which must come first. Here I have put emphasis on *place* because I think it somewhat peculiar to ethnography that *where* one conducts research plays such an important role. When place comes first, the fine-tuning that must follow comes about through knowing how to pose an ethnographic question. When the question comes first—a seemingly more logical way to begin for those who can't set out until they have a clear idea of exactly where they are headed—recognition must still be given to the fact that place will impose constraints anyway, so one's guiding question(s) must still be fine-tuned and adjusted to the situation.

The resolution of the nexus between setting and problem is *always* recursive and dialogical. For analytical purposes, I have separated them, and I must return to the question of what is an ethnographic question. But first I want to review what may be more familiar ground, how ethnographers collect their data. What are the customary techniques that ethnographers share with fieldworkers of other orientations? Part Two consists of two chapters. Chapter 3 provides a broad overview of the *techniques* of fieldwork. Chapter 4 examines what it is in addition to techniques that makes an inquiry ethnographic, and thus how some studies become "more" ethnographic than others. That is the place to ask, "What is an ethnographic question?"

Notes

1. For a review of the parallel and somewhat independent development of the ethnographic research tradition in sociology, see Prus 1996, especially chapter 4.

2. The idea of ethnographic reconnaissance is developed in Chapter 8.

3. See, for example, a special issue of *Anthropology and Humanism,* "Changing Contexts of Ethnographic Practice in the Era of Globalization," Volume 22, No. 1, January 1997.

4. Whenever asked for advice, Kroeber is also reported to have reached for his copy of *Argonauts* and said, "Go thou and do likewise" (Ann Simonds, personal recollection). Radcliffe-Brown's advice is quoted in Rubinstein (1991:14).

5. As the authors themselves note, not all of the cases presented are "rigorous examples" of ethnographic semantics (Spradley and McCurdy 1972:ix). For such an example, I recommend Spradley's own ethnosemantic study, *You Owe Yourself a Drunk* (1970). His portrayal of homeless men conducted through interviews on Seattle's Skid Road provides an excellent model of what the approach accomplishes as he describes the "life" (somewhat) and the "cognitive domains" (extensively) of his "urban nomads." For further discussion of their approach to teaching ethnographic research, see McCurdy 1997.

PART TWO: A WAY OF LOOKING AND A WAY OF SEEING

Ethnography as a Way of Looking

For anthropology, ethnography remains vital, not because ethnographic methods guarantee certain knowledge of others but because ethnographic fieldwork brings us into direct dialogue *with* others. . . .
—Michael Jackson
Things as They Are, 1996, p. 8

In the good old days mentioned in Chapter 1, the focus of ethnography was on the reports that resulted from field research, what Radcliffe-Brown referred to as "descriptive accounts of non-literate peoples." Ethnography was only tenuously awarded the status of "method" or "a method." One can still find anthropologists who prefer the phrase "ethnographic research" over "ethnographic method."

In the intervening years, an ongoing critique of how those early anthropologists went about conducting fieldwork has drawn attention from the *results* of their inquiries to self-conscious examination of the research *process.* When writing about ethnography today, the more anthropologically oriented writers are careful to make the distinction between ethnography as *process* and ethnography as *product.* In fields in which ethnography has only recently been recognized as an acceptable research approach it is viewed almost exclusively as a method. Thus, for many of today's qualitatively oriented researchers, to be "doing ethnography" has become a shorthand expression for describing how they intend to gather data, without necessarily suggesting or implying, and certainly without promising, that the outcome of their efforts will be framed as ethnography.

As already noted, I have long urged qualitative researchers to make a distinction both for themselves and for their audiences between *doing ethnography* and *borrowing ethnographic techniques*. The latter phrase emphasizes how data are gathered without imposing on how they are to be used, reserving the label of ethnography for accounts that, from the outset, are ethnographic in *intent*. The modest phrase "borrowing ethnographic techniques" seems both adequate and appropriate when the link with ethnography is essentially methodological. In employing it, the fieldworker claims only to be using—or, more likely, to be adapting—some of the standard fieldwork procedures for gathering data. The procedures may indeed be comparable to those originally employed in compiling "descriptive accounts of non-literate peoples," but using them implies neither taking so singular a focus on non-literate peoples nor insisting that the final product has been informed by, and therefore may be judged by, ethnographic tradition other than in taking a broad "fieldwork" approach.

I have held firmly to my position and may have been successful in imbuing it among a few others, certainly including my doctoral students. Matter of fact, carefully noting that the label was applicable only for this single dimension, students once dubbed me "Harry the Pure." Be warned, accordingly, that in the chapters that follow, I will endeavor to enlist you in support of distinguishing clearly between doing ethnography and borrowing ethnographic techniques. I hardly mean to argue that method is of no importance in ethnography, for most certainly it is. Fieldwork is a way of looking, and fieldwork is the mainstay of ethnography. But fieldwork is not exclusive to ethnography. Russ Bernard makes that point emphatically with the title of an article that has become his personal motto as well, "Methods Belong to All of Us" (1994a). I am even a bit uneasy about the claim that ethnography is a *method* in circles where method has more esoteric meanings than simply "a way of doing something." My resolution is to stick with the label "ethnographic research," the phrase with which I am most comfortable. I leave for others the question *when is a method?*[1]

Regardless of how steadfastly I may work on behalf of protecting Fair Ethnography's good name, I must acknowledge that ethnography has long since slipped out from under the anthropological tent. I cannot insist that it continues to mean only what it meant in the past or what I personally would like it to mean. To many who write on qualitative research topics more broadly, as well as to researchers looking for one term that best communicates how they intend to go about their research, ethnography has come to mean doing research more or less in the manner that cultural anthropologists are presumed to do it. If that is not exactly how anthropologists go about their research these days, then ethnography refers more generally to how they used to go about it in a day when there were relatively isolated groups of people willing to let someone come live with them for awhile. Ethnography is, for many, a rather highly romanticized (and technically impossible) idea about "living one's way into a culture." If you happen to be studying a "culture" that cannot be lived in, then of course you aren't really expected to live in it, but in some way you are expected to establish a presence.[2]

A distinguishing characteristic of ethnographic research, singularly undistinguishing as it may be, is that we expect the ethnographer to go somewhere to conduct the study. As underscored in the previous chapter, traditionally that meant not only going into the field but going far afield as well, to someplace new or strange. There is a further expectation that the ethnographer will gather his or her own data rather than become overreliant on data gathered previously by others. There is an implied sense of adventure, even of the exotic, in the imagery that comes to mind. I think that those of us who have conducted most of our fieldwork in the most ordinary, familiar, and easily accessible of places still carry around an idealized image of someone outfitted in safari suit and pith helmet stepping onto the shore and into the center of a circle of huts, with camera, binoculars, and notebook at the ready.

The idea of being there in person, relying on oneself as the primary research instrument, is sufficiently different from the prevailing image of how science should be accomplished that it has tended to overshadow issues of what one is expected to do upon arrival. As a result, for many researchers attracted to an approach in which the self is instrument, ethnography is simply a preferred label for an activity that goes by many names: participant observation research, descriptive research, naturalistic research, qualitative research, on-site research, field study, and so forth. The set of activities common to all these approaches emphasizes the field "methods" or "fieldwork techniques" employed in data gathering, not on how data subsequently are organized, analyzed, or reported. Fieldwork techniques constitute the aspect of ethnography of broadest application and appeal. For those unfamiliar with whatever more ethnography is than simply a way of looking, ethnography is synonymous with fieldwork, particularly in the sense of a researcher present, in person, to gather data.

This seems a good place to review some of these key research tools or techniques for readers who want to know more about fieldwork as a research approach because that is what draws them to ethnography. As the chapter title suggests, the focus is on ethnography as a way of *looking*, taking that term literally but also in a broader sense to encompass *all* the ways one may direct attention while in the field. With a clearer understanding of how ethnographers ordinarily go about fieldwork, researchers of other persuasions may feel encouraged to avail themselves of a wider range of ways of looking than they customarily have employed. One of the unsung features of ethnographic research is its embrace of multiple techniques. The very idea that one might depend solely on one source of data—survey research as a prime example, since so much research is conducted in that fashion—is anathema to anyone genuinely committed to the ethnographer's "multi-instrument" approach. But that cannot be taken to mean that ethnography is necessarily the best approach; everything comes back to purposes. Woe be to the researcher who invests the time and energy in long-term fieldwork yet has no more to show for it than what a skilled survey researcher could have produced far more quickly and efficiently.

Chapter 4 follows with a complementary discussion of ethnography as a way of *seeing*. There I take a closer look at what the ethnographer does beyond simply being on hand as observer. I will emphasize ethnography as *mindwork*, not merely a set of techniques for *looking* but, consistent with my chosen title, a particular *way of seeing* as well. But here the focus is strictly on fieldwork *techniques*.

Participant Observation: The Catch-all Label

The phrase one hears most often in references to fieldwork is "participant observation." Sometimes the words are hyphenated to emphasize the connection between two activities that might otherwise seem not only dissimilar but antithetical. And there is tension between them, an insurmountable tension for anyone locked into the notion that only a detached and uninvolved observer is capable of rendering an acceptable description of human social behavior.

Participant observation lends further confusion because the label is used in different ways, in some cases referring to *all* the activities in which fieldworkers engage, at other times being paired off with its complement, *interviewing*, to highlight the two major categories into which fieldwork can be subdivided, participant observation and interviewing. As a result, participant observation is sometimes employed as an umbrella term to describe *everything* that ethnographers do, and indeed, that *all* on-site researchers do, in the field. It is employed by others to refer to any fieldwork activity that is not some form of interviewing.

Interviewing in its broadest sense is taken to include everything from casual conversation to the formal structured interview. Although they are closely related, I favor maintaining a distinction between participant observation and interviewing. Not only does the distinction underscore the importance of interview techniques as a major aspect of fieldwork, it also helps to keep fieldworkers mindful of making conscious decisions about whether and how to use them.

Regardless of whether the phrase is used in its broad sense or paired with its complement, participant observation poses more of a problem than an answer for the unsuspecting researcher who lays store by it as a bona fide research technique. At best, it points only to a strategy, and it does so in only the most general way. True, the phrase is bandied about just enough, and has just enough highfalutin resonance about it, that it may prove adequate to allow a researcher access to a research site. It also may be explanation enough to answer the question of what one intends to do if allowed to hang around, at least during the initial stages when the researcher may be unsure about how to proceed. On the other hand, many a grant writer or graduate student defending a research proposal has been surprised to have that same explanation rejected outright as woefully inadequate to convince a critical reviewer that he or she has any idea of how to proceed.

Such ambiguity has made the problem of defining participant observation an inviting topic in the never-ending discourse on method. There has been an outpouring of books and chapters dealing with aspects of participant observation for the past 50 years.[3] The term can be traced back at least as early as 1924 in a casual reference by E. C. Lindeman (1924:191). It was identified as a fieldwork strategy in a 1940 article by Florence Kluckhohn and is superbly illustrated in Powdermaker's account of her professional career in *Stranger and Friend* (1966). A definitive statement by sociologist Raymond Gold in the 1950s proposed a continuum distinguishing the observer-as-participant from the participant-as-observer, such nuanced distinctions set between poles of the totally detached observer at one extreme and the totally involved participant at the other (Gold 1958; see also Gold 1997; Tedlock 2000). In my own review of the topic (HFW 1995), rather than single out participant observation for special attention I advised neophyte researchers to describe, with far more detail than is prompted by the phrase itself, precisely what they intend to do, giving specific examples of the kind of data they believe they will need and the procedures by which they intend to obtain them.

Earlier, when asked to prepare a chapter for another of the recent and helpful handbooks dealing with qualitative research (LeCompte, Millroy, and Preissle 1992), I found myself thinking about how various fieldwork techniques complement each other. I pondered how *few* categories might be adequate to encompass them all. Given my propensity for sorting things in threes, three categories seemed sufficient, especially keeping in mind that participant observation would be one of them. By itself that category is so broad that it can refer to everything and anything that a participant observer does in the course of field research.

Recognized by their most frequently heard names, the three categories I identified are *participant observation, interviewing,* and *archival research.* To free myself of stereotypes associated with terms already so familiar, I sought a different term to convey the essence of what the researcher does and what is expected as a result of each activity. I succumbed as well to the temptation of alliteration, reassigning the activities a new set of labels: *experiencing, enquiring,* and *examining.* Although my proposed terms are not likely to dislodge three such well-established ones, they do call attention to what one is expected to *do* to accomplish each of them. Without implicating what a researcher is to look *for,* they are, nonetheless, guidelines for looking. Let me note some contrasts among the three before discussing each in turn.

Experiencing, Enquiring, and Examining

Experiencing seems an especially appropriate label for drawing attention to what is gained through participant observation. Neophyte researchers indoctrinated so rigorously in rigor that they no longer appreciate or trust what each of us accomplishes through personal experience may need to be reminded of the human capacity for observation and to recognize that ultimately everything we know comes to us that way. Participant observation is founded on firsthand experience in naturally occurring events. Today, we no longer have to pretend to a level of objectivity that was once fashionable; it is sufficient to recognize and reveal our subjectivity as best we can, thus to maximize the potential of fieldwork as personal experience rather than to deny it.

Experiencing includes, of course, information that comes directly through all the senses. In spite of constant reminders that humans have other senses to which researchers seem largely inattentive, observational research plays out almost entirely in what we *see* and what we *hear*. That is not likely to change. We lack notational systems for what we taste, touch, and smell; we ourselves cannot record such sensations except by analogy to personal experience. We are at even more of a loss when we try to communicate them to others, especially when we cannot communicate face to face so that we can assess the effectiveness of our efforts. Nevertheless, we are also overwhelmed by how much we can take in through looking and listening, from the subtleties of body language to the organization of cultural space. We need not despair what we do poorly; we are bombarded by all we can take in through our eyes and ears.

Enquiring, or "interviewing," may at first seem such a natural adjunct of participant observation that one can fail to recognize the extraordinary difference that sets it apart as a way of knowing. I emphasize the major distinction between *experiencing* and *enquiring* (or *inquiring,* if you prefer) to underscore the critical difference between being present as a passive *observer* of what is going on and taking an active role in *asking* about what is going on. It is one thing to attend to the flow of natural activity and conversation in a group; it is quite another to intrude on or initiate activities and conversations with those among whom we study. Enquiring requires a different order of field-work. It poses a dilemma for a field researcher: whether to intrude by inter-jecting one's own agenda into a research setting, or to remain silent in the hope that what one wants to know may (eventually) be revealed in some nat-urally occurring way.

We experience this dilemma in everyday life and everyday conversation any time we make a decision, consciously or subconsciously, as to whether to interrupt or to let activities or conversations continue as though we were not present. Among fieldworker types, we can distinguish between the passively inclined observer who seldom or never asks a question and the aggressive researcher who does little else. Both culture and personality enter into the equation of how each of us goes about fieldwork, influencing even the way we pose our problems or devise strategies for investigating them.

Examining, the third element of my trilogy, points to an activity in which the researcher turns attention to what has been produced by others. Most cer-tainly that includes archival research, but archival research in its technical sense limits eligible sources to documents accessible to other investigators. That is far too limiting for a fieldworker who may be privy to personal letters, diaries, and photographs, to examining ordinary apparel or esoteric art objects, to listening to recordings of speech or music, to making or reviewing inventories of household items—all sorts of things that informants may have in personal possession that might be shared with the ethnographer but are not necessarily available to anyone else.

A brief review of each of these three basic fieldwork procedures follows. I have also noted additional references, for every facet of fieldwork now has a special shelf addressing its problems and potential. I have had my say in a book devoted entirely to a discussion of fieldwork (HFW 1995). Keep in mind that there is no "proper" ratio for allocating one's efforts among the three facets, no guarantee of success simply by giving dutiful attention to each in turn. More important, as I discuss in the next chapter, simply availing one-self of the three broad strategies is not sufficient to guarantee that the out-come of one's research will be satisfyingly ethnographic. The potential of ethnography far exceeds what can be achieved by attending only to method. On the other hand, when data gathering is restricted to only one (or even two) of these facets, there is probably some more appropriate label than "ethno-graphic" for describing how data were obtained and to point to expected outcomes. Even when used collectively, these tried and true ways of looking are necessary but not sufficient for accomplishing ethnography's potential.

Experiencing: Distinguishing Between Observers and Participant Observers

In *Stranger and Friend: The Way of an Anthropologist,* one of the earliest accounts in which an anthropologist revealed ethnography as a highly personal endeavor, Hortense Powdermaker stresses the need for a fieldworker to move back and forth between involvement and detachment, an idea incorporated into her title contrasting the roles of stranger and friend (Powdermaker 1966). I suspect that for many who decide to pursue fieldwork, involvement proves the more difficult aspect of the assignment, not because it is difficult to enter into the activities of others who interest us, but because it conflicts with deeply held and uncritically examined notions of how we believe we should act when we are trying to be "scientific." For anyone naturally reticent or shy, traits not uncommon among ethnographers of my acquaintance, it is all too easy to withdraw and become an onlooker, especially when the role you are trying to take seems to support exactly that behavior.

With participant observation identified as central to most of the approaches in qualitative research, we seem to have come full circle, for we sometimes hear of an approach described as "non-participant participant observation." Although the phrase does appear to be a contradiction in terms, I think it signals the difficulty some researchers have with the idea of interacting, or even accepting that they might or should or are *allowed* to interact, in any setting where they accept responsibility as observers. In an earlier day we would have been satisfied simply to label ourselves as observers. Under present circumstances, however, to identify oneself as an observer perpetuates the idea that *we* are studying *them,* and that is no longer the way we prefer to portray either ourselves or our work. Thus I take the label of the "non-participant participant observer" as a self-ascribed label for researchers who make no effort to hide what they are doing or to deny their presence, but neither are they able fully to avail themselves of the potential afforded by *participant* observation to take a more active or interactive role.

How much participation is participation enough? If at one extreme a fieldworker can be too aloof, might one also become so involved as to make observation itself impossible? There is an inherent paradox in the role of participant observer. As a general guideline, it seems preferable to stay on the cautious side, becoming only as involved as necessary to obtain whatever information is sought. Operating with that level of restraint allows a researcher to help everyone else to remain conscious of the research *role* as the work continues, rather than risk having someone later complain about having been misled by a pretense at involvement.

My experience is that although people may become accustomed to having an observer present, that does not mean they ever become oblivious to that presence, especially if the researcher makes an effort to remind them of his or her presence and purpose. I have often been consoled with reassuring phrases such as "We just carry on as though you aren't here." In such words, I hear a dual message, that although those in a setting where I am conducting research have remained conscious of my presence, they do not think they would have acted differently had I not been present.

One hears the concern that as long as an observer is present, those being observed will put on an act, and thus their behavior under observation is not "real." That likelihood must be acknowledged, but there are several points to counter it. First, ethnography is ordinarily conducted over a long period of time. People can sustain an act or maintain their best image only so long. Eventually everyone present, researcher included, is likely either to let their guard down or to assume a more natural stance. Second, the possibility that people have acted differently in the presence of the researcher is a question that can be raised with those in the setting, sometimes helping to incorporate other views into the inquiry and further validating the researcher as a thoughtful observer endeavoring to get as complete a picture as possible. What is more, people on their best behavior enact roles in what they perceive as *ideal* types. Witnessing such behavior can be extremely valuable to the ethnographer interested in teasing out beliefs about how people *should* act and the inevitable tension between what people feel they *ought* to do or *ought* to say, and what they do or say in fact.

There is nothing wrong with a researcher taking an essentially passive role and remaining uninvolved. In some settings or for some researcher personalities that may be the only realistic option. The seasoned ethnographer might want to inventory the advantages and disadvantages of various levels of participation in terms of the situation, the problem under investigation, and his or her own personality and research style. Although my general advice is to become only as involved as is necessary to obtain the information desired, each researcher must weigh what might be gained, and at what risk or cost, by acting more naturally, by becoming more involved, and by approaching the research setting more informally or casually. That is one of the particular advantages of employing a participant observer strategy. It is an advantage too often overlooked by researchers ready and willing to accept a more passive role in order to keep their distance and refrain from "interfering" in a setting.

I do not mean to point a finger. Except for my initial fieldwork, when I was the village teacher, research I have conducted *in schools* has been essentially of this non-participant observer type. I aspired to be the ever-present-but-nonetheless-forgotten observer, the shadow, the fly on the wall. In each of those settings, someone was kind enough to tag me with some comparable label, making me feel that my efforts to be seen as "not seen" were indeed a success. What I was especially anxious to avoid was to be put in the conspicuous role of evaluator. To accomplish that, I tried to keep as low a profile as possible. In an opportunity for non-school-related research in the racially segregated setting of southern Africa, I was not aware until long after the fieldwork was completed the extent to which my research opportunities had been something of a guided tour rather than the carte blanche I felt I had at the time. The realization prompted a reflective article titled "Feedback Influences on Fieldwork, Or, A Funny Thing Happened on the Way to the Beer Garden" (HFW 1975b).

A pull toward that distanced-observer role continues to exert itself in most field research, largely as a result of our efforts to reassure ourselves that we are really behaving like real researchers. Thus the tendency to overemphasize the observer dimension in participant observation is particularly inviting. The ethnographic tradition allows and even encourages a more active role, but it does not insist on it. The *idea* of assuming a more active role seems to have wide appeal, yet it conflicts with the ideal image of how most of us have been socialized to believe that research should be conducted. Such tensions in our underlying beliefs about how properly to enact the research role can help us realize that we do not have to go far afield to find culture at work; we need but take a closer look at how we ourselves believe we should go about the work of locating culture.

Given the complications that participation introduces, intimacy gained at the cost of objectivity, observer bias, or intrusiveness, does it really contribute to our efforts all that much? Absolutely! The relatively "harder" data gathered through techniques yet to be discussed must still be pulled together into a meaningful whole in the final account. Elsewhere I have described this as a process involving three closely related but distinguishable facets: description, analysis, and interpretation (HFW 1994, especially chapter 2). Descriptive data are the bedrock of the account; analysis is distinguished from interpretation by reason of what we make of those data. In analysis, we know what we are doing because we examine the data following agreed-upon procedures for reporting facts, figures, and findings. Interpretations, on the other hand, are what we ourselves make of the data, a sense-making attentive to carefully analyzed facts but not overwhelmed by them when controverted by our direct dialogue with others. Firsthand experience through participant observation is both the starting point and the filter through which everything else is screened as we make sense of all that we have observed.

Description, analysis, and interpretation are not unique to ethnographic research; they are critical facets in all qualitative inquiry. There is no fixed proportion among them that assures the quality of a study—everything always gets back to purposes. To make that point, I drew a comparison to the N-P-K (nitrogen, phosphorous, potassium) formula that horticulturists depend on for assessing the key ingredients in commercial fertilizers. There is no single combination best suited for all plant needs; the common 20-20-20 formula is no more than a best guess when purposes are diffuse. Similarly, as with any qualitative research, an ethnographer will variously emphasize experiencing, enquiring, and examining during fieldwork, and description, analysis, and interpretation in the write-up, according to the purposes of the study. To make a study ethnographic, the researcher must also have a sense of the kinds of data to gather, the kinds of analysis that are appropriate, and a sense of what is meant by the broad charter of "cultural interpretation." An examination of the role of these elements in ethnography is the stuff of the next chapter, but the recognition of the importance of firsthand experience gained through participant observation is common to many qualitative approaches.

Enquiring: When Researchers Ask

The second major activity and data source in fieldwork focuses on interview strategies. As noted, this activity is so integral as a complement to participant observation that it is often subsumed as an aspect of it. Yet interviewing is far too important not to deserve a separate category of its own. Furthermore, distinguishing between participant observation and interviewing helps draw attention to the fact that some studies rely almost exclusively on participant observation, with virtually no opportunity for interviewing, and some studies are conducted almost exclusively through interviews. Sometimes there is no setting or "scene" in which the fieldworker can effect a participant observer role, and sometimes the research focus, or the personalities of those involved, makes interviewing the best—or only—option.

Primarily for instructional purposes, I developed a typology for distinguishing among the major forms that interviewing can take. I wanted students to recognize a variety of approaches and to be able to assess the advantages and disadvantages not only for getting certain kinds of information but for the constant vigilance one must exercise in maintaining rapport. Direct questioning always involves a certain risk and tends to emphasize an extractive element in fieldwork in a day when fieldworkers are striving to be more collaborative. Further, although you may get exactly the information you need, you may damage your chances for learning more. Yet a failure to pursue some topic may inadvertently signal a lack of interest. Recognizing a range of strategies may help one to proceed cautiously while gaining insight as to how particular kinds of questions can best be posed. Here is the typology as it evolved through the years:

Casual conversation
Life history, life cycle interview
Key informant interviewing
Semi-structured interview
Structured interview
Survey
Household census, ethnogenealogy
Questionnaire (written and/or oral)
Projective techniques
Other measurement techniques

I assigned *casual conversation,* the first strategy listed above, a category of its own so that students would not make a pretense of treating everything said to them in the course of their research as though it was carefully elicited "interview" data. I placed it at the head of the list to underscore its importance not only as a source of information but in recognition of the everyday nature of fieldwork itself.

Life history interviewing focuses on the life of a particular individual; *life cycle interviewing* examines the events that mark stages in the lives of members of a group, whether physiological (e.g., birth, infancy, puberty, old age) or social (e.g., recruit, initiate, member, chief).

Key informant interviewing refers to the practice of making one or more informants a major source of information in one's research. A linguist may work almost exclusively with a single key informant, since the basic grammar of a language can be worked out from analyzing the speech of any one of its speakers. Similarly, life history research, including ethnographically based biographies and autobiographies, capitalizes on intensive key informant interviewing, sometimes to the virtual exclusion of other data sources. On the other hand, fieldworkers often rely heavily on one or a few informants without necessarily realizing how narrow a base they have drawn upon for their information. It is good to have a clear notion of whether or not you intend to use certain informants as more or less key ones and to make sure it is clear to your readers as well.

Semi-structured interviews have an open-ended quality about them, the interview taking shape as it progresses. In a *structured interview,* each interviewee is asked the same questions in the same way. *Surveys* usually have that level of formality but are designed to elicit information from a broad sample of respondents about specific topics. The *household census* or *ethnogenealogy* is designed to elicit information about the occupants of each household or to trace family histories. *Questionnaires,* as I think of them, tend to be less formal and to be administered and reported less formally than surveys. In practice, not all researchers distinguish between the two, referring instead to the *survey questionnaire* as a single category.

Projective techniques, especially such formal ones as the Rorschach or Thematic Apperception Technique (T.A.T.), have gone out of vogue as standard fieldwork procedures, but the wide use they once enjoyed serves as a reminder of how reassuring it can be to obtain comparable data *of any kind* from different individuals in the same setting (see Henry and Spiro 1953). A measurement instrument already "standardized" on other populations offers some promise of a comparative basis for reporting on the group being studied. Projective testing of a more informal nature also occurs any time fieldworkers ask respondents to discuss what they predict for the future or what they wish for themselves and for others, even with such straightforward questions as "How do you see yourself ten years from now?"

I have included a final category, *other measurement techniques,* in recognition of the variety of test instruments fieldworkers sometimes employ. These range from widely known (and "standardized") devices such as IQ or manipulative tests for assessing mental ability to culture-specific instruments like the Instrumental Activities Inventory developed by George and Louise Spindler years ago (1965). The Spindlers were interested in assessing "acculturative status" among the Blood Indians in Alberta, Canada. They did this through informant responses to a series of commissioned line drawings of people engaged in various activities ranging from traditional rural to modern urban.

The rationale for using standardized instruments in ethnographic fieldwork differs markedly from the purposes for which most of them were originally designed as instruments of evaluation. Fieldworkers surely have had sufficient personal experience with academic testing and the potentially dire consequences of test outcomes to know better than to inflict potential discomfort or embarrassment on others. Anything that resembles or suggests that kind of testing should be approached with care if it must be done at all. However, when used to assess consensus in the knowledge base among members of a community, or to gauge what one group knows about the ways of another, such tests—often reinterpreted as "tasks"—have a valuable contribution to make in assessing the extent to which knowledge is "shared" within a group.[4]

Widespread and essential as it is in fieldwork, interviewing is a time-consuming task. It requires arranging and conducting the initial interview plus the subsequent effort involved in transcription and analysis. Further, interviewing seldom happens in quite the way we hope and intend or as glamorized in a few widely circulated photographs of ethnographers in action. Disappointment can come from every direction: obtaining far too little from informants, even those who seemed promising as willing and well-informed interviewees, or getting so much material—and probably so much verbiage along with it—that one wonders how it can ever be sorted out and reported in a manageable corpus. There is always a question about the nature of the relationship between fieldworker and informant, why the one was willing to talk to the other, how much confidence can be placed in what was revealed, and who has benefited from the exchange.

It has not been at all unusual for a key informant to become a participant in the interviewer's subculture, rather than the other way around. Boas's Kwakiutl informants were often interviewed in his hotel room (when they remembered to keep their appointments!) and his key informant/collaborator George Hunt made several trips to meet with Boas at Columbia University. Yet as long as the interviewing has been face-to-face, neither the actual circumstances of the interview nor the place where it was held have usually been reported. As noted, fieldworkers have long wrestled with the question of whether interviewing by telephone is acceptable as an ethnographic technique, with an up-to-date twist that raises a parallel question in regard to corresponding with informants by e-mail (see Fetterman 1998).

The absence of a face-to-face encounter strikes me as a serious drawback to information gained this way. However, a compelling case was reported in the *Cultural Anthropology Methods Newsletter*[5] emphasizing how researchers were able to extend the regional significance of a study, augmenting face-to-face interviews through telephone interviewing of distant respondents that would otherwise have been prohibitively costly (Maiolo et al. 1994). Questions involving new Internet technologies will fuel the never-quite-resolved controversy over the role and legitimacy of telephoning, which by comparison may now become less objectionable, for it does at least entail voice-to-voice communication.

The underlying issue is not about the legitimacy of the telephone or Internet in research; no potential channel of information can be ignored. But one might wonder what constitutes an adequate basis for claiming a study to be *ethnographic* if researcher and researched are not in each other's presence. Ordinarily I would think that to meet a criterion as naturalistic inquiry of any kind, communication should be not only person-to-person but face-to-face as well.

A historical precedent was established for the study of cultures "at a distance" when anthropologists lent their talent to national interests during World War II by providing accounts of peoples and places that allied troops *might* be occupying. Perhaps the best-known study of this genre is Ruth Benedict's *Chrysanthemum and the Sword* (1946; see also Mead and Métraux, *The Study of Culture at a Distance,* 1953). In spite of that historical precedent, I suspect we will bemoan a loosening of standards as we watch a new generation of qualitative researchers conduct studies seated in front of their computers while an older generation fails fully to appreciate the significance of the remarkable opportunity technology offers for interacting both with and within a *worldwide* web of correspondents.

In practice, of course, qualitative researchers have been collecting interview data for years through techniques that surely stretch the limits of what constitutes an interview: carrying on extended post-fieldwork correspondence with informants, asking informants to maintain diaries, sending lists of questions to be answered by using a tape recorder, holding essay contests for school children, and sending early drafts of manuscripts back to the field for comment and reaction.

The umbrella term "interview data" serves both to legitimate and to obscure some of the channels through which information is obtained directly from others. The term handily implies a setting in which the researcher directs specific questions to an interviewee who understands that this *is* an interview and that responses are likely to be treated as authoritative and to be quoted. In practice, things are not always made so explicit at the time, although they may later come to be interpreted that way. Too late we may learn that we have been "interviewed," as I was reminded recently when my efforts to direct an inquiring newspaper reporter to a proper source appeared in print the following day quoting me as that source.

Perhaps because participant observation is so difficult to describe analytically or to pinpoint—except by gradations that might be stretched out to read like compass points (e.g., participant observer as observing participant or as participating observer)—efforts to examine and improve interview techniques have received a great deal of attention. Useful texts abound, some devoted to a broad overview, others targeted to specific categories of interviewees.[6]

The decision as to whether or not to conduct interviews is not always an option. If you were not present when something occurred, and your task is to find out what happened, you are pretty much limited to inquiring about what occurred from those who were on the scene. "Questioning" can be rude behavior, but not everyone whose inquiries require it enjoys the luxury of the ethnographer who can agonize over how much questioning to do, how direct and intrusive to be, even whether to ask direct questions at all.

Telephone solicitors and pollsters have become adept at timing calls to interrupt mealtime because they know that people are likely to be home. Journalists and detectives depend heavily on their ability to ask direct and penetrating questions, in no small part because, like pollsters, they do not concern themselves with image-making to the extent that ethnographers do. Indeed, reporters often turn their own negative stereotype to advantage. They can be rude with impunity, jamming their questions, microphones, and cameras in the face of virtually anyone, because people *expect* them to behave that way. Then by simply showing more courtesy than one expects from the stereotypes held of them, they may be able to elicit more cooperation than their interviewees intended. If that isn't effective, they may resort to real or imagined authority to obtain information through intimidation. There are ways to coax and, if necessary, coerce people to talk; such are not the ways of the ethnographer.

Why the difference for qualitative researchers, and for ethnographers in particular? All researchers have questions, multitudes of them, whether a specific set of questions to be pursued or an overriding question about another group's way of life. But an ethnographer who has feigned interest in a people's entire way of life should not suddenly light up when a topic of particular professional interest is broached. Practiced hands at interviewing have long recognized that turning attention to *any* topic can make it a sensitive issue or a subject of criticism, real or implied.

With the likelihood that there are too many questions they would *like* to ask—and hope eventually to have answered—ethnographers do not want to earn reputations as people who pester with incessant questioning. Furthermore, the questions we would like most to ask, the "Why?" questions, prove the most vexing. Seldom are people able to come up with neat explanations as to "why" that are likely to satisfy either themselves or a researcher. Endeavor as they may to make traditions explicit, ethnographers are not enlightened when tradition is proffered as explanation: "That is our way."

Question-asking is further complicated for the ethnographer because it is culturally based. Hell-bent as we are to discern aspects of other people's "cultures," we are not always all that aware of our own customs. Part of the baggage we take into the field is our personal version of the meaning of questions, including our convictions about what can and cannot properly be brought up in conversation. I admit to surprise at some of the questions people in other places have put to me in the course of ordinary conversation. Too late has that led me to wonder if there were topics that in other places I might have introduced that would have seemed impertinent back home.

Question-asking is culture-specific; we follow our own implicit rules in the absence of anything better to guide us. I wonder how often ethnographers have thought to ask explicitly what kinds of things are and are not appropriate topics within a particular group? Or to inquire how we may give offense by *failing* to ask, when an appropriately phrased question might have signaled interest or allowed an informant or host an opportunity to show or show off some achievement that might have been unseemly among our own associates? Our own habits can get in the way of efforts to study the ways of others, and our efforts at image-building sometimes have an effect exactly opposite to what we intend.

When I began drafting this chapter, a neophyte ethnographer was preparing to depart for a year overseas to conduct his first major fieldwork. He confided that his family had proposed the gift of a round-trip air ticket if he would like to return home for a brief visit during the holiday season, midway through his long intended stay. He was reluctant to decline the generous offer, yet ambivalent about accepting it, voicing concern that even so brief a departure might be interpreted in his host country as a lack of commitment and interest. Recalling similar concerns of my own some 35 years earlier, I reminded him that his host country had been able to get by without him for hundreds of years and would have to get by without him again after his fieldwork was completed. I expressed doubt that serious repercussions would result were he to take a short break. What he had done—and something we all do, all too often—was to supply an answer of his own to a question never fully explicated: What will people in this setting make of my leave-taking during fieldwork? Experience suggests that in addition to the advantages of taking a breather and regaining one's perspective, fieldworkers have sometimes reported a strengthening of relationships between themselves and the community by the very act of going away and then returning as promised.

How we handle the question of question-asking, both as a general strategy and as a problem to be resolved anew with each question we would like to ask, is a concern that never goes away. "Ethnography without questions would be impossible," Michael Agar informs us, further cautioning that "ethnographic question-asking is a special blend of art and science" (1980:45). That might seem to have settled the matter, except that in the next paragraph, in reference to his own research into drug culture on the American scene, Agar reverses himself to caution instead, "In the streets, though, I learned that you don't ask questions." Ann Simonds informs me (personal communication) that George Foster, one of her mentors at Berkeley in the good old days, "was not a great believer in asking people direct questions, and we were all encouraged to sit in bars and cantinas, wash clothes at the local laundry, keep a daily journal, etc., in short, to apply an indirect technique, hoping in the process to shift discussions in appropriate and useful directions. . . ." Asking questions, it would seem, is universally recognized as a way to get information, but it is not universally practiced among ethnographers. Any advice one might receive is almost certain to be accompanied by the well-worn caveat for *all* advice pertaining to *all* aspects of fieldwork: "It depends." Be prepared as well for the too frequently heard reply, "Who knows?"

Examining: Archival Strategies

One feature common to the work of all anthropologists is their attention to records or to "the record." That has quite different meanings within anthropology's various subfields: Physical anthropologists and archaeologists examine the fossil record, each with an eye for different stories to be told. Archaeologists take oral interviews and examine documents in the process of doing historical archaeology and they examine the history implicit in materials they unearth, just as they study paintings and petroglyphs, carvings, anything that helps them piece together life "before history." Linguists listen repeatedly to recordings made of near-extinct languages in order to work out grammatical structures. These activities all require careful attention to the work of others and, within all anthropological subdisciplines, go under the label of "fieldwork." Thus fieldwork can refer to research of far broader scope than the way I use it here as virtually synonymous with, but limited essentially to, ethnography.

The key feature of archival strategies is the relative importance given to sifting through what has been produced or left by others in times past, a sifting sometimes literal for the archaeologist, usually figurative for everyone else. Historians take pride in the seeming objectivity they achieve in comparison to ethnographers because they cannot be accused of making up their own data. They sometimes look askance at our reliance on participant observation as a *primary* data source. Within their own discipline, those who do oral history are similarly suspect because they interview living persons rather than confine their research to well-documented sources that can be substantiated independently by others.

The only response ethnographers can make to the charge that they create their own data is to shrug their shoulders and agree enthusiastically. I am yet to be convinced that relying entirely on data created by others is preferable! I doubt that historians and biographers think of themselves or refer to themselves as participant observers as they go about their inquiries, but a convincing case could be made that participant observation provides the basis for every move they make as researchers.

The essential criterion for those who stake their reputations on archival research is their reliance on "intersubjectively verifiable" data (Hill 1993:2). To the professional archivist, legitimate searching may be confined to formal archives listed in the *Directory of Archives and Manuscript Repositories in the United States.* My use of "archive" here is far broader, in reference not to the places where such documents are registered and held but to the documents themselves. In that nontechnical sense, for an ethnographer *any* document that proves valuable as a source of information can rightfully be considered an archive.

Regardless of whether the materials have been formally cataloged or casually handed to a researcher who had no prior knowledge that they existed—old letters, diaries, or photographs, for example—written records can be a vital source of data. Most often such materials supplement participant observation research but sometimes they are, or become, the major focus of it. The study usually cited as exemplar is *The Polish Peasant in America,* a work reported in five volumes based on the examination of correspondence between new immigrants and their homeland, as recorded and reported by W. I. Thomas and F. Znaniecki (1918–1920). Although personal documents such as letters or official documents like government and church records spring first to mind, researchers have made good use of written records everywhere: cemetery records and grave markers, for example, as in studies by W. L. Warner (1959) or Deetz (Deetz and Dethlefsen 1967).

There is plenty of opportunity, and need, for including history in the work of the ethnographer. Anyone with a proclivity for studying the influences of the past has the subdiscipline of *ethnohistory* in support, an ethnographic best-of-both-worlds that blends the study of historical documents with opportunity for fieldwork in contemporary settings and an emphasis on interviewing older informants. Would-be biographers among ethnographers have a similar opportunity to focus attention on individuals through the well-established genre of the anthropological life history.

Probably the biggest distinction between the ethnographer and the historian or biographer is the concern of the former with the ordinary and everyday. The historian or biographer is more likely to be interested in the especially significant or outstanding: the catastrophic event, the artistic or political genius, the magnificent scoundrel. Lines are not firmly drawn; historians and biographers may turn attention to the typical and ordinary, and the life history approach of the anthropologist works just as well with a world leader as with a worker in the cane fields, as illustrated in Mandelbaum's classic piece on

Gandhi (Mandelbaum 1973). However, there is an important difference. As Michael Hill points out in *Archival Strategies and Techniques* (1993), those who do historical research in conjunction with fieldwork tend to regard the historical work as adjunct: their archival research is conducted to augment fieldwork, which retains its centrality to the inquiry. Historians and biographers, by contrast, see themselves engaged in a creative and satisfying process of discovery complete in its own right (p. v).

This archival dimension to ethnographic research poses its special dilemma for the fieldworker. How extensively should one depend on or delve into archival sources, and how familiar ought one become with work done earlier, especially if such familiarity is gained at the cost of time that could be spent doing original research, or if the fieldworker is concerned about forming preconceived notions instead of making judgments of his or her own? For the field-oriented researcher, the answer is a pragmatic one: Priority must be given to one's own fieldwork as opportunity arises. Attention can be redirected toward archival sources later, if necessary, or as a standby activity, should obstacles to accomplishing one's work present themselves: problems of access when experiencing unanticipated delays in obtaining permission to begin fieldwork, problems arising when informants are not easily available, or delays if the ritual or event of special focus occurs only infrequently. I suspect that the (conservative?) voice of their academic elders drives beginning ethnographers into the archives as well. Dissertation committees express (or at least feign) surprise at candidates who seem inadequately informed about the prior work of regional or conceptual specialists. And senior academics in virtually any field can be counted on to express general (but persistent) concern that neither their graduate students nor their younger colleagues seem sufficiently well informed about the history and traditions of their discipline.

Of course, this latter ploy serves as well to mask the problem old-timers have with efforts to keep up. I don't believe I have ever heard an anthropologist claim to be "well read." These days I find myself overwhelmed simply trying to take account of the new *titles* in ethnography. I have suggested elsewhere that I believe academics are essentially *either* readers *or* writers (HFW 1990c:20). Both activities demand almost full-time commitment. Ethnographers are probably advantaged if they are among the latter group, preoccupied with reporting what they have experienced firsthand rather than preoccupied with trying to know all there is to know about a topic before being so presumptuous as to make a contribution of their own.

Archival purists might seem to have the edge in being able to *exhaust* a topic. They are shielded by a nicely accommodating set of professional guidelines that establish the criteria for determining where a source must be located—and therefore be available for verification by others—in order to qualify as an archive. Such total dependence on sources produced by others imposes a limitation on their work from which the ethnographer is freed. If such a constraint is rather obvious, it is nonetheless seldom discussed: not everything about human social life gets put into a form that is "readable" by another. Hill cautions would-be archivists to reflect on what he calls "the broad sedimentary processes via which materials come to rest on archive shelves" (1993:9). As he observes, "The routes by which materials come to repose in archives are neither certain nor systematic" (p. 8). If the routes themselves are not systematic, the bias most certainly is. And systematic bias is the enemy, whether bias in terms of what does and does not make its way into the archives (or get recorded at all), what does and does not get talked about, or what even the most attentive of observers may fail to observe and to record. Admittedly this problem of what does and does not become part of the permanent record is not restricted to archival work alone, but it is most glaring there.

The Appeal of an Ethnographic Approach to Research

How can we account for the broad and growing appeal of ethnography as a way of looking, an approach that has become widely known and reasonably well accepted beyond the disciplines in which it has been a mainstay for decades? There are numerous advantages claimed for it, including often heard ones such as these:

- can be conducted entirely by one individual
- does not require one to be trained or licensed
- can be carried out almost anywhere
- problem to be studied can either be taken to the field or uncovered there
- a long-term commitment is assumed but there is no specified minimum
- the researcher often has exclusive domain in the setting studied
- relies essentially on a human observer to observe humans
- researcher can draw upon personal skills and strengths to advantage
- can make research not only interesting but adventurous
- requires no expensive equipment
- may present opportunity to learn and/or use another language
- offers opportunity to integrate professional and personal life
- role is recognized and usually accorded status associated with research

- can variously emphasize scientific or humanistic aspects
- flexible criteria for judging the finished product
- opportunity to develop writing (and sometimes photographic) talents
- presentation style can fit the circumstances
- provides rich database for further research and writing
- end product results in a contribution to knowledge
- emphasizes working with people rather than treating them as objects
- can get you out of your campus office if you are languishing there

The appeal of the ethnographic approach lies in the very eclecticism that its critics find so disarming, together with the straightforwardness and lack of pretense in the terminology with which it can be described. Given the absence of technical language or sophisticated procedures in the techniques reviewed above, once past the initial hurdle of gaining entrée to a study site or locating a willing informant, how could a fieldworker ever go wrong?

I doubt that I have introduced any unfamiliar terms here. If "ethno" refers to people, and "graph" to a picture, then the challenge of presenting a picture of a group of people seems to provide direction enough for many a researcher eager to get on with it. The task can always be honed more sharply for those drawn to a problem focus in their inquiries. True, we hear reference to an "ethnographic mystique" but there is little mystery in an approach that encourages one to experience the ways of a group firsthand, to supplement what one is able to observe with interviewing to learn what those in the group make of their experience, and further to supplement what can be learned first-hand with information gathered or materials prepared by others. Experiencing, enquiring, and examining shouldn't prove all that difficult as guidelines for conducting research, if that's all it takes to do ethnography.

For anyone pursuing research in a field in which qualitative research is now an option, there are also some incidental benefits in these approaches if one appreciates what can be *avoided* by not following one of the more quantitatively oriented ones. The experimental design that characterized so much social research in the past necessitates "interventions" or "treatments" that are not every researcher's cup of tea, especially those with an affinity for complex social problems and for solutions that do not lend themselves to the formal language of hypotheses or concocted variables. It seems not an unreasonable question to ask, Would it be "research enough" simply to attach myself to some group and to study some phenomenon in which I am interested, with the intent of trying better to understand how it works, without having to tamper with it or to isolate some tiny facet amenable to statistical treatment or laboratory study?

Perhaps the appeal of ethnography is of an even more personal nature, the attraction and satisfaction for anyone willing, able, and insistent on conducting *independent* inquiry. How especially appealing to the American sense of self-reliance to have sole responsibility for a research project from start to finish, regardless of how modest in scope, without having to bow to the authority of others or employ treatments not well understood or measurements deemed of little consequence. No wonder an ethnographic approach finds such broad appeal if it requires nothing more than experiencing, enquiring, and making use of relevant archival material. It might indeed seem not only that anyone can do it, but that we are all doing it all the time. But notice how these aspects contributing to the broad appeal are linked to fieldwork *techniques,* a sort of just-get-out-there-and-do-it approach. The question to examine next is, is that all there is to ethnography?

Notes

1. See, for example, Russ Bernard's "On Method and Methods in Anthropology," the introductory chapter to his edited *Handbook of Methods in Cultural Anthropology* (1998) in which he argues that "anthropology has always been about methods" (p. 9). Part 2 of the *Handbook* contains seven chapters with detailed descriptions of all the techniques mentioned in the present chapter, including discussions on structured interviewing and questionnaire construction, person-centered interviewing and observation, and visual anthropology.

2. I note that technically it is impossible to live your way into a culture because cultures don't exist as such. I take up that argument in Chapter 4.

3. Among recent books and articles dealing with the topic of participant observation are a useful one by sociologist Danny Jorgensen (1989); anthropological perspectives on the activity by Michael Agar (1980, 1996), Kathleen and Billie DeWalt (1998), and Barbara Tedlock (1991); chapters in both editions of the comprehensive Denzin and Lincoln *Handbook of Qualitative Research* (Atkinson and Hammersley 1994; Tedlock 2000); and Russ Bernard's two authored texts on anthropological research (1988, 1994b).

4. See, for example, an exemplary study reported by Boster (1985) that examines knowledge as a matter of consensus.

5. The *Cultural Anthropology Methods Newsletter,* originally published three times a year, became the *CAM Journal* in 1995 and, in 1999, under the name *Field Methods,* became the first journal publication of AltaMira Press. A journal devoted exclusively to method would seem to lend support to Russ Bernard's argument about the centrality of method in anthropology (see note 1, above), so I hasten to add that he is the founding editor of CAM and continues in that role for *Field Methods.*

6. For interviewing in general, see, for example, Kvale 1996; Seidman 1991. For the long interview, see McCracken 1988; for focus group interviews, Morgan 1988; for conducting interviews with special groups, such as children, Fine and Sandstrom 1988, with elites, Herz and Imber 1995, with the downtrodden, Hagan 1986. For early discussions specific to ethnography, see Paul 1953; Spradley 1979.

CHAPTER FOUR

Ethnography as a Way of Seeing

Natural science does not simply describe and explain nature; it is part of the interplay between nature and ourselves; it describes nature as exposed to our method of questioning.

—Werner Heisenberg
Physics and Philosophy, 1958, p. 81

The way we see things is affected by what we know or what we believe.

—John Berger
Ways of Seeing, 1973, p. 8

The previous chapter dealt with ethnographic research techniques. Collectively, those techniques are sometimes referred to as ethnographic methods (as Malinowski did in 1922) and even as "the" ethnographic method (for example, Gold 1997). So this chapter might be called "beyond method." That ethnography is more than method is a major theme throughout this book, and the discussion here is pivotal to show how I intend to represent and present it in the chapters that follow. In order to get beyond method without seeming to abandon it or leave it far behind, I will press the distinction reflected in the titles chosen for these paired chapters of Part Two, the previous chapter addressing ethnography as a way of *looking,* this one addressing ethnography as a way of *seeing.*

Let me illustrate the distinction I am making between "looking" and "seeing" by referring to the Rorschach cards mentioned earlier. At one time, use of the cards as a projective technique was fairly standard practice, especially among the more psychologically or psychoanalytically oriented fieldworkers. The cards were also known, and are perhaps better remembered, as the ink-blot cards. Anthropologists often carried a set of these cards into the field, intent on inviting informants to describe what they saw in them, just as psychoanalysts were doing in their offices with patients back home. In an era when Freudian terminology and concepts were highly touted in the anthropological quest for a unifying theory of humankind, Rorschach cards offered a standard stimulus (the set of cards, each presenting an ambiguous black-and-white or color figure) that provided an opportunity to collect protocols from subjects anywhere in the world. The protocols could then be sent away for analysis by someone unfamiliar with either the individuals who volunteered them or with their "culture." Here indeed was objective science that could be used in the comparative study of societies.[1]

The cards are now passé; fieldwork fads change, and Freudian theory no longer holds the promise or prominence that it did. But the cards nicely illustrate the distinction between looking and seeing. The psychoanalyst (if you were paying her) or the anthropologist (if she was paying you) asked you to *look* at the cards, but it was up to you to report what you *saw* in them. Whether addressing patients or informants, one can give all kinds of directions for looking—where, when, for how long, even what one *should* give special attention to or *should* see. Here I go beyond ways of looking to discuss what ethnographers see, and should see, *because they are ethnographers* who (more or less) share ideas about a way of viewing human social behavior.

For another example in making a distinction between looking and seeing, consider what might result if one were to invite a biologist, a hunter, and a real-estate developer to visit and to render an independent appraisal of an attractive rural site. In spite of the fact that the setting is the same, we would expect each of them to see and appreciate something quite different. My point is that an ethnographer's ways of seeing tell us more about the doing of ethnography than do an ethnographer's ways of looking. An ethnographer's ways of looking are strikingly similar to the ways of looking shared by humans everywhere: observing, asking, examining what others have done.

What the ethnographer does, to be a bit disarming about it, is to think about how other ethnographers would see the setting, what they would make of it. To become an ethnographer one must acquire a sense of what constitutes an ethnographic problem, what guides an inquiry so that it results in ethnography rather than, say, the inventory of flora and fauna we might expect from a biologist, the stalking strategy proposed by the hunter, or the subdivision potential envisioned by the real-estate developer. One quickly realizes that, as important as fieldwork is to accomplishing ethnography, it is the mindwork (and the accompanying deskwork) that goes with it that is most critical. Ethnography is more than method.

Ethnography as More than Method

For the anthropologically oriented researcher, ethnography has always been associated with and intended for studying culture. Early assumptions that any research along these lines must necessarily be directed toward the study of "primitives" and their "tribal cultures" have given way to broadly defined concern for cultural scenes, microcultures, and to the interactions between and among groups with differing cultural orientations. The underlying idea is that culture is revealed through discerning patterns of socially shared behavior. That idea rests a bit uneasily in the absence of satisfactory resolutions to provocative questions such as how much "sharing" is necessary or how much agreement there must be as to just what we mean by culture to keep the concept itself viable.

As viewed from *outside* its discipline of origin, however, ethnography has slowly become dislodged from the conceptual framework once so closely associated with it. As a consequence, for some researchers, an ethnographic question may simply be a question that is amenable to study through *techniques* (or *methods,* if you prefer) comparable to those employed by the early ethnographers. The orienting question need not call for interpretation at all, only description, with finely *detailed* description substituted for, and perhaps even misconstrued for, carefully *contextualized* description.

Given the wide range of activities that anthropologists themselves are inclined to label as ethnography, we might feel resigned to define ethnography as "what ethnographers do," always a safe way to define an activity, if not a very enlightening one. Indeed, in perusing a periodical like the *Journal of Contemporary Ethnography* (formerly *Urban Life and Culture*) one realizes that today's ethnographers may be found anywhere, studying anything that can be studied through a fieldwork approach. That is how *Contemporary Ethnography* defines its mission, informing readers and potential contributors in its policy statement that it "publishes original and theoretically significant studies based upon participant-observation, unobtrusive observation, intensive interviewing, and contextualized analysis of discourse as well as examinations of such ethnographic methods." Approach has become paramount. For many, the ethnographic question is not *what* one studies, or *where* one conducts research, but whether the data are obtained by techniques consistent with standard fieldwork practice.

Taking ethnography to be a method of inquiry independent of the study of culture is a reasonable adaptation (or perhaps appropriation) of it in service to other disciplines and areas of practice. Nevertheless, that is not the tack I have taken in the past (e.g., HFW 1975a, 1982b) and it is not the tack I pursue now. Ethnography as presented here finds its orienting and overarching purpose in an underlying concern with cultural interpretation. That is not to say that an explicit cultural framework must be rigorously imposed on every study, but it does mean that to be ethnographic, a study must provide the kind of account of human social activity out of which cultural patterning can be discerned.

Culture is to be regarded for what it is, an abstraction, a perspective for studying human behavior that gives particular attention to ("privileges," in today's lexicon) acquired social behavior. Such a view does not dismiss those who equate ethnography with participant observation or any particular constellation of fieldwork techniques, but it goes beyond merely insisting that a researcher be on site to collect data. I join with Michael Agar to insist that "ethnography is much more complicated than collecting data" (1980:41 and again in 1996:51). All researchers, most certainly the qualitatively oriented ones, ought to have a clear sense of what Agar means. Beyond that, of course, anyone is free to draw upon any aspects of ethnography that prove helpful. In that sense, pursuing research through a fieldwork approach is a logical starting place for realizing ethnographic potential. If you are comfortable with the techniques, I hope I can expand your embrace so that for you, too, ethnography comes to mean more than method.

The underlying purpose of ethnographic research in this view is to describe what the people in some particular place or status ordinarily do, and the meanings they ascribe to what they do, under ordinary or particular circumstances, presenting that description in a manner that draws attention to regularities that implicate cultural process. One can *do* ethnography anywhere, anytime, and of virtually anything, as long as human social behavior is involved (or *was* involved, in the case of studies made by archaeologists and ethnohistorians). The important question is not whether ethnography is feasible in a particular instance but whether and how cultural interpretation might enhance understanding of the topic or problem under investigation. What, then, is an ethnographic question, and what constitutes the essence of ethnography?

What Is an Ethnographic Question?

To pose an ethnographic question is to ask a question in such a way that ethnographic research is a reasonable way—although not necessarily the only way—to go about finding an answer.

There is always a strong descriptive element in ethnography, so an ethnographic question must implicate what it is that the ethnographer is to describe as a result of exercising the two major fieldwork components described earlier, experiencing and enquiring. You haven't posed an ethnographic question until it is clear what the ethnographer is to look at and look for, at least with sufficient clarity to get an inquiry underway. There is a rather narrow window here, somewhere between posing questions hopelessly broad (e.g., "Does Buddhism account for the patience that seems to dominate the Thai world view?" or "How do leaders make their decisions?") or so specific that they can better be investigated by quicker means ("What is the prevailing attitude of the Japanese toward Americans doing business in their country?" "What television programs do Brazilians watch most?" or "Where can you buy postage stamps in Italy?").

In Chapter 2, I stressed the importance of serendipity and of place in the ethnographic career, but neither of these aspects of fieldwork can define purpose. Ethnography cannot proceed without purpose. However, in the course of assessing the possibilities of all that might be researched, researchable questions readily arise: As an ethnographer who now finds himself or herself in some particular setting, what aspects appear worthy of study? If time and resources allow the luxury of a traditional ethnography, such broad questions as "What is going on here?" or "What do people in this setting have to know in order to do what they are doing?" might be adequate for initiating an inquiry. Any such inquiry should go beyond simply developing a descriptive account to framing more provocative questions—descriptive questions as to *how*, and underlying questions, voiced perhaps only in internal dialogues among ethnographers themselves, as to *meanings* imputed to action.

I underscore that the purposes that guide ethnographic inquiry do not spring forth from the settings in which ethnography is conducted; they arrive with the ethnographer. Even so direct a question as "What is going on here?" has its origins outside the setting in which it is posed. As my own academic interests turned to processes in the acquisition of culture, I began to frame guiding questions that helped me attend to those interests. There were two questions I could address in virtually any setting. First, what do people in this setting have to know and do to make this system work? And second, if culture, loosely defined as "shared knowledge," is mostly caught rather than taught, how do those being inducted into the group find their "way in" so that the system is maintained?

Broad, descriptive, orienting questions like these help me attend to some aspects of what is going on and relieve me of feeling that I ought to try to observe "everything." And that introduces an important caveat in how ethnography proceeds, a quality not fully appreciated by those unfamiliar with it. Whether stated explicitly or not, efforts at description must be directed at something. One cannot simply observe. A question such as "What is going on here?" can only be addressed when fleshed out with enough detail to answer the related question, "In terms of what?"

I hedged my statement, noting a "strong" descriptive element in ethnography, rather than suggesting that ethnographers try to achieve "pure" description. Description can only be accomplished in terms of purpose. Our most intense efforts to achieve objectivity are foiled from the outset. Despite how scientifically satisfying it might seem to argue the purity of our descriptive efforts, we must concede that descriptive data are always "theory laden." I use theory here in its little "t" sense, not in its capital "T" Grand Theory one. There has to be an *idea* guiding what we choose to describe and how we choose to describe it. Ethnographers do not engage in what has been referred to lightheartedly as "immaculate perception." We do not and cannot simply *observe, watch,* or *look;* we must observe, watch, or look at *something.* That fact surely tarnishes any notion that ethnography has somehow transcended the inherent human limitations of those who conduct it.

Ethnographers may say they are not exactly sure what they are looking for when pressed to divulge what they expect to learn in the course of an inquiry. That answer is always partially true, and I think it becoming for us to preserve all we can of such tentativeness toward what we are observing and what we make of it. Nonetheless, without some idea of what we are about, we could not proceed with observations at all. To be accused of "haphazard descriptiveness," then, reveals more of a failure to convince one's audience of knowing what one is doing, or adequately to specify one's parameters. Observation is, of necessity, a zero-sum game: the cost of looking at anything is at the expense of looking at something else, or looking elsewhere. Kenneth Burke has it right: A way of seeing is, indeed, always a way of not seeing (1935:70). Anyone who insists, "I haven't a clue," most assuredly has a hunch or an intuitive feeling to guide his or her observations. When you become established at this, you can start calling those guiding hunches your "theories." But Charles Darwin long ago warned against pushing too hard on that term. In a letter written in 1863, he advised:

> Let theory guide your observations, but till your reputation is well established be sparing in publishing theory. It makes persons doubt your observations. [Quoted in Gruber 1981:123]

The same holds for asking an ethnographic question: One cannot ask an ethnographic question without some idea of what an ethnographic answer looks like, some idea of the circumstances under which it does and does not make sense to pursue ethnography beyond its commitment to thorough fieldwork. Given the customary limits within which ethnographic research has traditionally been conducted—one person working alone for an extended period of time—there are corresponding limits to the scale of the issues or projects on which one may reasonably engage. When topics grow in complexity that exceeds the scope of what a lone researcher can accomplish, a ready and willing ethnographer must assess the goodness of fit between the information needed and whatever contribution ethnography might make. Should conducting an independent inquiry seem to serve little purpose, another possible contribution is to help create a better fit between some other, more systematic approach and the issue to be addressed.

To broad social concerns such as ethnic conflict, stemming the tide of AIDS, or understanding why children of certain backgrounds do poorly in school, one can ask how (or whether) the particularistic nature of ethnography can shed enough light to warrant the effort. Even the most rigorous of quantitatively oriented researchers may be willing to concede that ethnography can play a role in shaping an inquiry: helping to identify common factors, dramatizing differences among cases in different circumstances, refocusing the research problem, or helping to prioritize questions in terms of time and resources available. There seems to be wide recognition of ethnography's potential contribution in the problem-forming stage. But among the more deeply committed quantifiers a lingering doubt remains as to whether "real" research results can be achieved by such means. Researchers who have no trouble accepting ethnography as adjunct continue to have trouble with the idea of accepting it as a full-blown research approach in its own right.

I do not share such doubts, but that is certainly not to claim that ethnography is the be-all and end-all of research. A conservative view might hold that ethnography is not well suited to most research problems, and that for many pressing problems it has at best only a modest contribution to make. It does no harm to be modest in claims about what it can accomplish. In those instances when it *is* well suited, I think ethnography achieves its fullest potential when the ethnographer is free to work independently. That seems a better use of ethnographic talent than simply having ethnographers run interference for large-scale studies or watch their efforts get swallowed up in number-crunching efforts that tell us too little about too many.

I trust you recognize such preferences as personal as well as professional. I like to do my own thing, to work in my own way and at my own speed, and to assume responsibility for seeing a project through from start to finish. For me, that one-person feature is an aspect that I find especially appealing about ethnography. It also presents a good argument for including ethnographic experience in the training of all would-be researchers and *consumers* of research, because it takes them through the entire research process from start-up to write-up.

Although fieldwork tends to be conducted as an individual activity, there have always been ethnographers—today in increasing numbers—who find team research appealing. (For more discussion, see Erickson and Stull 1997; Tedlock 2000.) The two-person fieldwork team (often husband and wife) is especially well institutionalized in ethnographic research. This includes the not-too-uncommon circumstance where one partner is professionally trained when the fieldwork begins, but out of the shared experience and working relationship the other partner acquires a working knowledge—and, later perhaps, formal professional credentials as well. Rather predictably, when the team consists of a male and a female, the guiding ethnographic question has been split into two, the male partner focusing on men's activities and beliefs, the female partner on women and children, in a seemingly "natural" division of the research task that, until recently, we seemed not to question for some stereotyping of its own.

In times past, other ethnographers, typically younger ones beginning their research careers, sometimes joined large-scale projects on site or participated in ongoing projects administered through an academic department. Consider, for example, the Indonesian research described in Chapter 2, and projects of even grander scale such as the Cornell University–Vicos project in Peru, or the Harvard Chiapas Project that began as a five-year program and lasted for 35 years (Vogt 1994). In such cases the overriding ethnographic task became a collective one, the project defined in such a way that cadres of fieldworkers could be sent to investigate a central topic through research conducted in different communities. Prominent among such projects were the five-cultures study at Rimrock (Vogt and Albert 1967) and the six-cultures study under the direction of John and Beatrice Whiting (Whiting and Whiting 1975).

In spite of the romantic appeal of researchers seemingly free to study anything they want, ethnographers have also performed admirable service conducting preliminary fieldwork to get a sense of the range and depth of community feelings on an issue before systematic study was initiated on a grander scale. Contributing an ethnography or two won't cut down on infant mortality or AIDS, but in communities where information is lacking about local practices, efforts to gather survey data or to modify prevailing practice may entirely miss their mark. An assumption that infant mortality is a *problem*—rather than an answer as, for example, in a society that values children of one sex more than another—warrants ethnographic attention, preferably from an ethnographer who can recognize some assumptions of her or his own. So although I remain partial to the idea of the ethnographer working as an independent agent, I recognize the contribution to be made when ethnographers hire on as consultants to larger projects or are incorporated into social science teams.[2]

Some uses of ethnography in applied settings are discussed in Chapter 8. Here I draw attention to its more or less "pure" state, as with community studies that once characterized much of the total ethnographic effort. Even in those ethnography-for-its-own-sake days, it had to accommodate a multitude of practitioners, problems, and motives. My chosen subtitle is intended to convey and underscore the idea that ethnography is *a* way of seeing. As I delve deeper into what ethnographers do and the kinds of issues they confront, I may seem to portray the ethnographer as not only the lone researcher but also the Lone Ranger, the troubleshooter with infinite skill, patience, and personal resources to get to the bottom of things before riding off into the sunset, the Compleat Researcher after all. Michael Agar seems to start out that way in the following quote, but he quickly pares the ethnographer's task—and thus the ethnographer as well—down to size:

> Ethnography is really quite an arrogant enterprise. In a short period of time, an ethnographer moves in among a group of strangers to study and describe their beliefs, document their social life, write about their subsistence strategies, and generally explore the territory right down to their recipes for the evening meal. The task is an impossible one. At best, an ethnography can only be partial. [Agar 1980:41]

Instead of envisioning the ethnographer as Superman or Wonder Woman, one must recognize that it is the scope of the ethnographic *question* that must be pared to what one individual, or a researcher working with a colleague or small research team, can accomplish in a limited amount of time. The range of fieldwork techniques that can be employed must be pared as well.

Of course, in an ideal world, *every* researcher would be sufficiently talented to be able to summon from a vast personal repertoire whatever combination of techniques seems appropriate for addressing the issue at hand. And such an ideal might seem most nearly attainable in the role of the ethnographer responsible for an inquiry in its entirety, from conception to final report. It would be splendid indeed to have at one's command all the research skills one might ever need. But think about it! If you, as sole or principal investigator, really did have all the skills of social research at your command—computer skills, language skills, statistical skills, survey techniques, ability to work with experimental and quasi-experimental design—let alone all the observer and interviewer and interpersonal skills an ethnographer is likely to need, why would you invest your time plodding along with ethnography? Whatever else it is, ethnography is a time-consuming way to conduct in-depth inquiry. If you already know what results you need, or are under the gun quickly to provide quantifiable "findings," ethnography makes no sense at all as your major strategy.

On the other hand, if you see yourself as a dyed-in-the-wool ethnographer who happily leaves to others the treatment groups or controlled sampling procedures of the survey researcher, then you need carefully to assess—and make sure that others understand—what you can and cannot accomplish by following this modus operandi. If world problems (hunger, violence, religious or racial intolerance) or broadly conceived variables (leadership, morale, power, resistance, corruption) intrigue you, then ethnography is probably not your thing. If ethnography *is* your thing and you are nonetheless attracted to such issues, then you need to assess how, and to what extent, small-scale study can contribute, whether by calling attention to problems seen in broader context, to exploring the range and variation extant, or to helping others frame better questions for inquiry conducted on a larger scale. You also need to recognize personal strengths and preferences in conducting fieldwork, so that in whatever ways you execute the research role you make the fullest use of what you do best.

Great Expectations or Mission Impossible?

Do you remember a popular television series years ago, or more recently the film by the same name, titled *Mission Impossible?* The story in each episode took shape as the special agent who was its hero listened to a brief tape recording advising him of his next assignment. The message always began the same: "Your mission, should you choose to accept it . . ."

Attempting to address the topic of ethnography as a way of seeing, to examine the numerous forms it may take, to review all the arguments over definition that it has prompted, or to weigh all its advantages and shortcomings, presents me with something of a "mission impossible." Small wonder that when invited to write about ethnography in general, we usually retreat to writing about fieldwork *techniques,* as I confess to having done in the past (HFW 1975a,b; 1981a,b; 1988; 1990a; 1995).

I noted Agar's warning that ethnography can at best be only partial. And so, alas, my effort to capture and communicate its essence must necessarily prove partial as well, not only in one sense but in several. First, like ethnography itself, the effort is partial by reason of being incomplete, one person's view, at one point in time, based on one set of experiences enhanced by a purposeful but serendipitous selection of experiences related by others. Furthermore, I still tend to frame ethnography in terms of the purpose for which it was originally developed, toward understanding Culture in general by studying cultures in specific. "A true ethnography is about something called a culture," writes Richard Shweder (1996b:19), and I couldn't agree more. Being the flat-footed ethnographer that I am, I have been rather impervious to the whole postmodern critique of the 1980s and 1990s with its "crisis of representation." I have no problem with the consciousness-raising and introspection the critique has generated, but I have been at this so long that I am now part of what has come under fire. We were not all that insensitive *then,* and I do not see much impact on ethnographic *practice* now, except in caution about ethnographic authority and a more penetrating concern about power in human relationships. The dust seems finally to be settling on the postmodern era (see, for example, Marcus 1997), but that part of the story must wait to be told by others.

I regard myself as a traditional or old-fashioned ethnographer in a day when the culture concept itself has come under increasingly sharp attack. Yet I rather doubt that my own studies would pass muster among the *real* old guard who searched out tribal groups that left no doubt in anyone's mind as to what constituted difference enough. Only by contrast with what sometimes passes today for ethnography do my own studies look all that traditional.

Even in my study among the Kwakiutl I spent a great many of those "days in the field" at what had become by then my customary post at the head of a classroom. Four years later, the idea that I claimed to be doing an ethnography of a principal in a local elementary school produced frowns among some senior anthropologists whom I had rather hoped would find the idea intriguing. "Can you do an ethnography of a person?" I was asked. I found myself offering what I felt was a convincing distinction between *the ethnography of a principal* and *an ethnography of the principalship,* the latter a seemingly more satisfactory way to describe what I intended to accomplish. In spite of the absence of dramatic cross-cultural comparison, however, culture remained, as it has always remained, at the core of my interpretations.

I find it impossible to think about ethnography in any other way; I cannot accept the idea that it is nothing more than a set of fieldwork procedures that can be applied anywhere. To me, ethnography entails *both* the way we study culture and the interpretive framework that ethnographers impose on everything they study. I do not set out to "observe" culture, but I take responsibility for making culture explicit in whatever I observe, because that is how ethnographers make sense of what they see. It has become a personal way of seeing, as well.

For my purposes, therefore, I assume that an ethnographer—any ethnographer—is *always* guided by a concern for cultural description. If you are going to conduct ethnographic research, that can be your mission—should you choose to accept it—but it does not have to be your mission. You are free to use ethnography to accomplish your research purposes, whether you draw only upon its most basic fieldwork techniques, model your work on existing studies without a corresponding investment in a cultural perspective, or pursue your inquiry intent on producing a contemporary equivalent of one of the early classics. You will, I believe, be better off following *any* of these alternatives if you understand how ethnographers have conducted their studies in the past, at least in the recent past when ethnography finally "came home." Admittedly, however, ethnographers have *always* felt free to fashion, or refashion, ethnography to suit their purposes. Even teams sent out with detailed handbooks designed to guide the collection of data and assure some uniformity of results have returned to write up accounts that bear their individual and unique stamp. It can be no other way. "Whatever else an ethnography does," notes James Clifford, "it translates experience into text" (1986:115), and experience is always idiosyncratic.

As central and unifying as it is, a commitment to cultural interpretation is not the clear mandate it might appear to be, even among those steeped in a sociocultural orientation. Were culture something one could observe firsthand, all any ethnographer would have to do is observe and record human interaction and bring back a detailed account of what had been observed. But culture is not "there" waiting to be observed, and no ethnographer can ever hope to catch so much as a glimpse of it. Overly enthusiastic researchers do succumb at times to representing culture that way, as though they not only have seen it but have watched it push (or in a stronger version, pull) people around, fill their heads with beliefs, or keep them from realizing their full human potential. The ethnographer's mission—the traditionally oriented ethnographer I am describing here—recognizes culture not as something to be observed but as something ethnographers *put there because that is the way they render their accounts.* Ward Goodenough explains this by saying that ethnographers *attribute* culture to the people among whom they study:

> In anthropological practice the culture of any society is made of the concepts, beliefs, and principles of action and organization that an ethnographer has found could be attributed successfully to the members of that society in the context of dealing with them. [Goodenough 1976:5]

Goodenough is careful to distinguish between "culture" and "society." Although often used interchangeably, these two terms serve us better when they are differentiated. As Goodenough has observed (1981:103n), people belong to *groups,* not to *cultures.* One cannot belong to a culture any more than one can belong to a language; cultures and languages are ways of doing things, not something one can join. Because culture has been "so strongly associated with social groups and communities," Goodenough remarks, we too-often read about people being "members of a culture," but he finds the idea "truly nonsensical." I trust that I have been consistent here in differentiating between what people can do and what they can belong to.

To make their mission possible, following this particular way of viewing culture, ethnographers must be able to posit the "concepts, beliefs, and principles of action and organization" they infer from what they observe firsthand and what others tell them. With so broad a charter as doing the ethnography of some group, the ethnographer must paint with a broad brush in order to communicate this essence to a reader. Among the more problem-focused ethnographers, attention is directed to those aspects of culture most relevant to the issue under investigation. In either case, the ethnographer will experience tension between getting the big picture and getting the fine detail. The advice I offer is to try to capture something of each, but to have clearly in mind which of the two warrants greater emphasis according to the purposes of the inquiry. Ethnography demands constant selectivity on the part of the ethnographer as to what to put in and thoughtful reflection about what must be left out.

More Expectations

How many qualities or characteristics or criteria are enough to nurture *great* expectations for ethnography and to guide ethnographers to achieve some reasonable ones? Immediately above I have reviewed two critical expectations, first and foremost that ethnography is a *field-oriented activity,* and second that ethnography has traditionally taken *cultural interpretation* as its central purpose. Yet even in the good old days when consensus rather than "deconstructing" was the prevailing mood, I doubt that these two characteristics necessarily would have received universal approval. "Field-oriented activity" might pass muster simply because the phrase is sufficiently ambiguous to accommodate scholars who rely on ethnographic data but are themselves not well suited for fieldwork or attracted to the field in any sense other than metaphorical. And assigning centrality to "culture" might meet unexpected resistance even among cultural anthropologists; some of them find too little power in the "tired old culture concept" to devote a career to pursuing it.

Thus even two seemingly basic expectations might variously be argued or interpreted. Yet a book that boldly proclaims *Ethnography* as its title can rightfully be expected either to identify ethnography's essential components or at least to distinguish between critical and merely customary features. I accept as part of *my* mission to try to identify the essential components of ethnography. Be aware, however, that what may at first appear to be its essential features will prove instead to be only *customary* ones. Ethnography is going to prove a bit elusive.

Take the two criteria discussed above as a tentative starting point—that ethnography is a field-oriented activity and that cultural interpretation is at the core of it. Do these criteria hold in every case? And where do we go from here? It might be tempting to give way to further sermonizing about what ethnography *ought* to be (have I overdone that a bit already?) or to draw up the equivalent of the Boy Scout Law for the Truehearted Ethnographer: an ethnographer should be clean, courteous, kind but skeptical, honest, trustworthy, etc., qualities that should be evident in the ethnographic account as well. Or I might turn to a ready-made list of research expectations that would be proposed by experimentally oriented researchers and cast in a familiar vocabulary calling attention to validity, reliability, objectivity, and generalizability, criteria that invariably find us scrambling to defend our approaches on their home ground.

Rather than dwell too obsessively on ethnography's essential elements, perhaps I can make more headway if I begin by identifying what I refer to above as *customary* features. For example, I do not have to stretch a point to say that customarily it is a field-oriented activity. That is not the same as insisting that there is no possibility of ethnography without the presence of the ethnographer in the setting, but it certainly is a customary expectation. As to cultural interpretation, that, too, is customary. But even among anthropologists, there would be little agreement as to whether there are better conceptual frameworks for holding an account together than a too-strict insistence that "culture" is adequate for the task.

Let me introduce three additional terms anthropologists use, not only in reference to ethnography but in conveying the essence of their discipline—that it is *holistic, cross-cultural,* and *comparative.* Seemingly, such qualities as these should be apparent in all ethnographic work, since ethnographies are the building blocks of cultural anthropology. Yet we must keep ethnography itself in perspective. Anthropologists strive to do some things *as anthropologists* that both depend on and greatly exceed the contribution that can be made by ethnography alone. Trying to be holistic, cross-cultural, and comparative at once gives direction to and exerts some strain on what any one individual ethnographer can hope to accomplish. Because I have some difficulty in distinguishing what is cross-cultural from what is comparative, I will treat those two terms together. The criterion of being holistic presents less of a problem. Let me begin there.

Ethnography as Holistic or Contextual

Drawing on the special meaning of the term as employed by anthropologists, Felix Keesing defined "holistic" as "an approach which emphasizes phenomena of wholeness or integration" (1958:428). Holism (I've also seen it spelled wholism in an earlier day) prevails on ethnographers to examine things in their entirety rather than only in parts, the very idea of wholeness implied in such all-encompassing terms as "culture" or "society," as well as in the everyday caution that instances of observed behavior are part of a larger picture and cannot be understood out of context.

Historically, anthropologists have long argued the "parts versus whole" issue. Their various resolutions are reflected in contested definitions of culture, especially Kroeber's brief for culture as *superorganic,* that is, as more than the sum of its parts. Holism underwrites the ethnographer's effort to get the whole story. While the term itself seems to point to completeness, what it really calls for is making *connections* between things, rather than, as Agar expresses it, tearing them into pieces (1994:112).

What holism is all about is *context,* a term I like even better. Context has always seemed to be the ethnographic long suit. Context is something one can expect (and insist on) from ethnography that is most apt to be stripped away in any more narrowly focused approach. I can think of no better advice to offer a would-be ethnographer than to attend carefully to context. I subscribe to the notion that human behavior is *overdetermined,* at least in terms of our ability as observers to analyze and describe it. Context opens the way for the ethnographer to present human social behavior as *more,* rather than as *less,* complex, to keep explanations from becoming simplistic or reductionist.

To be commended for well-contextualized reporting should bring satisfaction to any ethnographer for having successfully resolved the tension between providing irrelevant or excessive detail and providing too little. Holism is not an invitation to fill up a study; it is a call for tracing interrelated elements and fitting parts together. I trust I render valuable service by remarking on the tension between exhibiting an economy of style and providing an adequate level of detail. If you are inclined to offer your descriptions in great detail, then here is an activity that not only calls for but insists on it. Ethnography *is* a matter of detail. An *ethnographic* question begs for relevant and complex detail.

Personal styles, rather than training or theoretical orientation, probably underlie how each of us deals with detail. By nature, do you ordinarily take on, try to do, and inevitably report on, too much or too little? You don't have to restrict your assessment only to how you report. In my own case, I have a difficult time throwing away *anything.* As a consequence, my writing can become as cluttered as my carport or work space with material that probably should be tossed out. I know others who keep everything pared to the bare bone, their prose included. The critiques they receive of their written work generally ask for more detail, more context. My reviewers invariably call for less. The rendering of detail presents different problems to different researchers; not everyone needs to be more sparing of it. As general advice, I recommend attending to as much detail as possible in one's observations and notes—especially during the initial period of note taking—and then rendering as much detail as possible in the reporting, at least in early drafts. It is preferable to have an excess of detail and subsequently do some heavy editing than initially to skimp on detail that must later be recaptured.

Colleagues can play a helpful role by reading early drafts to identify details that receive too little or too much attention. We lose track of the fact that we bring more to our own accounts than any other reader can possibly bring. The details we include are often shorthand references for which only the observer has the complete picture. Events we have witnessed can be related to others only through the details we provide. As observers, we ourselves are immersed in a fullness of detail we cannot possibly communicate. We are always caught between needing to be less wordy and needing to provide sufficient context.

One place where this is likely to occur is when we repeat verbatim what several informants have said about the same topic. Because we were there, we "hear" the words as they were actually spoken, perhaps by informants strikingly different in appearance or circumstance. But to the reader, such accounts are likely to appear remarkably similar and, therefore, needlessly repetitious. The challenge is to find other ways to communicate whatever is significant about such differences if merely repeating informants' words fails to accomplish it. This is another advantage in having someone read drafts aloud. To any reader other than yourself, your informants will all speak in one voice. Much as you may have preferred to have informants speak for themselves, the nuances will be lost.

We can also get lost in detail in ways of which we ourselves are not always cognizant. One is in subtle efforts to effect sheer "dazzle," showing off how much information we have gathered through our unrelenting attentiveness. We want readers to recognize that we have worked hard, done a good job, been thorough in our endeavors. We want to provide ample evidence that fieldwork is hard work, and thus our accomplishment worthy of commendation. We also validate an implicit claim that we are trustworthy observers *in general* through the level of detail we demonstrate in our descriptions of *particular* people or events. By the time we are ready to present our more tenuous observations or interpretations, we hope to have brought readers along so they recognize and appreciate the authority of the authorial voice with which we speak. I suspect most of us are also guilty of employing our ability to dazzle by giving emphasis to what we *are* able to report so that the reader becomes less mindful of whatever might be missing. Attention to detail is a critical part of claims-making in an endeavor in which everything to be reported must be seen through our eyes alone. While it is currently popular in some camps to pretend to divest ourselves of all authority, we simply must be listened to if we are to present our cases.

Associated as it is with the gathering of detail, and criticized as it often is for excesses in that regard, ethnography and ethnographers often take a bad rap for a quality that ought to warrant celebration. Isn't a preoccupation with detail one of our strong points? We need to see that our efforts are brought to the attention of those who share our patience for detail, rather than acquiesce to our rushy culture's insistence on getting on with it. Hear Arthur Kleinman's eloquent plea on behalf of ethnographers who go "on and on":

> In order to build the scaffolding of scholarly materials that makes cultural analysis convincing and authorizes the ethnographer to apply that analysis to different problems and special themes, the author composes an iterative process that goes back and forth across ethnographic context, social theory, and key issues. The sedulous reader of ethnography, being a devotee of detail, expects to become absorbed in the intricacies of thought and experience that represent an alternative way of being-in-the-world. While coherence and analytic power count for something, so too do reflexive voice, style, thickly described ethnographic materials, and *aperçus* that illuminate a local world, often in order to challenge a putative universal or to critique the world of the ethnographer, a not-so-silent subject in many ethnographic monographs.
>
> If all this sounds old-fashioned, that is one of the arresting charms of ethnography. In place of our era's egregious emphasis on minimalist interpretation, ethnography develops, meanders, even circles back; it goes on and on. [Kleinman 1995:194–195]

Voilà! There is your authoritative footnote, should you find yourself meandering, going "on and on." I can't really recommend that you make a grim determination to get "everything." Yet I temper that advice with an anthropologist's own reflection on our era's "egregious emphasis on minimalist interpretation," everything coming at us byte by byte. If ethnography is a meander, acknowledging that characteristic might help sort out who is better suited to pursue it and who, as readers, are more likely to appreciate it. Maybe that explains why I resist some of the "rapid" approaches to ethnography that I review in Chapter 8 but present without advocacy. My problem is not with those techniques per se but with why those who rely on them too exclusively want to burden themselves with the label "ethnography."

Ethnography as Cross-Cultural and Comparative

Given ethnography's origins in the study of dramatically different others, whatever is cross-cultural has always seemed to me ipso facto to be comparative as well. Even as anthropologists began turning attention to studies conducted in their own societies, "cross-cultural" and "comparative" remained closely linked. It seemed reasonable to assume that one's prior (and prerequisite) cross-cultural experience invariably provided the basis for a comparative perspective.

In recent years I have found it useful to recognize a distinction between these two terms. All study is comparative, but the cross-cultural perspective that was once a definitive feature of ethnography can no longer simply be assumed. If it isn't there already, the ethnographer has to put it there, somewhat the way he or she must put culture itself into the interpretation. Today we find ethnographers whose experiential base and research experience are limited essentially to subsets of their own societies. The expectation that ethnography is cross-cultural as well as comparative has become something of a predicament.

A cross-cultural perspective drawn from firsthand experience continues to be recognized as highly *desirable* for anyone claiming to do ethnography, but the idea of insisting on it as prerequisite has been losing ground. Students well versed in anthropological literature have sometimes been able to compensate for a lack of personal cross-cultural experience by drawing upon appropriate concepts and by comparisons from their (required) grounding in area studies, much as their forebears had done through "library studies" of their own. As ethnography gained favor outside anthropology, however, researchers felt neither the obligation nor the need to bring a cross-cultural perspective to their work. Watching this happen early on in educational anthropology gave one of its "founding fathers," George Spindler, grave concern:

> It would be a grievous error to think that a generation of educational anthropologists could be trained without a solid exposure to this kind of [cross-cultural] experience. I suggest that no anthropologist-of-education-to-be should start with his or her first significant piece of empirical research in a school in our own society. It is essential for him or her to get turned around by seeing and experiencing differently. [Spindler 1973:16]

Anthropologists might have chosen to use culture as a wall to keep outsiders from encroaching on their sacred ground. It is probably just as well that they never became all that protective of either "culture" or "ethnography" as exclusive intellectual properties of their discipline. In many parts of the world, finding opportunities for experiencing another macro- or national culture firsthand *for the explicit purpose of conducting ethnographic research* has become increasingly difficult. A contributing factor to the perceived extent of this problem is the close association in the minds of many, anthropologists included, between culture and ethnicity. Ethnicity may indeed signal the presence of dramatic cultural difference of the sort on which ethnography was founded, but culture is by no means limited to differences rooted in ethnicity. I was surprised to hear a student in Australia lament that it was almost impossible these days to do cross-cultural research in her country because of difficulties in securing permission to work with Aboriginal populations. In her mind, the only opportunity for *real* cross-cultural research was with that group. Closer to home I have heard a similar lament for years about the difficulties of gaining permission to work with Native American groups. It is interesting to realize how narrowly we define the groups for whom we customarily expect a particular style of research to be employed.

A closely related misperception is that culture is found only among others and thus is defined implicitly as any behavior different from our own. I listened with dismay as a high school teacher who only recently had "discovered" ethnography reported how she had begun assigning her ethnically different students to do "ethnographies" in their own homes. She had mislocated the role that a cross-cultural perspective plays in ethnography. What she herself might be able to discern from visiting her students' homes, they are quite unlikely to recognize on (or in) their own. She does not realize that ethnography does not begin at home! It is in *her* home that her ethnically different students would be most likely to detect the kinds of differences she expects them to discover in their own.

I concur in giving high priority to gaining firsthand experience in dramatically different circumstances for anyone with a long-range interest in ethnography. Travel, overseas teaching and exchanges, volunteer programs like the Peace Corps—all kinds of possibilities offer glimpses into other ways of life and a reaffirmation that cultural differences are real, dramatic, and deep. For those who get hooked on ethnography at a time when their initial foray into qualitative research lacks the dramatic cross-cultural experience they might have hoped for, it may be possible to gain such experience at a later time. Several of my doctoral students in "anthropology and education" found (i.e., created) such opportunity *after* completion of their dissertation studies; it is never too late. Further, their dissertations were fieldwork-based, conducted in depth, and made excellent and appropriate uses of a cultural framework. In the absence of the opportunity for *dramatic* cross-cultural experience, those students did not lose sight of the fact that they were studying and interpreting behavior from a cultural perspective.

What exactly does a cross-cultural perspective provide? It should allow the observer to make problematic what might otherwise be taken for granted.

Years ago Clyde Kluckhohn provided the following oft-quoted rationale for the need to study among others in order to "see ourselves":

> Studying primitives enables us to see ourselves better. Ordinarily we are unaware of the special lens through which we look at life. It would hardly be fish who discovered the existence of water. Students who had not gone beyond the horizon of their own society could not be expected to perceive custom which was the stuff of their own thinking. . . . This, and not the satisfaction of idle curiosity nor romantic quest, is the meaning of the anthropologist's work in nonliterate societies. [Kluckhohn 1949:11]

Let me provide an example of how a cross-cultural perspective can lend insight when pursuing an ethnographic approach in familiar circumstances. In writing up my Kwakiutl village material I followed an anthropological tradition of organizing part of my account around the annual cycle of activities. I drew upon the economic cycle as a way to incorporate the seasons and to emphasize what the seasons meant, rather than simply to make some contrasts between long winter nights and long summer days.

In the research project in which I next engaged—my study of an elementary school principal—the annual cycle seemed at first so obvious, at least to any reader familiar with public schools in North America, as to warrant little or no mention. As everyone knows, school starts in the late summer and, except for a brief Thanksgiving respite (October in Canada, November in the U.S.), continues through until the holiday season at the end of December. That break ends abruptly within a day or two after the New Year. Teachers generally regard January as a "teaching month," with the distractions of the fall (Halloween, Thanksgiving, Christmas) safely past. A holiday or two, a weeklong spring break in March or April, and a combination of winding up and winding down through May, extending perhaps into early June, complete the school "year" and cycle. Although my attention was focused on the school principal, it seemed obvious that his calendar could not differ significantly from that of the teachers and students, save for remaining on duty a bit longer after school closes in the summer and returning to duty a bit before the teachers return at summer's end.

But was I really thinking about school the way a principal does, or had all those years spent as a student, followed more recently by five years as a classroom teacher, blinded me from taking more careful account of what the principal was doing that might differ from what teachers and students were doing? In October, with a new school year barely underway, the principal had complained about having to submit his budget projections for the *next* school year. Later he was assigned to a committee to interview candidates for administrative openings anticipated the following year. Later still, he was involved in the annual "spring shuffle" when some teachers transferred, retired, or were replaced. In May teachers grew impatient with his requests about class lists and assignments for the next school year, reminding him that they were totally preoccupied with getting through the present one! I realized that a more useful way to look at a principal's cycle of activities was to think of over-lapping cycles of about 20 months' duration that began in October of the pre-vious year and lasted virtually until the day school began the year following. Realizing the difference in their annual cycles helped me to understand some of the circumstances that often found principals and teachers out of step with each other.

Adopting a standard way to organize and process my data in a cross-cultural framework allowed me to uncover a pattern so obvious that it might otherwise have escaped attention. My study was also guided by a broader per-spective, thinking about the principal's role compared to the role of the vil-lage chief (who happened as well to be a seine boat skipper). Throughout the study I kept thinking about what constituted a problem for an individual in either role and how it was likely to be resolved. In the village, I had endeav-ored to make the strange familiar; in a local school, I needed to make the familiar strange. No matter how achieved, strangeness seems to be important to ethnography. Is it essential to it?

On a grand scale, some anthropologists devote almost exclusive attention to cross-cultural comparison through testing universalistic hypotheses, work made possible largely through the Human Relations Area Files (HRAF), a data bank that catalogs a huge sample of world cultures. In terms of overcoming the nonindependence of the societies sampled, the arguments concerning sam-pling procedures are so complex that they have their own shorthand label among anthropologists, known as "Galton's Problem." Computer technologies have increased the sophistication of the studies and of solutions to Galton's Problem, and the HRAF data have now been computerized.

Controlled comparison as a formal method has been a legitimate concern among comparative anthropologists for years, tracing its recognition in Amer-ican anthropology at least as far back as an article by Fred Eggan (1954). Radcliffe-Brown cautioned that "without systematic comparative studies anthropology will become only historiography and ethnography" (1951:16). Half a century earlier, Franz Boas had cautioned instead about the "limita-tions" of the comparative method (1896). But notice that I have slipped into a discussion of broad anthropological concerns. Radcliffe-Brown's caution that anthropology might become *nothing more than ethnography* is another reminder that, central as it is to their work, ethnography is but one of many things that anthropologists do, and not all of them are particularly talented at, nor necessarily interested in, doing it.

Conversely, if the conceptual tasks approached by comparativists working on a grand scale in multiple arenas are what most interest you, then ethnography seems a rather inefficient way for you to invest your research energy. Comparative efforts of such scale are beyond the pale of the lone ethnographer. Ethnography, which makes controlled comparison possible, is not in itself a *comparative* endeavor, except implicitly, in the sense discussed earlier of differences that call attention to themselves or a conscious effort on the ethnographer's part to view the familiar as strange. Paradoxical as it may sound, I suggest that ethnography proceeds best when explicit comparison is minimized rather than maximized. Ethnographies that are not overly comparative are the most helpful when it comes time to draw upon them comparatively—that is, when the ethnographer assumes the complementary role of ethnologist.

In the course of individual careers, anthropologists who continue to do fieldwork may build an observational basis for macrocultural scale comparisons of their own, a fact that helps to explain some of the unlikely comparisons that we find. One place where such comparisons appear are the introductory texts in which authors interject observations from their own firsthand fieldwork by way of illustration. Some authors are able to integrate their writing by focusing on a few societies they know reasonably well, a practice preferable to simply allowing comparisons to get out of hand by seeming to draw at random in a contemporary version of what was dismissed earlier as armchair anthropology.

Along more systematic academic lines within the range of possibilities for the experienced ethnographer, one can cite such examples as Clifford Geertz's comparisons between the role of colonialism in agricultural development in Japan and Java (1963) or his comparisons of religious developments in Morocco and Indonesia (1968). His comparative studies are beyond the scope of the beginning ethnographer, but they illustrate how ethnography can play a major role in the evolution of a career. Keith Otterbein has proposed a career trajectory for someone interested in pursuing comparative research:

> In my own teaching and research I advocate a research progression wherein case studies are followed by small-scale comparative studies . . . or longitudinal studies and then by world-wide cross-cultural studies. Finally, cases that deviate from predictions can be scrutinized in a new round of case studies. [Otterbein 1994:560]

Elsewhere Geertz offers critical advice about the proper role of comparison, whether cross-cultural or not. I read his caution as an effort to keep anyone from falling into the mindless, endless, and pointless task of simply inventorying similarities and differences:

> We need to look for systematic relationships among diverse phenomena, not for substantive identities among similar ones. [1973a:44]

The best way for the neophyte ethnographer to avoid the trap of mindless comparison is to endeavor to do as *little* comparing as possible rather than as much. Ethnographers need to recognize that when they conduct fieldwork they are *already* comparing what they know, or think they know, with what they are discovering. Geertz quotes what he refers to as Santayana's "famous dictum" that "one compares only when one is unable to get to the heart of the matter" (Geertz 1983:233). I have suggested taking that idea for a fieldwork aphorism of our own: Get to the heart of the matter if possible; if not, compare (HFW 1994:183).

I am not arguing against comparison. By nature, that is how we learn. As anthropologist Michael Jackson reminds us, "No human being comes to a knowledge of himself or herself except through others" (1995:118). The whole concept of ethnography hinges on recognition of aspects of human behavior capable of being noticed by another human observer, something far more likely to occur with differences than with similarities. What I am suggesting is that ethnographers draw explicit comparisons only to the extent necessary to make a case, rather than allow themselves to be distracted by a mistaken notion that more comparison produces a more satisfying product. To my way of thinking, the ideal unit of study for any ethnographic inquiry is *one* of something, whether it be one village, one key event, one institution (such as Malinowski's Kula exchange), or, under some circumstances, one individual. In a day when large sample sizes remain the vogue and computer capabilities entice us to substitute breadth for depth, ethnography offers an authoritative mandate to study in units of one, the single case studied holistically. That is also consistent with my general advice to ethnographers (as well as the advice I give to most everyone, about most everything) to do less more thoroughly.

I doubt that urging fieldworkers to restrict the scope of their studies will raise many eyebrows except perhaps for the quantifiers and closet quantifiers among us. From the outset, stepping into a strange community or group for the first time, seasoned ethnographers recognize that the scope of their work will have to be narrowed sufficiently to make it manageable. The unseasoned ones may have to learn that lesson as part of their seasoning.

As ethnography has come to be adapted more widely, this critical aspect of focusing in depth rather than breadth has become somewhat contentious.

Increasingly I found myself serving on dissertation committees for studies in the field of education purportedly *inspired* by the ethnographic approach but subsequently recast in terms of some other prevailing research tradition. Multiple cases were routinely called for where it seemed to me that one case would have been sufficient. Time after time I argued that those seemingly small increments in sample size, doing two, three, or four "little" cases instead of one case in depth, are not likely to increase the power of a study but unquestionably they diminish the attention that can be devoted to each case. In a situation where the researcher proposes a study of a single case but is "encouraged" (or bullied?) to do a comparison among four or five, the strength of each case is reduced proportionately, the number of cases serving as a denominator that reduces the time that can be devoted to each one. It took me forever to realize that the answer to the seemingly straightforward question, "What can we learn from studying a single case of something?" is the equally straightforward answer, "All we can!"

So much for comparison in the numerical sense, trying to compensate for our characteristically small sample sizes. Such modest increases in sample size do not accomplish an adequate basis for generalization, but they most certainly compromise the opportunity to report in depth. Another kind of comparison, less frequently found in ethnographic writing, is the *literary* one. Such comparisons do have the capability to lend power of a different sort to our work through helping us to communicate our understanding to our readers— or at least to the readers among them.

Comparisons are not as common as one might expect in accounts that sometimes seem to beg for parallels drawn from the literary classics. Perhaps the type of individual intrigued by the all-consuming activities of ethnography tends not to be a prodigious reader. And perhaps that is just as well, for when literary comparisons are done, they are often overdone, authors too facilely assuming a posture that implies that any well-read individual really *ought* to recognize the reference, the work, the full quote, or whatever. I am grateful for authors who strive to keep me informed by offering enough explanation (or sometimes simply the courtesy of a translation of a foreign phrase) so that I remain on the inside of the joke, or allusion, or reference, or whatever.[3] As you will discover in these pages, my preference in making comparisons is to draw analogies. I admit to occasionally getting stuck with an analogy, working a good one too hard or trying too hard to make a bad one work, but I try to avoid subjecting readers to being left out just because they may not have read what I happened to have read or studied a language I have studied.

Ethnography as Idiosyncratic

No single criterion among those examined to this point seems to have quite the stranglehold on ethnography that one might imagine from hearing a list of its customary attributes. What results from any *particular* ethnographic inquiry represents a coming together of a personality and personal biography in the persona of the ethnographer, interacting in a particular place in a unique way, for the purposes of preparing a study framed broadly by an academic tradition and more narrowly by how the assignment is perceived by the ethnographer and others in the setting. Some of those others play important roles in the final outcome. Still others not likely to be part of the immediate setting may exert an even greater influence on the form and manner of reporting, in much the same way patron audiences play a critical role in what artists produce as "art."[4]

The consequence of this idiosyncratic dimension in fieldwork is that if I were to ask permission to conduct an inquiry in which you were to be involved, you probably would not have much of a clue as to what will result. And, in terms of specifics, quite frankly I probably wouldn't, either. Recognizing my interest in cultural acquisition, you might assume that aspect of a broader cultural interpretation will be emphasized. Yet even in terms of cultural interpretation, you would probably have a clearer idea of what that might mean for someone in quite different circumstances from your own, for, as noted, we are inclined to view our own behavior as normal rather than as "cultural." Culture is an abstraction we reserve for describing the (strange) behavior of other.

Nonetheless, ethnography is, and will always be, something of a wild card. That makes it fun to engage in, but something of a risk as well. And fun, and somewhat risky, to fund, or commission, or direct, or even allow. One of the problems associated with cultural anthropology, and thus of ethnography, is the reluctance of those in positions of authority who are able but not always eager to employ ethnographers on research projects because "you never know what you are getting or what they will come up with." In Part Three, I will sample some of the range and variation in ethnography one finds today, but such information does little in helping to predict how any *particular* ethnographer will proceed with any *particular* inquiry. About the best one can do in anticipating what to expect is to examine the record for what has already been accomplished, leavened perhaps with some straight talk about what can go wrong, such as in Caroline Brettell's edited volume, *When They Read What We Write* (1993). What the ethnographic record has revealed, explicitly in most instances, is a preoccupation with culture. How, then, does culture, itself unseen, play such an important role in the ethnographer's way of seeing?

Thinking Broadly About Culture

Like ethnography, culture, too, is elusive, yet attention given to it is the best single criterion for distinguishing the more ethnographically oriented studies from the less. But I do not want to overdo its importance in this regard. It makes no sense to try to assess its presence in absolute terms; one cannot describe human social behavior without some notion of culture lurking in the background, at least implicitly. Rather than get caught up in never-ending debate, let me explain how I have come to understand the idea of culture and how I believe it provides an underlying cohesiveness not only to ethnographies individually but to the whole ethnographic enterprise. And this in spite of the variability we see in what is put forward as ethnography. I return to Malinowski's description of the ethnographer's task as one of pursuing evidence.

Malinowski was not above drawing an analogy or two, and there is some hint in the following quotation that he was well aware of the customs of the British gentry for whom he could presume to be writing.

> But the Ethnographer has not only to spread his nets in the right place, and wait for what will fall into them. He must be an active huntsman, and drive his quarry into them and follow it up to its most inaccessible lairs. And that leads us to the more active methods of pursuing ethnographic evidence. [Malinowski 1922:8]

The language of Malinowski's famous text no longer seems appropriate in a day when we are circumspect in our use of a word like "native" and have long since dropped terms like "savage" or "primitive." Today we prefer to represent ourselves as working in concert with those among whom we study, our *participants*, even our *collaborators*, but certainly not our *subjects*. Even our own special and well-intended term *informant* makes us uncomfortable. We know what we mean by it and acknowledge our immeasurable debt to those upon whom we depend to "inform" us. Nevertheless, as Michael Agar notes, the label "really does sound ugly now" and it would be a welcome relief to have a more suitable word in its place (1996:x).

I find a certain charm in thinking of ethnography as a kind of hunt or quest or, in Malinowski's term, "pursuit." I would not be offended were a reviewer to note that I seemed to have "captured" the essence of culture in the course of some ethnographic endeavor. Malinowski, intent on securing a place for ethnography in a scientific world, underscored its methodological nature and lamented then-current practice "in which wholesale generalisations are laid down before us, and we are not informed at all by what actual experiences the writers have reached their conclusion" (1922:3). In a subsection titled

"Active Methods of Research," he included the material quoted above as part of the important introduction he prepared for *Argonauts,* a chapter that has remained a standard reference on ethnographic research ever since.

What is the nature of this "ethnographic evidence" that Malinowski calls for? For anyone knowingly (or unknowingly) following the traditions that distinguish American anthropology from the anthropologies of other nations, ethnographic evidence is the stuff out of which one can render cultural description. The ethnographer who sets out to "capture" the culture of some group needs not only descriptive material adequate for composing a picture of that group's way of life but also an idea of how to frame that picture in cultural terms. There is no "one best way" to accomplish that, but I can suggest several broad conceptual avenues that lead there, each focusing on some particular subset of tangible behaviors. The three that I describe below are *cultural orientation, cultural know-how,* and *cultural beliefs.* Any text devoted to cultural theory will present one or more such approaches, and a sampling of such texts over time (e.g., Harris 1999; Kaplan and Manners 1972) offers insight into the intellectual history of the discipline.

Cultural Orientation

The notion of "cultural orientation" variously invites attention to description, analysis, and/or interpretation, depending on the meaning an ethnographer assigns to the question of *where* the people being described are situated. Taken literally, the reference might begin with a location in physical space; figuratively, it might locate people according to their major activities (e.g., hunters and gatherers) or their world view. Cultural orientation can begin with social setting, looking at anything from compass points or degrees of longitude and latitude to a cluster of houses in a village to cronies who meet regularly at a neighborhood restaurant (as, for example, at Slim's Table [Duneier 1992]). Taking cultural orientation in its broadest interpretive sense, the researcher may want to portray the "ethos" of the group, whether a tiny community (e.g., a rock band, a group of rock collectors) or a nation.

Cultural orientation can help the ethnographer define the outer physical and experiential boundaries of the lives of those being described, boundaries of time, place, and circumstance. One's family, one's place in that family, and that family's place in a larger community; one's first language; one's gender; one's stature; all these are prior conditions that influence what one can become and what family and community expect one to become. The necessary caution to today's ethnographer is to recognize such boundaries as an artifact of research, a convenience for the researcher. We have come to recognize that culture resists the tight packaging in which it was so often presented in days gone by.

Anthropologists no longer describe their "others" as encapsulated entities in which everyone inside behaves more or less the same and there is little or no contact with anyone different, not even anthropologists.

How the ethnographer chooses to situate the people being described in terms of their cultural setting—geographically, with physical landmarks; comparatively, among similar or dissimilar groups as to memberships, socio-economic status, modernization, and technology; or interpretively, reflecting on their world view and their underlying cohesiveness—also offers clues as to the orientation of the ethnographer. While the term "culture" may or may not be defined (nor necessarily employed at all), a reader ought to be able to assess the extent to which an underlying notion of culture has guided the research and writing. Now that it has become fashionable in some camps to downplay and even to disparage the notion of culture as a guiding force in ethnography, today's ethnographer writing *against culture* must articulate what concept or concepts are being substituted in its place.

Consider an example of cultural orientation offered in the most literal sense. "Let us imagine that we are sailing along the South coast of New Guinea towards its Eastern end," Malinowski writes, inviting us to join him in learning about the Kula district and its people (1922:33). He continues, "At about the middle of Orangerie Bay we arrive at the boundary of the Massim, which runs from this point north-westwards till it strikes the northern coast near Cape Nelson (see Map II)." A reader of contemporary ethnography may reasonably expect to find not only a comparable statement of orientation but one that concludes with the same parenthetical instruction, "see map." Little doubt that the reader needs to be "oriented," although that practice may be observed without much apparent thought as to exactly what orientation the reader needs, especially a reader unfamiliar with local landmarks. Malinowski properly discharged his duty, but I cannot get my bearings from "about the middle of Orangerie Bay," I do not know what the Massim is, and I rather doubt that it is marked with so obvious a boundary line as he implies.

Nevertheless, I do understand what Malinowski was up to in presenting this description. I admit to deriving a certain satisfaction in telling visitors to my home that the elevation where my graveled drive leaves the county road is 1,010 feet above sea level, a fact of little consequence to them and presumably even less to you. Yet any such physical description reveals something of what can or cannot reasonably be expected to occur in that setting. Malinowski's description strongly suggests that the ocean plays a key role in his account, while mine rules out the likelihood of the ocean playing any role at all in my "backyard" ethnography of a Sneaky Kid (HFW 1983a).

To "capture" and convey the cultural orientation of a group in a well-formed statement about a people's world view or *eidos* is the epitome of what ethnography is about—at least for the interpretively inclined ethnographer. Although anthropologists tend to be chary of such broadly conceived generalizations in their professional dialogues, I think they recognize, even when they resist, that this is what patron audiences want and expect. Ruth Benedict "painted" the Kwakiutl as "vigorous and overbearing," a "Dionysian" people for whom "life would have been impossible without the sea" (1934:173,175). "In their religious ceremonies," she reported, "the final thing they strove for was ecstasy" (p. 175). Like it or not—and in this case I can't help being uncomfortable with such broad generalizations about a people among whom I have many acquaintances—this is the kind of reporting that lay audiences have come to associate with ethnography. Those expectations egg us on to sweeping statements intended to capture and reveal a culture, regardless of whether the generalizations apply in a literal sense to so much as even one individual in it.

There is more precedence and pressure to report in such terms than one may realize. I was dismayed to receive an invitation to prepare a brief encyclopedialike entry about the Kwakiutl for yet another encyclopedic volume on the world's "cultures" and to realize the level of generalization that would be necessary to cover, in the number of words allowed, the categories I was expected to address. I declined the invitation. A contemporary ethnographer, heeding Richard Fox's admonition to attend to "the everyday life of persons rather than the cultural life of a people" (1991:12) is not so eager to make sweeping statements of the sort once made by early romantics among ethnographers. Nevertheless, the urge to generalize presents a fierce dilemma, damned if you do, damned if you don't. An ethnography lacking in generalization leaves something to be desired. It is as though the author has timidly held back, forsaking the opportunity to transform observed *instances* of behavior into inferred *patterns* of behavior, opting instead to take refuge in the aura of the meticulous scientist at work.

I think ethnographers should share whatever generalizations they have to offer, taking care only to distinguish between warranted ones and those put forward ever so tentatively. The important point is to state the basis on which generalizations have been formed and the extent to which they include impressions, emotions, and whatever other personal resources have been drawn upon. Intimate, long-term acquaintance with a group of people ought to enrich an account, not be regarded as a threat to it. Taking *cultural orientation* as an approach invites painting with a broad brush, with generalizations tentatively offered, but offered nonetheless, to be examined in terms of ethnographic evidence presented in support.

For the neophyte, however, as well as for the cautious chronicler, one's efforts to implicate culture may more conservatively be directed to either of two other dimensions: *cultural know-how* or *cultural beliefs*. With either of these categories, description and analysis alone provide opportunity for presenting ethnographic evidence, without the risk of inadvertently tripping over, or becoming tripped up with, the concept of culture.

Cultural Know-how

The task of inventorying cultural know-how virtually assures that in some guise or another the responsibility for reporting how various groups go about their daily activities—with a focus on the details of what they do and what they make in order to do it—will remain in perpetuity as a standing order for ethnographic inquiry. As Bernard Siegel observes, "We can never know all that is potentially knowable about any culture studied or to be studied by anthropologists, partly because of the continual flow of information (openness) and partly because individuals in them are variously exposed to what they know" (Siegel 1996:6).

From the earliest years in school we are introduced to some basic survival categories that outline what people must address in order to meet their human needs: food, shelter, housing, clothing, transportation. If we miss the message in those first lessons, we confront it more directly as we outgrow the dependency of youth and must make provision for satisfying such needs on our own. How people living in different geographical areas have conceptualized and met these needs, how they have adapted to their circumstances (wherever they could not adapt their circumstances to suit themselves), how our own forebears made these adaptations in the old (i.e., pre-computer?) days, these are fascinating topics. While the novelty-and-invention-minded seek constantly to create the new, there will always be others equally intent on capturing the past, celebrating the old ways while lamenting their passing. Ethnographers tend to fall in the latter category, more concerned with *what has been* than with *what is yet to come*. That is why we cannot shrug off Maitland's prophecy (1968[1936]) that anthropology will be history or it will be nothing—even if we agree with Evans-Pritchard (1962) that Maitland got it backward.

Current developments in cognitive science invite participation by ethnographers interested in how humans systematize their knowledge, so there are new links and new roles for ethnographers to explore as the sciences themselves jockey for position and compete for attention and funding. At the same time, the concerns that once drove efforts at salvage ethnography, trying to capture the last remnants of disappearing "cultures" before they were overrun or simply died out, are present today in everything but name. Social scientists scramble to get the stories (or lawyers scramble to get depositions, if there are juicy lawsuits pending) of older informants or to record the grammars and vocabularies of "dying" languages.

The good news and bad news are all one: there is no end to inventorying cultural know-how. Ethnographers are at once promised eternal occupation and shackled by the infinite nature of their self-imposed task. The extent of such inventorying becomes a real issue for the individual ethnographer working in a particular society. Where does the inventorying stop, either in scope or in depth? How much is enough?

Let me illustrate this pervasive problem of the level of detail as it surfaced in a study I was invited to read in the role of an invited external thesis examiner. In that capacity, I was asked to submit an independent assessment of a doctoral dissertation completed at an institution overseas.

The thesis topic was an ethnographic account of a military band. In the incident being reported (by the ethnographer, and now by me), members of the band were en route by bus to a performance they were to give later in the day. The researcher was given to meticulous reporting. Even the bus trip was described in some detail, including how different members of the band passed the time. As reported, one band member spent the time reading a magazine devoted exclusively to matters dealing with the instrument that he played. Having stated that much, the ethnographer went on to summarize the *content of the article being read*. I could not help but wonder at such attention to detail. Yet neither could I escape a sense of panic: When is enough?

In my letter of evaluation, I commended the study, including the researcher's capacity for detail. But I also raised a question for members of the dissertation committee to ponder. I acknowledged that this was the first time I had ever been able to look over the shoulder of someone sitting next to a researcher and been privy to the content of the article that person was reading. But why stop there? Given that the observer had gone to that level of detail, should there not have been a citation to page and volume number of the journal being read, as is customary in scholarly writing? How much description should be provided?

To draw attention to the underlying issue I was raising, I searched the thesis for an opposite instance, one worthy of what I have referred to elsewhere in this section (but not in my letter to the candidate's committee) as a "whopping generalization" supported by no evidence at all. I noted how, at one point, the researcher stated succinctly that "band morale was 'quite high,' " an observation left to stand entirely on its own. Recalling how often I have heard interest expressed in researching topics related to morale, I noted that, like "leadership" or "cohesiveness," I have always considered the assessment of "morale" to be a topic inviting endless speculation. The question I wanted to raise for the committee, and the lesson to remember for myself, was to ask where responsibility lies in helping a beginning researcher recognize and cope with this problem of how much detail is detail enough.

The best guideline I can offer is to bear constantly in mind the purposes for which an inquiry has been initiated. The stated purposes should provide the basis for establishing criteria as to what detail, and at what *level* of detail, *must* be included, what else *might* be included, and what is tangential. That practice calls as well for making the statement of purpose a subject of constant review and refinement throughout the fieldwork and writing. A guideline for assessing what detail warrants reporting is the question, "How important is it for the reader to know, and at what level of detail, whatever further information I am able to provide?" Recognize that such decisions are always made on a relative cost/benefit basis against the pressing need to get on with it, with time, space, ethical considerations, and readers' patience all viewed as precious resources.

As a guide for the overall research agenda, however, a more important question for the researcher committed to ethnography is whether the research is guided by a suitable *ethnographic* question. Level of detail is a problem for anyone working in a qualitative/descriptive mode: the answer does not lie with detail itself. Nor is it of much help to be advised not to get caught up in detail. If the research question can be addressed by giving painstaking attention to certain facets of behavior, then close examination of a few items may best satisfy the research intent. For the anthropologist drawn to cultural know-how as a way to portray culture, looking, say, at issues of consensus about what things are called, or how things are done within a community, one had better be willing to be caught up with detail.

Both the nature of issues explored and the methods employed to analyze them may exceed the boundaries of ethnography, especially in its more traditional form. Then again, ethnographers are not doomed only to conduct long-term, intimate studies of small groups, nor does their work necessarily exclude them from attending to problems requiring strict quantification. In the latter regard, some important branching into new facets of quantitatively oriented inquiry has been going on for several years, especially among the more mathematically inclined or computer-oriented anthropologists investigating cognitive structuring.[5]

Cultural Beliefs

For some anthropologists (such as those mentioned in the endnote to the paragraph immediately above), efforts to distinguish between cultural know-how and cultural beliefs might seem redundant at best. Their work is directed at consensus modeling of informant accuracy. For their purposes, what people *know* and what people *believe* are inexorably intertwined. Taken together, knowledge and beliefs provide the source of data for consensus measures that, in turn, allow researchers to study *cognitive sharing*. That is how these researchers address the question of what to study in pursuit of "culture." Researchers of other persuasions might be equally skeptical of my effort to distinguish between cultural orientation and cultural beliefs, arguing instead that the latter are nothing more than instances of the former.

One way to mark the contrast between a cultural orientation and cultural beliefs is to distinguish "knowing how" from "knowing that." There is a say-ing—intended, I have always assumed, to convey a different message from its literal one—that there is more than one way to skin a cat. Know-how refers to technical knowledge of ways to go about doing something . . . for instance, skinning a cat. "Knowing that" refers to a concomitant idea that puts skill knowledge in context. For example, one needs to realize that genteel folk do not skin cats; the idea of skinning a cat is as metaphorical as the expression itself. Know-how knows no limits: there are multiple ways of doing and of knowing. An underlying element in American thinking is not only that there may be other ways of doing things but that there are (or ought to be) better ways than whatever way we do it now. Thus Americans tend to be rejecting of the old ways with the same vigor that people in other societies may be rejecting—or at least wary—of new ones. American know-how resides in that broader context of a cultural belief that things not only can but *must* be improved.

I believe it was Erich Fromm who years ago wrote about getting people to *want* to act as they *have* to act. I have never heard a better shorthand expres-sion of the role of culture in human life, at once underscoring culture as an ideal system for how things are supposed to be and recognizing that "how things are supposed to be" is never exactly how they are. Fromm's observation also helped me to distinguish between two terms often heard in early discus-sions about cultural acquisition and (particularly) culture transmission: *social-ization* and *enculturation*. The term "socialization" seems best suited for describing how people *have to act,* the "know how" of the range of behavior acceptable within a particular group. That leaves enculturation to refer to a complementary set of beliefs and values linking the knowledge of what *must* be done with a set of shared values that recognizes such behavior as "good," "proper," "moral," and so forth, and thus how one *wants* to act. Beliefs are embedded in the values attached to them: notions of good and bad, right and wrong, better or worse; as well as beautiful or ugly, graceful or awkward, tragic or comic. Thus a society's projective systems—its art, music, literature, and so forth—are important in what is subsumed under cultural beliefs.

Given my interest in cultural acquisition, you might understand why I find cultural beliefs to be of special interest. How do particular groups convey to succeeding generations not only their know-how but a corresponding sense of their self-righteousness about the knowing? And what is the nexus between how one generation goes about transmitting such ideas and the way those ideas are actually acquired by the next generation?

Highly systematic procedures such as consensus modeling serve as excellent examples of fine-tuned cultural analysis that can produce percent figures as to the level of cognitive sharing, but they do not address my interest in how culture is acquired. In the tripartite schema just reviewed, there should be room for everyone interested in studying culture, and plenty of opportunity for ethnographers to make their contribution of the *instances* to which we can look, in searches that must ultimately exceed those bounds.

Culture and Ethnography Under Siege

I recognize some need to temper what may appear as my unbridled enthusiasm for the culture concept. I close this discussion by pointing to some lingering problems and criticisms before turning away from procedures, the focus of the two chapters in this section, to *outcomes,* the accounts that result from the ethnographer's efforts. That is the subject matter for the trio of chapters in Part Three.

A continuing debate over culture has to do with the *efficacy* of the concept. On that question there is wide-ranging opinion. Its severest critics dismiss it: If culture is both ubiquitous and unseen, how does it help explain anything? Those who regard the culture concept as moribund might seem its severe critics, but it occurs to me that their very word choice does allow that the concept did have its day, even if they perceive it as stagnant or near death at present. Since I remain a true believer, I have found the arguments of the skeptics more instructive than arguments of those who dismiss the concept outright. Skeptics tend to be more helpful by pointing out what they feel is lacking in argument or evidence. Hear the voices of two skeptical British social scientists who recognize major problems with culture's self-fulfilling aspect, a concept that in their view is defined in such a way that its very existence is reaffirmed in the act of searching for it:

> When setting out to describe a culture, we operate on the basis of the assumption that there are such things as cultures, and have some ideas about what they are like; and we select out for analysis the aspects of what is observed that we judge to be "cultural." While there may be nothing wrong

with such cultural description, the kind of empiricist methodology enshrined in naturalism renders the theory implicit and thus systematically discourages its development and testing. [Hammersley and Atkinson 1983:13]

Most certainly the concept of culture fares worse to whatever degree its promises are overstated. For example, if I modestly portray and defend (and commend!) culture as an "orienting concept" rather than as theory, then its shortcomings are mollified: we tend to be more forgiving of concepts than of theory. Similarly, by defining the ethnographer's task as "attributing" culture to a group, rather than insisting that culture can be "found" there, I steel myself against the criticism that ethnographers "select out for analysis the aspects of what is observed that we judge to be 'cultural.' "

My enthusiasm for giving culture its due does not extend to simply tossing the term about. Statements about how a people's culture makes them do this-or-that are highly suspect; humans do things, cultures do not. For the researcher willing to make allowance for sociocultural influences, but uncertain how to portray them, it may be sufficient to limit one's account to describing instances of observed behavior. Readers can draw their own inferences about what is cultural.

In spite of all the rhetoric, as Wuthnow et al. observed years ago in an overview to *Cultural Analysis* (1984:2), "the denial of culture has been difficult to sustain in actual practice." Rather than insist that ethnography *is* the study of culture, let me turn the argument to its gentler side to suggest that ethnography, both by tradition and by design, presents the opportunity and the challenge to pursue an inquiry in a manner especially attentive to broad social contexts. In times or places where the culture concept itself is in disrepute, there are other terms that one can employ (e.g., conventions, customs, folkways, lifeways, life styles, mores, practices, traditions) that point essentially to the same thing. The "idea" of culture in reference to the social context of behavior is not exclusively a property of the term culture itself.

Like culture, ethnography, too, has its critics, and it, too, has been declared moribund. Yet I think both ethnography and culture have been and will continue to be able to survive their harshest critics. The sometimes severity of the attacks raises questions for me as to what it is about academia that brings out such cynicism (is that word strong enough?) among otherwise genteel folk. Both concepts probably owe their longevity and vitality not to flat-footed ethnographers like myself who are inclined simply to take them at their best and get on with it, but to a loyal opposition who worry and argue over them with titles like *The End(s) of Ethnography* (Clough 1992, 1998) or *What's Wrong with Ethnography?* (Hammersley 1992) or debate whether to give "Culture—A

Second Chance?"[6] But then, I'm one of those who finds "nothing wrong with such cultural description." Indeed, what other kind of description is there?

Notes

1. For a retrospective account of such practice, see the Spindlers' (1991) article, "Rorschaching in North America in the Shadow of Hallowell." For an example of field reports of the day, see Clifton and Levine 1961.

2. For example, the Experimental Schools project of the 1970s placed resident fieldworkers in a number of American communities with the intent of studying the effects of educational change during a period of five years (for an overview, see Herriott and Gross 1979; see also Hennigh 1981).

3. In that regard, forgive me for having failed to provide a translation for *Sturm und Drang* noted in connection with Margaret Mead's study of adolescence in Samoa. The phrase is a literary one, in this case referring to the period of "storm and stress" associated with American adolescence. How easy to make assumptions about what everyone knows.

4. I have explored comparisons between the work of artists and fieldworkers in HFW 1995. See especially chapter 3, drawing on an earlier study by Howard Becker (1982).

5. For models of such work, see Boster 1985; Romney, Weller, and Batchelder 1986; or overviews provided by these authors (e.g., Romney 1994; Romney and Moore 1998; Weller and Romney 1988).

6. A supplement to Volume 40 of *Current Anthropology* (February 1999) titled "Culture—A Second Chance?" continues the never-ending debate with a special issue devoted to examining the viability of the culture concept.

PART THREE: REPRESENTING AND PRESENTING HUMAN SOCIAL LIFE

CHAPTER FIVE

Traditional Ethnography and Ethnographic Tradition

Artists do not paint what they see, they see what they know how to paint.

—Attributed to E. H. Gombrich
In Elliot W. Eisner, 1997

The aphorism above can be restated in terms of ethnography: Ethnographers do not describe what they see, they see what they know how to describe. The chapters of Part Three review ethnographic practice in terms of what ethnographers know how to describe, beginning in this chapter with long-standing traditions that, if observed to the letter, would virtually guarantee that tomorrow's ethnographies will bear uncanny resemblance to yesterday's.

I begin with a personal story. One of the most creatively satisfying things I have done in recent years was to design my own house. I have not been modest in boasting about that accomplishment. But I have learned to be more circumspect, for I have been reminded that others not only have done the same but have sometimes built their own house as well. My "design" efforts were limited to rough sketches and dimensions redrafted by the contractor's wife into an acceptable format, with her husband looking after structural matters and all of us consulting together about the details. Nevertheless, I proudly claim the house as "my" design. It received only a quick review by a professional architect to see if he could spot any major problems or errors. (He made a thoughtful suggestion for improving the kitchen entryway.)

If I did not at first appreciate how many others have designed their own home, and countless more who worked so closely with an architect that they feel the design to be "theirs" nonetheless, I have also been surprised, and smugly pleased, with the response of visitors who have exclaimed, in words such as these, "How could you ever do it? Why, I wouldn't have the faintest idea of where to start!"

I had never designed a house before, and as gratifying as the experience ultimately proved to be, I do not expect to design another. (Designing this one was not out of choice so much as out of necessity after the old house was destroyed by fire, a story related elsewhere [HFW 1990b].) To my surprise, planning a house, first in my mind, then on paper, came easily. Although I did relocate the house site, I had resided on the same 20-acre plot for the previous two decades, and that gave me a great advantage.

In addition to practical considerations such as cost, I discovered that there were all kinds of conventions to guide me. Most of them were out-of-consciousness. Others were quite explicit: materials to use, overall size (2,000 square feet seemed smaller than necessary, 4,000 square feet larger; I settled for 3,500), customs dictating the rooms one typically includes in a mainstream American home (kitchen, living room, bedrooms, bathrooms), and options according to personal preference and prevailing fashion (formal dining area or country kitchen; one story, split level, or two story; family room or study; garage or carport; full basement and attic or just crawl spaces, and so on). I quickly became aware that far too many decisions had already been made for me and were accepted as standard practice. I was not going to be consulted about most of them unless I made a special point of inquiring. For example, windows needn't be placed as high as they usually are, nor countertops and railings so low, but if you don't happen to state your preferences, no one is likely to ask.

If you have an overall "sense of house" appropriate for the region in which you intend to live, and a corresponding sense of trust in your judgment, including your ability to find a reliable and responsive building contractor, you can design your own house. If not, you can pore over hundreds of plans in commercial plan books, modify the design of a particular house that you like, or consult an architect and offer as much or as little input as you wish. You can also escape this ordeal altogether—should it begin to feel like an ordeal—by buying a suitable house already built, or choosing not to become a homeowner at all.

My experience in doing ethnography has many parallels with designing a house. I keep company with ethnographers who are variously impressed or unimpressed with my efforts, but none of them marvels that I do it at all. On the other hand, I meet people who have become interested in ethnographic research but have no idea how to go about it. Their reaction has a familiar ring: "How could you ever do it? Why, I wouldn't have the faintest idea of where to start!"

This chapter offers the equivalent of a "plan book" approach to ethnography, with clearly laid out models as guides for what to do, what goes where. I originally titled the chapter "Ethnography Without Tears" to suggest that this is the low-risk approach. It may not result in a custom structure (you pay extra for that) but neither are you likely to leave anything out. The result should be a well-crafted product with a basic but satisfactory design. You can always add on or do some remodeling later.

Chapter 6, "Ethnography from Inside Out," complements this one by describing approaches in which the ethnographer is less concerned with producing something customary or standard. Whether designing a house or an ethnography, there are risks involved in deviating from standard practice. In either case, freeing oneself from too-strict adherence to customary standards may enhance the possibilities for creating something especially well suited to the setting or one's personal style. In the case of ethnography, that may accommodate a more person-centered approach that allows for, and benefits from, good narrative. More to risk, more to gain, as long as one's results are not going to be judged by conventional standards.

I do not mean to draw too sharp a distinction between the standard approaches discussed here and the variations to be explored in chapters that follow. As with designing a house, no one is likely to be aware of all the questions that can arise or all the answers and assumptions already in place. There is lots of advice, almost too freely offered, and there is always a strong current of local tradition. There are also new materials and methods to consider and unforeseen problems to resolve as the structure begins to take shape. There is also a lot of common sense involved.

Nor do I mean to suggest that before ever attempting something out of the ordinary, everyone ought first to do a standard ethnography or build a standard house. What does seem essential is to have a good grasp of current practice, as well as a clear idea of what you intend to accomplish that may be better achieved by deviating from it. Standard procedures can underwrite your work so that you do not have to agonize over every decision or find yourself doing things differently just to be different. While you are in the planning or "mulling" stages, there is also ample opportunity for considering alternative approaches, for getting help, for making changes. No matter how you begin, there is always the possibility that the start itself is wrong, that at some point—preferably not too far along—you may need to scrap the whole plan and start over because your basic concept or approach isn't working. Far better in such cases to be developing a manuscript than actually building a house: Carpenters make expensive erasers!

Ethnography by the Numbers

I like analogies. I want to press this one between designing a house and designing an ethnography; there are insights to be gained. For example, one does not set out to construct either a house or an ethnography by stockpiling raw material (read "data" in the latter case). One must have a fairly good idea of how the finished product is to look and of conditions for its use. Experienced builder that he is, my contractor did not begin construction by calling a local building-supply company and ordering "a load of stuff for building a house." He needed to consult with me to learn what kind of house I had in mind for what location, to assure both of us that the house I wanted was one he could build, and to inform me about the myriad rules and regulations governing my options. My analogy may be better suited to planning a house like the one I presently live in, but even for the over-romanticized igloo builder of times past, it was not only snow that was needed; there was no shortage of that. What was needed was packed snow of the proper consistency for carving into blocks to form a shelter *and* a promising location for procuring food.

There are catalogs aplenty to assist in ordering what is necessary to build a house. Catalogs are a rich source of information about the names for various items, their cost, and their intended use. But randomly ordering from a hefty catalog would not enable a novice to construct a house, in spite of the fact that every necessary item might be inventoried somewhere among the pages. There are sources available for the ethnographer that serve a comparable function, so exhaustingly thorough that they attempt to provide total inventories, with not only a name but even a number for every "part." Their very thoroughness renders them sterile as guides.

I turn first to the clear forerunner of such catalogs, a manual that has undergone continuous publication and revision since 1874 and is currently in its sixth (1951) edition. It is known to experienced fieldworkers by the shorthand title of its first three words, *Notes and Queries,* and carries a full annotation lengthy enough to make anyone wary of having to cite it, *Notes and Queries on Anthropology, Sixth Edition, Revised and Rewritten by A Committee of the Royal Anthropological Institute of Great Britain and Ireland.* The table of contents of *Notes and Queries* might at first seem a dream come true in presenting a checklist of everything to be covered in a satisfactory (and very traditional) ethnography, albeit one overweighted with attention to material culture (that category accounts for about one-third of the text) and the importance assigned to social structure, consistent with its British origins. But present and past committees intent on revising it as a field guide that could be used *everywhere* go to such extremes of detail in attempting to list possible alternatives and exceptions that they have produced a manual too exhaustive to be used *anywhere*.

Obviously that problem has been confounded by the evolution of anthropology itself. As noted in the Preface to the Sixth Edition, the major section on Social Anthropology (Part II), 191 pages in all, "deals mainly with the sociology of non-literate peoples, though the methods described are also suitable in general principle to studies in an advanced society" (1951:v). Under that broad heading the book combines didactic summaries of every imaginable category (e.g., "Cosmology, Seasons, Weather and Calendar" in a chapter titled "Knowledge and Tradition"; or "String Figures and Tricks" in the major section "Material Culture") with an outpouring of questions on each identified topic sufficient to stun any beginner and terrify even an old hand.

The "current" revision of *Notes and Queries* was begun in 1936 and completed 15 years later. Perhaps today it has become a relic of the past. Even so, I think it worth a trip to the library to study its table of contents, thumb through its pages, and ponder the impact it had on ethnographers for some hundred years. For all the credit we assign to Malinowski for "pioneering" ethnographic research with the publication of *Argonauts,* it should be noted that he had access to and consulted *Notes and Queries,* in his day already in its fourth (1912) edition.[1]

As for its practical use, that day may be long past. I doubt that the Royal Anthropological Institute will take up the charge handed on by the committee that finally completed this edition. I recall a moment during our initiation into fieldwork when Ron Rohner and I became concerned that we were "drying up" in our capacity as the thorough observers we had intended to be. Ron had dutifully brought along a copy of *Notes and Queries,* and we consulted it to give us an ethnographic "jolt." Jolt us it did, for on whatever page of text we turned, it pummeled us with questions we had never thought to raise in our conversations with villagers. We also doubted whether we really needed to raise them.

In its function as a sort of Whole Ethnography Catalog, *Notes and Queries* has largely been replaced by another "outline." The replacement was far tighter in structure and was especially useful for anyone anxious to employ a *universal* category scheme for coding fieldnotes rather than have to devise a scheme designed specifically with his or her own fieldwork and problem in mind. This general inventory system, modified but essentially stable over several decades, is the *Outline of Cultural Materials,* or *OCM.* The *OCM* was developed in conjunction with the Human Relations Area Files (HRAF), an ongoing project initiated in 1937 to facilitate cross-cultural comparison. The *Outline* provides a universal set of major and minor headings for sorting data and a system for the uniform numerical coding of fieldnotes.

To anyone anticipating fieldwork for the first time, the *Outline of Cultural Materials* may seem like a godsend. There they are, all the major topics one might inquire into, from Anthropometry or Descriptive Somatology to Port Facilities, Postures, War Veterans, Weaning and Food Training, and Senescence. Each of 88 major topics (e.g., 57, Interpersonal Relations; 58, Marriage; 59, Family; 60, Kinship) is in turn subdivided into a subset of minor descriptive categories (as, for example, topic 57, Interpersonal Relations, which includes the subtopics 571, Social Relationships and Groups; 572, Friendships; 573, Cliques; 574, Visiting and Hospitality; 575, Sodalities; 576, Etiquette; 577, Ethics; 578, Intergroup Antagonism; and 579, Brawls, Riots, and Banditry).

Without observational data to fill them or test them, the categories look as though they must surely cover every circumstance a fieldworker would encounter. Alas! In the field, lines are often blurred (how to distinguish among group, friendship, and clique, for example), there are at once too many and too few categories, and fieldwork does not unfold in the orderly sequence of a universal and predetermined outline. My guess is that most fieldworkers modify or totally abandon such rigid systems, whether a standard one such as the *OCM* or one devised with a particular focus in mind (e.g., Hilger's *Field Guide to the Ethnological Study of Child Life,* 1960). However, instructors in fieldwork courses or summer field schools often use the *OCM* as a training device. Among experienced fieldworkers it has its staunch supporters who point out that as a taxonomy it becomes ever more useful as one becomes ever more familiar with it. Russ Bernard, for example, is a firm believer[2]:

> The *OCM* contains the coding scheme developed by the Human Relations Area Files for handling all ethnographic text, and I've always found the scheme to be easy to teach, and sensible to use. [Bernard 1989:29]

In pursuing my analogy to designing a house, I take *Notes and Queries* and the *Outline of Cultural Materials* to be more like parts catalogs than field guides. Each represents a gigantic effort that may have seemed exactly what was needed but proved unwieldy once completed. There is no question that *Notes and Queries* was intended as a field guide; the book jacket specifies that its intended audience includes "amateurs untrained in anthropology" as well as the "trained" anthropologist. The taxonomy that is the essence of the *Outline of Cultural Materials* greatly facilitated cross-cultural comparison on a scale never before possible. Its tight taxonomic structure also anticipated a computer age in which social categories could be assigned numbers in addition to names.[3]

The house analogy prompts consideration of several alternative ways for designing ethnography other than finding a catalog that attempts to list every possible topic and subtopic. One possibility is to replicate or adapt an existing model. Another is to combine features from several models. Still another is to adopt a standard plan. One can also work with a set of basic modules that can be combined in any number of ways. The discussion of these alternatives provides the substance of this chapter, with a focus on final outcomes, in this case, what the builder—or the ethnographer—intends to construct. Choosing the specific materials that will be needed follows from that; not ordering willy-nilly from a catalog, but working with an overall plan clearly in mind. Needless to say, materials locally available and the customary ways of using them are important considerations in selecting an appropriate plan. Although I remain somewhat dubious of step-by-step approaches to ethnographic research, there are also helpful sources for anyone interested in exploring them.[4]

Replicating or Adapting an Existing Model

One seemingly simple solution for designing a house—or an ethnography— is to borrow or adapt a model already used successfully. That is a good place to begin. Whether you are thinking about houses or ethnographies, if you are about to design one of your own, it seems reasonable that from the hundreds you have visited, you have seen at least one that would be just right or would provide a basic plan that could be modified.

As for houses, I know that I could live comfortably in many that I have visited. Yet I have never seen a house so superbly suited both to the site and to the lifestyle that I share with my partner Norman that I wished I might simply have transplanted or replicated it for the house I have now. And much as I commend the house I have designed, I have never felt that it would necessarily be a "better" house for someone else or that it would necessarily fit someplace else, without the particular trees, slope, view, access—or occupants—that constitute its present setting. I find the idea of adapting a model more appealing that adopting one.

I know I should have been impressed by several of the Frank Lloyd Wright houses I have visited, but to be frank myself, I am glad he did not design a house for me. Is it different with ethnography? Might one turn to the classics to find a template for a contemporary ethnography certain to satisfy the most demanding of reviewers (a doctoral dissertation committee, for example)? Let's consider how well some ethnographic classics might serve in that regard.

Suppose we consider what must surely be the most widely recognized ethnography of all time, Branislaw Malinowski's *Argonauts of the Western Pacific* (1922) as a model. Malinowski's introduction works well, focusing immediately on a discussion of how his study was conducted, "The Subject, Method and Scope of This Enquiry." Not a bad idea to start by defining the purpose and reviewing how the study was conducted. Yet Malinowski felt compelled to provide a methodological broadside, far more ambitious in scope and purpose than anything we expect or need to have repeated in every ethnography to follow. If Malinowski intended his work to serve as a model for others, it might have proven more instructive at the time (and remains a good idea today) had he restricted his discussion of method to how the information he actually *used* in his study was gathered.

Malinowski's chapter 1 seems to point the way to the next step, "The Country and Inhabitants of the Kula District." Chapter 2, "The Natives of the Trobriand Islands," follows logically from that. Its eight subsections promise the level of detail we have come to expect in all ethnography, although the topics and arrangement may differ from how we might organize the account today: arrival and first impression, position of women, gardens and gardening, magic and work, chieftainship and wealth, totemism, magic and spirits of the dead, and some discussion of the neighboring districts.

There are 20 more chapters to come, yet the reader quickly realizes that the general ethnography has already been completed. Starting with chapter 3, Malinowski's attention turns to the Kula trading ring:

> Having thus described the scene, and the actors, let us now proceed to the performance. The Kula is a form of exchange, of extensive, inter-tribal character; it is carried on by communities inhabiting a wide ring of islands, which form a closed circuit. . . . Along this route, articles of two kinds, and these two kinds only, are constantly traveling in opposite directions. [Malinowski 1922:81]

On inspection, Malinowski's much-revered classic proves not to be a general ethnography at all, but a study of *one* dynamic aspect of *one* particular subset of *one* particular group of people. Good for Malinowski and his ability to make the ethnographic task manageable, but no good as a universal model, for he did not write the ethnography he seemed to promise in his introduction. He did his thing, but it does not help us do ours, except for an important but implicit lesson about the need for focus.

Is there a further lesson to be gained from examining his chosen title? *Argonauts of the Western Pacific* is an impressive title for a book that might more modestly have been called *The Kula Exchange*. We seem to have been promised more, yet presented with only a piece of the action, something quite within grasp of the lone ethnographer. That practice of assigning grandiose titles is a habit that ethnographers (might it sometimes be their publishers instead?)

have never quite been able to shake, titles often promising to deliver an entire people: *American Kinship; The Central Eskimo; Coming of Age in New Jersey; The People of Alor; We, the Tikopia;* or *China: Its People, Its Society, Its Culture.* Well, at least we have someone to blame.

To examine another classic as a possible model, consider E. E. Evans-Pritchard's *The Nuer,* first published in 1940. Six chapters follow an introductory one, with a narrowing focus that clearly signals the British social anthropologist at work. Explanation leans heavily toward the study of social structure, the last three chapters in turn devoted to the political system, the lineage system, and the age-set system. A good framework for presenting what Evans-Pritchard had in mind; an unlikely model for the ethnographer of today.

Perhaps something more recent, such as Sherry Ortner's *Sherpas Through Their Rituals* (1978). As with the examples from an earlier generation, Ortner's table of contents is more helpful in revealing her focus than is her title. Her first chapter is devoted not to the Sherpas of her study but to the topic of ritual. Not until the second one, which she describes as "a general ethnographic chapter," does she delve briefly into such familiar subheadings as Economy, Social Organization, and Religion, having cautioned that to approach an ethnography through the standard categories "is problematic, not only because the categories are externally imposed but because they are undynamic" (p. 1). From that point, ritual provides the focus for examining aspects of Sherpa culture. Once again, a clear focus for the ethnographer and for the work, but not a transportable model, even for the study of ritual in other contexts.

How about examples from the contemporary American scene, such as Sue Estroff's *Making It Crazy,* its focus revealed in the subtitle, *An Ethnography of Psychiatric Clients in an American Community* (1981, 1985). Estroff's three broadly defined sections seem to hold promise, Part 1, Introduction and Orientation; Part 2, Ethnographic Material; Part 3, Interpretation and Conclusions. Does Part 2 offer the structure we have been looking for? Yes, if you are presenting the material Estroff has to present, but not much help to an ethnographer in any other setting. Its four chapters deal, respectively, with the clients in an outpatient program, the medications they take (and the difficult decision Estroff faced about whether to take them herself in order to experience what they were experiencing), subsistence strategies, and a final chapter titled, "Normals, Crazies, Insiders and Outsiders." Estroff accomplishes what is promised by her subtitle, but I hardly encourage any beginning ethnographer to build a descriptive account by simply adopting the unique chapter headings so well suited for her study, even for a comparable study of psychiatric clients. Similarly, the chapters of Philippe Bourgois's *In Search of Respect: Selling Crack in El Barrio* (1995) flow nicely into each other, but neither chapter titles like "Crackhouse Management" nor subtitles like "Learning to Be a Better Criminal" point the way for the next researcher.

A final example, another contemporary study, this one of modern Thailand written by an anthropologist who has spent a lifetime studying and writing about it, Charles Keyes. His *Thailand: Buddhist Kingdom as Modern Nation-State* (1989) has the same painstakingly thorough quality about it that characterized much early ethnography (for example, the Nuer mentioned above). It includes chapters devoted to social organization and economy such as one might expect in a comprehensive effort. Its particular focus, as indicated in its subtitle, is on the tensions between a Buddhist society and a nation-state with militaristic leanings. Thus many of the minor topics discussed might be suitable for other ethnographic inquiries (e.g., "Foundations of a National Culture," "Ethnic and Religious Minorities," "The Roots of Cultural Change," "Mass Media and Popular Culture"), but they are arranged to present Thailand as the unique country it is, with an emphasis on recent developments.

Every ethnography takes on that same uniqueness; no particular one can serve as a model for all, and no particular one can be singled out for having set the standard for all that follow. As might be expected, knocking down the giants of the past has become a more popular anthropological pastime than pausing in reverence, at least in these days of the postmodern critique when seldom is heard an encouraging word. Hear Clifford Geertz go after a trio of early heroes:

> Firth, not Malinowski, is probably our best Malinowskian. Fortes so far eclipses Radcliffe-Brown as to make us wonder how he could have taken him for his master. Kroeber did what Boas but promised. [Geertz 1988:20]

No ethnographic classic, past or present, will ever serve as a suitable one-model-fits-all. Yet any of the studies mentioned above, or the hundreds of titles available today, offers not only a proven and workable plan but an opportunity to validate your approach with a footnote acknowledging the work of an earlier ethnographer. And no one will ever insist that you must adhere rigidly to a single model. So, why not take the best features from several of them, like the musical recordings that sample well-known themes from dozens of symphonies or operas? Let me explore that option, returning briefly to my personal story.

Combining Features from Several Models

In the interim between the decision to rebuild on the property and the moment we were ready to submit plans for obtaining the necessary building permits, Norman and I sought to become acutely aware of design elements we did and did not want in the new house. We put our radar out to detect features in other people's houses that one ordinarily takes for granted. For a while I carried a tape measure for recording the exact dimensions of things we liked: countertop widths; shelf, cupboard, window, and railing heights; closet space and arrangement; and so forth. We also asked friends to identify features they particularly liked about their own home that they felt we might want to consider for ours. Although I would not recommend the approach as a way to design a house from the ground up, the idea of incorporating desirable features from other people's houses worked well for us; we already had an integrated design in mind.

I doubt that one could construct a satisfactory ethnography by borrowing ideas piecemeal, either. An ethnography ought to be a tightly integrated (i.e., holistic) work, not simply an assemblage of unrelated items. Seamless is a word that comes to mind, although seamlessness is difficult to achieve with the linearity of abrupt sentences, paragraphs, and chapters. One of the most difficult tasks in writing ethnography is to achieve that seamless quality and yet present an adequate level of detail. Better to borrow whole elements, such as a first-person narrative style, or progression from general description to individual cases, than, say, to borrow the idea of a section on magic and work from Malinowski, political system from Evans-Pritchard, hospitality from Ortner, mental disorder from Estroff, street history from Bourgois, and education and social class from Keyes. If you need help with an overall structure, I have better ideas to offer in the next section, "Working from a Standard Plan."

Nevertheless, as an ethnographer you need to be sensitive to what others have to offer by way of suggestions, and to be especially attentive to what others can impose by reason of their authority. That is no different from adhering to local building codes in constructing a house. I did not have to tell my builder how many electrical outlets to put in each room, except where I wanted *more* than the minimum required. Instead, he told me what I had to have or, more often, simply went ahead without bothering to inform me as to what a building inspector would look for. Only when we were told that the plan called for too many windows was it time to do battle with the county building department. Too many windows, indeed!

In like fashion, an editor or academic adviser, a dissertation committee, government officials, reviewers for a professional journal, some tacitly observed but unstated norms of the field, and, in recent times, the people in the setting where you are conducting your research—any or all of these may be in a position to propose, or impose, certain conditions as to what you study and what you report. The growing awareness of being read by those we write about is nicely reflected in the title and contents of the edited collection mentioned earlier, *When They Read What We Write* (Brettell 1993). We cherish so-called academic freedom and, as ethnographers, are inclined to overestimate how much freedom we have, probably because we have internalized the limits as to what we can do. As an unhappy informant told a contributor to the Brettell volume, what had been reported in the published account was not incorrect, but an ethnographer also has the right, and sometimes an obligation, *not* to report all that might be revealed.

Contributors to the Brettell volume rendered a valuable service in their discussion of ethics and responsibility by reminding us that our informants today not only can but do read what we write. As the editor notes in her introduction, "Ethnographic authority survived under the cloak of distance and difference because the 'natives' never knew what had been written about them" (1993:10). Today they do know, and we write more circumspectly or run the risk of publishing and, figuratively, perishing as well, like John Messenger, who was warned he might be lynched were he to return to the Irish community where he had been conducting fieldwork.[5]

Within academic circles, my advice is to be pragmatic and as flexible as possible in negotiating one's way through and around the mundane requirements and regulations that can seem like such stumbling blocks, "little" impositions often more political than ethical. Most such obstacles are small, and small steps are sufficient for getting over them, rather than turning every issue into a major philosophical one. Yes, I live in a democracy, and no one ought to be able to tell me how many windows I can have in my house, but neither was the issue one that needed to be brought before the Supreme Court. When we rose to do battle with the county, I paid a consultant's fee to an engineering firm for technical advice as to how we could increase the insulation factor somewhere else to compensate for the heat loss through "too many" (double pane) windows. If your editor or dissertation chair has a "thing" about material culture, or reviewers think it a shame that you didn't do more with art or religion, consider how you might accommodate them before you rush off to call in the engineers. But if those among whom you have studied might feel betrayed by the account you intend to construct, then you may indeed have some negotiating to do before construction ever begins. House plans are mute as to who stands to profit, who may be offended, or whether the plan you would like to follow is even allowed.

Working from a Standard Plan

Although you may never have thought about it quite this way, ethnographers have at their fingertips the equivalent of those ubiquitous books filled with page after page of standard house plans. The books I have in mind are not *advertised* as plan books, but they can be used that way. The only difference is that ethnographic plans in this format come one to a book. To compare plans, you must consult multiple sources. These ethnographic templates are to be found in introductory undergraduate texts, for the most part an overlooked resource. Some texts designed for general anthropology classes may do, but introductory texts focused specifically on cultural anthropology and taking an "aspects of culture" approach are ideal. Each such text presents a single "model," a detailed conceptualization of what cultural anthropology is all about that can also serve as a framework for organizing an ethnographic account according to that conceptualization.

I recall a reviewer's comment that anthropologists *write* introductory texts but they do not *read* them. That observation is probably true, and it may explain why more attention is not drawn to introductory texts as resources to guide the beginning ethnographer. Although I don't want to risk my credentials by being caught reading introductory texts, I do pay attention to how they are organized and to the major topics their authors identify. I pay particular attention to tables of contents and to the descriptive synopses that publishers circulate. Many of those tables of contents offer splendid outlines of topics that can guide a would-be ethnographer who feels at a loss for what to cover and how to organize an inquiry.

When I first began to study anthropology systematically (as a classroom teacher who had gone back to school as a doctoral student), Felix Keesing's introductory text, *Cultural Anthropology: The Science of Custom* (1958), was the newest text on the market. I do not know what reception it had nationally, but on the Stanford campus it was heralded as a great breakthrough. Little wonder, since Keesing was chair of the anthropology department at the time. Still, the book's fresh approach did seem a welcome change from the heavy and heavily authoritative texts anthropologists had been writing until then. My mentor George Spindler was using the Keesing text in his large introductory classes. He insisted that the book succeeded at Stanford (whereas it might not be so successful elsewhere) because the students were "so bright." Students didn't mind being told how bright they were, and the book did "work." It also worked for me, not so much because of its innovative style of posing questions rather than presenting answers—the discussion is built around 84 "problems"—but because of splendid choices Keesing made for his chapter headings. To this day, those headings still represent for me a model and outline of what cultural anthropology is about. I continue to recommend his table of contents as an excellent guide for anyone trying to discern the basic components for making ethnography their way of seeing.

Keesing developed his material in 17 chapters. To place cultural anthropology in the broadest social science context, the early chapters devote attention to culture and biological heritage, to the growth of culture, to universals and aspects of culture, and to culture in space. With these topics as a foundation, Keesing then proceeded with the chapters that constitute the core of the book.

I repeat the titles of Keesing's major chapters here to show how they also can serve as a guide for the ethnographer, both in the field and in subsequently organizing and writing an account. I have retained the order in which he originally introduced them, although I did rearrange and modify the topics (the "problems" he poses) examined in each chapter. The sequence, of course, reflects *his theory* (idea, hunch, notion) of how best to order the topics for *his purposes*. Even were you to adopt his plan in toto, you might want to rearrange the order to suit your purposes and help you to achieve emphasis on matters of most importance to your own work. An artist himself (he provided the illustrations for the text), Keesing was especially interested in art and aesthetics and he devoted more attention to those domains than do most anthropologists. That interest is reflected in his identification of a major chapter, "Art and Play," as well as special attention to a category for "Ceramics, Textiles, and Metallurgy" under "Material Culture" that I did not include in these encapsulated summaries.

- Material Culture: Food and food customs, clothing, housing, travel and transportation, tools and weapons
- Economic Organization: Systems of production, consumption, and exchange
- Social Organization: Kinship; descent; hierarchical or rank-order principles; age and generation; sex, marriage, and family; voluntary associations
- Political Organization: Power and status; localism, nationalism, and international organization; emergence of the modern state; war and peace
- Social Control: Forces of social conformity; social response to breaches of rules; deviants; crime and the criminal
- World View: Knowledge and belief; the ideational dimensions of culture; religion; magic
- Art and Play: Aesthetic aspects of culture; major arts
- Language: Distribution and dynamics of language; metalinguistics

Two additional chapter headings differ from the "aspects of culture" inventory outlined above but need to be added to this list to round it out for ethnographic completeness:

- Society, Culture, and the Individual: Culture and personality; the life cycle
- Stability and Change: Innovation; diffusion; cultural dynamics; the individual and change

Much as I revere Keesing's original headings, I realized while reviewing them for inclusion here that I did not want to recapitulate them without making modifications of my own. I trust you would feel free to do likewise, should you find the headings somewhat helpful. The sequence can always be modified or rearranged to suit the situation. A British social anthropologist might change the order of topics to introduce social organization first, a linguistically oriented ethnographer would probably start with attention to language, and so on, much the same way one might find a highly suitable house plan but take its mirror image or rotate it 90° to better fit a particular site. Archaeologists work essentially from physical evidence, so their attention might be devoted to material culture and what can be inferred from it, while the symbolically oriented anthropologist might give rather scant attention to food, shelter, and clothing in order to address questions of language and world view. From the moment one identifies a suitable set of categories they become subject to modification.

What the list *does* provide is a sound structure that encompasses the major categories that ethnographers have traditionally addressed. This is not *the* basic floor plan; it is *a* basic floor plan. This one was developed by Felix Keesing for the first edition of his introductory text. He did not live long enough to revise the book. His son Roger Keesing, a major contributor to anthropological thinking in the generation that followed, took up that task. Initially Roger planned only to revise the book his father had written, but he found himself transforming it as a coauthor, rather than simply updating it as originally intended (R. Keesing 1971). Nevertheless, in that first transformation, Roger felt that the resulting text was "more like the original in structure than it would be had I set out to write a new book" (p. v), noting specifically, "Starting anew I might well have abandoned the rather traditional chapter organization." By the next iteration Roger had rewritten the book to his own satisfaction, and he lived long enough to revise it once more before his own early death (R. Keesing 1976, 1981).

Roger followed a "growth of cultures" approach that served well for introducing students to the study of cultural anthropology. Although he continued to devote chapters to major aspects of culture as outlined above (social structure, economic systems, political organization, social control, religion, world view), his revisions no longer presented the ethnographic checklist that I so valued in his father's book. No subsequent text has ever struck me as being more singularly useful than Felix Keesing's. However, that reflects a moment in my personal history. His was the book I had at hand when I embarked upon fieldwork. The categories he developed became the categories I used as I first began to sort the information I was gathering in my village study and, more important, the topics I felt I *must* address if I intended to claim my research as ethnographic. The die was cast: Once having adapted Keesing's categories for my own, I have more or less continued to readapt and use them ever since. As with learning language, the imprint of the one through which we first find our way is like no other. (Bear in mind as you read that I cut my teeth on a text that was already judged "rather traditional" fully 25 years ago.)

Proposing One's Own Set of Categories

By the time I was organizing and writing a fieldwork account of my own in 1963–64, I realized I was not bound to any particular order of presentation. I also hoped I did not have to pretend to know more than I did about the Kwakiutl to satisfy my dissertation committee. A couple of ways to organize and present data seemed appropriate. One was to describe the *everyday life* of villagers, children and adult alike, in terms of their nonschool life, for it was apparent that school "organized" the life of most village households on school days. I wanted to be able to contrast "village" life with "school" life. Another idea was to present material in terms of the *annual cycle of activities,* focusing on a dominant economic activity of each season—fall fishing, clam season, springtime and eulachon time, and summer fishing—as well as noting important minor activities such as logging and clam digging that engaged some people some of the time.

In revising the dissertation for publication, I realized that a straightforward way to organize my village "data" had evolved under three major headings: Features of Everyday Life, The Annual Economic Cycle, and Social Activities of Villagers. Everyday Life, the first category, prompted a review of material culture (food, shelter, clothing) as well as a way to introduce villagers by family and household. Examining the annual economic cycle called for a review of seasonal activities as well as a discussion of the sources of villager income, including important government subsidies. The third section, Social Activities, described social gatherings held for both traditional and contemporary purposes (e.g., potlatches, Band meetings, sports, religious activities, travel). It concluded with a discussion of social control, a topic directly related to Felix Keesing's marking of its importance and my own realization that I needed to introduce social control as a significant aspect of village life, although its complexity exceeded my grasp.

My intent in that first part of the monograph was to provide an adequate descriptive basis for the discussion about schooling that was to follow (as part 2) without overplaying my role as an ethnographer of contemporary Kwakiutl society. Having survived both writing a dissertation and revising it to the satisfaction of a publisher, I thought I had succeeded. But my colleague and fellow fieldworker Rohner didn't let me off the hook so easily. In his review for the *American Anthropologist* he lauded how part 2 is "impressively sensitive to the problems created by an intrusive, formal educational system" (Rohner 1968:654). But he was less impressed with my efforts as an ethnographer as revealed in part 1:

> Although this section is solid and competent, it reflects the fact that Wolcott's major involvement was not with general ethnographic research. The reader sometimes gets the feeling that he is reading a catalogue of observable culture traits, interspersed with many stimulating anecdotal citations from the author's journal notes. But the reader is left minimally informed about important facets of life such as the tenor of interpersonal and emotional life within the family, or the major dimensions of contemporary Kwakiutl social structure. . . . [P. 654]

I took little delight in having my ethnographic efforts likened to a "catalogue of observable culture traits"—and by the very person who had been guiding me through the course of the fieldwork (but, then, what are friends for?). However, I survived the critique and discovered that any attention is better than no attention, for the monograph remained in print for 25 years and is still being translated for new audiences. Furthermore, an important point Rohner was making in his review was that my role as village teacher at once focused and limited the scope of my work:

> Obligation to a formal role other than that of ethnographer also reduces the potentiality for obtaining certain kinds of information in the richness and depth that the investigator would like. On the other hand, such commitment may allow him to achieve a more sensitive understanding of the subtleties and complexities of those areas defined by the community as being within the legitimate perimeter of his status. [P. 654]

One has to enter a system somewhere. I have always felt that "my" villagers were more comfortable with the idea that I was their teacher than were Rohner's with the idea that he was their ethnographer. They actually assigned him a different role, that of Boss of the School. Although Ron's wife Evelyn was the formally appointed teacher, villagers were inclined to defer to males in appeals to formal authority. Evelyn was in charge of the classroom, but Ron was deemed to be in charge of the school. To Evelyn's dismay, requests concerning use of the school building or of school equipment were always directed to Ron.

For purposes of this discussion, let me emphasize that even a "catalogue of observable culture traits, interspersed with many stimulating anecdotal citations from the author's journal notes" is a beginning, and that is something. With Rohner's words to haunt me, I also began self-consciously to make my work "more ethnographic" and to look for ways that might help others seeking to do the same. I have been doing that ever since.

Some years later, while developing formal guidelines to help anyone trying to infuse their work with more of an anthropological perspective—more, that is, than simply through their presence as participant observers—I prepared a list of the topics with which ethnographers of the day seemed most concerned. The list reflected my growing experience as an ethnographer and provided an opportunity to share with others some categories that were working well for me (HFW 1975a). The list was divided into three subsets. The first subset was designed to identify several relatively straightforward topics amenable to everyday observation and descriptive narrative:

allocation and distribution of resources
environment
material culture/technology
personal adaptations (in both words and action)
ritual behavior
social networks

The second subset traced its roots directly to Felix Keesing's original chapter headings. It was intended not only as a guide but also to alert would-be ethnographers to the kinds of conceptual schema they needed to bring *into* the field in addition to the kinds of information they needed to glean while there.

economic organization
ethos or world view/ideational systems
language
life cycle customs
political organization
projective systems (religion, art, folklore)
social control
social organization

The third subset was directed at a particular audience of researchers, colleagues interested in doing ethnography in schools or studying aspects of the educational process. I realize that I was outlining my own career interests as well, except that today I would substitute the phrase "cultural acquisition" where I originally used the term "enculturation":

culture and personality
cultural stability and change
cultural transmission/enculturation

I emphasized that an ethnographer was not duty bound to touch each of these bases. To know (and report) "a little bit about a lot of things" is not a particularly instructive guideline for making a substantial contribution to ethnography. It seemed more helpful to point out that an ethnographer might develop a comprehensive study around any *one* major activity, as Malinowski had done in his focus on the Kula exchange, or to focus on *one* major topic of general ethnographic concern, as, for example, the Bohannans' *Tiv Economy* (1968), Clifford Geertz's *Religion of Java* (1960), or studies focused exclusively on material culture (e.g., Buck 1930; Osgood 1940; Schlereth 1982).[6] I had already staked out two arenas of general ethnographic concern that seemed particularly compelling at the time:

> (1) the means by which people organize themselves into interacting social systems, what the anthropologist studies as *social organization;* and (2) the shared systems of beliefs and attitudes, the "ideational systems," that the anthropologist examines as *ethos* or *world view*. [HFW 1975a:123]

More than two decades later, social organization and world view still seem to me to encapsulate both the essence and the uniqueness of the ethnographic approach. Attending to those two aspects can help ethnographers with the necessary task, as Spindler has described it, of separating out "culture as an ideational organization from social behavior and interaction" (1971:1). Social behavior and interaction are amenable to observation—an ethnographer can record what people do and say and what they say they do. Ideational organization, as revealed in world view, is what the ethnographer infers from that observed behavior, and what people say about it. Pretty straightforward, eh? What you can observe, and what you make of it. So there you have another framework for organizing and presenting data in a way that privileges a cultural interpretation without having to beat the culture concept to death.

More Alternatives

Regardless of what they are searching for—automobiles, house plans, or new clothes—some people prefer to shop around and others stop looking as soon as they find something suitable. Thus far I have reviewed three sources of plans. If you are about to embark on your own ethnographic inquiry, perhaps following any one of these options is enough to get you started. They have already proved adequate as starting points for me by providing a base that has served as both guideline and checklist.

I pay close attention to what other ethnographers are doing. I pay even closer attention to what the field situation presents. But I have never felt that I needed to thumb through a dozen or more ethnographies every time I was about to initiate a new study. Like other old-timers, I often find it expedient to ignore all the newfangled approaches so that I can keep doing things the same old (aha, but tried and true!) ways.

We put our unique imprint on everything we do as individuals, and that certainly includes how we go about conducting an inquiry. I have a way of going about ethnography. Although no two of my studies are, or ever could be, quite the same, I am sure there is a recognizable style and character about them all. There should as well be evidence of my preoccupation with certain facets of social behavior that seem to me clearly deserving of attention.

If you want to continue shopping before you make a selection, I suggest you examine the tables of contents of other introductory texts until you find a suitable set of categories or feel confident in creating a set of categories of your own. Keep in mind that each table of contents reflects one particular way of conceptualizing the field, and that each author has had to identify particular aspects of culture deemed appropriate for some particular segment of a highly competitive text market.

Be aware as well of the period in which each text was written, along with any generational difference, such as those reflected in iterations of the Keesing text from father to son. Today, for example, one expects to find more emphasis on the biological contribution, and today's fieldworker needs to decide how that shift is to be represented in the ethnographer's task: whether to remain with the earlier tradition linking ethnography rather exclusively with culture, or to attempt a broader base in studying human behavior. My vote goes with those who feel ethnographers have enough in dealing with "minds," leaving brain research and DNA studies to others—including many cultural anthropologists whose work far exceeds ethnographic boundaries.

I realize I have a tendency to place boundaries around ethnography that others may find unnecessarily restrictive, especially in a day when disciplinary boundaries seem to be breaking down and new alignments are being formed, as with cognitive studies, computer simulations, and the like. Yet I was struck when I first came across the idea of fetal alcohol syndrome (Dorris 1989) and realized what a compelling alternative explanation it offered for some of the problems among the Kwakiutl that for 25 years I had attributed solely to culture. The best I can suggest in this regard is for ethnographers to strive to place their studies in the broadest possible context, just as they strive to put the broadest possible context into their studies.

If one turns to introductory texts as a source of ideas and plans for developing an ethnography, it is also useful to ascertain where the authors of those texts studied, where they conducted fieldwork, and what topics they claim as areas of specialization. These aspects usually become apparent as authors begin to draw upon case material to illustrate their points. It is important to recognize how an author's personal experience of ethnography influences his or her way of conceptualizing it. The "culture and personality" people put their stamp on the introductory texts they write; the "social organization" people or "material culture" people do the same. However, they sometimes forget to mention, and indeed may be somewhat unaware of, the extent to which those special interests, or their own particular set of experiences, have influenced their way of seeing. Textbook writing seems to invite authors to maintain a distance and to write in an authoritative third-person voice. If you are thinking about adapting a particular outline as a guide for your work, you need to examine the match between what the author set out to accomplish and what you want to accomplish.

The Introductory Text as Informal Field Guide

From introductory texts that happen to have found their way to my bookshelves over the years let me draw some examples of topics and sequences that might guide a beginning ethnographer who is searching for ways to structure a study. My purpose is not to compare texts, but to show how different authors have addressed a roughly comparable set of underlying themes, while the themes themselves undergo a gradual evolution from decade to decade. My sources include some old texts and some more recent or recently revised, although one needs to keep in mind that the basic structure of a textbook is pretty well set in its first edition. Revisions are important for the market, but that basic structure is unlikely to change dramatically as long as the author remains the same. Recall that it took Roger Keesing two cycles of revision before he felt that his text adequately reflected his own organization rather than his father's.

I begin with the second edition of a text originally published in 1969 and revised in 1974, Philip Bock's *Modern Cultural Anthropology: An Introduction*. Bock organized the core of his text around four headings that he identified as the major subsystems of a culture—and thus a set of headings that would serve as well for developing an ethnographic account: Language, Society, Technology, and Ideology (Bock 1974:431). Each subsystem was developed through chapters devoted to its major structural components:

- Learning to be Human
    Learning a Language
    The Process of Enculturation
- Social Systems
    Kinds of Persons
    Kinds of Groups
    Social Space and Social Time
    Stability and Change
- Technological Systems
    Tools and Human Needs
    Techniques and Skills
- Ideological Systems
    Belief Systems
    Value Systems

Next, I jump ahead almost two decades to William Haviland's seventh edition (1993) of *Cultural Anthropology,* which the publisher describes as *the* classic cultural anthropology text. Of the five major sections in the Haviland text, the middle three offer an ethnographic outline with topics that may already have begun to sound comfortably familiar. Here are the section headings and the titles of the chapters devoted to each:

- Culture and Survival: Communicating, Raising Children, and Staying Alive
    Language and Communication
    Growing Up Human
    Patterns of Subsistence
    Economic Systems
- The Formation of Groups: Solving the Problem of Cooperation
    Sex and Marriage
    Family and Household
    Kinship and Descent
    Grouping by Sex, Age, Common Interest, and Class

- The Search for Order: Solving the Problem of Disorder
  Political Organization and Social Control
  Religion and the Supernatural
  The Arts

For a related example, I turn to the fifth edition of Michael C. Howard's *Contemporary Cultural Anthropology* (1996). This book differs only slightly in structure from the text described above except for the absence of section headings that organize major topics into smaller units. The topics themselves and the sequence for addressing them are similar, as is the seeming logic (and tradition) of authors to start with introductory chapters presenting basic concepts and issues—and perhaps some discussion of ethnographic research—and a closing chapter or two devoted to culture change and modern world development.

Keep in mind that we are looking only at basic outlines in this sampling of texts, comparable to examining house plans rather than touring completed houses. As with two houses constructed from the same basic plan, ethnographies constructed from these plans might differ in important ways: format, style, cases chosen for illustration. In Howard's text, most chapters conclude with an example drawn from the work of someone else. In the course of reading the entire book a student will have been introduced to the work of a dozen other anthropologists. Orienting chapters in his text that might serve as a handy guide to fieldwork are, in order:

Culture and Communication (including linguistic variation)
Patterns of Subsistence
Economic Systems
Society (i.e., social groupings)
Socialization (including world view and values)
Kinship and Descent
Sex, Marriage and the Family
Ethnicity and Social Stratification
Politics and Political Organization
Law and Conflict
Religious Belief, Behavior, and Symbolism
Artistic Expression
Illness and Curing

Now consider Paul Bohannan's *We, The Alien* (1992). This anthropologist author made a self-conscious effort to achieve something different by way of an introductory text. He reminds his reader at the outset how important it is "not only to include the right stuff but also to get it in the right order—an order that makes repetition unnecessary, and that makes the subject grow from idea to idea" (1992:ix). Bohannan organized his text around five key words: people, kinship, power, meaning, and context. The middle three of these terms, and the chapter headings included under them, might serve any ethnographer who first takes time to understand what Bohannan means with some of his shorthand labels:

- Kinship
    Men and Women, Sex and Babies
    Marriage and Family
    Kinship and Community
- Power
    Bread and Work
    Conflict and Order
    Getting Control
    Born Equal?
- Meaning
    Symbols: Language and Art
    Meaning: Creativity and Performance
    Creed: Religion and Ideology

Many authors of introductory texts follow a format that takes a "growth of culture" approach, as Roger Keesing did in modifying his father's text to draw contrasts between tribal societies and complex ones. Textbook authors knowingly take a risk following a sequential approach, for it tends to lock the instructor into a predetermined sequence that must be followed for the text to make sense. Texts organized around standard categories tend to be favored by instructors who want to set their own sequence of topics rather than have their course outline dictated by a text author. This is an important consideration in marketing and a reminder of the influence consumers have over the form in which products are designed. It also means that not *every* introductory text can double as a field guide. It takes only a moment to glance through a table of contents in order to recognize whether it is organized around standard ethnographic categories.

Identifying categories is not the only service the introductory texts can perform for someone unfamiliar with anthropology as a field of study. My colleagues Sheldon Smith and Philip Young have oriented their introductory text *Cultural Anthropology: Understanding A World in Transition* (1998) around issues of global change, with major sections devoted to Africa, the Middle East, Asia, and Latin America, as well as to the U.S. Before turning attention to major cultural areas, they offer overviews on a number of topics critical to understanding anthropology as a discipline, including discussion of the culture concept, anthropological theory, and fieldwork, drawing upon their own broad experience. Thus no matter what approach is followed, all introductory texts offer an excellent opportunity for readers to see "culture at work" as anthropologists explain and employ the concept. But certain ones offer the special bonus of a fully explicated plan that is there for the asking.

The Modular Approach

Returning to the house-plan analogy, the texts with interchangeable parts—chapters or sections that do not *necessarily* have to be read in any particular order—can be compared to modular units used in simplified designing. One can pick and choose among basic units and assemble them in whatever combination fits the parameters. For several years, instructors of large introductory classes in anthropology have had a similar option to customize their own text by selecting modules from a growing list of titles initiated under the general editorship of anthropologists Melvin and Carol Ember, including Carol Ember's own *The Making of a Cross-Cultural Researcher* (1994).

One can write ethnographies that way, too. The first step is to identify the major topics to be included. These can then be arranged into suitable clusters, the clusters then put in some satisfactory sequence. Highly structured fieldworkers probably follow a similar pattern in organizing their data-gathering sequences, literally ticking off topics to be covered before the fieldwork comes to an end. As a fieldwork strategy, it may also make good sense to arrange topics to be investigated on a scale of anticipated difficulty, beginning with relatively straightforward headings such as material culture, kinship, art, or economic organization, holding off on sensitive issues (belief systems, power, social control) until one has become more familiar with the setting and more certain about how to ferret out relevant information. That also helps in prioritizing the time available for fieldwork. Should time in the field be cut short, as is frequently the case, the fieldworker nonetheless should have ample information to report, albeit of more modest consequence than what may originally have been planned.

Getting a Start and Building On Later

One usually hopes and intends to return to the site(s) of one's studies, especially if the fieldwork was conducted among what are to become the ethnographer's "people." But sustained efforts at fieldwork do not necessarily mean that the work becomes easier (should it?), and length of stay is no necessary guarantee that one's access or understanding is enhanced. Nor do ethnographers who remain in the field *necessarily* endear themselves to those among whom they study. Sometimes it is the other way around; the longer one stays, the greater the chance of making tactical errors or creating misunderstanding. Some parts of the original design of a research project may never be implemented. Ethnographers can also become their own worst enemy by inadvertently closing off topics or sources of information, by proceeding too quickly or brusquely with their initial inquiries, or by imposing unduly on hosts who may nurture second thoughts about the seemingly endless demands being made on them as the period of fieldwork lengthens.

Like dream houses started on small budgets, ambitious plans to produce definitive ethnographies must sometimes be realized through modest additions completed in phases. In such cases, it helps to know which modules are critical, which can wait, if construction is going to have to proceed in stages. For example, although to *me* my library/study is clearly the most important room in the house, had it been necessary to build in stages, that room might not have headed the list of work to be completed in phase one. When an ethnography is going to have to be developed this way, fieldwork should be designed to allow for interim reporting (for example, in journal articles and contributed chapters) on units of work as they are completed, rather than awaiting completion of a magnum opus that, like the house of one of my neighbors, may never be "finished."

The analogy to designing a house suggests various sources of ideas and ways to combine the essential elements of ethnography, leaving open the question of just what is, in fact, essential. Designing a house is the same; it is easier to reach agreement that there *are* certain essentials than to get agreement as to exactly what the essentials are. Agreeing upon some minimum standards for ethnography seems an obvious first step, and it is easy to muster arguments on the need for them, but reaching agreement as to exactly what those standards should be raises questions (see Stewart 1998; Werner 1998). Oswald Werner, for example, posits that establishing explicit standards should help to make ethnography more "vulnerable," a quality he feels is worth striving for. However, as soon as he identifies examples of some "fairly obvious" standards—in this case, two prompted by the earlier work of Raoul Naroll (1962): length of stay in the field and ability to speak the native language—the task of list-making becomes suspect. Length of stay cannot guarantee quality; competence in local language is mooted in much contemporary work.

An American friend writes of building a house in the mountains in the south of Thailand surrounded by "jungle, waterfalls, rivers, no electricity" and adds, "At times I sit in the house—as much as one can, since it's all open to the air—and try to convince myself that it's mine, that I designed it, and that it is where it is" (Bill Savage, personal communication, January 1997). With the clear objective in mind of designing a house, he and I seem to have come up with distinctly different results. Similarly, ethnographers today can worry about how to be holistic, or how to satisfy criteria for being cross-cultural and comparative, yet still agree that they know a good ethnography (or a well-designed house) when they see one. There is no universal standard for a house plan; there is no universal standard for ethnography. To play it safe and without risk, you won't go wrong if the house you design looks pretty much like other houses in the neighborhood, or the ethnography you design covers the same major topics as other standard ethnographies. Either can have a few idiosyncratic touches, but be prepared for criticism within your community if you are viewed as being too far-out.

Meeting Ethnographic Criteria the Low-Risk Way

Were I to proceed from this point by proposing my own revised set of categories for organizing the field of cultural anthropology, then fleshing them out as chapters, I might find myself writing another introductory text in cultural anthropology. And, like many of its predecessors, it also might double as a field guide for the novice ethnographer.

Had I set out instead to write a historically oriented review of the development of cultural anthropology, I might have turned back more than 125 years to draw upon E. B. Tylor's *Primitive Cultures,* written in 1871. The end products from organizing a new text or doing a historical review might prove surprisingly similar. Tylor's two-volume work was developed around the topics of mythology, philosophy, religion, language, and art and custom. His proposed set of topics is sufficiently flexible that even today it could provide an adequate outline for a text or fieldwork guide.

Like the authors of introductory texts, ethnographers are free to change the order in which topics are addressed, to combine certain topics and ignore others, or to single out one or two topics for attention, focusing specifically on *aspects* of culture rather than attempting that elusive holistic view. Ideally, any account should meld categories into a unified whole, integrated in the ethnographic account just as they are integrated in human lives. When comprehensiveness is the goal, pursuing a kind of "ethnography by the numbers" approach through systematically addressing some standard set of categories—any of the lists already reviewed, for example—virtually guarantees a satisfactory ethnographic account. Satisfactory, but not necessarily very satisfying. The ethnographer who attempts dutifully to address every major category runs the risk of the sort of "undynamic" presentation that may result in little more than a catalog of cultural items and cultural traits. There is a fine line to walk between providing *rich* detail and *endless* detail. What can guide one in assessing what is enough, when to stop?

To answer, we might look again at the extremes. In spite of the well-intended efforts of their compilers to be comprehensive, neither *Notes and Queries* nor the *Outline of Cultural Materials* offers a helpful guide for anyone who takes it too literally as *the* set of topics that must be addressed. Either of those sources may render more valuable service through helping a novice to *eliminate* topics, or to set priorities among topics to be covered, than to provide a comprehensive checklist to insure that nothing is left out.

The endless ways ethnographers have arranged their accounts, or that different authors have arranged introductory texts, underscore the idiosyncratic nature of ethnography: no two texts or accounts are ever exactly the same. Yet in some form or another, certain categories seem invariably to reappear; this chapter has provided ample evidence of that. One way to insure that you are "doing ethnography" is to address these standard categories, or some thoughtfully selected subset of them, quite explicitly. If you need an authoritative source to guide your selection, you might adopt the four that David Schneider identified as the traditional quartet: kinship, economics, politics, and religion (1984:181; see also Stocking 1992:362–372). If you feel more daring, you might reduce the list to the two categories I proposed, *social organization* and *world view,* updating and broadening those categories to direct attention to how people are organized to do what they are doing and to what they (say they) think about what they are doing.

One advantage of systematically attending to a broad set of categories is that they satisfy ethnographic criteria without belaboring the issue of criteria; everything is built in. The categories provide a cultural framework, and they are cross-cultural and comparative by design. They demand the direct experience of fieldwork. And they cannot help but be particularistic and idiosyncratic, because they are drawn out of the experience of a particular researcher working among a particular group of people. Even the extent to which each ethnographer feels constrained by the particular or tempted toward broad generalization is idiosyncratic.

In following the relatively risk-free approach of filling in standard categories, probably the most difficult criterion to meet is to achieve the integration called for in being holistic. Discrete categories virtually defy integration, tending instead to pull things apart into analytical elements that dehumanize the very processes they seek to understand. Ethnography as art yields to ethnography as science. But that admittedly plodding way to first set out on the ethnographic path worked for me, and I commend it to others unsure about how to get started on their own. Why not let some reasonable set of categories underwrite your ethnographic claim as you acquire firsthand experience and begin to appreciate the range of opportunities and the risks inherent in the options you can exercise?

For the inexperienced researcher committed to a fieldwork approach but undecided whether ethnography is necessary or even highly desirable as the outcome, the categories can serve another function On close inspection, the categories should seem both appealing and appropriate to the problem focus and one's own research style. No one is bound by any particular combination of categories, but if *none* of the topics that they address strikes a responsive chord, then the underlying cultural framework of ethnography may be out of place as well.

However, if problems related to the categories lie only in their seeming rigidity, then what one may need instead are alternative ways to organize and present information that fall within ethnographic boundaries. This chapter has focused on traditional ethnography and ethnographic traditions— ethnography "dead center," you might say. Ethnography reported this way enjoys the security of being on target, buoyed by tradition, but it runs the risk of proceeding rather perfunctorily, with results that can be, and often enough have been, as deadly dull as they are relentlessly thorough. This is how ethnography has been defined in the past, but it is not all ethnography is, has become, or can be. Time now to examine other ways ethnographers have found for pursuing their fieldwork and rendering their accounts without adhering so strictly to their own tradition.

Notes

1. Other than cost (five shillings), there are close parallels between the 1912 edition of *Notes and Queries* and the most recent (1951) one. The earlier publication is divided roughly into thirds, one section for "technology" (e.g., clothing, food, weapons), one for "sociology" (subsequently retitled "social anthropology," with subsections devoted to method, including "The Genealogical Method" and "Choice of Informants," and discussions on life history, social organization, economic organization, etc.), and one for "arts and sciences" (e.g., language, the arts, religion). Malinowski went into the field well coached.

2. As testimony to his faith in its efficacy, Bernard has reproduced a condensed version of the *Outline of Cultural Materials* as an appendix in both editions of his research methods text, making it easily accessible. See Bernard 1988, appendix C, pp. 463–479, where he also includes a description of how the HRAF works; see also Bernard 1994, appendix C, 519–528, where he provides only the code headings. See Murdock 1971 for the *OCM* version referred to here.

3. The Human Relations Area File *Collection of Ethnography* is now an indexed, full-text database available on CD-ROM and the World Wide Web and has been joined by a newer *Collection of Archaeology*.

4. See, for example, Fetterman 1998; Kutsche 1998; Spradley 1979, 1980. The best all-round source as a comprehensive handbook on fieldwork techniques with an ethnographic emphasis will undoubtedly prove to be Russ Bernard's edited *Handbook of Methods in Cultural Anthropology* (1998), or, for those who prefer a single-authored text, his earlier *Research Methods in Anthropology: Qualitative and Quantitative Approaches* (1994b). Two other handbooks with excellent chapters on ethnographic approaches are those edited by Denzin and Lincoln (1994, 2000) and by LeCompte, Millroy, and Preissle (1992). See also the seven-volume set edited by Schensul and LeCompte, *Ethnographer's Toolkit* (1999).

5. See Messenger 1989. For a discussion of similar cases, see Brettell 1993:9–16.

6. The topic of material culture also has its own special publication, the journal *Material Culture,* published in Great Britain by Sage.

CHAPTER SIX

Ethnography from Inside Out

Without an ethnographer, there is no ethnography. . . .

—Paul Bohannan
How Culture Works, 1995, p. 157

If I gave the impression in the previous chapter of seeming to dismiss traditional category-bound ethnography with such expressions as "ethnography by the numbers," let me hasten to reinvest it with its proper status. Traditional ethnography, presenting highly detailed accounts of how (other) people live, organized and presented in terms of a set of generally agreed upon categories for describing cultural behavior, will remain, as it always has been, at the center of things.

So central and inviolable a position also guarantees that traditional ethnography will continue to be, as it always has been, subject to a constant barrage of criticism. Not only is it vulnerable for being tedious and undynamic, the very idea of employing predetermined categories has been severely criticized. David Schneider, for example, has faulted the categories as "essentially undefined and vacuous," a set of "metacultural categories embedded in European culture" incorporated uncritically into social science thinking (Schneider 1984:184–185; see also Stocking 1992:362–372). Frankly, I cannot imagine how one proceeds without having some broad organizing topics in mind, and neither could Schneider, who argues only that "the first step, prerequisite to all others in comparative work, is to establish the particular categories or units which each particular culture itself marks off" (p. 184).

The comprehensiveness of the categories presents the would-be ethnographer with an unreasonable and unreachable challenge in completeness, a mission impossible. It seems safe to predict that there will be no end to the variations introduced, to fads and frills and fresh, seemingly innovative ways to collect and display data or otherwise render (and vigorously defend) partial, category-defying, sometimes hopelessly subjective accounts, and no end to the soul-searching accompanying such efforts.

I have come to think of those endless variations as extending outward like ripples on a pond, the close-in ones more clearly evincing the impact of traditional ethnography, others "far-out" both literally and figuratively that offer little evidence of the direct impact of ethnography but are discernible as qualitative/descriptive research nonetheless. No exact line needs to be drawn to define where ethnography stops. The analogy to ripples on a pond helps to convey the idea of taking studies to be *more* or *less* ethnographic. Employing the *techniques* of ethnographic research is sufficient to place a study somewhere in the pool, but, as noted, the strength of a claim to "ethnographicness" depends on more than technique alone.

Examining approaches that represent a departure from the relatively safe, comfortable, and exhaustingly thorough traditional approaches finds us confronted with our own version of the statistician's dilemma in having to choose between a Type I or a Type II error.[1] Either we report according to categories of behavior that ethnographers have traditionally addressed, running the risk of exhausting not only the list and the ethnographer but probably the reader as well, or we set an alternative course in an effort to achieve a sense of thoroughness by defying tradition rather than reifying it.

The ethnographer willing to eschew standard categories that offer a kind of academic insurance will recognize the questions posed in Chapter 4 as all the more critical: What is an ethnographic question? What is the *essence* of ethnography? Thus far in my effort to ferret out that essence, I have tentatively identified several characteristics. Two frequently mentioned ones are that ethnography is *cross-cultural* and that it is *comparative*. On close examination, however, these two seemingly obvious conditions create problems when we try to distinguish between them or to establish what is cross-cultural *enough* or ask whether "comparative" says it all. The underlying issue here revolves around the concept of *difference*. What is the role of difference in ethnography? What makes something different, and, for an ethnographer, what is "different enough"?

How Critical Is "Difference" in Doing Ethnography?

"Difference," writes Bradd Shore (1996:379), "is at the heart of all anthropology." Ethnography, too, is predicated on difference. Standard categories help ethnographers by flagging particular arenas of behavior for observation, but it is difference itself to which ethnographers attend. How, then, does one employ the idea of difference in the absence of categories for comparison?

Recall my earlier suggestion that in pursuing an ethnographic inquiry I recommend that the beginner try to do as *little* comparing as possible. Where does this lead?

Gregory Bateson was particularly intrigued with the notion of *difference* and the critical role such an abstract idea plays in the creation of what we call information. Discussions about difference appear frequently in his collected essays (Bateson 1972). By way of illustration, Bateson points out that in map making what gets onto a map is difference, "be it a difference in altitude, a difference in vegetation, a difference in population structure, difference in surface, or whatever" (p. 451). His observation offers a profound way to think about ethnography, for if one thinks of it as a process of "mapping" cultural territory, then what we mark on our ethnographic "maps" are differences.

Consider the role of difference as revealed in another dimension of human activity, that of the cross-cultural and comparative study of color. The human eye perceives color in a continuous spectrum. However, in order to identify colors by *name* (which is, by the way, a splendid example of culture manifested in behavior), it is necessary that intervals be far enough apart along the spectrum for differences to be detected. The spectrum must be segmented, the difference readily discernible. In similar fashion, ethnographers draw upon continuous experience, but not everything that happens can be reported, recorded, or detected. What we note are points at which something stands out, something changes or appears discernibly different.

Think how ethnographers hurry us through the "flat" places where differences are not of sufficient magnitude to mark. This is especially noticeable as the observer scurries across the plains of routine with phrases that catapult the account quickly ahead: "The pace of everyday life remains pretty much unchanged until . . ." or "The seasons come and go . . ." or "Several weeks later. . . ." Like storytellers everywhere, informants do the same when the anecdote, the story, or the storyteller is finished. Peter Nabokov's Crow informant Two Leggings, for example, completes his account abruptly, "Nothing happened after that. We just lived. . . . There is nothing more to tell" (Nabokov 1967:197). Marjorie Shostak's informant Nisa does something similar as she relates certain events of her life in great detail and then makes huge leaps in her narrative with such phrases as "We lived and lived" (1981:69), "But life continued and I kept growing up" (p. 71), "My mother lived on after that . . ." (p. 78), "My heart was happy, eating honey and just living" (p. 98), or "We lived and lived and nothing more happened for a while" (p. 137).

Bateson offered another important observation when he pointed out that difference itself is an idea. Although we can recognize that two things differ, the *idea* of their difference can exist only in the mind. In his typically profound, yet typically obscure way, he also made a distinction between mere differences and differences that make a difference. In fact, that is how he defined *information*:

> What we mean by information—the elementary unit of information—is a difference which makes a difference. [Bateson 1972:453]

I would never attempt to out-Bateson Bateson, but for purposes of understanding ethnography, we need to go a step further and inquire as to whom a difference must make a difference. If the difference is primarily of interest to anthropologists and other like-minded social scientists, then the standard categories outlined in the previous chapter serve a critical comparative function and give one kind of purpose to a study. But preconceived categories can blunt the keen edge of observation, ignoring differences important to those in the scene while giving undue importance to categories of less consequence. If, for example, you set out to show how the social organization of some group of people "determines" their world view, quite likely that is what you will find. To free yourself of that risk by freeing yourself of standard categories is to risk the almost predictable critique that your account, interesting as it may be, has failed to give adequate attention to certain basic facets of human social life.

Recognition of the importance of difference may provide a startling "aha!" notion. But this is a source of concern for anyone dismayed by the idea that the ethnographic enterprise is so dependent on the notion of difference that we *make* others different in order to pursue our inquiries. I am consoled by Bateson's reminder that difference is an *idea,* and therefore a conceptual tool critical to our ability to observe. (Admittedly, looking for differences is also in keeping with my sometimes contrary nature, a trait sufficiently well distributed among my anthropology colleagues.)

How to resolve the dilemma between employing traditional categories that call attention to differences or using a descriptive mode that downplays the comparative and aims simply to "tell it like it is"? Because the pull toward the comparative, drawing as it does upon the power of difference, exerts such a strong influence on ethnography, I recommend making a conscious effort to attend to the richness of detail *internal* to the account.

I am not calling for a moratorium on comparison. But I do urge ethnographers to maintain a focus on what is being described, rather than to become preoccupied with exhausting the limitless possibilities that a comparative approach invites. By the very fact of an interest in the lives of others, the ethnographer *already* works from a comparative perspective. That comparative dimension becomes quite explicit when employing the traditional categories described earlier: they tell you what you should be looking for and provide ready-made labels for what you report. If you follow the approaches examined in this chapter, the comparisons will be less explicit, less intrusive, but your approach will be comparative, nonetheless.

The opportunity of ethnography lies in a commitment and devotion to description that acknowledges—but endeavors not to surrender entirely to—comparison. Others can assess the potential of your work for (their) comparative purposes. All the approaches are founded on observable difference. The comparative approach is more explicit about it; so explicit, in fact, that comparison too easily may become an end in itself that draws attention away from what is going on. Certainly you will have the standard categories in mind, even if you heed the advice to keep them in the background as you explore other ways to conceptualize and organize an account. Simply put, try to portray what you have observed before you find yourself swept up by the influence of the ethnographic tradition itself. Or, if your interest is in ethnographic process rather than in conducting a study of your own, consider the approaches to be described in this chapter (and the next) in terms of the problems all ethnographers face in finding ways to render their accounts without letting the comparative potential overwhelm them.

Do you sense the tension here in a tradition that embraces both description and comparison but endeavors to distinguish between them, even recognizing them by different (but variously assigned) labels such as the one that contrasts ethnography and ethnology? Among cultural anthropologists, the issue of description versus comparison has been compressed into a short-hand label, the *emic/etic* distinction. There was a time beginning in the 1960s when sides were so sharply drawn that some anthropologists felt obliged to identify themselves as being exclusively in one camp or the other, as, for example, declaring oneself to be an "etic anthropologist." I recall meetings of the American Anthropological Association at which the mood was reminiscent of attending formal weddings where an usher inquires whether you are a "friend of the bride" or "friend of the groom" in order to know on which side of the aisle you should be seated.

With a softening that comes with time, the lines between emic and etic are no longer drawn so sharply. Where it once seemed fashionable to insist on being *either* an emic or etic anthropologist, it now seems questionable how one could conduct ethnographic research without being a bit of both. As with the case of looking for similarities or looking for differences, the issue is a matter of emphasis. However, there is much to learn from a look at the origin of the terms and the idea behind the distinction. Let me review how we arrived at something called *emic* ethnography as an alternative to imposing a rigid set of predefined categories.

Emic and Etic

The labels "emic" and "etic" were derived from technical terms that serve as guides to their origin and pronunciation: *phonemic* and *phonetic*. Linguist Kenneth Pike recognized a common problem facing ethnographer and linguist alike, the same problem inherent in the contrasting approaches discussed in this chapter and the previous one. In order to compare languages, one needs some standard categories. However, such categories are not sensitive to the specific differences critical to the speakers of any *particular* language. Ward Goodenough describes the difference as follows:

> Linguists refer to the task of isolating and describing the sound modalities of particular languages as "phonemics," and they refer to the study of sound production and the development of a metalanguage by which the phonemes and distinctive features of any language can be described as "phonetics." Both kinds of operation are essential to linguistic science, and neither is possible without the other. [Goodenough 1970:108]

As early as 1954, Goodenough explains—in a book of his own appropriately titled *Description and Comparison in Cultural Anthropology*—Pike realized that description and comparison of standards of human conduct *of any kind* involve similar considerations. Pike "generalized from phonetics and phonemics to what he has called the 'etics' and 'emics' of all socially meaningful human behavior" (Goodenough 1970:108):

> Whatever the names one may choose to call them, these concepts of the etic and the emic are indispensable for understanding the problems of description and comparison, of the particular and the general, in cultural anthropology. [Pp. 108–109]

Goodenough placed himself on what he considered to be the neglected emic side, emphasizing the basic ethnographic task: A science of culture rests on description (Goodenough 1970:110). He urged anthropologists not to think of that task as "simply a matter of presenting the 'objective' facts about a society, its organization, law, customs, and shared beliefs" (pp. 110–111). Instead, he advised them to attend to what an *individual* must know to behave acceptably as a member of a particular group. As a constructive development along these lines, he commended the then-new efforts at "ethnoscience" and "the New Ethnography," although he expressed reservations about their "somewhat misleading" labels (p. 111).

Insiders and Outsiders

The emic/etic labels are still with us. They point to differences that make a difference, emic to differences important *within* a particular community, etic to differences important to the social scientist interested in intergroup comparisons. One might think of the comparable distinction between common or folk names for flora and fauna and their so-called scientific names. The latter tend to be cumbersome to use and are often unknown except to specialists. But they are standard throughout the scientific community and they can be essential for precise description and, especially, for comparison. Common, local, or folk names used in everyday practice are linguistically and regionally specific. Big Tree, for example, has a special meaning to Californians interested in species of redwoods, but that label is not very effective for communicating to people in other parts of the world precisely the tree one has in mind (*Sequoia giganteum*), any more than reference to The City necessarily brings San Francisco to mind the world over.

The approaches discussed in this chapter emphasize the emic approach. However, what was once a more narrowly defined emic view, rigorous in both its data gathering and analysis, is now glossed more expansively as the "insider's" view, the etic perspective as the "outsider's" view.[2] Outsider status refers to an *orientation*, not to a *membership*. Against sometimes overzealous claims of insiders to remind ethnographers that "you can't really know us unless you are one of us," ethnographers may feel an urge to remind others (or reassure themselves) that there is no monolithic insider view, either. There are multiple insider views, multiple outsider views. Every view is *a* way of seeing, not *the* way. But most certainly there was a time when, by definition, the ethnographer was always an outsider for whom virtually everything could be regarded as "different."

It is not unthinkable today for the ethnographer to be an insider. For purposes of research in general, and for ethnography in particular, being an insider has obvious advantages. It also has serious drawbacks, especially in the absence of the kind of difference on which ethnographic research was founded. Here we are not examining ethnographer roles but are looking at the vantage point from which the ethnographer presents the account. Whether insider or outsider, what you want to convey is how things look to those "inside." You cannot accomplish that by simply filling in standard categories that you or another scholar might someday use for comparative purposes. The emic approach seeks to "get to the heart of the matter," literally as well as figuratively. Given their strong preference for identifying the problems they intend to study and their idiosyncratic tendencies about how best to pursue them, ethnographers may seem to be in a great position to do just that.

However, ethnography has traditions of its own, and few things are more hidebound than the academic disciplines. To be, or try to become, a nontraditional ethnographer is to take some risk, if the idea of a nontraditional ethnographer is not an outright contradiction in terms. The approaches to be discussed find us moving ever so gently away from standard categories, not because those categories are ambiguous, tired, or tiresome, but because standard categories tend to emphasize the comparative at the cost of the descriptive, putting behavior in too-neat categories more likely to hide than to reveal the genius of each group.

The discussion that follows is organized around three major headings: first, "The Ethnographer Tells the Story of a People," second, "The Ethnographer Helps People Tell Their Story," and third, "Informant-Centered or Person-Centered Ethnography." As "insider" approaches, each poses problems for an ethnography grounded in the study of differences.

The Ethnographer Tells the Story of a People

I have noted Bateson's concern with differences that make a difference. For the ethnographer, a further question asks: To whom must the difference make the difference? The canon to which we generally subscribe is that our concern is with differences that matter to those in the setting, rather than a more ethnocentric concern with how others differ from ourselves. Although his gendered language can raise hackles today, Malinowski stated that idea succinctly, setting it as the ultimate goal, "of which an Ethnographer should never lose sight."

> This goal is, briefly, to grasp the native's point of view, his relation to life, to realise *his* vision of *his* world. [Malinowski 1922:25]

So lofty a purpose notwithstanding, the ethnographic *reality* has been, and is pretty much destined to remain, to present the native point of view *as understood and related by the ethnographer.* That is because ethnographers traditionally have written with their colleagues and other social scientists in mind or, to a lesser extent, for those who constitute patron audiences for their efforts. In an earlier day, members of groups being studied sometimes expressed interest in what an ethnographer might say about them, but their more immediate concern was with the person actually in their midst, not on stories yet to be told. Certainly people did not depend on ethnography in order to go about their daily business, any more than we need to know the scientific name *Toxicodendron diversilobum* to warn of the irritating effect of poison oak on the skin. And in spite of the often lengthy explanations anthropologists have given for the purposes of their endeavors, I find it hard to believe that many people have really understood what their local ethnographer was up to. (Don't we have a difficult enough time just trying to explain our work to relatives or to administrators in our own institutions?)

Historically, ethnography finds the anthropologist telling someone else's story. The telling was, and continues to be, guided by the ethnographer's traditional set of categories and by traditional ways of relating an account that make it recognizably ethnographic. An ethnographic portrayal should not be confused with accounts rendered by travelers, missionaries, and adventurers, although ethnography grew out of the tradition of travel writing. Nor should such portrayals be confused with accounts provided spontaneously by the people themselves, even accounts that might never have come into existence without encouragement and support from the fieldworker. Spontaneous accounts are indeed the stuff out of which ethnographies can be made, but that does not make them ethnographies in their own right. What I am talking about here are accounts that from the outset are explicitly ethnographic in intent.

Without some identifiable group of people, of course, there would not be an account. There is an inevitable tension between telling the story in the manner ethnographers believe they should, in order to satisfy *their* audience, and telling the story in such a way as to satisfy those in the setting, regardless of whether they may actually see, or be assumed to have any abiding interest in, the completed account. We have Malinowski's words forever ringing in our ears, reminding us to grasp *the native's point of view*.

When we set out to tell their story, we are really trying to have it both ways and to circumvent the ultimate conceit of fieldwork that it is our calling and obligation to make sense of somebody else's sense-making. What we hope to accomplish might be described as a "soft" eticism. We recognize that there are categories or topics that should be addressed, but we exercise discretion in playing them up or down, emphasizing the more relevant ones, looking for sequences that make sense in local as well as academic terms, perhaps making the categories implicit except for explanation offered in an introduction or in accompanying notes. Today's ethnographers are inclined to put themselves squarely into the picture, substituting what Margaret Mead described as "disciplined subjectivity" in lieu of a pretense of scientific objectivity (see also Erickson 1984:61).

Because this effort at representing The Other generally has been well intentioned, endeavoring to maintain a fashionable objectivity, it is interesting to look at some of the criticisms now leveled against the thinking of the past, any resolution achieved in one era tending to fan embers of discontent in the next. For example, the original sense of the German term *Kultur* conveyed the idea that civilization was on "our" side. Those less fortunate struggled along the way to achieve what Western Man had already accomplished. I suspect that no small number of "Western men" still hold fast to this assumption, although most have learned not to express themselves with such blatant chauvinism or sexism. Yet each of the two senses in which we continue to employ the term "culture" tends to reinforce the association between culture and civilization: to be cultured is to be civilized, and thus to be like us.

Another problem arose over the close relationship that anthropologists had not only with colonialism but with the colonialists themselves, administrators in particular. That era is closely associated with the expansion of the British Empire, thus conveniently ignoring efforts on this side of the Atlantic to bring Native American groups under close government supervision. Ethical concerns led eventually to an epoch of self-criticism: What right do we have to go among others to collect and tell their stories? Most recently we began reprimanding ourselves for decades of fieldwork and reporting now judged vulnerable for being male-dominated and male-oriented. Taken to excess, these recriminations and periods of intellectual angst have nurtured a mood sharply critical of *everything* done earlier, rather than prompt a determination to achieve a better balance in the future. We seem to do our compensating only by overcompensating.

I do not know what lies ahead, but if the observation proves correct that in American society today the disparity between the haves and the have nots is growing dramatically, then another inevitable wave of criticism may be the realization that those who can afford to spend their time studying "others" are *always* an advantaged group, the leisure of the theory class, to garble Thorstein Veblen's classic title. Ethnographers have long enough been faulted for studying "down," turning attention to the subjugated, the underprivileged, the underdogs, none of whom are in much of a position to forestall such advances. Beginning at least with Malinowski, we have also prided ourselves for giving "voice" to the disadvantaged, making them our beneficiaries. In the future, we will surely be asked again and again to recount—and to re-count—what we took in exchange for our beneficence.

There have been good intentions aplenty in all this, kindness and altruism underwritten with genuine efforts not only to understand particular others but to understand ourselves as well. If initially we have emphasized the differences between ourselves and those we study, we have also been searching for elusive human universals. Cultural relativism is a lasting contribution from ethnography, the idea of trying to see things in a broad context and from the perspective of those within a cultural system. Carried to extremes, cultural relativism seemed to imply that anything goes, that any behavior can be justified if viewed within its cultural context. Once ethnographers recognized that even their own values could be stretched only so far, they began to temper their zeal for appreciating other ways of life with a notion of "deferred judgment" that better epitomized their efforts to understand before rushing to judge. Clifford Geertz ennobled the work of the ethnographer by commending "the power of the scientific imagination to bring us into touch with the lives of strangers" (1973b:16), but there is no corresponding insistence today that to know people is (necessarily) to love them.

I feel that emic ethnography is most successfully achieved when the effort is presented and clearly understood to be the telling of the *ethnographer's* version of a people's story. In spite of noble intentions that seem to require the ethnographer to disappear altogether, the storyteller in ethnography is the ethnographer. It is not that people cannot tell their own stories; they can and do. And it may seem haughty to imply that an ethnographer can tell other people's stories better than they themselves can tell them. But when ethnography is the objective, someone has to take responsibility to see that ethnography "happens." As Paul Bohannan has observed, "Without an ethnographer, there is no ethnography" (1995:157). For the ethnographer who wants to be free from the constraints of what may seem like the straitjacket of etic tradition, here is an excellent way to invest one's research efforts. The challenge is to accomplish what ethnography ordinarily accomplishes in a way that enhances the story rather than intrudes upon it.

Should you find this approach attractive, let me suggest how you might be able to incorporate more of *their* story in the one you tell. I can offer several points for consideration that do not require you mysteriously to vanish or to abdicate your role and responsibility for keeping an account on track.

One way to put more of their story into your story is to be quite explicit in examining how the final account is and is not like a traditional ethnography, thereby freeing yourself from the haunting constraints of tradition. For example, if you are going to dwell on certain activities to the exclusion of others, let your readers know right away what you are up to. That approach should reassure readers wondering whether you know what you are talking about. Quickly review what a standard approach might cover and explain how and why you have chosen to depart from it in certain ways, or why you have placed your emphasis on certain beliefs or activities to the seeming exclusion of others.

Be forthright about how you happened to initiate the study and how you happened to work particularly closely with particular individuals. Be revealing in important details about how you entered the field, your first contacts, and the impressions you assume you made—or tried to make—on those in the setting, as well as the first impressions you gained of them. And introduce your important informants—even if they are not "key informants" in a technical sense—early in the account, rather than camouflage them in a semi-confessional acknowledgment or dedication.

My hunch is that most of us gain most of our data from far fewer sources than even we ourselves realize. One way to lessen this as a concern is to explain in careful detail how you obtained your data. One of the occupational hazards for ethnographers is their reluctance to discuss (and perhaps even to recognize) the true *depth* of their knowledge base, expressed in terms of how much more there is to know, rather than how much they feel they have come to understand. A good antidote is to be so overwhelmingly up front about it that readers quickly realize it can be no other way.

To satisfy the need for *context* in ethnography, you may be able to introduce an individual or event with a brief description that invites and prompts further elaboration, such detail to be added as needed, with an emphasis on *as needed* so that endless detail does not become an end in itself. I like linking description to particular persons or groups or activities, so that attention is directed at *somebody's* enactment of culture rather than at *everybody's* enactment of it. Keeping the focus on a particular individual or event can help accomplish that. Under circumstances where this appears too intimate or personal an approach to satisfy one's immediate critics (e.g., a dissertation committee or a journal editor insisting on a more formal presentation), perhaps such material can be reserved for an appendix, thus preserving the formal record without provoking an informal crisis.

In professional fields where qualitatively oriented approaches are only now catching on, researchers looking for ways to give the individual a more prominent place might achieve that goal in stages rather than attempt too sudden a shift in focus or style. In reporting to an audience unaccustomed to having accounts rendered in so personal a manner, one might at first simply add as appendices a case study or two focused on key individuals or, again as an appendix, offer a first-person account of the fieldwork experience. In subsequent reports, one might introduce specific individuals and events in the body of the text by way of illustration. In a still-later study the entire account might be constructed around the life stories of one or two major players. One's "hard data" would be treated in complementary fashion, initially constituting the bulk of the report, later serving to augment case study data, and eventually relegated to appendices to provide technical background.

There are other ways to incorporate more of your informants' words into your telling of their story, assuming that you actually have their words at hand. If you have collected long interview protocols, you can intersperse or follow your explanations with excerpts in informants' own words. For example, Alicja Iwanska invited informants to tell the story of their village in their own way and appended their account to hers with a separate title, *El Libro del Nopal* (Iwanska 1971:163–211). Or you can let their narrative account move the story along, augmented with explanatory footnotes or interspersed with explanations in separate sections or chapters. If you have not collected lengthy narrative accounts, brief quotations can also serve as chapter or section headings, so that the reader is constantly reminded of the translation occurring as you interpret someone else's story (for an example, see HFW 1983a).

Another way to bridge the gap between your story and theirs is to solicit informant reactions to earlier drafts and to include those reactions, in part or in whole, in your final account. Alas, this is easier said than done, even among those well positioned to do it or who declare their intention to take advantage of the opportunity. I have never succeeded in having anyone in any of the settings of my studies answer a request for a *written* reaction to a working draft, and only occasionally have I been successful in getting anyone to read a draft at all. It is a bit ego-deflating to realize that, for efforts that we like to think as being on their behalf, our "subjects" regard us as working essentially in our own interest and for our own purposes. But I have always made an effort to have those in the setting review my drafts and, when feedback has been offered, either to incorporate it or report it or, as appropriate, to do both. From the subjects' viewpoint, the problem lies in differing purposes, our concern typically with getting the big picture versus theirs with correcting details of personal concern and impression management. Be aware that when made explicit, their corrections (or denials, if the impressions are on a grand scale) may make them come across worse than in the way we have portrayed them. An easy test here is to be aware of how much explaining we feel obliged to do by way of preface.

Such problems really get in the way when we want them to tell their story *through* us, the next step in this unfolding sequence. We may find ourselves seeming to move farther and farther away from what ordinarily passes as ethnography. That may not matter; not even devoted ethnographers are doomed *only* to do ethnography, and the anthropological life history is a worthy endeavor on its own. Everything still gets back to purposes. But when ethnography *is* the objective, I recommend looking for a suitable compromise between adhering too rigidly to standard categories and paying no attention at all to facets of life to which ethnographers ordinarily attend.

Sometimes the resolution lies in preparing different accounts for different audiences, meeting professional obligations in one and touching a more personal chord in the other. Colin Turnbull provided an excellent model with his popular account of *The Forest People* (1961), followed later with *Wayward Servants* (1965). The earlier account, as he carefully explained,

> was in no way intended as an academic study, nor is it suited for use as such, though it served a useful purpose in helping the field worker detach himself from the subject of his study, enabling him to examine it more critically. [1965:4]

Researchers who want to cast their accounts in an ethnographic framework need to have a good idea of what makes an account ethnographic. A first question to consider is how important it is to make that claim. For the anthropologist, this may not be an issue; by definition, anything anthropologists write professionally can be labeled as anthropology, which, for the cultural anthropologist, may be assumed (sometimes rather charitably) to have its origins in ethnography simply because that is the basis of so much anthropological authority. For the nonanthropologist, ethnographic markers need to be clear *if employing the ethnographic label is all that important.* If the label is not that important, the solution is easy: Forget the categories—if they are the source of your problem—and do not make the ethnographic claim. Merely note that you have drawn upon ethnographic techniques in your research approach. By means of a book-jacket blurb or an invited introduction, perhaps you can coax others to do your claims-making for you.

The approaches to be introduced next offer examples employing ethnographic techniques that raise provocative questions as to what else is necessary to make an account ethnographic. The underlying issue of difference is important here, an inevitable problem as the ethnographer endeavors to get closer and closer to the subjects of study and thus to minimize difference. But I remind you that the issue is essentially one of labeling. In a subsequent chapter (Chapter 9) I will consider the question, "Does it matter whether or not it's ethnography?" For now, let us assume that it does matter, even if we recognize that the issue can be viewed as strictly academic. Such issues are the stuff of academia, great areas for intellectual discourse but not great places to get caught, or caught out, should a professional reputation depend on it.

The Ethnographer Helps People Tell Their Story

Since the days of Boas and Malinowski, the notion has persisted that the *ideal* ethnography would be the story a people tell about themselves, the ethnographer acting only as catalyst or facilitator. The ethnographer disappears into the background as soon as the narration begins. No better example of a title that suggests the ideal than Raymond Firth's classic, *We, The Tikopia* (Firth 1936). Such a notion may have special appeal today to younger fieldworkers reared in liberating notions of postmodernism. It seems to appeal as well to researchers outside anthropology who tend to romanticize what ethnography is (or what they would like it to be) rather than make too close an inspection of what has actually been achieved.

In practice, the *ideal* of relating the stories that a people tell about themselves presents problems. Why, for example, does someone else's story need to be told at all? Who constitutes the audience for that telling? No doubt there can be a certain amount of ego involvement for an individual who becomes the subject of an account (the person-centered ethnography to be discussed below), but why would any *group* need to have its story told unless its members see something in it for themselves? And if a group enthusiastically embraces the idea of having its story told, how might that affect the vexing question of objectivity? What kind of portrait do you paint when the patron is also the subject? Others—biographers and historians, for example—can do this work; is it better left to them?

Standard etic categories that initially seem so constraining may, on consideration, provide a welcome structure for organizing an account after all. Standard categories lend a sense of detachment for the ethnographer who does not want to be, or to appear, too involved, perhaps even to have been co-opted. If one chooses not to develop an account using traditional categories, what else can provide some structure, some basis for comparison? An emic approach beckons us inside, sensitive to whatever categories people in the setting use. But it is difficult to pretend that we are not guided, perhaps even a bit intimidated, by frameworks already deeply imprinted through long-standing tradition. The same for sequence. We can voice enthusiasm for helping others tell their stories their own way, but it is difficult not to want to supply a logic of our own to insure that the reader does not get lost—as we ourselves may have done in the original telling.

There have been outstanding informants who have worked with ethnographers to provide a sort of "as told to" account in which the ethnographer seems to have been eclipsed. However, we are not privy to the interaction itself. We do not see the researcher nodding enthusiastically, redirecting the conversation, or responding to the repeated question, "Is this the kind of thing you want?" It is easy to find ourselves "using" our informants even when we try desperately not to do so.

It is perhaps more unsettling to realize how informants use us. Many an ethnographer has discovered that he or she is regarded as a potential pipeline, particularly as a means of access to power, either financial or political. It is more than a bit tempting to play on this notion, to promise to "do what we can" to obtain assistance or redress wrongs. Working among populations distant either geographically or politically from power centers, fieldworkers are often asked to provide medical services or to assist others in getting help. Almost invariably fieldworkers find themselves asked to provide needed and/or luxury items, ranging from cigarettes, fish hooks, or small cash "loans" to writing letters or providing transportation and accommodation. A certain feeling of vulnerability accompanies one's presence in the field, a garden-variety paranoia that cautions us about letting things get out of hand or to be put upon more than necessary for whatever information we want in return. That's the catch, of course; we have be sufficiently "giving" so that we can get what *we* want.

In short, altruism has its limits, and ethnographers, concerned as they are with reciprocity, do not make very convincing altruists. Much as we may like to think we work on behalf of our subject populations or to promote certain aspects of social justice, the stark reality is that we are pretty much in it for ourselves. That particular aspect of research is hardly unique to ethnography, but it is important to recognize it rather than to wish it away. Although we do desperately want to tell it like it is and to help others tell their stories through us, we remain in control of, and always have something to gain by, the telling.

The Idea of "Native" Ethnography

Anthropologists have long struggled with the idea of helping people tell their own story. Although Malinowski's words are better known on this topic, and his and Boas's life spans tend to meld into a single time frame (they died the same year, 1942), Boas was already conducting fieldwork among the Baffin Island Eskimo in 1884, the year Malinowski was born. The legacy each left to ethnography needs to be recognized separately. Let me briefly note Boas's influence in that regard (see also Wax 1956).

Boas recognized the "almost unavoidable distortion contained in the descriptions given by the casual visitor and student" (quoted in Codere 1966:xv) and sought to minimize the effects of such distortion through collecting texts dictated or recorded by a native speaker and preserved in the native language. Much of his own ethnographic material consists of such texts and translations.[3]

Boas's haunting problem was that of detail, a compulsion not only for getting it right but for getting it all. He was so reluctant to publish material when unsure of its authenticity that he made little use of material he himself had gathered during the earliest years of his Northwest Coast fieldwork. In that sense he was more of an ethnographer's ethnographer, collecting and correcting material that would later have to be integrated into a coherent account prepared by others. Given so rigorous an approach for himself, it is remarkable that his students saw their way to producing ethnographies of their own. Perhaps that is where their British counterparts set a more helpful example.

Malinowski's work was completed, if not always complete. Boas, by contrast, spent a lifetime accumulating pieces that he never managed—or apparently even tried—to pull together. At Boas's death at age 84, his manuscript for *Kwakiutl Ethnography* was still incomplete; he never produced an overall, synthesized account of Kwakiutl culture and society. That task remained for others, finally to be performed by Helen Codere following a suggestion made by Ruth Benedict several years after Boas's death. The work was not completed for more than two decades. Of the manuscript that she received, Codere wrote that it

> lacked certain essential topics, contained only fragmentary material on others, treated some topics—gestures, for example—so unusual that it must certainly have been intended that more usual but missing ones be included, and, as a final problem, had to be kept as a unit. It would have been possible to have had the completed sections published separately as articles or monographs, but they were all part of a unit, even though it was an unfinished one. [Codere 1966:vii]

To accomplish his intent to record the lives of the people he studied *as they saw themselves,* Boas concerned himself with collecting "texts"—materials recorded in the native language by a native speaker of the language. He was aided in this research among the Kwakiutl by his long association with George Hunt. Hunt served originally as his interpreter, then as his informant, and in time became something of a field ethnographer on his own. He produced thousands of pages of transcriptions on which Boas drew extensively (e.g., Boas 1897). Although Hunt was not Kwakiutl by birth—his mother was Tlingit, his father a Scot—he was raised at the Kwakiutl village of Fort Rupert and was a native speaker of Kwakwala, the local language. That insider-outsider status is not unusual among those who become ethnographic informants, but Hunt proved a most unusual one. In him, Boas found an intuitive fieldworker willing to be trained in data-gathering techniques, ready to learn how to write his (unwritten) language in a system devised by the ethnographer, and able independently to pursue topics of inquiry suggested by a correspondence and collaboration that lasted until Hunt's death in 1933.

Boas had other collaborators during the many years he devoted to fieldwork, but it is hard to imagine how his notion of ethnography might have evolved had the productive working relationship between himself and Hunt not have formed. Yet that opportunity also doomed Boas to the endless recording (in Kwakwala) of details of Kwakiutl life. Coupled with his determination to be utterly scientific in his investigations,[4] Boas's "scrupulous ethnography" (Codere's term, 1966:xvi), based on direct observation and verbatim reporting, resulted in a corpus of material rather deadly in its thoroughness, especially given his exhaustive efforts at recording family histories and mythology. And here is the paradox in the ideal of native ethnography: Just how much do we want to know, and of that, how much to report, when we insist, however ideally, that we want to record "everything"?

There was little enough precedent for doing ethnography at the time, and no precedent for doing what has become known as the anthropological life history. In any case, Hunt served far better as an observer and recorder of Kwakiutl custom than as the subject of a life history, for, as noted, he was not a native Kwakiutl. Yet the attention Boas assigned to family histories, the importance he gave to having informants record their stories in their own language, and his apparently never fully resolved dilemma of how to capture the essence of another way of life without having to describe absolutely everything, may have pointed the way for others to focus their accounts on an individual life story.

Paul Radin, one of Boas's students, noted the need among his fellow fieldworkers for an "insider's view, where informants could express their feelings and emotions, as they saw fit" (Bernard 1989:13). From his own fieldwork, Radin first produced a monumental ethnography of the Winnebago filled with direct translations. Subsequently he published his well-known study, *Crashing Thunder: The Autobiography of an American Indian* (Radin 1926). Radin enthusiastically described the monograph not only as "a document absolutely unique of its kind—the only account that has even been obtained from a so-called 'primitive' man," but also because "this particular individual took his task literally and attempted to give an absolutely and bewilderingly honest account of his life" (1983[1926]:xxvi–xxvii). Radin wanted readers clearly to understand his own role:

> No changes of any kind have been introduced. . . . Everything in this manuscript comes directly from him and was told in the original and in the first person. It is needless for me to insist that I in no way influenced him either directly or indirectly in any way. [1983(1926):xxiii]

We might not be as insistent today in claiming to have had "no influence" in the preparation of such an account. Most certainly these stories would not find their way into print were it not for the presence of an ethnographer. Even Radin seems willing to acknowledge having exerted some subtle influence:

Here is a man with an unusual capacity for articulate expression and fortunately free from our traditional conventions and proprieties, setting before himself the task of pleasing a sympathetic white man by writing down for him what he regarded as significant and important in his life. [1983(1926):xxxii]

There has been a steady outpouring of anthropological life histories ever since *Crashing Thunder*. Anthropologists have usually labeled and rendered them as "autobiographies," as though they sprang forth spontaneously, the researcher serving as little more than scribe. More accurately, they are someone's account of his or her own people—most often that individual's personal story—*as told to* another. Typically the ethnographer is present but endeavors to keep such influence to a minimum.

Under the topic "Person-Centered Ethnography" I will return to the life history approach at the end of this chapter. Here I want to say a bit more about "native ethnography" as a response to this pervasive problem of how to keep the ethnographer from coming between the informant and the reader. To do so, let me jump ahead almost a full century from Boas's collaboration with George Hunt to examine what the computer age has offered in efforts to let informants speak for themselves.

Achieving Native Ethnography

Russ Bernard has been working for years with a modern counterpart to George Hunt to accomplish what he calls "native ethnography." That phrase was incorporated into the title of a major publication, *Native Ethnography: A Mexican Indian Describes His Culture,* coauthored with Jesús Salinas Pedraza (Bernard and Salinas 1989).

The two collaborators first met in 1962, when 19-year-old Salinas served as Bernard's linguistic informant for a summer of study in Mexico devoted to learning Nähñu phonology. Bernard, 22 at the time, was completing fieldwork for his master's degree. Following that summer, the two corresponded, but Bernard did not return to the area for five years. When he did return, he brought with him a group of graduate students to form the Ixmiquilpan Field School in Ethnography and Linguistics. Salinas was hired as a native informant.

By 1971, Bernard reports that his interests had expanded beyond formal linguistic analysis, and he discussed the possibility of doing an ethnography of the Nähñu with the help of Salinas. He describes the project as he originally anticipated it:

I envisioned myself teaching Jesús how to take fieldnotes and how to observe his culture. . . . I would instruct him in the subtleties of ethnographic reportage. I would teach him to conduct unstructured interviews with old people, to make detailed observations of ceremonies, to record the mundane aspects of life (what people eat, what time they go to work, etc.) that outsider anthropologists might miss, to enlist the cooperation of other "informants" (particularly women) so that he could cover more ethnographic ground, and to integrate his observations into a coherent whole.

I saw him writing up a bunch of raw facts and me guiding him in the analysis of those facts, as we teased out the "underlying meaning" of the texts produced by his unschooled efforts. I saw myself guiding Jesús, monitoring and supervising his work, and seeing to it that the ethnography he would produce would meet the high standards of modern anthropology. [Bernard 1989:24]

That was the plan, but, as Bernard succinctly summarizes, "That's not how it worked out." Salinas had become interested in writing about his culture on his own, anxious to help preserve it, to correct impressions formed by others, and to provide something other than the Bible for his people to read (p. 23). Recalling his efforts to resist becoming a "professional informant," Salinas proposed an alternative:

I suggested that I would like to write about the culture of my own people, in Nähñu. Bernard could serve as my "informant" about writing ethnography, entering my writing into a computer. [Salinas 1996:177]

"The fact is," Bernard writes, "this ethnography was written by Jesús Salinas, with very little active coaching from me on how to do it. As all readers will surely note, this ethnography looks nothing like the ethnography that I, or any other university-trained anthropologist, would have written" (Bernard 1989:24). Note in this assessment that in spite of its problematic title, *Native Ethnography*, Bernard states that it looks "nothing like" the ethnography he would have written. For purposes of teasing out what makes some studies more ethnographic than others, that makes this case ideal for examining "ethnographicness," although that question is tangential to recognizing the substantial contribution of the work itself. It is unfortunate that this publication did not become more widely available so others could ponder and debate its lessons, for there is much to consider here, and there is growing interest and support for pursuing insider studies of this kind. Let me highlight some issues the study raises for me.

The first concerns Bernard's influence on the outcome. Discount that influence as he may, Bernard does not deny his influence on Salinas over a period of what had by then become a quarter of a century: "I'm sure that through our long conversations during his writing stints I indirectly influenced his selection of topics for this book" (p. 24). Anyone acquainted with Russ Bernard, whether personally or through his writing, ought to be highly skeptical of the suggestion that Bernard exerted no direct influence as well. Russ describes himself as an "unrepentant positivist" and he has devoted much of his career toward developing a stronger scientific basis for fieldwork (e.g., Bernard 1988, 1994b, 1998). It is also important to keep in mind that for the first decade of their acquaintance, Salinas was primarily Bernard's *linguistic* informant. That is a far more circumscribed role than the one to which informants customarily are subjected.

Consistent with his penchant for categorization and order, Bernard has always used and frequently expounded on the benefits of the *Outline of Cultural Materials,* the widely recognized set of categories described in the previous chapter, for coding fieldnotes.[5] It is hardly surprising to have Bernard report that while he was "still harboring notions of training Jesús as an ethnographer" he presented him with a version of the *Outline* in Spanish so that Jesús "could learn about the various components of ethnography" (Bernard 1989:29). Presumably without knowing that there was any other kind, Salinas had been indoctrinated in rigorous fieldwork methodology by one of ethnography's most rigorous fieldwork methodologists.

The impact of that indoctrination is evident in the way that Bernard relates the story of what happened next, for he reports: "After a short time Jesús became impatient and said that he preferred to get started writing." Bernard felt he should offer a sense of direction, "I thought that the 'setting' (rather than, say, politics, economics, or family life) would be less complex and easier to do for a start" (p. 29).

With the advantage of hindsight, I might have suggested that Salinas begin however he wished and write the story entirely his way. If we believe in capturing our informants' view of their world, then no category is necessarily easier than any other, although a more personal starting place might help get the writing underway. But the project this particular duo envisioned was not intended as a life history, the story of one individual, it was to be *an ethnography of a people.* Bernard was already framing the ethnography from what was for him a "logical" starting place. When Salinas asked him to explain what he meant by "the setting," Bernard reports, "I told him that it consisted of a discussion of the physical characteristics of the region in which he lived—the geography, the fauna, and the flora, for example, and referred him again to the *OCM* guide" (p. 29).

Restated as "The Geography," the discussion of physical characteristics forms a major section of *Native Ethnography.* Off to a good, safe start, Volume

II describes "The Fauna," Volume III, "The Flora." Only in Volume IV, "Religion," does Salinas leave the safety of such impersonal topics, and even here he carefully notes, "This description deals with the years before 1950" (p. 409). Their years of working together had produced a sympathetic mindset in the informant. What I might view with dismay in this approach to achieving ethnography, Bernard found so exciting that he reports being "nonplussed," for Salinas's response was to ask "if it were legitimate to discuss the various kinds of winds and frosts—where they came from and what they meant for crops, animals and people in the Mezquital" (p. 29). Of this example Bernard writes, and the emphasis is his,

> The fact is, *I could not have formed the appropriate questions in Nähñu that would have retrieved that kind of information* from a Nähñu person. I was totally unprepared for the richness of detail that his ethnography would provide, and for the questions it would answer that I would never have thought to ask. [P. 29]

A second point has to do with Bernard's role as facilitator of the project, both through introducing computer technology and in his role as translator. Bernard is straightforward in noting that in his role as translator his influence on the outcome is anything but indirect: "I am conscious of the risks that I've taken trying to convey what I *think* Jesús meant at so many turns" (p. 25). In the end, efforts to free the informant of dependence on the ethnographer had to give way as Bernard relates decisions made in the translating strategies necessary for resolving the technical problems of rendering a native language through available computer letters and symbols.

As Boas did with Hunt, Bernard had to develop with Salinas a way to transcribe a previously unwritten language, a process enhanced in its later stages through the use of a Nähñu/Spanish word processor (Bernard and Evans 1983). Their task was complicated by the need for an intermediary language, since Salinas did not have sufficient command of English to insure that Bernard was capturing his intent, and Bernard did not have sufficient command of Nähñu. Yet without an English translation, the audience for the work would be limited almost exclusively to linguists interested in native languages of Mexico. Thus the work spanned three languages, with Spanish as the intermediary. The work of translating also consumed far more time than had originally been estimated—fair warning to others who may dismiss the task of translation too lightly.

The idea that generated the project is one more effort to realize the long-expressed ideal—envisioned by Boas a century earlier—to have native speakers record stories in their own way and in their own language, *under the aegis of ethnography.* I underscore that *ethnographicness* is the issue here, not the worthwhileness of causes such as helping people to tell their stories, to describe various *aspects* of their culture, and to record and actively use previously unrecorded languages, efforts at which both collaborators have continued to devote attention throughout their careers (Bernard 1996, Salinas 1996). Certainly ethnography can be an avenue for reaching such goals, but it has no corner on that market. The question here is, what is it that the ethnographic intent adds?

Recall that Bernard makes the claim that the work *is* ethnography. An enthusiastic reviewer for the *American Anthropologist* lauded the accomplishment as that and more, describing it as a "compact, well-grounded, and well-written ethnography" that is "by a seeming paradox, both maximally objective and maximally subjective" (Friedrich 1991). The paradox eludes me, but I certainly concur that the work is maximally objective. It is objective to a fault, relentlessly encyclopedic. That is what I see as its problem. The account overflows with detail on aspects of culture but seems to lack an adequate notion of culture to integrate them. Like Boas's work begun a century earlier, this is *the stuff out of which ethnography is made,* yet to me the presentation is not "satisfyingly ethnographic," not "ethnographic enough."

It would be a rare ethnographer indeed to ever achieve and report in such full and intimate knowledge as Salinas does here. But it would be an even rarer "native" who would have an intuitive grasp of ethnography. Salinas's prior experience as a linguistic informant, and his mentor's careful attention to method, shaped the outcome to demonstrate both the potential and the limitations of simply relegating the task of ethnography in toto to a native informant. Salinas's own references to his contributions seem to take that into account as he reflects modestly on writing about "the environment of the Nähñu, their customs, festivals, and other ethnographic themes" (Salinas 1996:177). Indeed, the work he has continued to engage in is designed not so much to contribute to the ethnographic shelf as to "move away from the traditional anthropological methods that involves an external observer and an observed culture" and instead to bring "indigenous people directly into the study of their own people" (p. 182).

Salinas originally envisioned seven volumes in the total project. Four were completed, collected together as *Native Ethnography,* a 648-page publication that also includes a preface and introduction written by Bernard.[6] If the end product fell short of expectations, that in no way diminishes what was achieved in this remarkable and remarkably accessible fact-filled account, internally indexed so that each entry can be identified (283 separately identified entries for Volume I, 1,369 for Volume II, and so forth). And like Boas's work, the level of detail presented is crushing. Yet somehow we have a story-teller keeping us at a distance, the docent giving us the carefully arranged tour. In spite of the intrusiveness of, say, Vincent Crapanzano relaying the "story" of his informant Tuhami (Crapanzano 1980), each descriptive chapter sandwiched between the author's own meditations, I come away feeling I know, and know about, Tuhami far, far better than I know, or know about, Salinas. For all the promise of the approach, I missed getting what Malinowski called "the native's point of view." The lesson I draw is that the idea of ethnography springing forth spontaneously and untutored from a native's own hand is likely to remain just that, an idea. As an idea, it can guide future efforts to capture the native's point of view in ethnographic terms without enticing us into believing that we can ever entirely relegate the assignment.

In an informative introduction to *Native Ethnography*, Bernard describes another, and slightly different, collaborative arrangement. In this case, an anthropologist actively trained a local fieldworker, identified the phenomena to be studied, and developed a specific set of topics to be addressed. The two researchers then conducted independent studies of the same phenomena. The result in that instance achieved a parallel insider and outsider perspective of the same set of events. The reference is to the work of anthropologist Fadwa El Guindi and her colleague Abel Hernández. Their joint effort resulted in ethno-graphic descriptions of four Zapotec rituals: a baptism, a wedding, a child's funeral, and an adult's funeral (El Guindi 1986; see also Bernard 1989:14). Per-haps this approach, in which the ethnographer takes a more authoritative role, offers a way to shape an account into recognizable form *as ethnography,* albeit at the risk of the intrusiveness that Bernard was so careful to avoid. But hear again the caution of the chapter epigraph, "Without an ethnographer . . ."

The "Native" Goes Anthropologist

In another variation on native ethnography the roles of native and of ethno-grapher are fused in one person. No other ethnographer is involved except perhaps as colleague or formal mentor. Here the teller of the story is *a native who studies to become an anthropologist* and who then relates a story from a per-spective infused with and informed by that professional orientation. This approach has gained favor as more "minority" and Third-World students seek access to programs of graduate study and recognize the potential in ethnog-raphy as one way to tell the story of their own people.

As with their nonrandom selection of sites for their studies, American anthropologists have also devoted more attention to some ethnic groups than to others. Noticeably less attention has been given to Asian Americans or American Blacks, for example, than to Native Americans or Spanish-speaking populations. Anthropological attention to Blacks has been directed more to the African roots suggested by the term "Afro-American" than to American Blacks at home. Conversely, urban Blacks have received more attention from sociologists accustomed to conducting research in cities long before there was widely shared interest in urban anthropology. Internationally, anthropology in Africa has always been more a British concern than an American one, and anthropology has never attracted the number of Black scholars that sociology has.

One might ponder the extent to which the label "native" may have helped such a division of labor to seem "natural," at least until "native" itself began to be perceived more pejoratively than only in reference to something or someone indigenous. Nonetheless, there have been anthropologically trained individuals whose ethnographic research was conducted among their own native people. Prominent among them is Fei Hsiao-Tung's study, *Peasant Life in China* (1939). From Africa, Victor Uchendu wrote an ethnography about his people in Nigeria, the Igbo (1965). Probably better known is Jomo Kenyatta, a student of Malinowski's at the London Institute of Economics who published an ethnography of the Gikuyu of Kenya (1938) in the years before he became president of his country.[7]

Through the years a growing number of Native Americans have trained in anthropology and pursued professional careers, including studies among their own people in the scope of their work. I mention two such individuals now deceased, both Tewa, both with Ph.D.s in anthropology, both of whom I met many years ago, Alfonso Ortiz and Edward P. Dozier. Ortiz was born at San Juan Pueblo, New Mexico, and wrote a major study of that community, *The Tewa World* (1969). Dozier was born in the Tewa Pueblo of Santa Clara; his mother was a full-blooded Tewa, his father a school teacher in the pueblo. He authored a major study of the Hano Tewa, the same "people" but distant in time and place from his own (*Hano: A Tewa Indian Community in Arizona*, 1966) after first conducting fieldwork in the Philippines (*The Kalinga of Northern Luzon*, 1967).

The feature in common among all the individuals named is that they were formally schooled in anthropology. Their foray into academia furnished them with a formal cross-cultural perspective for studying their own people. No matter that the native in these native ethnographies is the ethnographer as well, for it is the native *community* that presents suitable differences (of the out-of-mainstream sort, preferably ethnic, perhaps only class or regional) that renders it suitable for study. To whatever extent the ethnographer achieves a cross-cultural perspective in these cases, its roots are in social science.

In trying to tease out criteria for assessing ethnographic adequacy, we are drawn back to Bateson's question, "What kinds of difference *make* a difference?"

Does the curiously ambivalent term "native" bring us closer to revealing the ethnographic essence, or at least to ruling out that ethnography has always and only been a study of The Other?

Informant-Centered or "Person-Centered" Ethnography

We have become accustomed (or conditioned!) to the broad, generalized "outsider's" view of a culture offered from the perspective of a traditional etic approach. Examination here of the emic perspective calls attention to the fact that such a view must be *somebody's* view. It cannot be *everybody's*. As a consequence, the research, and the researcher, must become more person-centered.

Person-centered ethnography is achieved through a researcher who works closely with only a few informants and most often with one individual who becomes a key informant. A problem with this approach is that culture may be overwhelmed by personality and personal history. On the positive side, that is one way to heed Geertz's admonition to cut the culture concept down to size, although it does so at the risk of ignoring culture altogether. Evidence for some wrangling with the dilemma is evident in efforts of anthropologists through the years to find a suitable term to join *culture* with *personality,* or *individual* with *society.* Which of these word pairs is preferable, and within each pair, which term should go first? What further significance is added by the choice of connecting words: Culture in personality, or personality in culture? Culture and personality, or personality and culture? Society and the individual, or individual and society?

If one takes culture to be the central orienting concept in ethnography, how heavily should we invest in one informant for revealing it, or, in the case of the anthropological life history to be discussed next, on one personality for portraying it? Fieldworkers remain divided on this topic as an academic argument, but in fact a large part of the ethnographic literature is the direct result of just such an arrangement. Take, for example, Cassagrande's 1960 volume *In the Company of Man,* in which 20 anthropologists portray the individuals who helped them in their studies. Such close reliance on a single informant reaffirms the importance of a question raised years ago by Clyde Kluckhohn, "What sort of Hopi or Navaho or Kwakiutl will tell his story to a white man?" (Kluckhohn 1945:99).

I do not mean to make it sound all that easy to locate a willing informant, should you decide that is the approach you would like to pursue. Few of us are likely to stumble upon such remarkable individuals as George Hunt or Jesús Salinas for a sustained collaborative effort. We may or may not find *anyone* willing to serve as key informant, let alone someone able to achieve an "outsider" sense of his or her own culture, as have outstanding informants like Taso of Sidney Mintz's *Worker in the Cane* (1974). Should you unexpectedly happen upon someone whom you believe might prove an excellent informant, you may face a difficult decision deciding whether to refocus your study accordingly.

I faced that decision when I decided *not* to pursue opportunities for doing life histories that presented themselves. Chief Henry Bell told me straightaway that he would be willing to tell me his life story, just as his nephew James Sewid had related his story to James Spradley and watched the effort come to fruition, first in Spradley's doctoral dissertation, then as a scholarly book (Spradley 1967, 1969). Over the years, several of my Kwakiutl acquaintances have expressed interest in such a project or have made hints in that regard. I was delighted and flattered when the first such suggestion came from Henry himself. I also anticipated the time and effort that would be involved, and that the project would compete with, and might not necessarily enhance, the work I felt I should pursue along the lines of an evolving "anthropology and education."

I did not avail myself of that opportunity. However, the fact that Henry suggested the idea helped me realize the extent to which he had already been responsible either directly or indirectly for so much of what I appreciated about the Kwakiutl. That left me wondering whether my situation was much different from other fieldworkers. I was making some whopping generalizations about the Kwakiutl largely from the perspective of the Bell family, and I had been greatly influenced by Henry himself. That thought prompts a whopping generalization I am willing to make about ethnographic research in general: *Ethnographic research is heavily influenced by the ethnographer's interactions with some particular individual or one individual in a closely knit group, such as a family or age cohort.* I think the extent of the influence of one or at most a handful of individuals is far greater than most fieldworkers themselves realize. It is certainly far greater than they customarily report, in spite of frequently intimate and typically generous acknowledgments and dedications.

Note that I did not say "unduly" influenced, or add a reproachful note about "bias." I feel more hesitancy toward accounts from fieldworkers who seem never to have achieved a close attachment with at least *someone* in the group. What I underscore is that any pull toward telling *someone's* story is a pull away from the ethnographic objective of describing an entire social system. Conversely, in our efforts to get closer to a person, we risk getting farther from "the people." It is a dilemma as old as anthropology itself, arguments on the one hand—British social anthropologists, for example—cautioning against overattention to persons and personalities, and on the other hand recognizing, with Sapir and Goodenough and American cultural anthropologists in general, that

> People learn as individuals. Therefore, if culture is learned, its ultimate focus
> must be in individuals rather than in groups. [Goodenough 1981:54]

I have labeled this section "Person-Centered Ethnography," an old descriptive phrase that seems periodically to be rediscovered and to stir up a new set of concerns about the nagging issue of the locus of culture (and thus the proper boundaries of ethnography). Informants become special to us, and we make them special in our attention to them. It has usually been true that they are drawn from the rank and file. Yet they often hold somewhat marginal status within their own community, as with both George Hunt from his Metis family and Jesús Salinas, a native who went outside his community to receive a formal education and subsequently took a post teaching literacy.

There is an as-yet-untold story in studying how these early field-recruited assistants not only contributed to ethnography but actually helped shape it. Ron Rohner, in his *Ethnography of Franz Boas,* containing the translated letters and diaries of Franz Boas written on the Northwest Coast from 1886 to 1931 (Rohner 1969), refers to a manuscript he drafted but never completed, "An Anthropologist's Anthropologist: George Hunt's Influence on the Ethnography of Franz Boas." Our present-day historians have a challenge to revisit such relationships. Meanwhile, we can all do a better job of reflecting on and reporting how those we have met in the course of fieldwork have helped to shape our notions of what fieldwork is and how it should be practiced.

A further distinction can be made between the native ethnography of people like Jesús Salinas and person-centered ethnography of the type discussed here. In the former case, local "natives" study anthropology and subsequently produce ethnographies of their own *societies.* They do not conduct studies of themselves. As with Salinas's work, they tend to distance themselves from their people to produce objective—although clearly sympathetic—accounts from their advantaged, insider positions. As discussed, Salinas became a sort of walking encyclopedia of Näñu knowledge, providing the reader with hints of a Näñu world view and an exhaustive inventory of their physical world.

An even finer distinction can be made between informant-centered and person-centered ethnography, not to befuddle but to help ethnographers keep clear in their own minds, and to communicate with each other, just what they are up to. An informant-centered account does not dwell so single-mindedly on the informant's life as much as it uses a life story as the vehicle for describing a culture. That differs from the more customary approach of the person-centered ethnography in which the cultural scene is filtered through personal experience. Russ Bernard illustrates the difference in describing an account provided by Refugio Savala, a Yaqui poet who was encouraged to write his autobiography. "In his narrative," writes Bernard, "Savala tries to describe Yaqui culture in general by showing his family's participation in it" (Bernard 1989:14; see also Sands 1980).

My early study, *The Man in the Principal's Office: An Ethnography* (HFW 1973) provides another example in which one individual serves not only as a major informant but as the central figure, although the focus is on a role and its cultural setting. The account is not a personality sudy, yet neither does it deny the importance of the individual acting in a professional role. In a person-centered account, by contrast, we expect the individual to hold center stage. When that individual's life provides the basis for organizing and presenting an ethnographic study, anthropologists have traditionally assigned it to a special category mentioned earlier and discussed next, the anthropological life history.

The Anthropological Life History

> The ordinary man, whose existence is far removed from centers of power, is rarely prompted to recall his days. . . . While men of renown have always documented their experiences, or storytellers have done it for them, only recently have representatives of a culture been asked to relate the rhythms of their lives. The request has come from anthropologists, whose primary concern is with revealing the social behavior of a people, not individual peculiarities.
>
> —Peter Nabokov
> *Two Leggings*, 1967, p. xi

What makes a life history "ethnographic"? What distinguishing features mark it off from biography, autobiography, or oral history? And for whom do such differences make a difference? One might entertain the idea that an anthropological life history simply allows anthropologists—and anyone else conducting an inquiry under the aegis of ethnography—to "do" life history. In that sense, the life history can be viewed as *an extended form of key informant interviewing,* perhaps an "extreme" form of it (A. P. Cohen, in Ellen 1984:224). On the other hand, one might insist that a defining feature of an *anthropological* life history is that there must be an ethnographer on hand, either seen clearly or clearly behind the scene. With the ethnographer comes the expected concern for cultural interpretation. As noted earlier, what Refugio Savala tried explicitly to do—to describe his culture in general by showing his family's (and his own) participation in it—is the underlying idea and ideal of the anthropological life history. Here would seem to be the solution to presenting the emic perspective:

have insiders tell their own stories, in their own way, and let culture filter through, to be rendered explicit through independent interpretation superimposed after the fact by an ethnographer.

Using ethnographic techniques, with a heavy reliance on key informant interviewing, ethnographers have been collecting life stories, or helping informants frame their own stories, throughout most of the 20th century. Sometimes the anthropologist disappears altogether from the final account, or seems surreptitiously to slip away after a brief introduction, somehow managing nonetheless to retain authorship as editor or collaborator. There is a delicate balance to achieve in the disappearing act, for the reader does want to know how the account came to be, how words originally written (or, more likely, originally spoken) were then arranged or rearranged to produce the final sequence, and what was left out—and by whom.

One of the most effective accounts from the standpoint of literary achievement, Oscar Lewis's *Children of Sánchez* (Lewis 1961), suffered academic criticism because Lewis never really leveled with his readers to reveal his part in producing so compelling and sympathetic a story.[8] We know that these stories do not tell themselves; in today's mood we expect full disclosure rather than any pretense that such things just happen. Fact is, they do happen, of course; people don't need an ethnographer in order to tell their own stories. But ethnographers are interested in stories not likely to have been told had they not asked. And whenever such autobiographical as-told-to accounts have been completed, an ethnographer is likely to have been a major player, regardless of how modest the researcher subsequently may want to portray his or her role.

Through the years ethnographers have become less reluctant about making an appearance of their own in these life histories. Today they tend to provide lengthier explanations about their role and to disclose more of the research dialogue, perhaps taking turns with an informant in narrating the account, as with Shostak's *Nisa: The Life and Words of a !Kung Woman* (1981), or alternating between descriptive sections provided by the informant and interpretive ones provided by the anthropologist, as with Roger Keesing's *!Elota's Story* (1978) or Crapanzano's *Tuhami: Portrait of a Moroccan* (1980). These same years have seen a growing interest in biography, life history, and life story accounts among qualitative researchers in other fields, and a growing recognition of these approaches as legitimate forms of research (see, for example, Kridel 1998). Historians seemed to have a difficult time accepting oral history as a legitimate form of inquiry within their discipline, but it is well recognized today.

I applaud these various efforts at biography and remind researchers that there are excellent sources offering an anthropological perspective on this approach. One source that offers both a framework for writing an anthropological life history and an illustrative example, albeit an exceptional one because it deals with an extraordinary individual rather than an ordinary one, is David Mandelbaum's "The Study of Life History: Gandhi" (1973). Langness and Frank's coauthored *Lives: An Anthropological Approach to Biography* (1981), offers five helpful chapters and a splendid bibliography of materials published to that time. Readers may be surprised to discover how well Clyde Kluckhohn's earlier (1945) discussion on the topic has held up over the years. Looking now at some of the autobiographical life histories completed with and by Native Americans is a reminder of how long that work had been going on, how extensive the collection has become (Brumble 1981, 1988).

The authors of *Lives* introduce their discussion of an anthropological approach to biography with this important opening sentence:

> *Lives: An Anthropological Approach to Biography* comes out of a movement at
> this time toward what might be called "person-centered" ethnography.
> [Langness and Frank 1981:1]

Life histories, or person-centered ethnographies in some form that does not hinge so singularly on an entire life span, can bring a sharp focus to research efforts during fieldwork and a workable format and alternative to writing a traditional ethnography. The approach also introduces some uncertainty; the ethnographer is wise to work in such a way that a more general ethnography can be salvaged on the chance the focused life history does not pan out. Numerous things can go wrong when working with an unknown informant on such an ambitious undertaking. Too late one may discover that the informant is not well "informed" after all (and may be inclined to make up answers rather than admit to not knowing); loses interest in the project along the way; grows reluctant to divulge information; becomes concerned that the ethnographer has too much to gain, the informant too little; or begins to draw the account out, quite possibly in more than one way. So while one should always be on the lookout for an exceptional informant, it may be prudent to keep a more traditional ethnography in mind as a fall-back option. Person-centered ethnography represents a fortuitous relationship that may or may not present itself.

Be aware also that the only models of life history we have are the successful cases. Virtually no information is available about life histories never completed. Nor do I recall ever reading an ethnography in which it is stated flat out that an initial effort aimed at producing a life history had to be scrapped in favor of a more general treatment.

Perhaps we should call these "life stories" to keep the historians happy, since a personal history usually turns out to be far more personal than historical. Informants know about themselves, and that is what they talk about, another condition that cannot be fully assessed until interviewing is well underway. Regardless of hope or intention, informants do not simply spew out ethnography. As comforting and time-tested as the traditional etic categories may seem in guiding our professional work, that is no more the way others tell their life stories than the way we tell our own. If someone asks, "Well, what have you been up to lately?" I do not need to consult one of the sources described in the previous chapter in order to form my response.

One might argue that traditional ethnography and life history compete rather than complement each other, each pulling the ethnographer in a different direction. I don't see them as mutually exclusive, but they do require different emphases in fieldwork and in the write-up. The researcher can have it both ways, by incorporating a life history into an ethnography or by systematically moving an informant's account through every aspect of a traditional account. I think the better strategy is to weight the emphasis clearly in favor of one approach or the other. One way to accomplish that is to work with general ethnography as the overall goal, and to include brief sections drawing illustrative material from collected life histories or from the life history of one individual. In that way, the ethnographer can show how aspects of a cultural system are played out in some particular individual's life.

In my own work, I have played on either side of the line. *The Man in the Principal's Office* is just over the ethnographic side. Although that study is focused on one individual, the emphasis is on his behavior within a cultural system, not on presenting a life story. The "Brad Trilogy," on the other hand (HFW 1983a, 1987a, 1990b; and collected together in HFW 1994), not only focuses on one individual (almost exclusively) but focuses on his life story. It is based on ethnographic research, draws on an anthropological perspective, and offers a cultural interpretation; it is in the ethnographic tradition, but it is not traditional ethnography.

I was not always so attentive to distinguishing life history and other person-centered approaches as a special form ethnography in guiding students in their choice of class projects in ethnography. I did insist that they label their work properly, but for years I allowed them to present *either* a modest ethnographic inquiry *or* a brief life history in fulfillment of the class requirement for a hands-on project. I stressed the desirability of finding a dramatically different (i.e., culturally different) scene or individual, but I stated no preference for scene over person. Matter of fact, I often recommended that students who felt lost in the assignment concentrate on finding a willing informant. Doing so invariably led to a life history. Culturally different or not, most informants were conveniently located near the campus and shared much in common with their proto-ethnographers. As a consequence, "culture" came through only as what had been left back in the old country, or what informants related of what they remembered hearing about and from their grandparents.

Those taped interviews, edited and rearranged, made for neat term papers. Eventually (notice a timeless and unmarked "flat place" here) I realized that students who took the life history approach were doing an end run around my effort to have them grapple with the elusive notion(s) of "culture." I revamped the requirement and began to insist that all projects had to describe a cultural scene (à la Spradley and McCurdy, as described in Chapter 3). For instructional purposes, I think we can lead students to a better understanding of ethnography by making a clear distinction in our course offerings or project assignments between "The Anthropological Life History" and "Ethnographic Research."

Beyond setting up a class exercise, if you are successful in locating an ideal informant, then life history can be a highly focused, efficient, and satisfying way to pursue research, one that offers a more clearly defined objective than the broad mandate to do ethnography. To accomplish either is, of course, a major undertaking, but I realize why I always felt that my goal to write an *ethnography* of a Kwakiutl village and school afforded greater opportunity to appreciate and experience the full potential of fieldwork than did Jim Spradley's goal to report the *life story* of one of its prominent former residents. However, that is not meant to disparage his efforts or those of anyone else taking a life history approach. Let me offer a few suggestions about pursuing an ethnographically oriented life history as a special form of ethnography.

In all person-centered ethnography, risk and empathy converge in what should be a self-conscious and thoughtfully considered decision on the ethnographer's part either to play up the ethnography or to play up the person. How one perceives the ethnographic task and the ethnographic contribution is critical; one can never escape the ultimate test: the purpose(s) for which the inquiry is being initiated. The risk involved is related to how closely one feels bound to ethnography as essentially a scientific, analytical, and traditional exercise, or how compelling one finds it as an essentially humanistic, interpretive, and exploratory adventure.

In the hands of a skilled ethnographer, a life history can prove an excellent way to achieve the comprehensiveness of the standard ethnography and yet avoid the risk of seeming simply to fill in categories. Morris Opler's *Apache Odyssey: A Journey Between Two Worlds* (1969) has been cited by Langness and Frank as "undoubtedly the best example of the presentation of a life history for purely ethnographic purposes" (1981:71). Although the material is presented as a biographical narrative of one individual, accompanied by the author's running interpretation, the result is "an extremely detailed ethnography of

Mescalero Apache culture," with "no focus on the subject as an individual personality" (p. 71).

Ordinarily, shifting from a broad ethnographic approach to focus on a life story involves a certain surrendering to another's personality as well as to someone else's set of categories and perceptions, categories unlikely to be satisfyingly "ethnographic" to an etic purist. The ethnographer has to be ready to defend and celebrate that approach. In itself that can be a cause for concern or celebration, depending on whether the ethnographer wants, sees, and seizes an opportunity to be free of traditional constraints.

We shed one set of problems only to take on certain new ones. With our minds filled with orderly academic sequences, it is easy to assume that our informant's logic *must*—logically—approximate our own. Should that happen, we are likely to realize too late that our informant, if non-Western, was too Westernized, or, if already like us, was too well informed, too savvy about what we wanted. We imagine being able to find the *ideal* informant, not only someone willing to divulge the intimacies and intricacies of his or her life—and thus of another culture as well—but also to be someone we can present as "typical." Yet never have I found anyone willing to represent himself or herself that way. And in years of reading life story accounts gathered by students, I have never failed to find either these very words or some close equivalent: "Of course, my case is different from most others," or, "I'm afraid I'm not what you'd call 'typical.' "

Informants tend also to dwell on personal tragedies and hardships, differences that made a difference to them *personally*. What the ethnographer may have intended as a celebration of another life, and another *way* of life, may become instead a self-serving statement showing an informant either constantly put upon and demeaned or someone able to surmount all obstacles. Our invitation invariably unleashes both ego and Ego as we discover that, just as we have been using our informants, they are quite capable and adept at using us.

On the other hand, in the very way ethnographers locate their informants those stories might otherwise never be told. In 1985, James Sexton sent me a copy of a book continuing the story of his informant Ignacio Bizarro, with whom he had then been working for the previous 15 years (Sexton 1985; see also Sexton 1981). Sexton chose the following selection from his informant's words to begin that account, under the heading "Reflections about Publishing My Life History":

> . . . I am very grateful to God and to the good-natured James D. Sexton.
> This señor has tried to help me with my diary. Also, I am thankful that all
> of this work is going well for publication. Soon they are going to publish
> this sad story of a humble peasant. [Sexton 1985:17]

The stories do tend to be sad, the histories so personal that except for their I-was-there testimony they can be difficult to use as historical documents. We often miss a point when we try to make them into something they are not, or worry that without a heavy hand in editing, our readers will not be able to discern for themselves what we discern. Once ethnographers have freed themselves from feeling professionally obliged to transform such works into recognizable ethnography, I would urge them to play with various ways to present the data so that the informant emerges more clearly as the ethnographer begins to let go. Of course, this introduces new problems. Informants may not portray themselves in the best light, especially given that the audience for ethnography is ordinarily assumed to be looking across cultures. But with just the right touch in the form of a recognizable "assist" from the ethnographer, there ought to be a good chance that the cross-cultural message does get through and that some new level of appreciation for diversity is achieved.

The life cycle approach in ethnographic description exerts a strong and obvious influence on the way personal stories are told. Many a narration begins with "I was born on . . ." How else to begin such an account? For one thing, beginnings need not be so literal. Before assuming that the sequence needs to be rearranged, the sensitive ethnographer ought carefully to examine how the narrator has put his or her story together. Although that is *likely* to be a chronological account at the hand of most informants, others might start at the present and work backward.

Radcliffe-Brown's purported advice, quoted earlier, suggests still another possibility for organizing a life story: "Get a large notebook and start in the middle because you never know which way things will develop" (quoted in Rubinstein 1991:14). The middle needn't be a literal midpoint, but it is worth giving a thought to beginning a life history account at some point related to one's present position or circumstances, filling in background detail later. In recounting my own life, for example, and giving it a characteristically American middle-class occupational slant, I might begin my story at the point when I completed my doctorate and accepted a full-time position in post-doctoral status. Since I taught at the same institution for the next 32 years, that event proved a major turning point in my life. That would seem to be as good a starting place as going back to a family genealogy, early schooling, summer jobs, backpacking in the Sierra Nevada, or military service. By contrast, I cannot imagine any Kwakiutl elder relating a story in which either occupation or formal educational achievement would receive any mention at all.

The idea of developing a life story around such turning points is one of the three perspectives that David Mandelbaum has suggested for organizing and reporting life history (Mandelbaum 1973). Collectively, his three perspectives offer a way to present an account by superimposing a scholarly analysis that can accompany a first-person narrative without having to resort to chronology. I summarize his strategy below, but anyone interested in a life history approach ought to read this classic article in its entirety.

"Turnings" provide the most obvious circumstance for analysis. Mandelbaum uses this label to refer not only to single events but also to any period in an individual's life when a major but gradual change is taking place. "Dimensions," another of his categories, asks the researcher to attend to biological, cultural, social, and psychosocial factors and thus to insure that the analysis emphasizes sociocultural rather than psychological aspects: "The biological factors set the basic conditions for a life course; cultural factors mould the shape and content of a person's career" (p. 180). The book is not closed on the relative contribution of biological and cultural factors, but calling explicit attention to them suggests how an anthropological life history can, and should, differ from life history presented from such perspectives as historical biography, literary biography, psychobiography, or autobiography.

Mandelbaum's third category points to "adaptations." In the course of their lives, he notes, all individuals alter some of their established patterns of behavior in order to cope with new situations. "Each person *changes* his ways in order to maintain *continuity*, whether of group participation or social expectation or self-image or simply survival" (p. 181).

Writing in 1981, Langness and Frank commended Mandelbaum for offering "probably the most important scheme available for gathering and interpreting the lives of others" (p. 72).[9] Especially with his category of "turnings," Mandelbaum provided a way in for ethnographic interpretation other than simply chunking up someone's life in terms of obvious life cycle categories like birth, puberty, courtship and marriage, etc., and without over-psychologizing either the individual or the analysis. I think we remain essentially unaware of the invidiousness of our own seemingly "natural" categories, especially for cross-cultural analysis. They introduce bias that is both undetected and unremarked, especially when we make note of what an individual has *not* done, such as "never finished high school," "never belonged to a church," "never learned to drive an automobile," "never married." If puberty, courtship, or marriage ought to be a bit suspect as universal markers, consider that birth itself may go relatively unheralded. In some societies children are not given individual identities until they have managed to survive the perils of early infancy.

Under any circumstance where it is a viable alternative to a standard ethnography, a person-centered approach should receive serious consideration, perhaps even be given priority if everything points to it as a way to achieve one's intended purposes. Once again, serendipity plays a major role.

You must be able to recognize a potential informant *if* one happens along at a time in your work when devoting time to collecting and telling a life story can be fitted into your own agenda. You must also be able to make a commitment to assure that the effort and result will achieve whatever expectations your informant holds, or to insure that your informant has realistic expectations about the outcomes you anticipate. We gloss over the incredible investment of time involved for researcher and researched alike in this approach. There is no way to tally the failed efforts, the partially completed accounts, tapes never transcribed, informants or researchers who moved on or passed on before a substantial corpus of data was collected and organized.

Nonetheless, such accounts offer the opportunity to develop a sensitive human document and to circumvent the attendant risk of producing a sterile one. A beginning fieldworker may also experience the satisfying feeling of holding in hand the tangible record of hours of taped transcription, rather than having to rely on fieldnotes from that ambiguous activity known as participant observation.

This is a good stopping place for making the transition to ever-widening circles of ethnographic practice through adaptations to be discussed in the next chapter. Such variations pose a considerable threat to traditional ethnography as reviewed in Chapter 5 and even to the kinds of "insider" approaches reviewed here. At the same time, they also suggest a vitality that virtually assures there will *always* be ethnography in some form.

Notes

1. Type I and Type II errors point to the statistician's dilemma in setting a level of significance that risks either rejecting a (null) hypothesis that is true or accepting a (null) hypothesis that is false. Among qualitatively oriented researchers less enchanted with hypothesis testing, one occasionally hears lighthearted reference to the Type III error in which the research is not relevant to the problem (Kirk and Miller [1986:30] attribute the idea to John Tukey). Alex Stewart discusses the error types in connection with the indexing and coding of ethnographic data (1998:41–43).

2. From a folklorist, for example, "An emic approach considers material from the insiders' point of view; an etic approach, on the other hand, relies upon the researcher's perceptions as an outsider" (Goodwin 1989:89).

3. I have seen mention of 3,000 pages of such material. From firsthand experience, Ron Rohner informs me that the number is more like 10,000 pages (personal communication, 1998).

4. Boas's exasperation with the progress of his fieldwork and his own preoccupation with physical measurement such as cranial circumferences is expressed in writing

to his wife in 1890, "I am measuring a lot of Indians, but that is all" (Rohner [1969:129]).

5. Recall that Bernard has reproduced the *Outline of Cultural Materials* in both editions (1988, 1994b) of his authored text on research methods.

6. An earlier publication (Salinas 1978) presents volumes 1 and 2 of the study (*Geography, Fauna*) with Salinas's Otomí account and Bernard's free English translation on facing pages, plus brief introductory material printed in both English and Spanish. In subsequent publication, local preference was recognized in substituting the name Nähñu in place of the earlier use of Otomí, as the people are more often referred to in the literature.

7. For more on indigenous anthropologists in the field, see a volume with that title edited by Fahim (1982).

8. See the discussion by Juliet du Boulay and Rory Williams in Ellen (1984:247–257).

9. Langness and Frank's own text, *Lives: An Anthropological Approach to Biography* (1981) was another major contribution. Subsequently Watson and Watson-Franke added *Interpreting Life Histories* (1985) to that literature, calling special attention to life histories with women.

CHAPTER SEVEN

A Widening Circle of Ethnographic Practices

Ethnographies are getting weirder, both for disjunctures between subject and object and for blurrings of subject and object.

—Lawrence Hammar
from a review in *American Anthropologist,* March 1998

There is just a lot more variety now in the nature of research projects that begin as ethnography, and in the textual forms that these are taking.

—George E. Marcus
Ethnography through Thick and Thin, 1998, p. 232

Waves emanating from a pebble dropped into a pond—that is the image and the analogy I pursue here, to suggest how ethnographic practice has become like those waves, each one showing less evidence of the impact that originally produced it. The work of the early ethnographers had that effect, setting in motion successive waves of ethnographers in what has become an ever-widening circle of applications and adaptations.[1]

It is the *circle* of ethnographic practices that grows wider. It is hardly the intent of most ethnographers to get too far "out" or to risk having their work labeled as weird. Conversations heard among anxious students completing graduate programs in anthropology reassure me that long-entrenched traditions are not about to disappear. Qualitatively oriented colleagues unfamiliar with ethnography press for more precise definitions than those that seem adequate to insiders (e.g., James Clifford's "an especially deep, extended, and interactive research encounter" [1997:187]). But the extent of variation in the ways ethnography is applied, adapted, and reported seems to know no limits. This ever-widening circle confounds my efforts to tease out ethnography's critical attributes.

In this chapter I explore a few of what might collectively be called "ethnographic adaptations." The list could be longer or shorter. An intentionally "incomplete" list of ethnographic genres compiled years ago by John Gatewood (1984) identified nine such forms, including several that receive no attention here, such as the chronicle, the log, distribution studies, and phenomenal ethnography. A similar list compiled today probably would give more emphasis to styles of reporting than to the type of data gathered, following either the historical moment (classic/traditional, modern, postmodern) or a classification scheme such as John Van Maanen's (1988) trio of confessional, realist, and idealist "tales." More recently, we find attention given to specific ethnographic forms, such as feminist ethnography, interpretive ethnography, or phenomenological ethnography, each of which has accumulated a specialized body of literature.

The five adaptations I discuss should be sufficient to illustrate how ethnography's practices and potential have moved out in directions that would have astounded that group from Oxford, Cambridge, and London convened years ago to discuss issues of definition. Each such adaptation is drawn in service to some purpose that mitigates the importance of adhering too strictly to ethnographic tradition—flattens the wave, if you will. If research is driven by purposes, and purposes are subject to change, then here is ample evidence that ethnography has the capability to adapt to changing circumstances.

The adaptations to be discussed are, in order, ethnography of the self, ethnographic evaluation, critical ethnography, ethnographic futures, and ethnographic fiction. The five are not equal contenders in the unfolding ethnography of ethnography, but each provides opportunity to illustrate how ethnography has been adapted to achieve purposes other than its original mission to provide "descriptive accounts of non-literate peoples."

Ethnography of the Self

With its origins in the study of *others,* particularly of others less well mannered or stationed, the thought of focusing ethnographic attention on others *like themselves* would have been quite unthinkable to our anthropological forebears. The idea of studying ourselves—in the sense of studying our own people—is not all that preposterous today, when members of all kinds of different groups (e.g., native populations such as American Indians, or occupational groups such as educators or nurses) study anthropology and conduct ethnographic research among their "people." A few brazen "foreign" ethnographers have been presumptuous enough to come study "us." Today's ethnographers not only conduct research in their own society, they may go back to their own hometown (Foley

1995), report in ethnographic fashion on life in their own academic discipline or department (Fried 1972; Wallace 1972), or focus exclusively on some particular aspect of professional life such as "the meeting" (Schwartzman 1989). I have referred to my own efforts in this regard (HFW 1983a) as "backyard ethnography," although we now find that phrase being appropriated for a particular form of richly detailed autobiographical accounts of an author's direct experience—the "ethnography"—in which the focus is on everyday life—thus, the "backyard" (see, for example, Smith and Watson 1996).

It has not proven any easier to agree on suitable labels for turning the anthropological mirror on ourselves than it has been to rationalize that such study fits comfortably under the ethnographic umbrella (or in the ethnographic pond, to stay with my metaphor), no matter how broadly defined. To native anthropology discussed earlier we can now add other labels, sometimes used interchangeably, such as indigenous anthropology and insider anthropology. Lacking the possible confusion with terms like "indigenous" and "native," the label "insider" appears to have become the preferred one, as found in the title of a monograph edited by E. L. Cerroni-Long, *Insider Anthropology* (1995).

In an article titled "How Native Is a 'Native' Anthropologist?" Kirin Narayan cautions that *all* such terms "imply that an authentic insider's perspective is possible, and that this can unproblematically represent the associated group" (1993:678). If we recognize that we are all more or less insiders in some settings, and more or less outsiders (even when enacting the role of participant observer) in others, Narayan's advice seems well given to keep us mindful of what the issue is: "Rather than try to sort out who is authentically a 'native' anthropologist and who is not, surely it is more rewarding to examine the ways in which each one of us is situated in relation to the people we study" (Narayan 1993:678).

Although Narayan does not propose the label "hybrid anthropology," she does argue on behalf of "an emerging style in anthropological writing that I call the *enactment of hybridity*," reminding us that we are all "incipiently bi- (or multi-) cultural in that we belong to worlds both personal and professional, whether in the field or at home" (p. 681; see also Goodenough 1976). On the other hand, Cerroni-Long does not want ethnographers to lose track of critical differences in recognizing and reporting how knowledge has come to them, through attending to what she calls "locating cultural knowledge" (p. 9). She argues against glossing *native* and *insider* anthropology as one and the same:

> A true insider anthropology . . . is a reflexive form of native anthropology, implying so much more than simply "practicing at home." It means that it is

done on the basis of constant reflection upon one's biases to discern whether they may be personal or culture specific. It means that results are specifically offered for inspection to both the fellow natives under study and cultural outsiders. It means that it is built upon cross-cultural expertise on how the problem under study has been addressed in different cultural settings. It means that it incorporates systematic comparisons of native and nonnative research. It means that it clearly locates cultural knowledge both in terms of "where" it is and "how" it should be retrieved and organized. [P. 11]

Whenever we turn the mirror for a look at ourselves, we need to report how we are situated vis-à-vis the group we are studying. The best way to accomplish this seems to be to avoid labels like "insider" or "native" that invite confusion rather than dispel it.

Another label that invites confusion is the term "autoethnography." Like the terms mentioned above, autoethnography was intended to refer to the study of *one's own group*. In a brief article that appeared in *Human Organization* in 1979, David Hayano develops the idea of autoethnography, although he acknowledges having first heard it in a seminar several years earlier. Hayano's interest in the term was related to what had by that time evolved into an ethnographic inquiry of his own into the lives of professional card players in the "legal and abundant" public cardrooms in southern California (Hayano 1982:145).

Hayano had found a way to have his cake and eat it, too, for he admits to a lifelong fascination with "risk-laden proclivities" (p. 144), which to me sounds suspiciously like a euphemism for an addiction to poker playing. After completing dissertation research in the Papua New Guinea highlands and securing a teaching position, Hayano found himself turning again to his former pastime: card playing, poker in particular. He eventually realized that "it might be both interesting and feasible to undertake a systematic social study—an ethnography—of the cardroom and its players" (p. 147), combining work and play in an inquiry that seemed ideally suited to his involvement as a participant. "To my knowledge," he writes in the methodological appendix to the completed account of *Poker Faces: The Life and Work of Professional Card Players,* "the degree of intensity and involvement, empathy, and actual participation I had attained had rarely been duplicated in most ethnographic and sociological studies of subcultures" (p. 149).

Hayano admits to profound self-doubt as to the integrity of inquiry into an activity in which he was so completely immersed. "I was not even sure that the terms *fieldwork* and *research* could properly convey what I was involved with," he writes, haunted by the nagging question of whether he was simply rationalizing the time he devoted to poker playing by having it double as an academic pursuit (p. 151). His self-described autoethnography did, however, require—or at least accommodate—a genuine participant observer approach. Hayano assures his reader that the understanding he gained of poker players "could not have possibly taken place in any way other than full, complete, long-term submersion, even communion, on the part of the ethnographer. . . . My attempt to present an insider's view of the work of professional poker players could only be accomplished by prolonged immersion and, most important, *by being a player*" (p. 155).

There is nothing to stop researchers from putting themselves squarely into their inquiries, an approach that has become increasingly fashionable (see, for example, Hayano's own *Road Through the Rain Forest,* 1990), and there is ample precedent today for studying within one's own group. Some advantages and disadvantages were outlined in the previous chapter and are elaborated further in references cited above (e.g., Cerroni-Long 1995; Clifford 1997; Narayan 1993).

Unfortunately, the *label* autoethnography generates confusion by suggesting that a proper focus of ethnographic inquiry can be *oneself.* That is not the meaning Hayano intended. He was quite insistent on distinguishing autoethnography, referring to the study of one's own people or group, from essentially autobiographical accounts presented as ethnographies of the self. But it was inevitable that so ambiguous a phrase would be subjected to multiple interpretation. Deborah Reed-Danahay, in an edited collection, *Auto/Ethnography: Rewriting the Self and the Social* (1997), reports that autoethnography now has "a double sense—referring either to the ethnography of one's own group *or to autobiographical writing that has ethnographic interest*" (p. 2, emphasis added). She offers a definition sufficiently broad to encompass both aspects, describing autoethnography as "a form of self-narrative that places the self within a social context" (p. 9). For insiders who agonize over the best use of such terms, careful explanation as to what is being researched and who is doing the researching can clear up any confusion created by this plethora of related terms: indigenous ethnography, native ethnography, insider ethnography, autoethnography. But I worry that the labels tend to hide rather than highlight the vexing question of how intimately involved the ethnographer can or should become.

This problem is not unique to researchers interested in the ethnography of the self; *every* instance of ethnography needs to be understood in its own context. Like researchers of other persuasions, ethnographers have been known to report on themselves and their everyday experience, both private and professional, as, for example, A.F.C. Wallace's detailed accounts of driving to work or a day at the office (1965, 1972). Although such accounts provide good examples of the ethnographer at work—or play—that is not sufficient to make them good examples of ethnography.

Most anthropologists have heard a colleague exclaim, in the course of heated debate in a departmental faculty meeting, "Someone ought to be doing an ethnography of us!" And at least one anthropologist, Morton Fried, has produced an ethnography of anthropology as a discipline (1972), although all he claimed for the book was to "tell it like it is, to give the details about this particular field of endeavor" (p. v). Fried's efforts achieved both ethnography and success. We could use another such account today, an updated "ethnography of anthropology" to be placed in the hands of students seeking an insider perspective of the anthropological career. Such a study might warrant the label of autoethnography; however, I think it preferable to present it under a different label or, better still, to avoid using any label at all.

Although the term autoethnography is not widely used, it does point to the lack of a suitable label to describe those (increasingly frequent?) occasions when ethnographers lapse into narrative accounts of their own lives to make a point, or when they take center stage in accounts purportedly devoted to portraying the lives of others. "Microethnography" is sometimes used in that sense, as when Renato Rosaldo employed the term to relate a personal story about family breakfast with his future in-laws (Rosaldo 1989:46–48). As he used the term, however, the qualifier "micro" was meant to caution readers that he was providing nothing more than an ethnographic tidbit, the kind of observation an off-duty ethnographer might make because ethnographers simply can't resist making such observations. But "microethnography" has already been appropriated, and although there is no confusion in the manner that Rosaldo used the term, it has generally been reserved for studies of microcultures, especially classrooms (see, for example, Erickson 1992), rather than for relating personal anecdotes in the lives of ethnographers.

More problematic is where to draw the line between ethnography and reflexive account, or how to signal an intentional crossing of that line when the reflexive alternative takes the upper hand and the account becomes highly—and almost exclusively—personal. One way to accomplish that is to observe a distinction between the ethnography itself and the account of the ethnographer's experience of it, for which there is already a body of writing and a suitable label, "the anthropology of experience."

The Anthropology of Experience
My concerns about autoethnography should not be misconstrued as discouraging ethnographers from studying any activity in which they are personally engaged or leading them to deny their personal engagement in, and affection for, any topic they address. I simply want to know who is telling me all this in accounts I read, and I assume my readers want to know something about me in

the accounts I write. As Vincent Crapanzano has observed, "However objective they may seem, there is an autobiographical dimension to all ethnographies" (1977:72). The question is how much to say in that regard and when to say it.

I have tried to be forthright in my reporting, sometimes almost painfully so (e.g., HFW 1990b), with a style I call "heady candor."[2] In one study based on extended fieldwork, my biases were so pervasive, yet so vital as a source of personal energy, that I opened the account with a chapter titled "Caution: Bias at Work" in order to explain how my misgivings had served as a launching pad for what was to follow (HFW 1977). Such efforts were not intended to transform the account into a personal one; they provided a way to handle the important task of positioning the ethnographer within it.

Some ethnographers found the reflexive turn that anthropology and anthropologists took in the postmodern 1980s so tempting that the person in their person-centered account became themselves, either in the way their accounts were presented or in a new genre of sometimes devastating critique of the work of others. This may not have been a bad thing for anthropology in general, but I wonder what the effect will be on a generation of ethnographers reared in an atmosphere in which indignation became a substitute for firsthand experience. Will they continue to believe that the most important thing to report in their ethnographic accounts is the understanding they gain of themselves?

Of course, the most important thing gained through the fieldwork experience may very well have been—and will continue to be—the understanding ethnographers gain of themselves. Nonetheless, I hope we have returned to a day when ethnographers find ways to report their revelations without letting them interfere with, or become a substitute for, their ethnographic accounts. Boas found an outlet for his feelings in personal letters written in German; Malinowski did it through a diary never intended for the public (1967). Some of today's ethnographers adopt so personal and confessional a style that as readers we can only wish they would get out of the way and allow us to see for ourselves what is happening.

Admittedly, these shifting styles reflect changing fashions of which we are not always aware at the time. But there are precautions fieldworkers of any era can take to achieve sufficient balance so that their accounts will not seem totally out of fashion when the styles change again. One obvious place to signal readers as to what you are up to is in your choice of titles, both for the work itself and for subsections within it. Titles like Barbara Gallatin Anderson's *First Fieldwork: The Misadventures of an Anthropologist* (1990) or Jean-Paul Dumont's *The Headman and I* (1992[1978]) make quite clear that the account is constructed around the experience and perceptions of the ethnographer. The reader cannot fault the first-person orientation or personal nature of such reporting when the title so boldly announces what is coming. Dumont underscores the orientation promised in his title with his opening sentences: "This book is about the Panare Indians of Venezuelan Guiana and me, the investigating anthropologist. I have already written a book about the Panare" (1992:3). He goes on to outline the course he intends to follow:

> I emphatically do not intend to dwell myopically on either of two extremes: neither the self-indulgent emotions of a fieldworker vainly attempting, by confessional narratives, to create an introspective travelogue, nor the simpleminded obsession for the hard, computerizable, and computerized data which, with their positivistic aura, pass for the ultimate in scientific sophistication in some anthropological circles. Between these two different forms of the same monologue there must be room for something else. [P. 3]

Accounts such as these parallel an ethnographic report completed separately; they are not to be confused with the ethnography itself. Writing a separate description of the fieldwork experience is one satisfactory way to handle the personal dimension, although it is probably better suited for those well established in their careers than for those reporting first fieldwork of their own or transforming a dissertation into a first monograph. In such instances, the beginning ethnographer who wishes to include a personal dimension must decide how personal to get and where those personal revelations fit best. To whatever extent the account is to be advanced as evidence of one's professional competence, it may be prudent to minimize the personal aspects and to keep ethnographic intent clearly in mind, even when following a more emically oriented approach.

Surely, however, there ought to be some appropriate place for revealing personal insights and feelings, even in an academic thesis. Dedications, acknowledgments, forewords, prefaces, and introductions serve that purpose quite well. I recommend writing a separate methodological section that deals explicitly with the personal dimension, a section that subsequently may be appended to a formal chapter dealing with method, added as a closing chapter, or included as a separate appendix. To underscore that separateness, I suggest that such highly personal narrative be regarded, and formally presented, as a different genre, one that fits comfortably within an already-existing body of work that deals with how individuals actually experience their culture, *the anthropology of experience* (Bruner 1986:4; see also Behar 1996; E. Turner 1985; V. Turner and Bruner 1986). Should none of these alternatives be acceptable (to a stern editor or thesis committee, for example), the researcher nonetheless will have captured such feelings and made them a matter of written record while they are still fresh. Perhaps they can appear later, either on their own or incorporated into a different writing task.

Wherever and however these personal dimensions are addressed in your own work, don't allow the reflections you intend to share publicly to become trite. Look at what others have written under similar circumstances, both to recognize how easy it is to become maudlin and to remind yourself that fieldwork of any sort usually (often? always?) has its most profound effect on the researcher. If you have nothing more profound to add, it may be better to keep your private feelings private, rather than to effect a shallow or clichéd style or to suggest that you have been overwhelmed by the humanity—or inhumanity—of it all. If only for yourself, however, I do urge you to make the personal aspects of your experience a matter of record; they may someday prove a valuable resource for helping you to recall details of your experience or give counsel to others. If you are not going to incorporate them, they also may be getting in your way, so it can be doubly helpful to attend to them and then set them aside. If you have promised ethnography, that is what your readers expect, and the more scientifically oriented among them won't be impressed with a gusher. Let Pertti Pelto speak a caution on their behalf:

> Why go out to do fieldwork at all, if the ethnographic reporting is to be a totally subjective rendition, in which any order or pattern results solely from the ingenuity of the researcher's interpretations? [Pelto 1992:263]

I should note that Pelto's advice appears as a concluding chapter in an edited volume (Poggie, DeWalt, and Dressler 1992) *dedicated to him,* so it is not that the more scientifically oriented do not have their soft side, they simply remain more circumspect about when and how they reveal it. There is no room in their quarter for effusive ethnography. I doubt whether they have any interest at all in how the ethnographer felt personally about what is reported, just as long as those feelings do not interfere with the accuracy of the reporting. The focus is on data from empirical observation, the descriptive and analytical generalizations that can be derived from such observation, and the processes by which the latter are derived from the former (Pelto 1992:263). When ethnographers of this orientation reflect, they reflect on method. And when they project what ethnography must look like in the future, they see an even greater need for scientific research methodology. No introspective travelogues for them.

How personal and revealing you become in your reporting is quite up to you. Recognizing the distinction suggested here between the *doing of ethnography* and the *anthropology of experience* may help you communicate to your reader what you have drawn on for information and inspiration, much as you also need your reader to understand your relationship with those among whom you conducted your research.

Ethnographic Evaluation

The important aspect of what to emphasize within the broad scope of "ethnographic evaluation" is not how information is gathered but how information is to be used. Here, those uses are related directly to evaluation, assessment, or adjudication.

"Assessment" seems to be a favored term these days. Efforts by some ethnographers to distance themselves from any negative connotation associated with evaluation procedures are revealed by labels such as "ethnographic monitoring" heard in the past, or what is sometimes referred to as "engaged anthropology" today. But anthropologists have not been reluctant to work on behalf of advocacy causes, and the courts have become a new client for ethnographic research. The Traditional Cultural Properties evaluation studies being conducted in the U.S., and similar work in Australia and in western Canada in connection with land-use claims of Aboriginal and First Nations people, are examples of current applied interests. Ethnographers in Canada work under the label "T.U.S."—Traditional Use Studies—to determine precontact conditions in support of "rights claims" to places (e.g., traditional seasonal hunting grounds), materials, and practices. Such studies ordinarily entail some traditional ethnography as well as ethnohistorical methods and a heavy emphasis on mapping.

Evaluators employing ethnographic techniques (and sometimes employing ethnographers, as in a study to be discussed in Chapter 9) avail themselves of a wide array of techniques to accomplish purposes that are anything but traditional. Most of the ethnographic work done in formal educational settings, for example, is either explicitly evaluative or has evaluative undertones, reflecting the preoccupation (obsession?) with evaluation in the educational community. Ethnographic evaluation may take either of two forms, as an *alternative to* evaluation or as an *alternative form of it*. The latter, more customary use employs ethnographic techniques as an interesting but admittedly time-consuming approach for gathering information to be used in standard ways to make judgments. It has achieved the status of an acceptable evaluation procedure but is recognized as one best suited to long-range and amply funded studies.

The potential of ethnography as an alternative to evaluation is less widely recognized. In this approach, research is undertaken to present a descriptive account in lieu of more customary assessment procedures designed to render some form of judgment. Michael Agar is one of a number of anthropologists currently swept up in what he calls this "ethno-boom," and his approach is more in keeping with traditional anthropological approaches that seek to defer judgment rather than rush to render it. Although he now spends most of his time as a paid consultant invited to do formal studies of organizations, Agar reports that he continues to emphasize the descriptive aspects characteristic of an ethnographic approach. He initiates his studies by recording and documenting what he has observed to produce an "organizational ethnography," which, in turn, becomes the basis for an "organizational diagnosis" that follows from it. The diagnosis offers an interpretation of what is going on, without the customary evaluative overtones of what is "wrong" and what must be done to remedy it.

During the 1960s, educators began making a distinction between two major directions that evaluation can take: *formative* evaluation to provide feedback in shaping a project underway, and *summative* evaluation completed after a project's termination. Summative evaluations were intended to provide an independent documentation of what had happened throughout the duration of a project, without providing interim feedback. Ethnography can, of course, be used to accomplish either objective, but it was a remarkable breakthrough in educator thinking to recognize the potential of using research in a developmental way *to make something work better* rather than to focus so singularly on consequences. It was not unusual for ethnographers, or ethnographically oriented educational researchers, to be invited to join research projects with specific instructions to ferret out and immediately report anything they could learn that might remedy a problem or help to make a project more effective. That was a far cry from the traditional ethnographic stance of noninterference and deferred judgment.

Given that successful projects can be a boon for people whose careers are built on proposing and conducting them (versus the threat posed by having an independent ethnographer gathering who-knows-what-kinds-of-data), there were tensions aplenty between the ethnographers' preference for conducting and reporting research in the summative mode and project directors' preference for formative feedback to help underwrite success. A seeming resolution, far more satisfactory to project directors than to ethnographers, was to invite fieldworkers to occupy both roles, leaving researchers in the paradoxical position of documenting the success of their own efforts to make projects succeed.

If the motives behind every project ostensibly designed to improve some aspect of public education were all that praiseworthy, those recruited for ethnographic evaluations should have found themselves in happy and rewarding work. However, education is big business for institutions that provide or service it, with high stakes for those who achieve recognition in its highly competitive environment at the national, state, and even local levels of the larger school systems. Ethnography became an uneasy adjunct to well-funded research and development proposals, yet it had such enthusiastic support in some quarters that for awhile in the '70s and '80s major funded projects often were *required* to include an ethnographic component within their proposed scope of work.

The generous funding for educational research that began with President Lyndon Johnson's Great Society in the early 1960s is long past. In the ensuing years, educational researchers began adapting ethnography for their evaluative tasks, their long-standing preoccupation with evaluation tending to over-shadow its potential for descriptive work. Evaluation has maintained its power-ful position. The relatively little descriptive ethnography that is conducted in school settings today is carried out essentially by university-based researchers, including graduate students engaging in ad hoc studies of local programs study-ing "educational change" of modest consequence in time frames too short to matter. In such circumstances, the techniques of field research support the ethnographic claim as a way of looking, but ethnography as a way of seeing is seldom realized. In any such evaluatively focused studies, traditional ethno-graphic concern with the local tends to become *too* local to produce the well-contextualized studies that have been its hallmark. One noteworthy shortcoming is a rather consistent failure to recognize evaluation itself as part of the ethos of schooling, North American schooling in particular.

The long-term effect of ethnography in educational research has proba-bly been to soften, if ever so slightly, the preoccupation with evaluation. The ethnographic emphasis on context may also have encouraged educators to become more attentive to what *else* was happening, rather than remaining too narrowly focused on short-term results related to the effects of special atten-tion itself, a phenomenon known as the Hawthorne effect.[3]

I do not report this as a sad tale—the ethnographer in me is still drawn to that summative side to look at what happened, rather than rush to divulge what did not, to disclose what went wrong, or to mock the disparity between what was supposed to happen and what actually occurred. But it is interest-ing to note parallels between the development of ethnography in the broader social setting and the development of ethnography in education. Recall that it was Margaret Mead who first ventured forth with a particular problem to investigate, rather than in pursuit of a traditional ethnography. In the course of her career, she moved away from a problem-focused approach in favor of broader ethnographic inquiries. While ethnographers enjoy the luxury of being able to debate the merits of these diverse approaches, research con-ducted under the auspices of the schools must be argued on the basis of its immediate relevancy. Thus the questions to be addressed are usually so focused, and so limited in time and scope, that they offer little opportunity for gaining the broad perspective that can be achieved through ethnographic research. And invariably they are conducted under an educator aura intent on identifying what is better, what is best.

There is, I believe, a major contribution still to be made from ethnography simply by helping educators (and others in comparable positions) to understand the sociocultural systems in which they live and work, in this case perhaps drawing educator attention to how a preoccupation with the evaluation of school *effects* detracts from efforts to realize more of the potential of the school *experience*. That is why it is important that at least some ethnographic research related to matters of schooling continue to be of the old-fashioned type in which the ethnographer's attention is drawn to what is going on, rather than with a preoccupation as to how good (or bad) it is and how it can (must?) be improved. The ethnography *of* schools (and of schooling, and of education) is by no means limited to ethnography *in* schools.

The same observation applies to any of the settings in which ethnography has, to date, been recognized solely for its contribution to method and thus, almost invariably, to evaluation. The lingering notion that ethnography only "makes the obvious obvious" disarms the contribution to be made by looking closely at what everyone takes for granted, or for recognizing that people tend to be unaware of sociocultural forces at work in the social systems in which they themselves are participants. The idea that a social setting ought to seem more complex rather than greatly oversimplified as a result of ethnographic inquiry is a step in the right direction, especially when accompanied by a corresponding commitment to understand how things are before setting out avowedly to change them.

Critical Ethnography

The very act of observing anything, since it necessitates drawing attention to something and thereby diverts attention from something else, has evaluative overtones. Critical ethnography has no patience with overtones; it is undertaken on the presumption that whatever is identified as the target for research warrants attention precisely because it is recognized as being in need of repair. With critical ethnography, the effort to understand is cast in a prejudgmental framework; the ethnographer seeks not merely to understand, but to understand *what is wrong*, and to link the problem to some greater wrong operating at some grander level. Marxist sociology is a clear demonstration of this orientation. "For some scholars," notes Jim Thomas in his concise monograph on the topic, "critical ethnography must remain a Marxist ideology to justify the label *critical*"; for others, broad socialist or human concerns drive the research

(1993:32). A telling quote from Marx sets the tone: "Why should we be content to understand the world instead of trying to change it?" (Marx 1974[1846]:123). Stated so bluntly, it is easy to see the distinction Thomas makes between what he calls "conventional ethnographers" who describe what is, and the critical ethnographer with a vision of what might be (1993:4).

My ripples-on-a-pond analogy precludes my having to identify "mainstream" ethnography, but there would be many ready to put critical ethnography in that category, positioning it between extremes that Arthur Kleinman identifies as "no-nonsense naturalism" and "vexed postmodernism" (1995:95). Critical ethnography has ties to history, philosophy, education, and, of course, to ethnography itself, particularly in its research approach. Today's feminist scholars constitute one identifiable group drawn to the critical metaphor that "directs attention to symbols of oppression by shifting and contrasting cultural images in ways that reveal subtle qualities of social control" (Thomas 1993:20). Ethnographically oriented researchers among them are drawn to critical ethnography. Conversely, critical ethnography that "foregrounds the question of social inequality vis-à-vis the lives of men, women, and children" can be characterized as feminist ethnography (Visweswaran 1997:593).

Educational research has its critical ethnographers; I turn to them for illustration. Their efforts add another dimension to educational evaluation by casting a wide net that looks at social ills—and invariably at inadequate educator responses to them—without getting bogged down in the nitty-gritty of monitoring programs and projects at the school and school system level. Critical ethnography aligns itself with broad social movements, pursuing its cases in ethnographic fashion but drawing lessons (and pronouncements) more universal in scope, in what are sometimes referred to as "totalizing" ethnographies. Two examples are Peter McLaren's *Schooling as a Ritual Performance* (1993) and Deborah Britzman's *Practice Makes Practice* (1991). Britzman's intent, revealed in her subtitle, *A Critical Study of Learning to Teach*, takes form in a critique of student teaching and is illustrated with two case studies of "practice" teaching. In the author's words, "This text represents a theoretical journey into the practical world of the student teacher and my attempt to critically narrate some of the tensions, contradictions, and dilemmas that make this world so persistently problematic" (Britzman 1991:xiii). She makes clear how the assignment she accepts as a critical ethnographer differs from the work of the traditional ethnographer in a school setting:

> Unlike traditional educational ethnographers who enter the familiar world of school and linguistically render this familiar experience as strange, my

project is to take the familiar story of learning to teach and render it problematic through cultural critique and by asserting multiple voices. [P. 10]

One would hardly claim that the early ethnographers found nothing "problematic" among those whom they observed. But I think they felt called upon, even obliged, to rise above whatever bothered (or offended) them to try to understand how behaviors and practices they personally found reprehensible might at least be examined, if not necessarily understood, from another perspective. To that extent they were romantic optimists, looking for the best in other ways of life even when evidence was hard to come by.

Today's critical ethnographers turn that around to find their energy in ferreting out what is wrong with the social order in which they themselves are engaged, with nary a doubt that plenty is wrong. If that is a less romantic notion, it is nonetheless a powerful source of energy and motivation; there is a kind of self-righteousness in believing that one is *actively engaged* in trying to make one's own world a better place, rather than simply assuming that things would seem OK if everyone would just look hard enough for evidence of how well the system functions. As Thomas notes, conventional ethnographers generally speak *for* their subjects (and, usually, to an audience of other researchers), while critical ethnographers "accept an added research task of raising their voice to speak *to* an audience *on behalf* of their subjects. . . . Critical ethnographers use their work to aid emancipatory goals or to negate the repressive influences that lead to unnecessary social domination of all groups" (Thomas 1993:4).

It has become increasingly acceptable to speak out on behalf of those with whom one has conducted research, to engage them in the research process, to attend more carefully to what they seek for themselves rather than simply to assume that the ethnographer knows best, and to help the downtrodden to reach their goals or realize their rights. To move in these directions poses a quandary for the observer committed to the idea that description alone is enough. Critical theorists insist that ethnography invariably stops one step short, while *their* critics wonder instead whether they overstep bounds in creating their own "regime of truth."

Ethnographic Futures

Since the late 1970s, spearheaded in part by Robert Textor who was then at Stanford University, ethnography in another form evolved under the label EFR or Ethnographic Futures Research (see, for example, Textor 1990). What distinguishes Ethnographic Futures Research from Futures Research more generally (e.g., Fowles 1978; Bell 1997a,b) is its emphasis on culture. In its early days, Textor referred to inquiry of this type as "anticipatory anthropology."

As Textor has been careful to point out, this "anticipatory" dimension is at the heart of the procedure. EFR is not a claim to study the future:

> In our epistemology, that would be technically impossible, because in our ontology there are no future facts; the future does not exist. What *do* exist, though, are people's *present* images of possible or probable future cultures, and their preferences among those hypothetical cultures. Statements about such presently held images do fall within the realm of the factual. It is these images and preferences that an EFR project elicits, describes, analyzes, interprets, and diagnoses. [Textor, Ladavalya, and Prabudhanitisarn 1984:10]

The eliciting is done through semi-structured interviews. In terms of fieldwork technique it resembles the anthropological life history as another "extreme" form of informant interviewing, characterized in this case by research carried out in a brief period and on a highly focused topic. To be relevant at the level of sociocultural *system* change, the interviewing must be done by an ethnographer already well informed about local conditions and able to put the interview data into a broader cultural context (Textor 1995:463).

The procedure asks informants to describe alternative futures in terms of three probable "scenarios," *best* case, *worst* case, and *most likely* or *most probable* case:

> In the EFR interview, an "Optimistic Scenario" and a "Pessimistic Scenario" are elicited, about which no probability assessment needs be made, other than that, in the interviewee's judgment, the scenarized events or trends are merely *possible*—that is, have a probability greater than zero. After these two scenarios have been completed, a "Most Probable Scenario" is then elicited. These three scenarios comprise the bulk of the record, or "protocol," of the EFR interview. [Textor et al. 1984:12]

Textor is a Thailand specialist, and he has carried out major efforts with EFR there, in one case working with a team of Thai scholars to produce "conglomerate scenarios," in another, working with a single high-ranking scholar-statesman to produce one individual's vision for his country (Ketudat 1990). The intent of the probes is to elicit the three distinct projections described above: best case, worst case, and most likely case. Experience suggests, however, that the two extremes establish a continuum that renders the "most likely" scenario rather predictable. Having once painted a rosy picture of how things might be, interviewees seem drawn in that direction, wanting to believe that is more or less how things are likely to turn out.

In Chapter 8, I discuss some ways that ethnography is being brought up to speed so that applied or practicing anthropologists and others who find their métier in these approaches can compete with the more nimble efforts of quick-and-dirty (quick-and-clean?) researchers. For rapidity alone, it would be hard to beat Textor's own work as reported in a pilot study conducted with two Thai coworkers (1984). In this early effort to demonstrate ethnographic futures, the team of researchers sought to investigate alternative sociocultural futures as envisioned by the faculty of Chiang Mai University in northern Thailand. Determined to complete their survey *and report back to their constituency* within the 40-day time period available for the work, the research team conducted 90 taped hours of interviews with 24 interviewees, had each interview transcribed and subsequently reviewed by the interviewee, organized their data to provide conglomerate scenarios, and wrote and revised a preliminary version of their report in time to circulate it among an invited workshop of participants on the 39th day of the project. The report was revised overnight and distributed the following day to a university-wide colloquium.

Readers more accustomed to Thai style may appreciate that the final published report did not appear until three years later. Nor will it be a surprise to learn of some disappointment on the part of the research team when their audience seemed preoccupied with clarifications about the futures *approach* and aspects of EFR *methodology*, rather than with the substantive findings and policy implications that had been the goal of the project (p. vi). How often has it been the experience of ethnographers—or researchers venturing in front of any audience unfamiliar with a new and seemingly neat approach—to find attention diverted from substantive findings they hoped would prove a revelation, and redirected instead to their listeners' preoccupation with the methods of data gathering and analysis?

The graduate student looking for a formula for a 40-day dissertation is well advised to ascertain in advance whether projective interviewing of this sort will satisfy academic requirements. Writing in 1985, Textor and his student coauthors forecast that "by 1995, we expect that for an anthropologist to build an anticipatory stance into his or her research, using real data and prudent caution, will be viewed as commonplace" (1985:27). Now 1995 has come and gone. Although the predicted groundswell never occurred, there is still some interest in this work, evidenced in a long-standing committee on Cultural and Educational Futures of the Council on Anthropology and Education and by an accumulating shelf of completed studies.[4]

Since the days when anthropologists carried Rorschach ink-blot cards into the field and asked informants to describe what they "saw" in them, fieldworkers have used projective tests or have made inquiries concerning how people in a setting believed things might be or become in the future. EFR serves as a reminder for any fieldworker to ask informants to reflect on what they project for the future. But to dwell so singularly on that one aspect, with responses confined only to brief, impressionistic interviews, seems too narrow an adaptation to qualify as ethnography in its own right. As the basis for a study presented as ethnography, EFR must be reserved for the ethnographer already well acquainted with the local scene who wants to add another dimension to long-term research. For most fieldworkers, the approach might best be regarded as simply another eliciting technique for informant interviewing.

Ethnographic Fiction

I experienced some personal distress after publication in 1973 of *The Man in the Principal's Office* when a reviewer commented that what I had reported was so utterly obvious that I might just as well have written the study by holing up for three days in the library. He did not accuse me of having made up the data; his point was that everything reported in my study was so commonplace that as far as he was concerned I might just as well have made it up.

The very implication that *anyone* would ever make up an ethnography seemed preposterous to me at the time. As a relative newcomer both to research and to anthropology, I was anxious to demonstrate how an ethnographic approach could broaden the scope of research conducted in school settings. My self-appointed mission was to help ethnography put its best foot forward as a rigorous, reliable, and productive way to conduct research.

That may explain why I was not enchanted at the time with the then-emerging accounts of don Juan, the Yaqui shaman, being revealed through his anthropologist-interpreter, Carlos Castaneda. Castaneda's writings were drawing attention to the ethnographic endeavor, including both his acclaim in the popular press and a growing suspicion in academia that ethnographer and informant were one and the same. Richard deMille, who dubbed himself "don Juan's loyal debunker," reports that when Castaneda's first book, *The Teachings of Don Juan: A Yaqui Way of Knowledge* (1968), went from a university publication to a popular press, it sold 300,000 copies in its first three years, "transforming an obscure graduate student into a pop-lit, quasi-scientific, neomystical cult figure, as he pressed on to publish his second, more novelesque adventure and to talk about his third" (deMille 1978:79).[5]

The first book was followed by *A Separate Reality: Further Conversations with Don Juan,* in 1971, then *Journey to Ixtlan: The Lessons of Don Juan,* in 1972. Another work, *Sorcery: A Description of the World,* was completed in 1973. "Though they may contain a fact here or there," deMille observes, Castaneda's works "are abundantly and essentially fictive and must be classified as fiction if we are going to classify them at all" (p. 35). The problem is not with their fiction but that *Sorcery* was submitted, and accepted, as Castaneda's doctoral dissertation. However, as deMille reports, "except for its title, five faculty signatures endorsing the fieldwork, a five-line vita, a four-item list of Castaneda's prior publications, the 500-word abstract, and a few minor editorial changes in the text, *Sorcery: A Description of the World* was indeed *Journey to Ixtlan* and nothing more" (deMille 1978:68).

Outside academia no one really cared; deMille compares the hoax to that of the earlier anthropological foible of the Piltdown man and concludes that "the scientific cost of Piltdown man was high, of don Juan low" (p. x). "Few anthropologists subscribed to don Juan: no pits were dug to find him or monuments erected to him; trifling research funds were diverted by him. The spate of Juanist writing has been literary, philosophical, or occult, seldom scientific" (p. xi).

In spite of growing concerns about the apparent absence of any scientific basis for his work, Castaneda was acclaimed as something of a model fieldworker who, through patience, attentiveness, and an apparently uncanny ability to recall the words of his mentor—in spite of the psychedelic circumstances under which they were uttered and recorded—had been able to achieve the fashionable emic or insider's view. DeMille makes specific mention of the three appearances of the term "emic" in Castaneda's 500-word dissertation abstract, noting that he did not find the term in the dissertation itself. DeMille quotes a personal communication from an academician identified only as "an impeccable ethnographic warrior" in explanation:

> I don't know how Castaneda got away with calling *Journey to Ixtlan* "an emic account," since it fails to meet the usual emic criteria of scientific rigor and narrow scope, but he certainly got farther into his native informant's head than most of us do. Of course, if don Juan was already in *his* head to begin with, he didn't have far to go to share the native reality, did he? [Quoted in deMille 1978:73]

One of Castaneda's severest critics was anthropologist Weston LaBarre, who wrote, "As for finding cosmic truth by searching 'inner space'—often deplorably unfurnished—with the aid of drugs, this epistemology is too noodleheaded and naive to merit comment" (quoted in Wilk 1977:84). Little was to be gained for anthropologists to act as spoilsports, however, for Castaneda spoke directly to a counterculture generation. Many readers were drawn to anthropology in search of other such teachings, and a few went off in search of don Juan himself. DeMille, describing himself as a complete novice and utter outsider to anthropology, "rightly and gladly" admits to calling Castaneda his teacher and don Juan his benefactor for creating the opportunity for his own inquiry into *Castaneda's Journey,* which saw two editions (1976, 1978) as well as an edited collection of papers (1980).

The academics closed ranks. Ralph Beals, one of Castaneda's early teachers, acknowledged giving initial approval for his student to focus on a single informant, the Yaqui shaman who became don Juan, rather than to develop "some more conventional ethnographic problem" (Beals 1978:357), but goes on to absolve himself of subsequent events, noting that he himself retired in 1969, the year after Castaneda's first book appeared:

> I pressed him to show me some of his fieldnotes, but he became evasive and finally dropped from sight, not too difficult in a large department. I assumed that he had dropped out the of [sic] University. . . .
>
> Next, I was surprised to learn that Castaneda had obtained the Ph.D. For the record . . . I did not serve on his doctoral committee. . . . I was also surprised by the writing in his book and dissertation, in view of the barely acceptable quality of the seminar reports he had written earlier for me. . . . [P. 357]

Those with any lingering recollection today of these events seem to carry all sorts of different versions of how—or whether—the case was ever resolved. Castaneda himself never went public. Nor did he pursue an academic career, preferring instead to continue with his writing, tricking us, as deMille concludes, for our own good. "Castaneda becomes Coyote, the original Amerindian shaman, a trickster who abuses people's trust while teaching them valuable lessons" (deMille 1980:23).

What might have happened to the status and reputation of ethnography as a consequence of the Castaneda capers did not happen. Castaneda went his way, to his own separate reality, and ethnographers since that time have not had to assure each generation anew that their work was based on real people in real places. There is a genre called "ethnographic fiction" to which I turn next, but Castaneda's work stands apart from it. I might have been inclined to say his name is all but forgotten, but on the day I first drafted this section, my morning paper happened to include a reference to having one's own "Carlos Castaneda Don Juan" (syndicated columnist Maureen Dowd, 12 April 1996), the two identities now melded into one.[6]

There are other facets from the Castaneda story worthy of note, especially for a volume like this, which, I hasten to remind you, is subtitled *A Way of Seeing*. Castaneda's second book, *A Separate Reality*, the one immediately preceding the completion of his dissertation, is a book about *seeing*. Mary Douglas, writing before the full controversy broke, underscores that point, the ability to "discern a realm of being which other men miss by applying too ploddingly the criteria from their ordinary life" (1980[1973]:27). Were I writing on some other topic, I might not be as inclined as I am to read her statement as only slightly veiled criticism of conventional ethnographic reporting. "This balance between strict control and strict readiness to take on any vision that is offered and sustain it as long as possible is the condition of *seeing*," Douglas writes, and she commends Castaneda's "suggestions about how different forms of visual experience are induced, by squinting, focusing and unfocusing and rapid sideways scanning" (p. 31).

I take note as well of the effect of ethnographers observed: It was not an anthropologist who chose to do the stalking of Castaneda. It was an investigative journalist, an outsider looking in, and apparently not a welcome looker in all quarters, judging both by the responses deMille *was* able to solicit and more so by those who refused to talk to him. "We are fortunate it is deMille who is doing the looking," states an unattributed accolade from the *American Anthropologist*, but I suspect the sense of good fortune was not shared by all.

Ethnography, and ethnographers, are fortunate that the excitement eventually died down. But the success of Castaneda's reported journeys remains as mute testimony to what many readers outside of anthropology continue to seek in ethnographic accounts—guides to worlds of their dreams, rather than the too often sterile accounts of the too often harsh realities of the real worlds of others. Castaneda came to that juncture from what began as a dissertation on ethnobotany, a study of hallucinogenic plants, especially peyote. It remains something of a mystery why he persisted in his anthropological pursuit through nine years of imaginary fieldwork once he realized his preference for and success at imaginative writing.[7]

The writing of Carlos Castaneda aside, or the writing of might-have-been anthropologists like Kurt Vonnegut[8] or might-have-been novelists among the many anthropologists who have tried their hand at fiction writing, there is an established genre of literature that goes under the name of *ethnographic fiction*. More than the anthropologically focused stories of authors like science-fiction writer Chad Oliver, authors writing in this genre base their accounts on solid ethnographic research but add plot and character to create stories—in the form of novels, short stories, even plays—that are themselves fictions. The genre is hardly new. Alfred Kroeber dated it back to Swiss archaeologist Adolf

Bandelier's story of the Keresan Pueblos, *The Delight Makers,* first published in 1890 (Kroeber 1922:13). The distinguishing feature of such writing in the ensuing years was the emphasis on ethnographic rather than historical detail during a period when ethnographers were not averse to being recognized as good storytellers. Efforts to make ethnography more "scientific" following World War II engendered some resistance to the notion of ethnographic fiction, but over the years, and depending on just how one draws the line, there has been a steady outpouring of such works. Barbara Tedlock makes a good case for the link between that earlier writing and the interest emerging today in the form of the ethnographic narrative.[9] One especially well-known example of this genre is Laura Bohannan's fictionalized account of fieldwork, *Return to Laughter,* published in 1954 under the nom de plume Elenore Smith Bowen.

I had the good luck in my initial sampling of ethnographic fiction to read two pioneering works written by anthropologist/authors, Oliver LaFarge's *Laughing Boy,* originally published in 1929, and Carter Wilson's *Crazy February,* originally published in 1966. Unlike the factually based ethnographic "reconstruction" of the ethnoarchaeologist (for example, Tilley's *Ethnography of the Neolithic,* 1996), the author of ethnographic fiction weaves a "likely" story that relates events in an ethnographically informed account: If things didn't happen exactly as the story suggests, they nonetheless *might* have happened that way. With ethnographic veracity satisfied, the author becomes novelist, and readers are privy to dialogues never spoken and first-person eyewitness accounts that give us access even to what the actors are (i.e., might reasonably have been) thinking.

Here the ripple effect from traditional ethnography might seem to become less discernible, for the writer of ethnographic fiction *is* a serious storyteller. But ethnographic fiction is based on fieldwork. Presumably in answer to questions raised after the initial publication of *Crazy February,* Carter Wilson makes that point clear in an introduction added to a later edition: "The book grew directly out of experience" (1974:1). It is the mode of presentation that bows to creativity, not the accuracy of the information. Wilson was able to report satisfaction on that score: "I was very happy when anthropologists with greater experience in the Mayan area found the book essentially exact and, more important, true to the spirit of the place I had written about" (p. 2).[10] The ethnographic record is the resource, the story determines how that resource is used. But the reader feels no didactic authorial and authoritative presence lurking in the shadows with a checklist of categories dutifully waiting to be covered.

As fiction, the ethnographic novel must compete with the works of storytellers whose works are neither hampered nor enhanced by allegiance to accuracy, but we cannot help but be filled with admiration and awe for those novelists whose works are recognized for their authoritative observations, as with the novels of Charles Dickens or George Eliot in an earlier day or, closer for me in place and time, Wallace Stegner or Ken Kesey. It is our own preoccupation that prompts us to use ethnography as a yardstick for applauding the work of novelists for their attention to detail or to commend them for being "intuitive" ethnographers. Being lauded for ethnographic acumen is probably the farthest thing from their minds.

Exactly how people "become" novelists remains a mystery to me. Does serendipity play a major role for them, too, as with an ethnographically intuitive author like Anthony Burgess whose wonderful *Malayan Trilogy* was prompted by a medical misdiagnosis that set him on a writing course because he was told he only had a few months to live? Note as well some uneasy ground for the academic writer who *does* succeed at the writing task. Writing too well, too engagingly, invariably raises eyebrows among fellow academics that one is pandering, selling out, trying to appeal to the masses. Anthropologists are not alone among social scientists who have a problem with colleagues who draw undue attention to their works or to themselves. I am not so sure that every ethnographer today desires to be recognized as a good storyteller, or to be accused of being a "storyteller" at all.

Within a couple of months of pondering these very thoughts, one of anthropology's hard-line "scientific" ethnographers commended me for being just that, "a good storyteller." I now rest uneasily; I will never know for sure whether the comment was intended as a compliment, and I will never know for sure whether, as intended, the comment meant that as a consequence I am therefore a good ethnographer or that, because I tell a story well, my competence as an ethnographer doesn't really matter. Given my choice, I would prefer to have it said of me that I tell my ethnographies well, rather than that my stories read almost like ethnographies.

An Ever-Widening Circle

> Thinking back I wish less time had been spent in graduate school arguing whether it is scientists or humanists who make the best ethnographers. I wish more time had been spent spelling out the character of a "true ethnography."
> —Richard Shweder
> "True Ethnography," 1996b, p. 17

It is hardly a coincidence that this chapter and this major section of the book should conclude with the concern for how ethnography is presented rather than how it is conducted in the field. And readers interested in what has been called "ethnoperformance" may be disappointed that I have not followed out other waves to describe forms of presentation in which ethnographic materials are read or performed as instructional theatre or variously presented in plays, poetry, and short stories. These experimental modes of representation speak directly to the underlying problem of finding audiences for our efforts and for doing a more exciting job of reaching the audiences we find.[11]

While I applaud those efforts, I leave them for others of artistic bent. Following the wave analogy, I choose to stay out in the deeper water rather than risk being washed ashore. If you are new to ethnography and are about to "take the plunge," I suggest you do the same, at least for your first project. Don't eschew convention just to be different. If you have set out to conduct ethnographic research, your work needs to be *reported,* not produced, for there is no such thing as unreported research. To warrant the claim, anything labeled as research must be accessible to others. I am an avid theatregoer, and I have no doubt that my understanding of human social life has been deepened by theatre and film experience, but I find it extremely difficult to cite or even refer to such experience without feeling that I am excluding rather than including my reader. I have also used sociodrama in the classroom with students of all ages. But those experiences are ephemeral, great for getting lessons across but limited to whomever happens to be present. Ethnographic research in readily accessible format can provide a solid foundation; what we do with it beyond that necessitates our assuming evangelical roles to get the word out or bring others in.

There is renewed interest in the short story as an alternative way to present ethnography (e.g., Ellis and Bochner 1996) and there are now models of ethnographic data presented in story form, not quite fiction, not quite nonfiction (e.g., Angrosino 1998). Experienced ethnographers can even get their "poetics" published in the *American Anthropologist* (e.g., Richardson 1998). Nevertheless (and quite predictably, I suppose) I recommend that you establish yourself solidly in the ethnographic tradition before venturing into these waters. There is no substitute for demonstrating that you know your tradition before you set out to transcend or transform it.

The variations reviewed here can be taken as evidence of how flexible ethnography is, how adaptive, how able to evolve with changing orientations as to whom we study and how we best proceed, and how we then communicate what we have learned. At the same time, such variation can also be taken to show how ethnographic practice has moved in so many directions that any trace of the original charter—to undertake the scientific study of others dramatically different from ourselves—is sometimes barely discernible.

What makes a study ethnographic when ethnography's limits seem to know no boundaries, resembling instead endless ripples no longer traceable to whatever source initially produced them? Autoethnography, studies in which we are not only key participants but become key informants as well? A tradition of deferred judgment reformulated as ethnographic evaluations conducted explicitly to render judgment? Critical ethnography to rectify circumstances prejudged to be wrong? Engaging informants in contemplating the future in lieu of documenting what they have experienced in the past? Making up stories describing what people were saying—alas, even what they were *thinking*—in the absence of any possibility of ever garnering factual evidence in support?

No wonder that researchers interested in ethnography but lacking familiarity with its origins or past accomplishments feel little constraint about labeling almost any approach that requires their presence on site (or prolonged interaction with an informant) as ethnography. No wonder ethnographers sometimes have a hard time convincing their readers (or each other, and sometimes even themselves) that their work has a legitimate claim to be labeled "ethnographic." In some ways, tradition itself is ethnography's worst enemy, at least in the sense of allowing ethnographers to become responsive to changing structures in the way research is defined and supported. Almost any study proposed as ethnography can be greeted in either of two ways today: dismissed for being clearly beyond the pale, or embraced for extending ethnographic boundaries into new realms.

Of particular importance in the past has been the idea that doing ethnography requires time. Yet each of the approaches discussed above circumvents time by finding the locus of ethnography to be in some other sphere, either by capitalizing on what the ethnographer already knows or is doing, defining purposes more efficiently, or locating the study in a place or era that precludes the researcher's living presence. So, too, the cross-cultural and comparative aspects characteristic of early studies seem missing in many of these adaptations. They offer no argument against the desirability of being "holistic" in perspective, but it is less clear how to achieve holism as inquiries become more highly focused.

A related question has to do with how "close" an ethnographer can be to what is to be studied, whether close to an individual or group, to a place, to an ideology, to an event, to a practice. One can read encouraging words for turning the ethnographic gaze inward to an even greater extent than we witnessed during the efflorescence of reflexive ethnography. Hear this challenge from enthusiast Richard Quinney in the introduction to what he describes as an ethnographic essay designed to "take you beyond questions of participant-observation, unstructured data, case size, and interpretation. It will encompass your emotional and spiritual life, your very being":

> Try writing an ethnography of something very close to you. A story from the
> beginning of your life that takes you to the present moment . . . This is ethnog-
> raphy as the lived experience of the ethnographer. [Quinney 1996:357]

My own counsel is not meant to discourage you from such personal writing but to encourage you to recognize some limits as to where ethnography
stops and some other genre begins. The resolution I have proposed is to distinguish the doing of ethnography from the anthropology of experience. That
puts me on the side of researchers like Hammersley and Atkinson, who argue
on behalf of an essential strangeness:

> There must always remain some part held back, some social and intellectual
> "distance." For it is in the "space" created by this distance that the analytic
> work of the ethnographer gets done. Without that distance, without such
> analytic space, the ethnography can be little more than the autobiographi-
> cal account of a personal conversion. This would be an interesting and valu-
> able document, but not an ethnographic study. [Hammersley and Atkinson
> 1983:102]

With the introduction of *Composing Ethnography: Alternative Forms of Qualitative Writing* (1996), editors Carolyn Ellis and Arthur Bochner have introduced a new series devoted to exploring broad ethnographic alternatives. At
the same time, others (e.g., Grills 1998; Stewart 1998; Werner 1998) are
bearing down on efforts to establish more rigid criteria for future ethnographic work. With ethnography drifting off in ever-widening circles, there is
ample evidence that ethnographers themselves are alive and well . . . and still
making waves.

Notes

1. Analogies exert their own subtle influence. The imagery I follow suggests waves
radiating outward, moving farther and farther from the epicenter of ethnographic tradition. With something similar in mind, James Clifford cites examples of "exotic fieldwork at the edges of changing academic practice" (1997:199; see also Marcus 1998).
By contrast, in writing about the growing importance of narrative ethnography, Barbara Tedlock describes that genre as having "emerged from the margins and moved to
claim the center" (Tedlock 2000).

2. The phrase "heady candor" is a play on the name of Eddie Cantor, a radio come-
dian popular in the '30s and '40s whom no one seems to remember, thus rendering
my humor obsolete.

3. The Hawthorne effect recognizes that being included in an experimental treatment may affect performance, regardless of the treatment itself (Roethlisberger and Dickson 1939). Coincidentally, the Hawthorne studies of the 1930s marked the foray of American anthropologists into the factory and workplace, where they introduced long-term observational research aimed at understanding interpersonal relations in change processes rather than occupy themselves as "change agents" (see Chapple 1953:819).

4. See, for example, the discussion and citations in Riner 1991; see also a dissertation by McKeown 1988.

5. I always assumed Castaneda to be not only younger than myself but in a state of perpetual youth. Following his death in April 1998, our local newspaper carried the caption "Carlos Castaneda, mystical writer, dies" and noted the confusion still surrounding the date of his birth. Official immigration records gave the date as December 25, 1925, making him slightly more than three years my senior. He might not have been dismayed at my mistaken impression; apparently he preferred to mark his birth from as much as a decade later than the recorded one (deMille 1978:28).

6. Similarly, the revival of the film trio "Star Wars" in 1997 brought forth the reminder, or at least serious speculation, that the idea of *a force,* which became "The Force" in the film story, had been inspired by Castaneda's writing some 25 years earlier.

7. The direction Castaneda set for his own journey was established in his first book (1968), as suggested by the titles of those that followed, including, in addition to works already mentioned, *Tales of Power; The Second Ring of Power; The Eagle's Gift; The Fire from Within; The Power of Silence: Further Lessons of Don Juan; The Art of Dreaming; Silent Knowledge; The Wheel of Time: The Shamans of Ancient Mexico—Their Thoughts about Life, Death and the Universe; The Active Side of Infinity;* and *Magical Passes: The Practical Wisdom of the Shamans of Ancient Mexico.*

8. Vonnegut is another author who discovered writing while studying for an advanced degree in anthropology. Reportedly, his subsequent accomplishment as a published author was the basis on which the degree was awarded. It has been suggested that *all* ethnographers are frustrated novelists. Not me, of course, although I do have this idea . . .

9. See her informative essay on this topic, Tedlock 2000; see also an earlier statement on the ethnographic novel by Langness and Frank 1978.

10. In addition to other writing, Wilson produced two further works in this genre (1972, 1981) as well as a children's novel about the Netsilik (1969) based on Rasmussen's early account. For years he has also taught "Community Through Imagination," a class for fiction and nonfiction writers.

11. For more on the topic, see the discussion on performance texts by Denzin in chapter 4 of his *Interpretive Ethnography* (1997).

PART FOUR: THE BIGGER PICTURE

CHAPTER EIGHT

Hurried Ethnography
for Harried Ethnographers

The demand for quick results from ethnographic work is one of the major influences current in the applied social sciences.

—Pertti J. Pelto
"Anthropological Research Methods and Applications," 1992, p. 264

In professional lives as in personal ones, each of us grapples constantly with issues of time. Ethnographers face the problem at each step of an inquiry. On one hand we confront the impatience of others and even ourselves: as a time-consuming approach to research, ethnography seems to make unreasonable demands. Yet even if we are willing to make the necessary commitment, need our inquiries invariably take so long?

Must an ethnographer *always* spend months and months in the field in order to claim ethnographic validity? If so, is there an *absolute minimum* length of time required in order for a study to qualify as ethnography, an implicit guideline if no explicit rule exists? Correspondingly, for the compulsive field-worker, is there some *maximum* period of time that should be allotted to it? In the absence of such a guideline—or any recognition of the problem—should one set an arbitrary and self-imposed deadline after which data gathering must come to a stop? Is there a point at which some kind of report writing must begin, in effect either to stop the losses or to face the music, depending on the nature of the problem?

In our professional responsibilities, as with other aspects of our lives, we find ourselves caught between two extremes, feeling constantly rushed and harried, on the one hand, or, on the other, seeming to be totally oblivious to the demands of time. Time can pose as serious a problem for ethnographers who recognize no limits on it as for those determined to circumvent it. The former invest it with the power to guarantee outcomes: given enough time, you can learn all you would ever need to know before proceeding to write about a topic. The latter, buoyed by the realization that it is impossible to exhaust any topic of inquiry, fail to recognize that time is always a necessary, if never a sufficient, element—and constraint—in ethnographic research.

Ethnographers need to adopt a matter-of-fact attitude toward time, appreciative of and realistic about whatever time can be devoted to the research, with purpose and agenda adjusted accordingly. The total time available for conducting a study can be written directly into the statement of purpose. A broad ethnographic inquiry might be designed with the caveat, "To provide as full an account as can be obtained in a period of 12 months of sustained fieldwork" or "To describe the cycle of activities based on observation during the period (date) to (date)."

The critical issue explored in this chapter deals with what might be termed "ethnographic accommodation": how ethnographers have been trying to speed up their work without risking the opprobrium of a label Ray Rist suggested years ago, "Blitzkrieg Ethnography" (Rist 1980). Can those who find themselves pressed for time, aware of being unable to conduct a full-blown ethnography yet committed to an ethnographic perspective, employ some of its techniques and enjoy some of its advantages under speeded-up circumstances?

As with anything, there can be too much of a good thing as well as too little. An ethnographer embarking on a project that might take years and years might also end up with no ethnography at all. Time alone cannot guarantee ethnographic accomplishment. So let me begin by examining circumstances when it may be the ethnographer, rather than ethnographic research, that needs to be speeded up. In pursuing a research approach that conceivably might take forever, what can the ethnographer do to insure that it doesn't?

How Having Too Much Time Can Work Against the Ethnographer

Time poses a threat for the ethnographer for whom it becomes an excuse rather than a condition. That can happen to anyone who confuses spending the long period of time customarily required to accomplish fieldwork with actually accomplishing it. There are some telltale signs to suggest when time has become a problem rather than an ally. You may detect some not-so-subtle bias in my outlining of such indicators. They reflect the maxim that there is no such thing as unreported research, and a corollary, that fieldwork is never an end in itself. To keep time from working against the ethnographer, the purposes and limitations of an inquiry not only must remain paramount but must be cast in terms of reasonable expectations within the time available. Time itself must be co-opted if the ethnographic task is to be accomplished.

As long as reporting is recognized as an essential aspect of *all* research, then time constraints must exert a *major* influence on the scope of work to be undertaken. To face that reality squarely, the best advice I can offer is to reverse ordinary priorities. In planning an inquiry, the amount of time that can be devoted to fieldwork should be calculated not as the first priority but as a *residual*. That is, the maximum time available for fieldwork is limited to whatever time will remain *after* making allowance for time that must be set aside for organizing and writing.

In thinking about time as a scarce commodity rather than an abundant resource, it is critical to recognize when it is time to stop gathering data and to turn attention to using the data already at hand. Here are four possible indicators:

- It is time to start writing if you have not begun to write, yet you feel that you are not learning anything sufficiently new to warrant the time you are investing. Start writing up what you already know. Such writing should not only test the depth of your knowledge but should also help you to identify areas requiring attention or warranting study in greater depth. That is also why writing is best initiated while you are in the field or still have easy access to it.

- It is time to start writing if you have not begun to write but you realize that you will never get it all and the possibility has crossed your mind that you may now be using fieldwork *as an excuse for not writing*. You would be better off to begin making sense of data already gathered than to bank on suddenly becoming a more astute fieldworker. If you are serious about turning to writing, this very moment is the time to begin, not tomorrow or the day after that.

- It is time to start writing if you have not begun to write, but you have convinced yourself that after attending "only a couple more" big events, or investigating "only a couple more" major topics, you will begin. If you feel you are that close to getting started, then there must be certain topics about which you are already well informed. Start by addressing those "comfortable" topics, rather than putting the writing task off for a few more days (or weeks, or months). Remember that the point at which you begin organizing and writing need not mark the end of fieldwork. Far more likely, turning attention to organizing and writing may help you focus your fieldwork efforts during whatever time remains.

- It is time to start writing if you have not begun to write, yet you realize that you are now at the midpoint of the total time you have allocated for completing the study. Years ago, Rosalie Wax offered cogent counsel about apportioning time in *Doing Fieldwork: Warnings and Advice* (1971):

  > It is a horrid but inescapable fact that it usually takes *more* time to organize, write, and present material well than it takes to gather it. . . . The sensible researcher will allow as much free time to write his report as he spent in the field. If he is really astute and can get away with it, he will allow himself more. [P. 45]

Simple arithmetic can turn that advice into an easy-to-follow formula: Allocate the total time available so that one day is set aside for organizing and writing for every day scheduled for fieldwork. Should you reach the midpoint between your start-up date and the date when you must complete the project, then deskwork must immediately become the order of the day. Wax also offered advice about the folly of devoting *all* the available time to fieldwork, even during the fieldwork phase, with intent to complete the writing "later": "The notion that one can work in the field for a year and then write a good report while one is carrying a full- or part-time teaching load is idiotic" (p. 45). To which she added, parenthetically, "People do write in this fashion, but this is one reason why so many monographs are uninspired."

Interpreted too literally, Wax's advice might seem to cut fieldwork time in half. In a pure arithmetic sense, of course, it does just that. But no one ever insisted that a conscientious ethnographer must be "on duty" every minute of every day, and no seasoned ethnographer would ever offer or follow such advice. The ethnographer who devotes some time every day to organizing and writing also stretches out the period over which at least *some* time can be devoted to keeping up with what is going on at the field site.

There is another maxim hiding here: *It is never too early to begin writing.* Were you to press me on this point, that it is never too early to begin writing, you might think you could push me to the absurd, "Well, surely you don't mean that on the very first day of fieldwork you might begin writing?"

Yet that is exactly what I mean: *never* too early. At the least, you should be recording first impressions, along with your personal reactions and any anxieties you are experiencing about the projected work or the circumstances in which you have placed yourself. Even when recording your thoughts in a journal or personal diary, keep in mind that you most certainly will return to that material again. You may even want to quote yourself from those early entries as a way of leading your reader into the setting in much the same way that you originally encountered it.

When I say "*Never* too early," I really mean it. I have written elsewhere (HFW 1990c:20 ff.) about what seem to me the obvious advantages of writing a preliminary draft of an account *before you even begin fieldwork*. Clearly, such a draft is intended for your eyes alone. But consider what such writing may accomplish for you. For one thing, it propels you into the field already focused on the ultimate purpose of the research, which is to make available to others what you have observed and understood. For another, it prompts you to think about how you will organize your final account, what you intend to emphasize, and what sequence you intend to follow as the story unfolds. For another, it establishes a permanent and accessible record of what you already know and what you need to find out. Closely linked to that point, it invites you to examine your own biases, assumptions, emotions, and so forth, and to make them a matter of record in a form readily accessible for your own future use.[1]

With that much written material already in place, it seems unlikely that your fieldwork could come to naught. Conceivably, early writing might also help you to discern whether you are about to embark on a diatribe rather than on ethnographic description. You may discover that your intended inquiry has been designed to prove rather than probe. If you suddenly realize that you are on a soapbox, your mind already made up and no real need for further inquiry, why not simply remain there. Go ahead and write your essay. Avoid the pretense of having to represent yourself as conducting impartial research. Save the limited opportunities you will have for ethnographic inquiry for pursuing problems suited to and deserving of the time and commitment it requires. Regardless of the many forms it may take, ethnography should always serve as a rich source of detail; it is never *simply* a platform for pronouncements. It promises an exploration into the less well known, rather than a reaffirmation of convictions already vigorously held. Critical ethnographers and ethnographic evaluators already push the limits in this regard, but they build a database from which they can explore or test their assumptions.

What often seems to be time's worst feature, that eventually it will run out, might well be turned to advantage. Under all circumstances, time exerts a major influence on ethnographic inquiry beyond the control of the researcher. Far better, I think, to recognize and capitalize on that fact, rather than bemoan the obvious. If there is never quite enough time for anything, then there is never going to be quite enough time for ethnography. We have to get by with what we can get.

Working Within Rigorous Time Constraints

Ethnography always takes time. The discussion thus far was intended to remind traditionally oriented or otherwise slow-working ethnographic researchers that *no one* ever has enough time. Ethnographers need to remain sufficiently focused on the essential task of *reporting* their research that fieldwork does not ever-so-gradually become an end in itself.

As Pertti Pelto notes in the epigraph chosen for this chapter, the more pressing problem these days is quite the opposite: What can be done to retain some of the advantage of ethnographic thoroughness in the face of rigorous time constraints? Is it possible for today's applied anthropologists, for example, to work within their disciplinary tradition and yet compete in a hurry-up world? Is there any way those in applied settings can develop an adequate ethnographic base before having to recommend or endorse some new course of action? Can ethnographically oriented researchers stay competitive under circumstances where time is of the essence, or must all action-oriented researchers, within or outside of anthropology, turn their backs on ethnographic approaches and rely on the same quick-and-dirty techniques used by everyone else anxious to report in a hurry?

The resolution is an uneasy one, another instance of methodological accommodation to changing circumstances and shortened time frames. This dilemma has produced such seemingly self-contradictory labels as "rapid ethnographic assessment." Whatever else it is, ethnography is never rapid. Pairing the terms "rapid" and "ethnographic" strikes me as about as near as ethnography will come to having an oxymoron uniquely its own.

I realize as I write—with writing itself as a prime example—that I never do anything rapidly. (No one who has nervously watched me eat an ice cream cone will disagree.) But I do get things done. Given enough time, I can even write a book. Although I was not drawn to ethnography simply because it is time-consuming, neither do I have a problem with it on that score. I don't like being crowded or rushed. I like to take my time to try to do things well, most certainly including efforts at ethnographic research. That leaves me with serious reservations about anyone who claims to be able to do it quickly.

I wish we could avoid terminology that gives the slightest hint that ethnography can be done rapidly, as implied in phrases like "focused ethnographic study" and announced unabashedly with labels like "rapid ethnographic assessment" or "rapid ethnographic procedures." However, we cannot ignore mounting pressure to be able to provide quick results, lest ethnographers be forever excluded from any inquiry in which time is of the essence. Can we capture something of the *essence* of ethnographic research when ethnography itself is out of the question? To this end, I propose what I call "ethnographic reconnaissance," to be discussed later in the chapter.

Admittedly, not everyone shares my reluctance about the speeding up of ethnography or how we might achieve such efforts (cf. Pelto 1992, for example). Personally, I do not feel the same reservation about a closely related label that substitutes the term "anthropological" for the more restricted term "ethnographic," to become "rapid anthropological assessment." Indeed, that label, pointing more broadly to anthropology rather than indicting ethnography, helps me underscore that not everything anthropologists do is necessarily connected with or based on ethnography. To whatever extent the nexus between anthropology and ethnography serves as a liability, forever dooming the former because of a dependence on time-consuming fieldwork, today's anthropologists need more than ever to be able to demonstrate a capability for producing quick results if they are to remain competitive in applied settings. This has led them to adopt or adapt some of the so-called rapid field procedures that originated in agricultural development and more recently have been adapted for research into health-care systems.

In terms of origins, the basic idea of employing rapid survey procedures, especially for social-impact assessment and farming-systems research, is best known under an earlier label, "rapid rural appraisal." Subsequently, as applications were extended into a broader range of problems and settings, the more commonly heard label has become "rapid assessment procedures" (RAP). Following the appearance in 1987 of the *RAP Manual* addressed to workers in nutrition and primary health care (Scrimshaw and Hurtado), a number of alternative labels and adaptations have appeared as guidelines for the rapid initiation of research projects on specific problems in animal husbandry, forestry, horticulture, and marine resources, in addition to fund-driven interests in topics like AIDS. Among other labels employed are the exploratory, informal, or "modified" survey; commodity systems assessments; rapid marketing appraisals; and market-needs assessments. One also finds bold titles such as community diagnoses, first-cut assessments, needs analyses, shortcut methods, targeted intervention research, or "time-effective" ethnography, along with a somewhat obscure term "soundings," including its rendering in Spanish, *sondeo*. The proliferation of titles is hardly surprising, given the ad hoc purposes for which such procedures are employed. Thus the informal survey in its generic form becomes an informal *agricultural* survey or an informal *forestry* survey in its specific applications.

As with research in Ethnographic Futures described earlier, guidelines and field manuals are often easier to trace through networks of people engaged in ongoing projects than through library searches.[2] Consonant with the trend favoring participatory approaches in both research and development work, participatory rural appraisal invites greater sensitivity to what local communities themselves can contribute toward identifying and solving local problems (see Chambers 1990, 1997).

Whether the reasons offered as rationale for developing and using rapid *anthropological* assessment prompted its formulation or followed along later, a good case can be made on their behalf. Support comes largely from those in the more scientific quarters, data crunchers impatient with ethnographic inefficiency and constantly urging the rest of us to be more systematic—and thus more efficient—in our data-gathering efforts. No ethnographer can completely ignore the call to be more time- and cost-effective or to find ways to make information available early enough to *inform* decisions rather than to supply only summative reports of how and where some well-intentioned effort went wrong.

Ethnographers also achieve a competitive advantage when they are seen as able to work in flexible time frames rather than regarded as singularly committed to fieldwork of long duration. It is interesting to note, however, that ethnographers who previously have done fieldwork in a region where a rapid assessment is to be conducted are recognized not only as potential recruits for research teams but also as ideal informants. Thus ethnographers are considered an excellent data *source* for teams conducting appraisals. In any number of ways, informed fieldworkers can find themselves in the role of informant, and even key informant (see Hennigh 1981).

The most engaging argument I have heard on behalf of promulgating greater use of rapid techniques into the fieldwork repertoire is Pelto's, that instructing and encouraging others in the use of such techniques can help to demystify ethnography and make its practice more readily understandable and thus available to a wider circle of researchers and developers (Pelto 1992:264–266). I am not exactly sure how one can maintain ethnographic integrity and, at the same time, get it up to speed; to me, that seems more apt to mystify than to demystify it. But it is comforting to realize that the facets of an ethnographic approach on which the proponents of rapid techniques focus their attention still rely on its two basic elements: *interviewing* and *direct observation*.

Rapid techniques require a clear sense of purpose. Even a seemingly innocuous label such as the "focused ethnographic study" hints at something different from what ethnographers ordinarily do, especially while initiating a study. When the time available for interviewing is limited, attention goes not to seeking out informants in general but to the careful identification of key informants. When even the time available for interviewing key informants is limited, then *focus groups* are substituted in their place, with focus-group techniques employed in what is reinterpreted as "a simple extension of the key informant idea":

> The difference is that the anthropologist interviews a set of key informants at once, thus increasing the potential that the data are representative. It is more than simply adding numbers for it seeks to increase the representativeness of the data by exposing the statement of the individual to the response of the group. [Van Willigen and Finan 1991:4]

Having sometimes watched domineering individuals run roughshod over my classes and seminars in more than 40 years of teaching, I have never been a big believer in group processes for getting at what *individuals* are thinking. I learn something about customary group interaction in such circumstances (turn taking, deference, and so forth), but I am not inclined to gather interview data that way. Still, an argument can be made that group interviewing is a good antidote to the overreliance that ethnographers often place on data obtained from a single informant. Nor is information-gathering necessarily the only objective of such group-process activities. The subtleties of constituency-building under the guise of research are not lost on those who do developmental work and who recognize the importance of winning local support through community involvement. An article titled "Rapid and Participatory Rural Appraisal" (Chambers 1990) that appeared in the journal *Appropriate Technology* reminds us not only that developers are fully aware of this need but that rapid rural appraisal is itself a form of "appropriate technology."

I like to think that ethnography exerts a strong and positive influence whenever field-oriented researchers do some interviewing they might otherwise not have done, even if they narrow their interviewees to key personnel in the setting, and even if they conduct their interviewing in groups. I would caution only about the possible confusion between *key informant*, the term ethnographers have traditionally used to refer to one or two individuals with whom they worked intensely for long periods of time, and persons who play key *roles* and who are interviewed only briefly during rapid appraisal procedures. It has been suggested that we use the term "individual respondents" to describe the latter, so that "key informant" retains its special meaning (Beebe 1995:45).

Observation must proceed in the same quick and focused manner when employed to augment other rapid field procedures. Traditional ethnographers may enjoy the luxury of simply wandering about, but observations conducted in concert with rapid appraisals are systematically recorded on tightly designed schedules and inventories. Such "purposeful" observations are typically noted on some kind of survey sheet or are otherwise structured through specific questions to be answered, items to be inventoried, or circumstances confronted. With rapid appraisal as the objective, field observations are focused, logically enough, on what is to be appraised. Again quoting van Willigen and Finan:

> The rapid appraisal is a generic category for a research methodology that involves short periods of fieldwork, usually less than one month . . . and exemplifies a truncation of the formal survey process combined with some of the useful aspects of key informant interviewing. [1991:5]

The fieldwork component in rapid appraisal relies basically on two techniques: directed observation and the informal, open-ended survey (rather than a formal questionnaire) conducted individually or in groups. Whatever time is devoted to field observations is "directed" not only figuratively but literally, as researchers record data according to pre-established categories deemed relevant to the research focus. Sampling strategies to accomplish these objectives are purposive rather than random or statistically representative. At the hands of the experienced researcher, it is assumed that "culturally meaningful and important categories" will emerge (p. 5).

As with Ethnographic Futures research, information gathered through the interviews presupposes that at least one member of the appraisal team is sufficiently well informed to be able to provide the necessary context and to recognize elements critical to moving the work ahead. Thus the fieldworker engaged in an appropriate application of rapid appraisal procedures is anything but an autonomous independent researcher. By definition, rapid appraisal cannot be accomplished by one person (Beebe 1995:47). Conversely, its strengths are argued not only on the basis of the greater speed with which multiple observers can complete a survey but on the kinds of interaction the requisite teamwork fosters. Advantages cited for the team approach include opportunities to train newcomers, to recruit local participants who will join a research project, and to pair less-experienced fieldworkers with old-timers.

For the types of project in which rapid appraisal has proved most suitable, research teams are composed of individuals representing different disciplines or agencies. Should there happen to be an anthropologist on the team, quite likely he or she will be the lone representative of the discipline. As noted, anyone who has previously conducted ethnographic research in the local setting is more likely to be regarded as a *source* of data than as a *gatherer* of it. Of course, an ideal team as one might envision it in the planning stage of a project may differ markedly from what may seem the motley crew that constitutes a real one. On the local scene, being literate and, especially, being immediately available, may be the only realistic criteria. However, fieldwork is not necessarily impeded by untrained assistants who speak the local dialect, may be able to interact with far greater ease, and may enjoy far easier access than the sometimes aloof professionals who direct such projects.

No doubt ethnographically oriented researchers will continue to seek ways to speed up aspects of their work, most certainly in applied fields where grant proposals or research contracts focus on highly specific topics within time frames too short to accommodate a traditional approach. I have no problem with that. I do urge, however, that we restrict the term "ethnography" to research carried out in the ethnographic tradition and in more or less traditional ways. We can use other phrases to describe work in which haste is prerequisite to taking the assignment at all.

On the other hand, much stands to be gained for *any* researcher who pauses long enough to have a look around, with the intention of putting an inquiry into some broader perspective. If ethnography both promises and asks too much in that regard, then we need a different label to describe an initial look around that may be followed by a more detailed inquiry as circumstances warrant or resources allow. For this purpose I propose and turn next to the idea of *ethnographic reconnaissance*.

Ethnographic Reconnaissance

Although the label "ethnographic reconnaissance" is not entirely new (Pelto cites an unpublished 1981 field manual prepared by Thomas Marchione in which the phrase appeared), neither has it received much attention. I reintroduce it here in the hope of infusing it with a slightly expanded meaning. I propose that ethnographic reconnaissance become a standard part of the fieldwork repertoire, not simply one more option among an ever-expanding number of rapid appraisal procedures but a fieldwork technique in its own right, one that every ethnographer seriously considers employing at the outset of any study. Most fieldworkers have been doing ethnographic reconnaissance all along.

The noun "reconnaissance," and related verb "reconnoiter," are often heard in reference to obtaining information for military purposes by inspecting, observing, or surveying an enemy position. Such close association with military practice may prejudice some readers against the terms, but these better-known meanings are certainly not the only ones, and use of the word is hardly new to social science. Writing in 1946, Kurt Lewin referred to reconnaissance not only as the necessary fact-finding stage of action research but a critical element in a cycle ("spiral," in his words) of activities that included planning, action, and assessing consequences in plotting further action, similar to what has more recently become known as formative evaluation. Here I propose it in its more customary sense—a preliminary examination or survey, usually followed by a more detailed inquiry.

Regardless of how one feels about the term, the *act* of reconnaissance is rather customary behavior for anyone in unfamiliar circumstances. Whether finding myself in a strange hotel, a strange town, or simply thumbing through an unfamiliar text or journal issue, I do a bit of reconnaissance as a matter of course, a brief exploration intended to orient me. The purpose of such reconnaissance, whether the rapid appraiser's so-called windshield survey of a new community as seen from an automobile, or my own strolling or casual browsing, is to get one's bearings and thus be able to make a better-informed decision as to whether or how to proceed with more thorough investigation. It is not hard to see why "reconnaissance" is another of several labels used for rapid appraisals (see, for example, Honadle 1982; van Willigen and DeWalt 1985), although they are sometimes simply referred to as "surveys without questionnaires" or, more modestly still, as "organized common sense."

To convey the notion of *getting oriented* for the purpose of designing a strategy for how to proceed, reconnaissance seems an excellent term. Paired with "ethnographic" I think it serves ideally to communicate the need and practice of making a preliminary survey at the first stage of any field-based investigation. Most certainly that can include the traditional scouting party—whether advance military unit, rapid appraisal team, or stroll down a hotel corridor in search of an ice machine—following which these preliminary observations are reviewed to inform a more carefully planned course of action. But just as there is no reason to restrict the idea of reconnaissance to an operation carried out by the military, it need not be regarded as something conducted only by a team, conducted only at the outset of a study, or conducted only once. Ethnographic reconnaissance seems an appropriate and useful strategy for every ethnographer to keep in mind *all the time*. It may also remind and encourage other researchers to take advantage of any and every opportunity to have a look around. Thus I commend it not to speed up ethnographers so much as to encourage other researchers to slow down, if only for a few days or a few hours.

Carefully separated from the term "rapid," the notion of reconnaissance directs attention away from the speed with which it *may* have to be completed to underscore instead the importance of assuring that, in the initial phase of a project, time and resources will be set aside for scouting the territory. Along with a commitment to early reconnaissance should come recognition that the accuracy and adequacy of certain features identified in a preliminary "sounding" may require more detailed examination. As a general strategy, ethnographic reconnaissance can serve not only as a fieldwork technique but also to help fieldworkers of any persuasion to mark the suggested distinction between *doing traditional ethnography* and *borrowing or adapting an ethnographic fieldwork technique or two* when time allows for no more. And anthropologists—especially the applied or "practicing" ones—can feel free to borrow from their own kit bag without fostering the impression that anything they do by way of research automatically becomes ethnography. Anthropologists who do applied work today under circumstances where there may *never* be opportunity to undertake traditional ethnography can still keep their hand in, drawing upon their ethnographic heritage without fretting that in doing so they may be compromising it. Similarly, the idea of ethnographic reconnaissance offers the researcher who has a carefully focused topic to investigate, yet who would like to infuse a project with a dash of ethnography—an almost literal dash, in this case—an appropriate label and some encouragement for pausing to take a broader look around.

The *term* reconnaissance meets some resistance among those who cannot divorce it from its militaristic connotation. But it is the *idea* of reconnaissance that I want to promote; there are other terms one might use. The verb "to canvass," for example, can refer to soliciting opinions, to investigating by inquiry, and to examining closely. All three activities are consistent with what I have in mind, although they downplay the importance of observation in favor of a more intrusive interview mode that may not be appropriate, especially in the initial stages of an inquiry. Some qualitative researchers refer to the practice of "casing" a situation or making initial "probes" before beginning more systematic work, and repeated probing may be incorporated into the research regimen through the practice of "spot observations" (see Whiting 1984).

As *idea,* ethnographic reconnaissance offers a strategy for anyone engaged in field research of any kind, including survey work. It ought to encourage all researchers to use more common sense, to employ more of their own senses, and *always* to have a look around *for themselves* regardless of time constraints or the depth of the inquiry. A suitable motto might be, "A little ethnographic reconnaissance is better than none at all." It never hurts for any researcher to have a look around, and the "re-" in reconnaissance and reconnoiter calls attention to something to be done again (and again). Both terms convey an intent to return for a more thorough look when and as warranted. Whether further study is warranted must be assessed in terms of research purposes, but no one need suffer the accusation of doing *rapid* or *superficial* or *hasty* ethnography, provided that preliminary work is carefully identified for what it is. Researchers otherwise hesitant to endorse qualitative procedures may feel comfortable trying on the role of fieldworker this way if they are otherwise concerned that their very presence on site might be misconstrued as an endorsement of "soft" approaches. Thus, ethnographic reconnaissance offers a way in for researchers reluctant to stray too far from what they regard as more rigorous approaches.

I trust that no ethnographer would ever insist that anyone could remain in the field long enough to get the whole story or get everything just right. But that idea needs to be turned around to recognize as well that there is no length of time too short to derive some insight from even the briefest effort at ethnographic reconnaissance. Russ Bernard, strong proponent of scientific approaches to data-based ethnography that he is, absolutely *insists* that his students engage in some form of participant observation activity in the course of their research. And he adds a concession difficult for a seasoned ethnographer to make, "At the extreme low end it is possible to do useful participant observation in just a few days" (Bernard 1994b:140).

Certainly, the more time available for fieldwork the better. What Bernard underscores is that there is no substitute for being there, on site and in person, regardless of how short the time available for doing so. That is a lesson ethnographers want to share with researchers of all orientations, many of whom regard their presence at a research site as a potential source of data contamination. In a sense, perhaps they are right. There is always the possibility that they might learn something that would screw up otherwise nice clean results, or that they might discover anew that things are hopelessly more complex than their studies are designed to reveal!

Suggestions for Incorporating Ethnographic Reconnaissance as a Research Strategy

If you participate in a research project that includes provision for rapid survey procedures, most likely you will receive prepared guidelines directing you to conduct a predetermined number of interviews among informants who have already been identified for you, by role if not by name. Or you may be handed an already-developed observation schedule to guide you in systematically gathering data someone else has deemed to be of potential use. If you are a seasoned fieldworker, you may take umbrage at having to give up your accustomed autonomy. On the bright side, you might rejoice at the opportunity (or excuse) such an assignment affords for having a look around. Regardless of how structured your schedule, be attentive to your intuitive feelings about what is going on, to how suitably the research has been designed, and to what new problems the project itself may create for researchers or for those in the setting.

I once had an opportunity to observe at the local level the efforts of a private organization interested in community development worldwide. That organization was willing to make as much as a five-year commitment to certain preselected communities based on one intense *week* of planning that included only *one day* for interviewing local residents (HFW 1983b). Yet the more I saw of the organization's rather lockstep approach to development—"rigid and doctrinaire, but in a benign sort of way," as one observer described it—the more I appreciated that at least *some* time had been allocated for such activity. Certainly one day was better than no time at all. And who knows: perhaps such rapid entrée served notice in the community as to how the project would operate.

Should you be assigned to develop a survey to initiate a team project (along with a predictably short deadline for completing the task), you might first check whether schedules already exist for the region and/or the general nature of your project. Given customary expectations for quick results, adapting a previously developed schedule for the particular circumstances might prove more expedient than starting from scratch. Recent issues of the two journal publications of the Society for Applied Anthropology (SfAA), *Human Organization* and *Practicing Anthropology,* as well as contacts made through SfAA itself, might also be of assistance in locating networks linking others actively engaged in the field development and field testing of such techniques.[3]

Although one underlying premise of rapid assessment methods is that the work is always conducted by a team, the advantages to be gained from ethnographic reconnaissance seem every bit as great for the individual researcher who views the strategy as another dimension of fieldwork. Ethnographic reconnaissance is not restricted only to the initial phase of a research project. It can and should serve as a constant reminder for an ongoing assessment of events, viewed in a context broader than the immediate focus of a research inquiry. Researchers need to remain vigilant about scouting the territory long after an initial program or course of action has been determined. It doesn't hurt to take stock not only as to whether you are still on the right track, but also whether you are getting somewhere. Arthur Godfrey and Will Rogers are variously credited for reminding us that even if you *are* on the right track, you can get run over if you just sit there.

As envisioned here, an ethnographic reconnaissance report might consist of a set of notes or memos comparable to what ethnographers make for themselves as informal working documents. On a large-scale project, such reports may be assembled as a set of semi-public documents pertaining to a particular region or community and intended for wider circulation. In what is probably the largest scale on which rapid rural appraisal procedures were employed over an extended period of time—the Khon Kaen University–Ford Rural Systems Research Project in Thailand initiated in 1983—the accumulating topical reports collectively formed an impressive set of regionally oriented technical papers. The status of 32 such reports was summarized (see Grandstaff 1988) to provide an important outcome from the research effort. With field projects of broad scope it is always prudent to devise ways to demonstrate both progress and accomplishment, and such reports can prove handy both for guiding the ongoing fieldwork and for purposes of accountability. As with any kind of document that might become widely available, fieldworkers need to be sensitive from the outset to the audiences who might eventually have access to them.

Let me suggest some pointers for initiating fieldwork that should help the individual researcher realize the maximum return on ethnographic reconnaissance:

- Ethnographic reconnaissance offers an opportunity to draw heavily on what Robert Chambers calls "organized common sense, freed from the chains of inappropriate professionalism" (quoted in Beebe 1995:43). Common sense isn't invariably the best guide, but it never hurts to hold our fieldwork procedures and interpretive efforts up for inspection. Newcomers to research have been known to try so hard to be "scientific" and "objective" that common sense sometimes departs them altogether. Too often we turn simple tasks of "finding out" into complex procedural issues. One criterion as a test of common sense is to think how your grandmother might have gone about finding things out, or how you would go about explaining to her what you felt you were up to, in plain, everyday talk about straightforward ideas, simply expressed, absent of academic pretense and posturing.

- When conducting reconnaissance efforts of your own, try to assume the role of an interested and curious human being, not to be confused either for a tourist or an opinion-poll taker, yet not trying too hard to achieve a special identity as a social scientist or researcher. There is some acceptance (or at least tolerance) for the latter role in professional settings, but it does not always wear well in the real world. Clipboard or notepad, tape recorder or camera, too businesslike in dress or manner—any of these is more likely to set a wrong tone than to foster natural dialogue. Experienced researchers even caution against arriving in a chauffeur-driven automobile: "Oversized vehicles bearing official looking numbers driven by chauffeurs should, if possible, be avoided" (Rhoades 1987:119).

- Don't feel you must "sample" on any basis other than a purposive sample when you begin. If formal sampling is warranted, do it later. Let intuition and your own natural way of going about things guide you. Recognize, however, that you may have no other choice than to talk to self-appointed informants who present themselves not only as willing to talk but probably insistent that they are the very people you most need to meet. Whether or not that is how you would prefer to begin, you may have to give both official and unofficial gatekeepers their due.

- Be prepared to answer all questions directed at you, most certainly questions having to do with what brings you there in the first place and what you plan to do with the information you seek. You ought to be able to satisfy such questions as "Why us?" and "Why now?" Such questions need not put you on the defensive (unless you have something to be defensive about). Spare long explanations for later, after people have a better idea of what you are up to and may want a fuller account. Keep in mind your relative unimportance in their lives, not the great relevance their lives have suddenly taken for you.

- As quickly as possible, write up notes about what you have learned, including first impressions, problems you anticipate, leads you might follow, analytical concepts you may later want to consider. Keep track as well of your emotional responses and information gained through *all* your senses, not just what you have "seen."

- Outline how you would go about doing a more thorough ethnography if time allowed. Possibly some of the topics you identify can be included within the time limits you have. You might set priorities, listing topics in order of importance to the work planned, distinguishing between marginal or optional ones and topics essential to the project. Remember that, unlike the rapid appraiser intent on completing a brief but formal report for others, you are doing this to enhance a relatively longer-term effort of your own.

- As early as possible, consider drafting your final report as it would look if it had to be based only on what you have learned to date. You probably know more about some aspects than you realize, just as you undoubtedly know less (or know with less certainty) about other critical topics. Writing based on even a brief reconnaissance should help you review what you already know and help you to inventory what remains to be investigated.

- Keep in mind that you are there to learn and to understand how those in the setting make sense of their world. If you are asking questions that informants cannot answer, then you are not talking about their world. What they know, and how they have come to know it, are what matter, not what they do not know, and not what you know. The real art called for here, as in all ethnographic interviewing, is to get people to talk without having to ask a lot of direct questions, and to frame the questions that you do ask in ways that make sense locally. That is the essence of the semi-structured interview. That might also be what distinguishes ethnographic reconnaissance from the rapid techniques noted earlier: rapid appraisers have their questions already developed for them; an ethnographer ought to be intent on trying to figure out what the right questions *are*.

- Just as you seek out informed people to help orient you, seek out information already available in archival sources. Developers and researchers pressed for time provide a good example, for they routinely search for *existing* resources so that they do not duplicate work already completed by others. Ethnographers sometimes get hung up with the idea that they must discover—or rediscover—everything for themselves. Do you really believe you are morally obligated to make your own maps if satisfactory ones are available? Do you feel you must prepare a new version of a community history if one already exists? Of course, take a critical stance toward information you receive from any source, but do look at, and look for, a wide array of existing resources there for the asking.

- In the absence of the interdisciplinary perspective that you would expect in conducting a rapid appraisal through a team approach, be your own interdisciplinary "monitor" by thinking how researchers with other problem orientations or academic commitments might be drawn to the setting you are studying. The very criticism that ethnography is overly broad in scope gives you license to pursue multifaceted interests. Reconnaissance, particularly of the "aerial photo" kind, allows you to keep the big picture in mind as your inquiry takes sharper and sharper focus. A reconnaissance mind-set offers a way to keep your own orientation in perspective.

Reconnaissance usually results in reports and maps, and it seems useful to think of ethnographic reconnaissance as a sort of exploratory map-making activity, figuratively if not always literally. Recall Bateson's observation that what gets recorded on a map is differences. That's what ethnography is about, too.

Systematic Data Collection

Another way to speed up fieldwork is to persist at refining the research question(s) and/or defining and refining the issue of what constitutes the kind of "data" the research question calls for. Precisely what ethnographic data consist of is so ambiguous that I sometimes wonder if the phrase presents us with another oxymoron, one that tempts us to refer to our research as though it really exists in tangible form. For researchers oriented to accumulating data rather than to achieving purposes, questions can be stated in such a way that quantifiable data can readily be identified and "collected." Many of the so-called systematic procedures used in social science investigations have this convenience about them. The data they call for are relatively easy to obtain if one can find willing subjects—and here the term "subjects" seems more appropriate than informants—and they can be gathered quickly and subjected to systematic procedures for analysis. They also have the advantage noted in earlier chapters of providing the fieldworker with a standard stimulus for engaging subjects, so that intra- and intergroup comparisons are possible, the advantage anthropologists discovered years ago through using Rorschach ink-blot tests.

The systematic procedures in vogue today tend to be used by fieldworkers preoccupied with measurement techniques and bolstered by the accumulation of large data sets. They work with models designed to explore the content and organization of cultural knowledge, joining with the efforts of other cognitive scientists. To pursue such approaches is, of course, to buy into the theories that drive them as to what constitutes culture and how it can be mapped in a population. The eliciting techniques of the earlier ethnoscience are an example, reflected in such approaches as "free listing" ("What kinds of _____s are there?" or "How do you prevent _____?"), componential analysis, or belief frames ("Can _____ cause _____?").

A related set of procedures can be used to explore subjects' judgments—easily systematized by having them sort objects or cards containing names or pictures in terms of what goes with what, or sorting them by groups, ordering them along some specified dimension. Both the tasks and the analysis can become quite sophisticated. In a simple pile sort, for example, selected members of a group might be asked to sort the names of all members of the group into different piles and then to explain to the investigator the basis on which the sorting was done. In a more directed task, the investigator might ask each subject to make a similar sort but to rank order the groups according to an assessment of power and/or prestige within the group.

Similarly, an ethnographer interested in the distribution of cultural knowledge in a community might employ any number of familiar testing modes to assess who knows what, whether by using a dichotomous format (Yes/No, True/False), a multiple-choice format, fill in the blanks, matching (what item in column A goes with what item in column B), estimation, or selecting appropriate items from a list. An important difference in the ethnographer's use of such approaches is that, ordinarily, at least, they are not administered as tests in which answers are to be scored as correct or incorrect but are intended to reveal what subjects know or how they assess others within the group.

These approaches also give the fieldworker lots of data to analyze, data that can be obtained quickly and are amenable to standard statistical treatment with comforting degrees of certainty underwritten by agreed-upon procedures for analyzing them. Although their *social* significance may remain somewhat dubious, diligently following such procedures allows one to achieve satisfying levels of *statistical* significance. Ethnographers who discover that they derive more sat-isfaction from understanding their data than from understanding the people who generated them may find themselves increasingly preoccupied with sys-tematic approaches until the approaches themselves become all-consuming research activities.

Such caution also can be turned the other way, to remind the less system-atically inclined fieldworker to be systematic when the occasion warrants, to count what counts, to measure what deserves to be measured. It is not so long since anthropologists routinely measured cranial circumferences simply because that was one of the things other anthropologists were doing (recall Boas's com-ment about "measuring a lot of Indians"). Anthropologists who specialize in the field of anthropometrics may still be found measuring heads, but the databases they build today are far more purposeful.[4] Conversely, some time-and-motion studies that might seem the very antithesis of what ethnography is about were initiated by the applied anthropologists of an earlier day.

The influence of the computer as a research tool has made ethnographers even more self-conscious about the question of exactly what "ethnographic data" should look like. One cannot help but wonder to what extent those data are beginning to look more and more like the kind of data that computers like. As long as purposes continue to guide ethnographic research, then com-puters will remain in the service of ethnography. Gigantic efforts such as inventorying cultural items, tangible or intangible, should benefit from com-puter capabilities for managing huge amounts of data. When problems begin to be defined (or redefined) in terms of computer capabilities or existing pro-grams, then we can expect to see ethnography making accommodations likely to move us still farther away from our orienting traditions.

Efforts at making ethnography more systematic are not new. Anthropol-ogist Pete Murdock reportedly offered a course on systematic ethnography in 1935, the year he established his Cross-Cultural Survey (Darnell 1998:362). I remember some discomfort of my own in the 1950s as we began to realize that still photography and filmmaking were carving such inroads that it seemed they might *become* forms of ethnography rather than be mere tools in fieldwork. Ethnography has not suffered because of film or videotaping. No doubt it will survive the computer age—as well as be adapted for (and by) it.

To date, whatever constructive force the computer age has exerted seems not so much to have made better ethnographers out of researchers, but to make more rounded researchers out of ethnographers. This undoubtedly has been an adaptive advantage for ethnographers now able to work more quickly and to handle more data, but it has been made at the cost of ethnography. Perhaps these are today's *new* New Ethnographers, committed to an approach but dubious about traditional ethnography itself, interested instead either in investigating issues of broad consequence or looking at pervasive social problems in more meticulous detail than was previously possible. Such efforts have been enhanced not only by the enormous amounts of data that computers can handle but also by computer simulations that can explore both real and hypothetical relationships and outcomes.[5]

Stepwise Research

One further idea that the harried ethnographer might borrow from rapid assessment approaches and other highly structured fieldwork techniques, an idea that fits nicely with the notion of ethnographic reconnaissance, is the concept of *stepwise research* (see van Willigen and Finan 1991:7–8) or of *staging* research. Stepwise research suggests a way to plan for and realize most of the advantages of long-term inquiry when the anticipated duration of each field trip is expected to be brief but there is the likelihood of opportunity for return visits. This involves plotting a strategy that begins with identifying major topics for inquiry, then arranging them in an orderly sequence that can be addressed topic by topic over an extended period.

This is another instance in which time constraints can be reinterpreted as an ally, for they not only force one to parcel or "chunk out" an ambitious scope of work in manageable units, they also require one to think about sequencing. The extended duration of a long-term project also invites directing more attention to issues of stability and change than is possible in a continuous time frame. One might devote special attention to aspects deemed most likely to change. That would maximize the opportunity to track what does change and what does not, with observations conducted over an extended period. As has too often been the case, short-term studies of directed change tend to confirm that change has occurred. Ethnographers engaged in long-term fieldwork make finer distinctions between change *efforts* and changed *results*, or between *change* and the *rhetoric of change*.

When first setting out, already feeling the constraints of time, few ethnographers make adequate provision for the possibility that their research of a particular topic or setting may continue for years, perhaps extending throughout the duration of a professional lifetime. I would never have dreamed in 1962 that I would still be writing about the Kwakiutl 34 years later (HFW 1996). Nor did I anticipate how quickly the passing of years would bring about a day when the youngsters in my classroom would be adults with school-age youngsters of their own. Experienced ethnographers may feel a sense of regret when reflecting on missed opportunities to study culture change simply because they gave too little attention to their own futures. Too bad we do not make better provision for the "most likely scenarios" in our research careers, in recognition of the likelihood that someday we, too, shall return to witness the effects of time.

Notes

1. I believed this to be an original and daring idea but have discovered that someone beat me to it: "Sol Tax used to advise his students to write the first draft of their dissertations before going to the field" (Bruner 1986:147).

2. Sources offering useful overviews and bibliography include a bulletin titled *Soundings: Rapid and Reliable Research Methods for Practicing Anthropologists* edited by van Willigen and Finan (1991); James Beebe's efforts toward establishing a conceptual foundation for rapid appraisal work (1995, with a follow-up by Harris et al. in 1998); Pertti Pelto's summary chapter on method in the edited collection dedicated to him (Poggie, DeWalt, and Dressler 1992); and a manual describing ethnographic methods for investigating women's health (Gittelsohn et al. 1998). An entire issue of *Practicing Anthropology* (Volume 18, No. 3, 1996) is devoted to "Handbooks and Manuals in Applied Research," giving emphasis to methods that can be applied in "relatively brief" periods of time and providing illustrative field reports of some applications and a bibliography of specialized materials.

3. Another source of assistance is the Applied Anthropology Documentation Project at the University of Kentucky, which, since 1978, has been collecting and making available through interlibrary loan the so-called fugitive literature (e.g., technical reports, research monographs) produced in the field.

4. For example, see Bradtmiller 1998, a report on improving children's bicycle helmets.

5. For fieldwork-oriented overviews of some of these structured, time-efficient interview techniques, see Bernard 1994, chapter 11 ff.; Weller and Romney 1988; or issues of *Field Methods,* published quarterly beginning in 1999, and its predecessor, *Cultural Anthropology Methods.* For discussion in greater detail, see, for example, the two volumes on systematic fieldwork by Werner and Schoepfle 1987a,b. For studies that have employed systematic procedures, see Boster 1985; D'Andrade 1987; Garro 1986, 1988; Romney, Weller, and Batchelder 1986.

CHAPTER NINE

Does It Matter
Whether or Not It's Ethnography?

I'll never understand your perverse, incessant desire to become "more anthropological." Despite all the good cultural analysis and description, you always seem a bit preoccupied with that issue. Perhaps someday you will explain it all to me.

—Doug Foley
Letter to HFW, August 29, 1996

L ike a modern-day Don Quixote, have I been tilting at giants of my own making, for years fearlessly protecting Fair Ethnography's good name and reputation against nameless foes and imagined threats? Doug Foley is but one of several researchers, both in and outside of anthropology, with whom I have long engaged in dialogue about ethnography and how rigorously it should be defined or defended. His comment, quoted above, set me to wondering. Why, indeed, have I held so firmly to the position that ethnography has more to offer to the world of research—particularly to researchers outside anthropology—to the extent that its distinctive features are emphasized? What stands to be lost when it is taken as a synonym for participant observation or used even more broadly to describe anything that any qualitative researcher does in pursuing a field-based inquiry? Why have I struggled here to find its "essence," especially when that essence seems so elusive?

I applaud researchers of any persuasion who borrow ethnographic techniques in the conduct of their inquiries. It is hard to imagine how anyone could pursue a field-oriented approach *without* borrowing ethnographic techniques, except that the very idea of borrowing suggests that fieldwork techniques somehow "belong" to ethnographers or to cultural anthropologists more generally. Anthropology has no special claim on either participant observation or interviewing, and in one form or another, those two activities

encompass what fieldwork is about. Turning the tables, it is difficult to identify any field technique that is *exclusive* to ethnography. There are a few special terms ethnographers use, such as "*key* informant" or "*genealogical*
method," but extensive interviewing with one individual, or collecting family
history data, hardly require a graduate degree in anthropology.

The basic fieldwork techniques are available for all. If ethnographers have
a special message to share, it is to encourage researchers of every persuasion
to avail themselves of the widest possible range of techniques, rather than rely
too exclusively on single sources of data, such as the overworked and over-
rated opinion survey. "Triangulation" is a term frequently heard in association
with ethnography, not to be taken as literally as it implies, but a reminder of
the need to corroborate findings. Similarly, the idea of incorporating ethnographic reconnaissance as a standard practice in *all* field-based research is
intended to encourage more researchers to give more consideration to the
benefits of having more of a look around, and thus to take more cognizance
of context in studies of even the shortest duration.

The caution I extend—and the implicit plea that drives it—is to use discretion in what gets *labeled* as ethnography in the final product. Under certain
circumstances, it *does* matter whether or not it is ethnography. This chapter
begins by setting forth some reasons as to why, or when, it may matter. I hope
I can present a compelling brief for treating ethnography with due regard. But
rest assured that my "incessant desire" to preserve ethnographic integrity is not
shared by all. The opposing point has been argued, that treating ethnography
as special can have the effect of excluding other qualitative researchers—those
lacking an anthropological orientation, in particular—when they are the very
researchers who should be recruited and made welcome. It has not been my
intent to portray or to idealize ethnography as an exclusive club. Still, I cannot
endorse the notion that anyone with good intentions and plenty of time can
suddenly begin doing it. So let me pose some answers to the question, "Does
it *really* matter whether or not it's ethnography?"

Yes, it matters whether or not it's ethnography if that is the claim you
intend to make for the finished product and that is the label you attach to it.
Ethnography is served best by those who use the label prudently. Outside of
research circles, and to some extent even within them, the term is neither generally well known nor always well understood. Anthropologists can appreciate that fact, for they are frequently confronted by people who take the
special interests of the archaeologist (or paleontologist) to be the sole preoccupation of the entire discipline. As research associated with study among living groups of people, ethnography helps remind the general public that not
all anthropological concerns—not even all archaeological ones—are limited

to the past. A clearer understanding of the role ethnography plays can help convey a more accurate picture of all that is encompassed in anthropology's four-going-on-five major subfields: *physical,* or what is becoming known as *biological, anthropology; archaeology; anthropological linguistics;* and *cultural* (or *social*) *anthropology.* Heretofore any applied efforts were regarded as simply the practical applications of the other four, but today the traditional four-field subdivision has been augmented through recognition awarded to *applied anthropology* as a distinct career field.

A qualitative researcher whose interests and efforts are painstakingly thorough, yet hopelessly descriptive and largely atheoretical, may buy a certain amount of protection in working under the aegis of ethnography as a label appropriate for such endeavors. The relationship between ethnography and theory remains an uneasy one, with faultfinding leveled at both extremes—theory getting in the way or theory too blatantly ignored. There is not much point in trying to reach agreement on what an optimum balance might be, since that depends on purposes. Nonetheless, the label "ethnography" offers fair warning, and thus some defense against criticisms of work not convincingly related to the theoretical spheres in which many academics prefer to travel.

On the other hand, to label as "ethnography" studies more likely to be distinguished for thin description than thick does a disservice not only to the discipline but to the researcher who makes the labeling error. If we lack confidence in the ability of researchers to situate their work in its proper context, how much confidence can we place in the accuracy of the material presented? And as clearly preferable as thick description might seem over thin, careful and thorough description is neither the answer to every problem nor every researcher's forte. Studies lacking adequate description may nonetheless have a significant contribution to make through their problem posing, their conceptualization of an issue, their theorizing, or, far too seldom, through a brilliant synthesis and critique of previous work. By definition, ethnography asks too much of the researcher who attempts it—mission impossible. The charitable reader can look for the ethnographer's strong points and be drawn to them; rigorous academic reviewers can be counted on to ferret out shortcomings.

Yes, it matters whether or not it's ethnography if ethnography is how you have described your intent and/or made your professional claim. If you say you are going to do ethnography and are capable of doing it, then do it you must. There are ethical dilemmas enough in conducting research when people do not know what you are up to or do not wish to have their stories told by others. In these times of cultural angst, such issues have become ever more sensitive. But as an ethnographer I am sorrowful indeed when I learn of instances where people have posed as ethnographers (or cultural anthropologists) but have engaged in undercover work of another sort. Similarly, I have been distressed on occasion to find research organizations doing contract work that specifically called for ethnography, yet did not have anyone associated with the project who had the faintest idea of what ethnography is about other than having an observer present at a research site.

To confound the issue, there have been instances in which no one who initiated the call for ethnography or who was subsequently charged with monitoring it seemed to have any idea of what it is all about. To illustrate: There was a period, dating back to the 1970s, when ethnography became a sort of fad in educational research. Calls for nationally funded projects routinely required an ethnographic component. On one occasion when I was invited to serve on a site-review team for a large-scale, federally funded project, I brought materials of possible interest to those responsible for its ethnographic facet. Alas, I found no one to give them to. No member of the research team had any idea of, or expressed the least interest in, what ethnography entailed other than "lots of description" or Gilbert Ryle's phrase that Clifford Geertz's then-new essay had popularized, "thick description" (Geertz 1973b). Ethnography was stuck at the techniques stage, a way of looking but not a way of seeing. Sensitive observers hired for the project were dutifully recording voluminous fieldnotes, but they were unable to convey any sense of purpose in their observations. Nor did that really seem to bother them; they were being paid by the hour.

I do not mean to put things out of balance. The world does not turn on ethnographic accomplishment. As anthropologist Michael Jackson has noted, "Many ground-breaking ethnographies are providing us with timely and ironic reminders that for the most part human beings live their lives independently of the intellectual schemes dreamed up in academe . . ." (1996:4). There are relatively few times when ethnography is even wanted, let alone needed or allowed.

For another project that I describe more fully below, I was invited to participate in an independent evaluation to document what actually occurred in classrooms during the implementation of a new series produced for instructional television. The programs were targeted for pupils in the upper elementary grades and were designed to promote problem-solving skills. I was asked (i.e., hired) to observe in one or more local classrooms where the program was being used. The invitation carried a strange stipulation: "We want an ethnographer, but we don't want you to give us a full ethnography!"

To be commissioned as "Ethnographers sans Ethnography" (as I titled a subsequent account of the experience [HFW 1984]) struck me as paradoxical. In the long run, I had to concede that those directing the evaluation had done some thoughtful problem solving of their own. By recruiting individuals who had previously conducted ethnographic inquiries in schools, they sought out researchers who were practiced in conducting classroom observation without succumbing to customary supervisory overtones. They were also sufficiently well informed about what ethnographers *ordinarily* do to realize that they would need to instill in these researchers—myself included—a tight problem-oriented focus. They did not want the treatises on school culture that we probably would have written (and might have preferred to write) had we been left to our own devices. By candidly informing us that they did *not* want ethnography, they were circumventing a problem conveyed in the title of a paper I recall hearing some years ago at a meeting of educational researchers, "Who Wants to Read a 600-page Ethnography?"

Continuing on, yes, it matters whether or not it's ethnography if you claim ethnography as an area of competence in your professional career and are prepared to take responsibility either for conducting research or for teaching others. With an academic appointment, you will probably to do both. Should you find yourself surrounded by colleagues for whom theory is central, clinging steadfastly to your ethnographic heritage may help you to explain—and may help explain you to others dubious about—the contribution to be made through your commitment to descriptive research.

And yes, it matters whether or not it's ethnography, and is clearly labeled as such (preferably in the title or subtitle), if you wish to call your work to the attention of other ethnographers and to be included in the ongoing dialogue about what ethnography is or how best to go about it, defend it, or teach it. Ethnographers need to be in touch with others actively engaged in such efforts and to situate themselves within those networks. Publishing in professional journals is one way to accomplish that, although establishing yourself that way may seem to take forever. In the interim, and along with doing your own writing for publication, I recommend that you search out opportunities to attend professional meetings with sessions devoted to ethnographic concerns and where you can begin your own networking.

Until you have something unique to contribute from your own research, don't hesitate to turn close attention to the work of those a few steps ahead of you in their ethnographic accomplishments. Study what they have done and be generous in your admiration. That may sound contrived, but most researchers work with scant recognition for their efforts. We can't help but savor the comments of people who read our studies; most of us are remarkably susceptible in this regard. After a professional lifetime of presenting formal papers or informal seminars and having people raise questions ostensibly about my work, or inform me about how interested they are in hearing what I have been up to, I have come to realize that the majority of one's seemingly laudatory listeners are really looking for an excuse to tell you what *they* are doing, or seeking your blessing for *their* research. Ethnographers, too, constitute a "community of practice," and you need not only to locate that community but, to borrow Jean Lave's phrase, to find your "way in" to it (Lave and Wenger 1991:72). Finding one's way in pretty well describes the whole fieldwork strategy. Don't become so preoccupied in your study of others that you fail to attend to your own need for a sense of community.

Yes, it matters whether or not it's ethnography if you intend to, or remotely think you might *possibly,* devote a major career effort to studying among a particular group of people (ballet dancers, the Kwakiutl), studying aspects of some human process amenable to ethnographic inquiry (cultural acquisition, cognition, kinship), or studying some fashionable conceptual scheme, past (acculturation, diffusion, national character, power and status), present (agency, entitlement, globalization, participation, violence and abuse, the distribution of power), or, with extraordinary luck or vision, future (ecological issues, human genetic technology, identity and identity work, or "your hunch here").

You will never go wrong building up, and building upon, a solid foundation of descriptive work. That foundation is most likely to be formed while you are entering or beginning a new phase of a professional career. Labeling your work as ethnographic serves public notice of what you do and by whom you wish to be judged. It also serves as a reminder for yourself of the need for the thorough descriptive base on which you later may develop longitudinal studies, more powerful interpretations, or a contribution to theory.

Ethnography also helps to mark territory, letting others know of your professional interest and establishing your claim on some group or problem, whether inadvertent or intentional. As noted, ethnographers have become more circumspect in such claims-making; they no longer make reference to groups of people as "theirs" in a manner suggestive of ownership or exclusive rights, although they may feel some proprietary interest in a group where they are engaging in long-term fieldwork. If today one is advised to soft-pedal these feelings, you may nonetheless appreciate that researchers have never been fond of tripping over each other in the field. I think the tacit message of the big fieldwork controversies (e.g., Freeman/Mead over Samoa; the earlier "debate" between Oscar Lewis and Robert Redfield over Tepoztlán; a more recent one between Gananath Obeyesekere and Marshall Sahlins over Captain Cook) is the longing to be left to do one's own thing and to be one's own critic, rather than become too engrossed in argument over territory or interpretation.

That longing is at once part of the appeal and yet a fatal drawback of ethnography, for whatever cannot be verified by others remains suspect. Thus the good news also becomes the bad: The lone ethnographer lives in his or her own little world. Regardless of whether or not your personal style is to keep your efforts largely to yourself, the people or problems that interest you will become part of the professional image others form of you. And you cannot simply be "an ethnographer," you must be an ethnographer *of* something. No matter how guarded you might prefer to be, sooner or later others will be nudging you about interests you may have believed (and perhaps hoped) were your exclusive domain.

Yes, it matters whether or not it's ethnography if you are a methodological purist and intend to model for others—your own students, especially—what you consider to be appropriate standards for conducting and reporting ethnographic research.

To get personal again: At one point in my career, I realized that I was spending too much time ranting and raving and fretting about the tendency of educational ethnography to feed on itself. Our citations were increasingly to each other's works, and we seemed to be losing sight of the characteristic cross-cultural perspective of the anthropologist. (Hmmm, maybe Doug Foley was right!) The alternative to further ranting was to conduct an inquiry well grounded in the traditional anthropological literature, thereby to model and demonstrate advantages of the approach. The outcome of that inquiry was *Teachers Versus Technocrats* (HFW 1977), an ethnographic account of an effort to develop and implement a highly structured management system adapted for schools. Although well intended on the part of its developers, the project seemed to pit instructionally oriented teachers against management-oriented administrators. In my analysis, I compared the social organization of educators to a traditional two-part moiety system as described in the anthropological literature. The book that resulted from that research is probably the least known of my studies (it was published and distributed through the University of Oregon's Research & Development Center rather than a commercial publisher, and it did not remain long in print). Nevertheless, I consider it my most purely anthropological accomplishment. It mattered to *me* that it was ethnography.

I have never hesitated to commend *Teachers Versus Technocrats* as a prototype. For students with a background in anthropology, the account demonstrates how an ethnographer can infuse a study conducted in a familiar contemporary setting with a traditional anthropological perspective. I have also brought the monograph to the attention of students who lacked a background in anthropological study yet were desirous of affixing the label "ethnography" to their work. My intent in those instances was to encourage them either to immerse themselves more deeply in the anthropological literature or to make a more suitable claim about the nature of their work (e.g., confidently labeling their work as a case study rather than seeing if they could get away with calling it ethnography). A researcher uncertain as to whether or not a study achieves an acceptable standard as ethnography can always refer to it by a more general label and hope that readers or reviewers will insist that it is something more. Series editors, publishers, and publishers' reviewers quoted on book jackets are great ones for commending studies as "ethnographies." Can you arrange to have them do your claims-making for you?

Yes, it matters whether or not it's ethnography, or, in this final example, whether or not you should be the one to label it as such, if you are intentionally setting out to test the limits of ethnography as presently practiced or to explore some potentially new facet of it. This is what others have done in the past in exploring such alternatives as life history, autoethnography, critical ethnography, ethnographic fiction, and ethnographic futures.[1] You can't be both judge and jury with such efforts, but you do need to put your ideas forth, to make clear what you are proposing, and to present your best case.

Reasons enough? Not an exhaustive list, but sufficient, I trust, to make the point that for certain circumstances, and to certain people, it *does* matter whether or not it's ethnography. Should you be inclined to insist that such arguments are "only academic," keep in mind that ethnography is essentially an academic enterprise and therefore is neither taken nor treated too cavalierly by other academicians. Be judicious in categorizing your own work. Select the labels under which you advance your studies with the same care you use in selecting the materials you incorporate into your descriptive account. If you are not sure whether your work will satisfy your critics as to its "ethnographicness," choose a label about which you feel more confident. Somewhere in your text you may want to make a brief explanation about your choice (and temptations) concerning how you decided upon an appropriate label. You can always refer to *following in the footsteps* of the early ethnographers, or report that you have adapted some basic fieldwork *techniques* in your work, without having to make a full but tenuous ethnographic claim.

Years ago I asked a colleague to read a draft of a paper I was preparing based on my study of the school principalship. I pressed him for an opinion as to whether the paper seemed adequately grounded in its anthropology. "What do you care whether or not the paper is 'anthropological'?" he queried. "What you really want is a good paper! Right?" He was both right and wrong. I did want to present a good study, and in that I seem to have succeeded, for the article, first published in 1974 (see HFW 1974b), has remained in print ever since (most recently in Creswell 1998). But I also wanted the study to be a good example of an *ethnographer* at work. It *did* matter to me whether I was achieving the quality of ethnographicness that I sought.

The underlying issue here has to do with the labeling of research accounts, not the curtailing of research efforts. I cannot truthfully claim that great harm has been done by applying the word "ethnography" too cavalierly to studies that might, with becoming modesty, have been labeled participant observation studies or case studies. Efforts to make ethnography user-friendly undoubtedly have helped bring about the remarkable acceptance of qualitative inquiry as a legitimate form of research in fields where previously nothing counted except counting itself. Nonetheless, one of the purposes of my writing here is to urge that the label be applied with care, even a bit more awe, to studies both "seen" and interpreted in a cultural context. When ethnography is merely another synonym for qualitative study, that special attention to context is likely to be sublimated to pressing concerns that look for explanations less complex.

I commend any effort to introduce or devote attention to contextual analysis—the stuff out of which ethnography is made—in any study, qualitative or quantitative. Toward that end, I encourage researchers to consider beginning every research project with an ethnographic reconnaissance (or ethnographic canvass) even if that is all the attention that ethnography is likely to receive, and even if the reconnaissance consists of little more than a windshield survey. Any nod in the direction of culture—the recognition of sociocultural context—is a step in the right direction, for it acknowledges that whatever has been observed and reported is, in turn, situated within some broader social system. A researcher who gives only scant attention to sociocultural influences in one study may be willing to give more attention in the next.

If ethnography is what you set out to do, and in spite of its challenge as "mission impossible" you are reasonably satisfied that is what you have accomplished, don't be bashful about saying so. While it is true that there is no ethnography without an ethnographer, keep in mind that neither must one *be* an ethnographer to do ethnography, any more than one must be a baker to bake a loaf of bread, a writer to write a book, or a painter to paint a house—or a canvas. It is the final product that must be assessed, not the credentials or the past accomplishments of the individual conducting the work. To be sure, one only *becomes* an ethnographer by doing ethnography, but not every career calls for or necessarily even recognizes ethnographic credentials. In some circles of hard-nosed quantifiers, the reverse may more nearly be the case: would-be ethnographers must feign admiration for quantification in spite of an intuitive attraction and talent for ethnographic work.

Can You Do Ethnography Without Embracing the Culture Concept?

In spite of my fervent endorsements of the culture concept throughout these pages, my response to the question above is a reluctant "Yes." Yes, you can do ethnography without directing any explicit attention to culture. Nor must you acknowledge in any way the role or historical importance of the culture concept for understanding the framework in which ethnographers traditionally have cast their studies. But that raises a question for me: Why would anyone who has no interest in the concept of culture want to insist on such a time-consuming, obsessively detailed, and contextually oriented approach when there are so many alternative—and quicker—ways to conduct research?

Perhaps a distinction is needed here between culture in its broadest sense, referring to sociocultural dimensions of behavior, and a narrower sense concerned strictly with the *term* culture. The culture concept is neither particularly nor uniquely American, but nowhere is culture given so central a role or argued so vigorously as in anthropology in the U.S. To insist, therefore, that the words "culture" or "cultural" must appear explicitly in order for a work to qualify as ethnography would be to ignore the anthropologies of other nations. Even within our own shores, researchers who equate ethnography strictly with method—a set of fieldwork techniques—feel no more obligation to attend to the culture concept than to any number of competing concepts that may guide or influence their interpretations. In my book—and thus, of course, in this book—that considerably constrains their basis for the ethnographic claim. But no matter how you try to pry ethnography loose from the study of culture, those of us who insist on their mutual interdependence stand ready to argue on behalf of the pervasiveness of culture in all human social behavior. For us, culture is as much part of the unseen scene as are the humans whom we do observe in interaction.

The potential for cultural interpretation is always there, though not always recognized. Allow me to share a case in which culture was explicitly excluded from an ethnographic inquiry, with no great harm done to the research, the researchers (myself included), or to ethnography.

An Assignment to "ThinkAbout"

Most of my own research has been involved with projects in which I had a major say as to outcomes, even when the parameters were set by others. That is not to say the projects simply "happened." All research is the result of some serendipitous combination of time, place, and station. Ethnographers are no more free to do as they please than are other colleagues in science or the arts.[2] My sense is that today's ethnographers feel far more constraint than I ever felt.

One factor contributing to that sense of constraint is the way government-sponsored research is funded. Today ethnographers negotiate their own contracts under highly competitive circumstances and myriad rules. By contrast, during the first decade after I completed my doctorate—roughly the mid-

1960s to the mid-1970s—research aimed at national health interests and at educational improvement was generously funded. Most funding went to institutions. Agenda-setting was essentially local, and research ideas were negotiated with colleagues down the hall rather than with project officers in Washington, D.C.

As one of a new breed of educational anthropologists proposing and conducting investigations at the time, my attention did have to be narrowed to topics related to schooling, education, and enculturation, but those expectations did not seem unreasonable. Concurrent teaching responsibilities also restricted any ongoing research forays to whatever could be studied close to home. These were realities of the workplace, and although they did little by way of expanding a broad cross-cultural perspective, I was able to set my own course, including not only the focus I would take but also the decision as to how the results would be reported.

What I describe below is a study in which my research assignment was indeed circumscribed by others. I was invited to participate, on a part-time basis, in a research project designed as a "summative evaluation." Summative evaluations, you recall, are conducted and reported independently of an ongoing project, as contrasted with formative evaluations designed to provide feedback while a project is underway. In this case, the assignment was to document the classroom use and initial impact of the first year in the introduction of an instructional television program called *ThinkAbout*. The intriguing, if somewhat startling, aspect of my assignment was that although the project directors specifically sought ethnographers to conduct classroom observations, they carefully stipulated that they did *not* want ethnography. They wanted the focus of the inquiry closely tied to the television series.

I admit to mixed feelings, relief coupled with panic, in agreeing to conduct some local "field observations" to be written up in case study fashion as my contribution to the project. My report was to be based on interviews and observations during the 1979–80 school year when the series was first telecast. My sense of relief arose from knowing I would not be responsible for producing another ethnography of schooling. By then I had published three such studies (HFW 1967, 1973, 1977), and I was all too aware of the time required for doing the fieldwork and writing, activities that now had to be sandwiched in among teaching and other faculty responsibilities. So ambitious a goal was obviously unrealistic for a project in which fieldwork was limited to part-time observations and a *final* report was due the following summer. Yet I also felt a sense of panic in being stripped of responsibility for writing about school culture. I found myself wondering just what I would look at, look for, and report on, as an ethnographer expressly prohibited from doing an ethnography.

I didn't have a suitable name for it then, but initially the situation seemed to call for what I have described here as ethnographic reconnaissance. That meant to have a look around to find out who was actually using instructional TV in classrooms, what information teachers had about the new series, and what they thought of it if they had watched any of the programs. In spite of the hype I had been hearing from everyone closely associated with the project, it was not easy to locate teachers using it or even to find teachers who knew anything about it. That posed my first task, to be accomplished pretty much by hearsay. Although the producers at the Agency for Instructional Television (today the Agency for Instructional Technology) had endeavored to get the word out to teachers everywhere, and there was enthusiastic support from the 38 consortium-member state (U.S.) and provincial (Canada) educational agencies that had sponsored the series, word had filtered down only slowly and unevenly to school districts, to schools, and to the target audience of fifth- and sixth-grade teachers. There was no way for word to filter back up as to who was using the program in classrooms except by word of mouth or by tracking teacher requests for a study guide available for the asking from the state and provincial agencies that had sponsored the project.

The agency that produced the program had contracted with an independent educational evaluation center for the follow-up study. The evaluation team split its efforts into two complementary studies. One facet was devoted to the proposed set of classroom observation studies; the other was addressed to the development and administration of a national survey that would include a mailed questionnaire and some before-and-after testing to assess program effects. Interesting to note that in one nearby school district where the program was used, that link to a "testing" program resulted in information about the new program channeled through school counselors. In a neighboring district where the program was *not* promoted, the announcement was channeled through the media specialist. The consequences of labeling, in one case emphasizing a *testing* program, in the other just another *television* program, provided a reminder of the importance of taking school culture into account, even if I was not expected, encouraged, or apparently even going to be allowed to produce a "culture of the schools" study.

By the time I was able to identify any local teachers reported to have expressed interest in having students view the program in the fall, most had stopped showing it. They voiced no complaints. They consistently applauded the high quality of the production and its lofty goal to help fifth and sixth graders "acquire and use skills necessary to become independent learners and problem-solvers." More than a decade later, I still remember the frequently repeated slogan put forward as the key strategy in problem solving (and a basic guide for any researcher): "What do I know? What do I need to know?" Even by early fall, however, teachers were feeling overloaded with things to do and, especially, with topics they were required to cover. Having pupils become independent learners through watching a 15-minute television program twice a week was not one of them.

Teacher views about any educational television program, this one or a host of others sometimes confused for it, seemed to correspond with their views about television in general, in or out of school. Proponents felt there was merit in, and something distinct about, *instructional* television. For detractors, "Television is television, period." There was no doubt in many minds that children already watched far too much of it.

Proponents stood their ground, any absence of supporting technology notwithstanding. Neither of the two classrooms in which I conducted observations during the next several weeks had a cable hookup; pupils watched the program on bulky old black-and-white TV sets with uneven rabbit-ear reception. In one case, the classroom in which pupils watched the program happened to be the only classroom in the entire school that did *not* have a cable hookup. In another school that I contacted by telephone, the media specialist polled teachers on my behalf to inquire whether anyone was watching the program and might be willing to meet with me or allow me to visit their classroom. She later reported that one teacher had explained that although she was not using the program this year she had "watched it last year and liked it very much." Recall that this was the first time the series was shown. I noted in my report, "Such unbridled enthusiasm may not be helpful, but it most certainly is instructive."

How wide a swath to cut in considering cultural context? The winter of 1979–80 saw a (contrived?) worldwide oil shortage, and topics of fuel and energy were on everyone's minds, including my own. The most consistent user of the program was a male sixth-grade teacher in a community 25 miles from my home. Although the project reimbursed me for mileage, my real concern was not the escalating price of gasoline but that there was little gasoline to be had. Gas stations opened and closed sporadically, and some neighborhood stations (in a day when there seemed to be gas stations at every major intersection) restricted sales to known customers on an appointment-only basis. Quite indirectly, my preoccupation that winter with the oil crisis and issues of energy conservation provided a perspective for thinking about teacher use of instructional TV. During the course of my observations, the crisis also had a *direct* effect on the viewing practices of the teacher in my small sample who stayed with the series the longest.

The program was telecast on the local public broadcasting channel twice a day, two days a week, a late-morning showing repeated at 1:30 P.M. the same afternoon. Since my reason for visiting his or any classroom was related solely to the implementation of the TV program, I initially arranged to arrive no more than half an hour before the program aired. Afterward I remained only long enough to observe any related follow-up activity or discussion and perhaps speak briefly with the teacher during a short afternoon recess that followed.

Although each visit to that school took about three hours, including driving time, the ethnographer in me was not satisfied catching so brief a glimpse of the school day. Eventually I asked the teacher if I might spend an entire day or two in class. He did not seem the least bit bothered by my presence; in fact, whenever I was there he usually asked me to assist by helping pupils individually with problems, listening to them read, or reading a story aloud to the entire class first thing after lunch. (One of his choices was the same story I had read aloud when I taught sixth grade 22 years earlier!) I was introduced to the pupils as someone doing research about the television program. They assigned me the nickname "Harry, the TV Guy," but they remained unconvinced that I could really be "doing research" simply by watching the program with them. They reasoned that I must be a TV producer with a major role in making programs like this one. They made a point of insuring that I had correctly recorded each of their names, should I need pupil-actors for my next production.

From my own days as a classroom teacher in the mid-1950s I well remembered the feeling of exhaustion at the end of a school day spent with 11- and 12-year-olds. I was sympathetic to the teacher's laments when he seemed to run out of steam in the afternoon. He was candid in his personal assessment of the problem, noting on one occasion immediately after lunch, facing almost three hours yet to go before the final dismissal,

> Now comes the part of the day I don't like. The afternoon drags on, and I'm tired. And by evening I am too tired to do a lot of preparation.

Arriving one morning before school began in order to get a sense of how the TV program fit into the full round of classroom activity, I found a far stricter, more businesslike atmosphere than what I had become accustomed to during my afternoon visits. That helped me understand a contrast the teacher made between what he called "the morning program" and "the afternoon program."

> If this series came only in the morning, I probably wouldn't use it. There's just so much under language arts and math that you have to cover—passing district objectives, all the things you want to cover that the kids will be tested on—that you don't want to give up the morning as much as you would in the afternoon.

The morning program was highly structured, devoted entirely to the three R's. The afternoon was given over to "fun" subjects or subjects the teacher himself valued less highly: social studies ("so-so studies," as one academically oriented pupil mumbled under her breath and intended for my hearing), science, health, art, music, games, library.

> It's a lot easier to give and take in the afternoon. If kids miss a lesson in social studies or science, it's not going to hurt them at all. Whereas, if they don't get their math one day, I almost always have to be sure they get it later.

By lunchtime, he had virtually exhausted his teaching energy for the day, and exhausted himself as well. While the outside world was experiencing its energy crisis, I had happened upon a teacher with an energy crisis all his own. Teaching demands energy, a fact well recognized within the teaching ranks; here was a teacher willing to talk candidly about how *very* tired he became during the course of the teaching day. By regional standards this school district had an exceptionally long day for pupils in the intermediate grades. School began at 8:30 A.M. and ended at 3:30 P.M., with a 40-minute period for lunch. The new television series offered a partial amelioration of one teacher's personal energy crisis. As he stated flatly one day, "The program provided 15 minutes twice a week that I didn't have to plan or teach."

And how does a world oil shortage affect the classroom television viewing of one teacher in a small town in western Oregon? That particular year, in that particular classroom, in that particular school district, it affected it just this way: For years, the teachers of grades four, five, and six had been pleading with the school superintendent and school board for a shorter school day. Their argument was not only that the instructional day was unnecessarily long but that the schedule unfairly deprived them of preparation time regularly scheduled for teachers at every other grade.[3]

Pleas to reduce the length of the school day for intermediate-grade pupils had always fallen on deaf ears. Now, unexpectedly, the combined threat of a continued fuel scarcity and the realization that fuel costs had risen 25 percent since the beginning of the school year gave school-board members a different (and more easily defended) basis for reversing a staunchly held position that might otherwise have been perceived as "caving in" to teacher demands. The board approved a plan to dramatically reduce the cost of operating its fleet of buses serving 11 widely scattered elementary schools by sending *all* elementary school children home at the same time. Prior to that, the buses had doubled back after taking primary-grade children home at 2:30 P.M. to run the same routes for intermediate-grade children dismissed one hour later.[4] The world's energy crisis inadvertently provided relief for an "instructional-energy" crisis about which the intermediate-grade teachers had been complaining for years.

The first thing to be eliminated was the brief afternoon recess; a break was no longer needed for a session shortened from three hours to two. Neither was the respite offered by watching a 15-minute television program twice a week. With classroom instruction time reduced by 45 minutes each day, television viewing now had the effect of crowding the afternoon schedule, prompting a quick review of the time it consumed, the instructional benefits it appeared to offer, and whether additional time could be devoted to suggested discussion topics or follow-up activities.

Suddenly a number of rather incidental reasons could be mustered in further support of dropping it. In spite of the intent of producers to make the series an integral part of the instructional program, teachers uniformly perceived it as interesting but strictly enrichment—if not outright entertainment. In spite of a carefully designed set of program objectives organized into clusters, there had been mix-ups when programs were repeated or shown out of sequence. Teachers had come to feel they could never be certain which program was actually going to be presented on any given day. Some programs had to be missed during December while the entire school worked on a Christmas program. Furthermore, the novelty of the plots had begun to wear thin as problem-solving challenges like "finding patterns" gave way to topics like "collecting information" that dramatized little more than after-school trips to the library.

After the bus schedule change, the only programs the class saw were shown out of the teacher's consideration for my research. I always checked in advance by telephone before making my visits, and the teacher's responses came to be predictably the same, "We haven't been watching it regularly, but I was thinking about showing it today." (Translation: "We haven't watched a program since you were last here, but I can work it in if you need it for your research.")

The ethnographer in me was concerned that my brief afternoon visits focused too exclusively on the television program itself and therefore gave undue emphasis to its prominence in the broader spectrum of classroom events. During some of those visits, as the scheduled time for the telecast approached, I recall becoming a bit antsy if the teacher had not dispatched student monitors to hunt down the cumbersome TV cart in some other classroom and get it set up—and to get such a vintage TV set sufficiently *warmed up*—in time for the program's opening. Neither the teacher nor the pupils seemed as focused as I was on that aspect of the school day. I rather suspected that where they watched *from,* and who they watched *with,* loomed more important to the children than whatever problem was about to be teased out and solved by the young actors on-screen. In spite of the great height of the television set perched atop the cart, the pupils were allowed to leave their assigned desks and to sit or lie on a carpet in the center of the classroom to watch the program. In some writing I asked the children to do comparing TV watching at home and at school, one boy wrote, "At home I watch television with my mom and dad. At school I watch television with Steve and Tom. Well, the whole class watches." And another wrote, "At home I watch television because I like to and there's nothing else to do. At school I watch television because we have to."

The opportunity for me to be back in the classroom afforded some other observations that I slipped into my report. It was apparent to me as never before, in every classroom I visited, that in spite of the careful efforts that had gone into preparing the series and the teacher materials to accompany it, *the teacher is the curriculum.* Other than the priority different subjects receive in the daily schedule, the teacher's command of the instructional program may be less obvious for subjects like arithmetic, more pronounced for subjects like social studies and the arts. But whatever the case, the teacher calls the shots. That was especially evident for connections made between the classroom instructional program and the TV program. To illustrate: Ignoring the questions suggested in the teacher's guide for a follow-up discussion of a program concerning the *reliability of sources of information,* the case study teacher gave an impromptu written assignment about the *sequence of events* in the story just presented. His brief explanation: "I needed a break."

At a different school, another teacher informed me prior to the broadcast that she intended to discuss the questions suggested in the study guide. The moment the TV set was turned off, however, she announced instead, "We're not going to discuss it. That's all." And they didn't discuss it, and that was all. Another teacher who used the program during its morning telecast had no class time for follow-up discussion because her pupils went immediately to the cafeteria for lunch. "The program is so good that it doesn't need further discussion," she explained. (That was probably the kind of testimonial the producers hoped we would gather, but not for reasons so incidental to their instructional objectives.)

In spite of having been involved with issues of "directed change" in the schools for years, I became aware of another facet of the change process as this study progressed: Early adopters of anything—even something as straightforward as watching a new series produced for instructional TV—are likely to be early adopters of the next comparable thing to come along, and the next, and the next. Educational researchers, like agricultural extension workers in previous decades, study innovations one at a time: Research on adoption is linked to particular innovations, not to the innovation *process.* It had not occurred to me that the early adopters of one innovation are the most likely to be the early adopters of the next, that early adopting is itself a form of patterned behavior. I was astounded to realize that by the end of the year *everyone* who earlier had expressed interest in the new instructional TV program was talking about some other new instructional TV program instead. Even the faithful teacher-user of my case study was far more enthusiastic about a new program he thought he might try next. However, he was quick to reassure me that because he was now familiar with *ThinkAbout* he would "probably" see if he could request videotapes of certain "shows" (his term) that he felt were especially provocative. I wondered if he, too, thought I had a hand in producing these materials and might make him a star of instructional TV? (I also wondered if he would be able to secure videotapes from the local or county instructional materials centers. Directors of those centers were in a quandary about whether they could, should, or by law were prohibited from taping the program for future use in their schools. At the school district level, instructional benefit was totally overshadowed by concern about litigative risk.) ·

I completed my report the following summer as contracted. It was 117 pages typed, double-spaced. It was graciously received by the contracting agency and forwarded exactly as submitted, along with the reports from two other classroom observers and the independent results of the national survey. Each piece constituted one volume of the final report. I assume the reports were reviewed by people required to read them as a function of their position, but the director of research who originally commissioned the studies on behalf of the agency later confessed to difficulties in getting his associates to read such "long" reports. I do not know whether the reports were distributed out-side the agency. I cannot imagine that the producers were particularly taken with parallels I drew between teacher energy and the oil crisis, but those parallels struck me as important contextual dimensions of this study and a superb illustration of the complexity of change.

The emphasis we three "classroom ethnographers" put on context and our matter-of-fact reporting did not provide the sort of testimonial the producers had hoped to receive. But neither were we faulted for having to capture something that we did not—and realistically could not—observe. In that regard, we were on yet another mission impossible. As another of the ethnographers candidly wrote in one of her field reports:

> I have never observed a child act perplexed, strive to understand a "cluster"
> of programs or the series as a whole, or apply one of its skills in a new con-
> text. [Sylvia Hart-Landsberg, Field Report, February 6, 1980]

I liked the reports we submitted. In my case, I endeavored to slip in plenty of cultural context (without, of course, ever using the term "culture"). I also offered the sponsors the benefit of what was at the time fast approaching 30 years' experience as an educator and ethnographer. I hoped that my report would offer ample evidence of how ethnography can contribute to understanding the processes of schooling. Further, although I did not expect anyone to recognize it, I felt that the report demonstrated how an ethnographer can work in a familiar setting, yet maintain an anthropological perspective, if not exactly making the familiar strange, at least making things appear strange enough to be recognized and reported.

Alas, our efforts went the way of most reports and commissioned studies, filed away in fulfillment of contractual obligations. In a chapter I later prepared for David Fetterman's edited collection, *Ethnography in Educational Evaluation* (Fetterman 1984), I was able to capture the essence of the study and to tie it in with the broader issue of ethnography as an *alternative* to educator preoccupation with evaluation. I was tempted to reproduce the report here in its entirety, either in this chapter or as an appendix. I received the gracious permission of the Agency for Instructional Technology to do just that. I was also informed that when the Agency moved to larger premises in 1994 only one copy of all research reports was kept. That was 12 years after they had been submitted; I probably should have been pleased that any record at all had been preserved.

The New Ethnographer[5]

Even today, whenever I think of ethnographers in action, I am inclined to think of someone pulling a canoe up onto a beach while curious inhabitants peek out of village huts. I do not think of myself driving 25 miles on the interstate, one eye on the freeway, the other on the fuel gauge, to "record what happens" two times a week when a classroom teacher turns on a 15-minute television program. If ethnography is to play a role in your career, you, too, probably opt for the canoe version over the freeway one. To be realistic, if you work in a professional field in which ethnography has, or may someday come to have, a contribution to make as a complement to more traditional research approaches, the freeway (or subway; see Passaro 1997) version is probably closer to what you will find yourself doing. Your own good sense will have to guide you as to just how "ethnographic" to be in what you report, just how heavily cultural or contextual to make your interpretations.

Ethnography was not compromised in our classroom study of instructional TV. It made good sense to invite experienced ethnographers to conduct the observations. As the head of the evaluation team originally explained to me, "We want a case study, limited in setting, time, actors, and to selected issues, but still open-ended to add new insights." I did hope that our reports might serve as "models" of ethnography in action. On that score, I guess I'm still waiting for someone to tell us that we did a great job that shows what ethnographers can contribute and what insights can be gained through a cultural perspective, even when expressly requested *not* to do a "full ethnography."

We *did* do a great job, even in the absence of tumultuous applause. There's no reason for not giving one's best to such assignments; we all pass this way only once. Apparently those of us who produced the case studies did achieve something in the way of a new level of objective reporting, for the director of research wrote the three of us a lighthearted appreciation that described us as "uncommitted, unfamiliar, and, in fact, completely uninterested in the use of television in the classroom." Yet he also expressed personal appreciation for (unspecified) insights he felt he gleaned from our accounts. In spite of chiding us for failing to see "how the technology and the curriculum in this project might have a use in the classroom," he wondered if we had been "too kind." He wished we had in some ways (also unspecified) been more critical (reported in HFW 1984:209).

I trust I have presented this case in sufficient detail to illustrate some of the dilemmas of a new era in ethnography when those with a stake in the results (the developers of instructional television, in this instance) have the resources and power to tell ethnographers what they want them to do and have little to suffer if they don't like the results. I tried to offer food for thought in my report. I called attention to the importance of contextual dimensions both within and beyond the producer's control. I had to turn a blind side to the fact that producers of instructional television are not likely to be any more receptive to a report that suggests how *little* an impact they may be having than forestry officials might be to an ethnographer's report on how *great* the potential impact of some proposed development might be on traditional tribal properties and practices. Today's new ethnographer can wonder who now calls the shots.

In response to the request for suggestions or recommendations for producers of instructional TV, I pointed again to the (perhaps, to them, seemingly irrelevant) issue of teacher energy. I suggested that they pay more attention to teachers who *do* adopt such materials, rather than strive to produce materials so good that everybody will want to use them. If teacher-adopters of instructional television tend to be people on the lookout for a boost for themselves or their instructional program, then attending specifically to who those teachers are, and what kind of help they seek, might provide a better focus for efforts at program development.

Together with staff of the evaluation center, we ethnographic "hired hands" had two productive meetings, an intense planning meeting held before and a work session held midway during the observation period. I felt that a further opportunity was lost when no subsequent effort was made to bring ethnographers and producers together after the reports were completed. It would have been satisfying both to give and to receive feedback, as well as to be able to elaborate upon our observations and reflections. Looking back, I wonder whether we had any real audience at all, especially when the sponsors realized that we had neither produced testimonials nor documented any instances of problem-solving behavior. Were we simply part of an evaluation ritual? Such a thought has crossed the mind of more than one ethnographer in recent years.

And as far as getting feedback about one's work as an ethnographer, it occurs to me that no one has ever told me *exactly* what any ethnographer would most like to hear, that in at least one of my studies I have (finally?) gotten it right. No one possibly could. There is no way any other person could ever judge precisely how well I understood what I was up to, how adequate or accurate was my description, how perceptive the interpretation, how discreet my discretion.

For this project, on which I was hired as a part-time "ethnographer sans ethnography," I simply took the money and ran. The work was well paid at the time, and I rejoice at opportunities to be paid to do something I like to do anyway, in this instance looking into processes of teaching and learning that have always fascinated me. Somehow, though, that seems to have more to do with leading the ethnographic life than with doing ethnography. That will be the subject for the final chapter. Before turning to that topic, I want to take a culminating look at the "doing" of ethnographic research and at my effort in these pages to distill its essence. As by now you may have come to suspect, that calls for introducing another analogy.

Notes

1. Recall from the discussion in Chapter 6 that this is what Bernard and Salinas did by titling, and thus boldly proclaiming, their study *Native Ethnography* (1989). I made a similar claim for *The Man in the Principal's Office* by subtitling it *An Ethnography* (HFW 1973).

2. Some similarities between support for fieldwork and support for the arts is discussed in HFW 1995, drawing especially on Howard Becker's *Art Worlds* (1982).

3. The primary grades were dismissed one hour earlier. Teachers of grade seven and above all had a "prep" period built into their daily schedule.

4. The school district extended throughout a huge rural area said to be about one-seventh the size of the state of Rhode Island.

5. In an essay, "Ethnography Reconstructed," that introduces the revised (1996) edition of *The Professional Stranger,* Michael Agar writes in specific terms of a "new ethnography" in which narrative approaches are replacing an earlier tradition he describes as "encyclopedic ethnography" (see also Tedlock 2000). For discussion he singles out as exemplary Dorinne Kondo's *Crafting Selves* (1990). My use of the phrase "new ethnography" here is more sweeping, intended to include anyone finding a "way in" to ethnography today.

CHAPTER TEN

Ethnography as a Piece of Cake

What we should do is make ethnography relevant and accessible. There is much ethnography to be done, and there are so many untrained enthusiastic people ready to do it.

—Sidney Mintz, Invited address
American Anthropological Association, November 1996

One of several people invited to critique the first draft of this book reacted to the way I seemed to be putting ethnography just out of reach of the audience most likely to want to learn about it. His estimate of the support for my case on behalf of ethnographic "purity" was limited to "about 30 ethnographers, worldwide," and he doubted that any of them really needed my approval for what they were already doing. Unfortunately, that reviewer happened not only to be an anthropologist but also my editor and publisher, Mitch Allen. His concerns sent me back to the drawing board.

It had not been my intent to tantalize readers by telling them about ethnography, only to insist that few people—certainly more than "30, worldwide" but admittedly some limited number, all well schooled in cultural anthropology—were capable of producing the real thing. That was neither what I had set out to do nor what I thought I had accomplished in that writing. However, if that is what my earliest readers saw, then I had somehow gone off track in spite of any good intentions.

In the course of editing and revising, I gave more emphasis not only to examining ethnography as it seems to be evolving but also to providing direction—and occasionally advice—for anyone considering adopting (or adapting) it as a research strategy. If you have been reading with that possibility in mind, I hope you feel both encouraged and better informed. If your initial ethnographic forays entail little more than selecting among a wider array of fieldwork techniques or doing some ethnographic reconnaissance, that is a beginning. But I trust you have heard my message: Although there is no substitute for fieldwork carefully done and carefully reported, ethnography encompasses more than fieldwork. That important "more" entails not only what *follows* from fieldwork. Ethnography *begins* with a researcher's ability to frame an appropriate question or to recognize what contribution ethnography can make toward understanding some larger issue. Ethnography begins with intent (see also HFW 1987b).

If my early draft tended to situate ethnography out of bounds, I began to wonder whether, in revising to make it more user-friendly, I had gone too far and made it seem a piece of cake, something too easily accomplished. Perhaps there is no harm done if I have. Today the label "ethnography" can be found on descriptive studies of many kinds. If I can encourage researchers already anxious to appropriate the *label* to become equally anxious about how to make their studies more ethnographic, not only through their ways of *looking* but also through their ways of *seeing,* so much the better.

In an earlier day, "naturalistic" approaches tended to be devalued against the contribution of the laboratory scientists. Ethnography has played a role in helping the more descriptively oriented approaches to gain recognition as legitimate. That interest in studying living things in their natural habitat may explain the curious association between natural history and ethnography. A reminder of that close association is the fact that many museums of natural history feature a hall of ethnography in recognition of their broad charter to study all objects in nature, humans included. Those museums are one of the few places in which, under the formal title of curator, an individual can claim full-time employment as an ethnographer or ethnologist. For example, although she lectured at institutions all over the world, Margaret Mead's permanent position was Curator of Ethnology at the American Museum of Natural History, a post she held from 1926 to 1969, when she became Curator Emeritus. Holding such a position does not necessarily guarantee opportunity for continued fieldwork; as in most things, Mead was exceptional in this regard.

Today ethnography is regarded as one among a number of approaches variously labeled as naturalistic, descriptive, or qualitative. I trust I have given adequate attention to pointing out features these approaches share in common, particularly in their fieldwork techniques. But even as I worked over the manuscript to insure that ethnography was presented as both understood and accessible, I reaffirmed my original commitment to tease out and thus help to preserve the qualities that make it unique. From the outset, I have been in search of those critical attributes, that "essence." My expectation from the day I began writing was that with each succeeding chapter my list of criteria would become more elegant and more definitive. You saw evidence of that in the conclusion of Chapter 4, "Ethnography as a Way of Seeing," as I began to inventory some of ethnography's seemingly essential elements: holistic, cross-cultural and comparative, long-term, based on firsthand experience, undertaken with explicit intent, and so forth. From that point, however, my explorations into ever-widening circles of ethnographic practice began to reveal exceptions to and adaptations of my evolving criteria rather than to reaffirm them. My dilemma was as old as ethnography itself: whether to describe things as they are, or to filter them through the eyes of those with strong feelings about how they should be—those "30 ethnographers, worldwide"—perhaps even narrowing the portrayal to how I personally feel things ought to be.

My tentative criteria never seemed able simultaneously to capture that elusive essence and yet accommodate the range of accounts that are satisfyingly "ethnographic." One especially elusive quality was "strangeness." In an earlier day, ethnography *was* the study of The Other. Ethnographers still study The Other (or, as many prefer to represent themselves today, study *with* The Other). Insisting on otherness as a critical attribute, however, is confounded by research in which we study not only Ourselves—social groups with which we may not only be familiar but may hold membership— but even Ourself, both as we experience ethnography and as we experience life. I don't feel I must (or could possibly) account for how ethnography evolved from a tradition intent on objective scientific study of The Other to accommodate a passionate reflexivity in revealing something about ourselves. But I did feel I should be able to identify a set of elements common to the full range of practice that would capture this elusive quality of ethnographicness.

Unless I wanted to pretend that I had become the standard setter for ethnography, establishing and defending a set of rigorous criteria of my own invention, I realized that my task did seem too narrowly conceived for the realities of ethnography as it is evolving. Simply put, there are many features *ordinarily* associated with it, yet no single one asserts itself as absolutely essential. Even the obvious ones had their exceptions: not *every* ethnography met *all* the customary criteria. Sometimes there was not even a "there" where an ethnographer could be situated, so the seemingly inviolable prerequisite that the researcher be physically present proved not to be inviolable after all. For every customary expectation there seemed to be notable exceptions as well.

Had I been trying to make things too neat, running the risk of rendering ethnography sterile by reducing it to a rigid formula or standard recipe? On reflection, I realized that even recipes can be changed, ingredients substituted, depending on purposes, skill, and available materials. Perhaps I needed a fresh perspective rather than such grim determination to isolate the essence of a process and product so resistant to rigid specification. In the process of revising, I began searching for another analogy. The analogy would have to be to something that, like ethnography, is made out of rather ordinary ingredients, has customary features by which it is generally recognized, and yet is dependent on no single ingredient and, *in every instance,* takes its unique shape and form at the hands of the individual who crafts it.

Analogy to the Rescue, One More Time

Now the catch: It is the analogy, rather than ethnography, that is the "piece of cake" promised by my chapter title. And the analogy is not strictly to cake, but to the process of bread making. Nevertheless, if the analogy helps to foster the idea that ethnography is not only doable but something you can and might do—and in that sense a "piece of cake"—so much the better. The discussion in the previous chapters was intended to make ethnography more understandable and better understood, something within reach of any researcher willing patiently to explore its possibilities. In this culminating chapter on ethnographic *process* (in the final chapter I discuss more personal dimensions) attention is drawn to the broad question of what goes into the making of ethnography. What must be present, what can be left out, among the many features (ingredients) ordinarily associated with it?

"Yet another analogy?" you might wonder. Already in these pages ethnography has been likened to designing a house and to ripples on a pond, and now I am about to compare it with the making of bread? Well, surely you recognize that I find analogy an extremely useful tool. I do not hesitate to draw analogies and then push them to their limits. Be patient as I risk doing that here: the analogy between making bread and doing ethnography invites a host of comparisons.

Perhaps this is a place to put in a word on behalf of the service that analogy renders more generally. Analogy offers a way to achieve ethnography's characteristic comparative dimension, especially for the researcher working in familiar territory. The task of the early ethnographers was to *make the strange familiar.* For the more traditionally oriented ethnographer, that will always be the task. As ethnographers began conducting studies closer to home, however, and still others began appropriating ethnographic techniques for study among groups in which they held membership, the strategy often had to be reversed. It became necessary to *make the familiar strange.*

The comparative dimension assured by the "strangeness" of those among whom the early ethnographers conducted their inquiries can be met in other ways. Analogy is one of them. Analogy invites comparison by looking for similarities and differences that help us see something familiar—perhaps too familiar—in a different way or from a fresh perspective.

Case in point: I feel I can make both a better and a clearer explanation here by suggesting comparisons between making bread and doing ethnography than were I to compare ethnography with, say, ethnomethodology or investigative journalism, two closely related approaches in qualitative inquiry. I am not concerned that you will come away with the idea that ethnography *is* a loaf of bread (or, except figuratively, a piece of cake). But drawing an analogy between making bread and doing ethnography suggests comparisons that help me explain why ethnography itself is difficult to explain. For here are two products made from widely varied but nonetheless readily available ingredients in which the selection and combination of them is subject to a range of practices, the final result more a consequence of what is done with them than with the ingredients themselves.

Essential Ingredients and Ethnography

Cake, technically defined as "a sweet, baked, breadlike food, made with or without shortening" (*Random House Unabridged Dictionary,* 2nd ed.), would have served adequately as analogy. But by drawing an analogy to bread rather than to cake, I am able to relegate one more customary and rather ordinary ingredient—the sweetener in this case—to the not-absolutely-essential category. Of course, breads *usually* contain a sweetener, just as they *usually* contain a number of other quite ordinary ingredients. The important thing is that *not a single one of the usual or customary ingredients we associate with bread making is absolutely essential.* There is no single ingredient common to all the world's breads. And that, of course, underscores the point of the analogy, for neither is there any single essential ingredient common to all the world's ethnographies. *Most* of the features of ethnography reviewed in these pages are present *most* of the time. But it is what is done with them that produces the desired result.

Toward producing something that can pass—as bread in one case, as ethnography in the other—there are numerous ways to get the process started, numerous ingredients from which to choose, and an almost endless variety of final shapes, sizes, tastes, and textures. For bread making, the basic essentials call only for something in each of two broad categories: There must be a grain of some kind, and there must be a liquid of some kind. It is as simple as that!

Ask most Americans about the basic steps in bread making and you will probably be told, "First you start with the yeast." That priority is awarded not because yeast is essential, which it is only if you intend to make a yeast-risen bread, but because the yeast can begin activating while one continues with

other preparations. Wheat is also essential for yeast-risen bread. Sugar acti-
vates the yeast, so it is important. Salt appears in virtually every recipe. Yet
no one of these items *customarily* included is absolutely essential, not yeast, not
sugar, not salt, not even wheat itself. All that is necessary is some form of flour
ground from seed, and some form of liquid. Yes, the flour is *usually* ground
from a grass seed, but technically (i.e., botanically) even that seeming essential has exceptions, since buckwheat and quinoa, starchy seeds as far as the
baker is concerned, are not members of the grass family.

While pondering whether an analogy might help in examining and
explaining an ethnographic essence that had become so exasperatingly elusive,
I happened to visit our local county fair. Ours is a community that still recognizes its agrarian roots, at least for a few days of celebration every August. As
I passed rows and rows of home-baked breads submitted in the foods and can-
ning division, the thought occurred that here might be my answer, comparing
what goes into the making of bread with the making of ethnography.

I confess some initial surprise at the variety of breads entered for judging.
I jotted down the labels assigned to them, some rather specific—banana,
banana nut, French, corn, zucchini, cranberry, sour cream raisin, yeast, and
fruit breads, plus gingerbread or cinnamon rolls—others identified only as
white, dark-but-less-than-100-percent whole wheat, 100 percent whole wheat,
fruit, rye, sourdough, along with several varieties of rolls, and still other categories loosely classified only as yeast breads. Reflecting more globally, perhaps
I should have been surprised at so *narrow* a range of entries or official categories: how similar the shapes of the loaves or selection of grains. But county
fairs are parochial affairs, and our local competitors are guided by an exhibitor's
handbook that provides a category for "foreign and holiday" breads almost as
afterthought. Nonetheless, if the display wasn't expansive, the potential of the
analogy was, for I realized that in bread making a distinction can be made
between what is *essential* and what is *customary*. A further distinction in bread
making sets the customary apart from any number of *optional* ingredients
sometimes referred to as "improvers." The use of improvers was evident among
entries at the fair; I could not help wondering whether unusually warm summer days had something to do with the many banana bread entries.

The absolute essentials in bread making offer no hint of the array of
ingredients that can be used, locally or anywhere. But flour and a liquid are
sufficient. As noted, not even yeast is essential. Kept in a warm place, a mixture of flour and water will, in time, become somewhat acidic (thus, a "sour"
dough) due to the action of ubiquitous bacteria. Of course, in bread making
as we usually practice it, the leavening process is both underwritten and has-
tened with a rising agent such as yeast, baking powder, or sour milk and soda.

And most recipes call for some form of sugar, for salt, and for fat, lard, or butter. For purposes of the analogy, however, it is important to recognize that there are recipes that specifically *exclude* one or more of these ingredients. Along with the range of possible variations are a host of possible substitutions as well. For example, the home baker can substitute a mixture of cream of tartar, bicarbonate of soda, and salt for baking powder itself. Hmmm, I wondered: How widespread is a comparable practice of making substitutions among ethnographers and ethnographic filmmakers when they discover, all too late, that they do not have at hand the transcripts, rich detail, or film record called for and must make do with whatever is available?

Take a closer look at the two essential categories of ingredients. First, there must be some kind of starchy seed. Second, a liquid must be added that allows the grain to soften and form into a resilient mass. In the analogy, I see the grain as comparable to the raw material an ethnographer gathers. To make this (coarse? dry?) material workable, something comparable to the liquid necessary for forming dough must be added, so that tiny bits of data can be worked into a cohesive whole. The ethnographer must also decide whether and how much of a rising agent to add, and for the same reason that the baker does, to contribute the life (or "soul") that causes a freshly made dough to "come alive" rather than remain flat. (Woe be unto ethnographers who think their material will come alive without further help, or who fail to recognize how the judicious use of seasoning or improvers can augment their efforts.)

Sugar in some form (including molasses, honey, barley malt syrup, or maple syrup) and salt add flavor and help control the action of the yeast as the dough alternately rises and falls. At this "deflating" stage in bread making, the material must be worked over (punched down) or the end product will have big holes in it, a phenomenon not unknown in ethnographic interpretation as well. And there are "quick breads"—biscuits, corn pone, muffins, scones—that do not require the time-consuming process of traditional bread making. Faced with a comparable problem in the time-consuming process involved in traditional ethnography, today's harried researchers also look for ways to turn out something produced more hastily.

Guided by a clear sense of purpose, the baker makes appropriate selections as to types and amount among the grains available, something like the fieldworker who must sort through the total "harvest" of data and decide what to use, what to set aside for another day, and what to discard. From one researcher to the next there is variation both in the quality and quantity of what might be collected and the manner and extent to which it requires further processing, not only to sort out the chaff but to have material refined in terms of preferences and purposes. This can vary from unsorted impressions, to headnotes, to scratch notes, to journal notes, to formally recorded field-notes, to carefully indexed archival material. Like bakers catering to different markets, one fieldworker may prefer data refined so as to yield something equivalent to the kernel containing the bran, germ, and endosperm. Another may insist on more-refined data, comparable to the baker who uses only the pure endosperm of refined white flour. Others may insist on keeping their data as near the natural state as possible, like the baker whose hearty loaves are made from stone-ground whole wheat, oats, buckwheat, or triticale.

As with the wide variety of grains and the ways they can be refined, there is no end to what can be collected and subsequently processed as data. One can go in search of data (or grains) of a familiar type, selected with a specific end product in mind, or one can gather whatever is available locally and see what can be made of it. The early ethnographers worked in the latter style; they sought remote locales in search of the strange, which they then rendered familiar through what they added and how they worked with it. The basic ingredients in their ethnographies may have been exotic; the form in which they rendered them was not.

The act of making bread does not implicate any particular grain, any particular combination of grains, or how polished the grain must be. The act of ethnography-making does not implicate what constitutes a suitable grain (i.e., kernel of "truth"). Yet the analogy helps to emphasize that simply gathering facts is necessary but not sufficient to accomplish ethnography, any more than simply collecting grains or obtaining flour guarantees production of an acceptable loaf of bread. As with baking, it is in what is selected, what is added, and how the forming mass is worked that the raw ingredients form something new and whole out of what begins as nothing more than a collection of tiny seeds. And it is in the process of bringing together and refining myriad empirical observations that ethnographers realize their potential to craft something new and whole. Perhaps it is understandable why today's ethnographers sometimes devote such attention to making the *form* seem exotic when working with material otherwise so familiar.

For ethnography, I suggest that some one or a combination of many different conceptions of "culture," like some one or a combination of many liquids from which the baker may choose, serves as the bonding agent that allows disparate bits of data to be formed into a cohesive whole. Researchers of other persuasions work up their data in comparable fashion, but they rely on other concepts to provide unity and thereby achieve somewhat different results. Symbolic interactionists, investigative journalists, folklorists, and ethnomethodologists each have their preferred concepts for rendering rather similar raw materials to achieve particular outcomes. They have characteristic ways of handling and shaping what they create, and existing markets ready to sample—and all too eager to critique—the results.

Different as their final products may seem—in their own eyes, if not always to outsiders—the basic data with which ethnographers and their allies in other qualitative endeavors work is pretty ordinary and pretty much the same. The variation extant in the finished products is not inherent in the data themselves, any more than bread is the inevitable or only possible product from a measure of grain. Variation derives not from rigid specifications as to ingredients but in how, at the hands of the ethnographer, folklorist, symbolic interactionist, and so forth, such common ingredients can be combined, worked over, and given shape to achieve results sufficiently different to be recognized for what they are intended to be, and even to be judged as more and less satisfactory, like entries at a county fair.

When Paul Bohannan observes, "Without an ethnographer, there is no ethnography" (1995:157), he writes about *intent,* not about role. One can make the same observation about making bread. Bread does not "happen" unless someone is intent on making it, but one need not be a baker to make a proper loaf of bread. There is much baking to be done, and there are many untrained enthusiastic people ready to try their hand at it. Recall Sidney Mintz's observation quoted in the epigraph suggesting something similar: There is much ethnography to be done, and there are many untrained enthusiastic people ready to do it.

And yet, neither ingredients nor intent nor enthusiasm is sufficient if unaccompanied by adequate know-how. What has changed over time, for bread maker and ethnographer alike, is the wider range of ingredients (and substitutes) acceptable, the wider range of variations, even some loosening of the character-building aspects once associated with following proper procedures or enduring personal inconvenience and hardship. Raw materials gathered (and refined) by others are readily available. Bread-making machines can now do the "sticky work"; some of today's ethnographers envision software that will do the same for them. Bread making and ethnography making also can be highly personal and fulfilling experiences, but here I want to keep the focus on what goes into the finished product, not on whether those who make it feel good about themselves. Personal satisfaction is a great basis for recruiting future bakers and ethnographers, but it does not guarantee results.

What has remained constant about ethnography over time, that elusive essence for which I have been searching, proves to be neither in the ingredients selected nor, except in the most general way, in the circumstances under which they have been collected. Rather, it is in how the ethnographer selects among the data available, and how the data so selected are brought together to take shape *as ethnography*.

As with any number and combination of liquids suitable for making bread, any number of concepts can be used for holding a descriptive/interpretive account together, but *if ethnography is the desired result, then culture must be among them*. And culture must be *added*; it does not spring forth from the data. Researchers of other persuasions often sprinkle culture into their accounts for good measure, but they rely on other concepts to make their accounts cohere. For the ethnographer, culture is the basic one, although there is no precisely specified amount needed. Nor is there any *particular* selection or mix of ingredients, no predetermined ratio of new to already-familiar data, no exact shape to which every account must conform. Nor need culture, in any of the varied definitions the concept may take, be the *sole* bonding agent for holding everything together. It need not necessarily be identified by name, and it may be introduced under another label—social system, for instance—but in some form it *must* be present.

As in everything else about the making of good ethnography, even the culture concept can be used to excess, in effect overpowering the unique qualities of the raw material by making it dense and hard to handle. So it must be added in balanced portion, neither overwhelming the descriptive material nor used too sparingly in a mistaken notion that the data are so complete and compelling that they speak for themselves. Nevertheless, if the end product is to be ethnography, some underlying conception of culture must be present.

There are many, many ways to render data malleable and give it shape. Researchers new to qualitative inquiry often feel overwhelmed by the alternatives, especially if they lack a strong orientation in one of the social sciences. That may explain the preoccupation with "method"—the search for surefire recipes—one finds in applied fields in which everyday urgencies far exceed the conceptual resources for dealing with them. Nonetheless, individuals lacking formal disciplinary orientation are never the naive investigators they may perceive themselves to be. Had they not already been surrounded in their professional lives with problem-solving styles and reporting formats, they would not find themselves in a position where they are expected to undertake research and are presumed to have some idea of what that means. It is difficult to imagine how someone who has never seen a loaf of bread would go about trying to make one. It is difficult to imagine anyone baking a first loaf of bread that does not bear strong resemblance to loaves seen previously.

Drawing on training, experience, and/or intuition, the researcher intent on producing ethnography must, in each situation, decide how much raw material to gather, how much of that to use, what needs to be added to make the material cohere, how to keep the end product from being either flat or full of holes, and what seasonings or improvers might enhance it. One soon evolves ways of going about all this that accommodate personal styles and preferences. That may explain why old-timers become less dependent on standard recipes or formulas, yet sometimes offer formulaic advice rather than reveal deep personal meaning the activity may have or divulge how they *personally* go about their work. Let an authority on bread making summarize the process in a way that speaks for ethnography as well:

> Although making bread is fundamentally simple, it remains a mysterious and exciting process, even to the most experienced baker. Each dough feels and behaves somewhat differently from another; and even the experience of making a particular kind of bread is never quite the same from one time to the next. [Shulman 1995:10]

"Adding In" Culture

Not only ethnographers but *every* researcher must decide how much emphasis to give to cultural interpretation. There is no way to inquire into human social action that ignores the influence of culture, if only to the extent of recognizing inquiry itself as a social process—the nonrandomness of the topics we investigate, for example. The question every researcher must address is how prominent a role to assign culture versus how much credence to give to competing alternatives calling attention to psychological, biological, ecological, or other ways of seeing and interpreting. For an ethnographically oriented researcher, a sociocultural framework is the perspective of choice.

At one point my colleague John Creswell confronted me boldly with the question, "Harry, will your book have a chapter on how to study a culture?" I assured him that not only the whole book but the whole purpose of the book was about studying culture, because that is what ethnography is about and what ethnographers do. But his question haunted me. I wondered whether he would find the straightforward answer about "how to study a culture" that I had so quickly assured him would be here.

I also wondered how literally to take his question. John, a professor of educational psychology, was trained as a measurement-oriented quantitative researcher. Like many others involved with both the doing and the teaching of research, not only has he "found" qualitative inquiry and become an enthusiastic proponent of it, he has made his own substantial contribution through two texts addressing issues of research design (Creswell 1994, 1998). But did he really want, and do his fellow converts or his students being introduced to qualitative research really need, a treatise on anthropological inquiry and the concept of culture?[1] John wants his students to know something about *several* major approaches in qualitative inquiry, including ethnography; he is not trying to make ethnographers of them.

A good starting place for examining qualitative approaches is to examine fieldwork techniques. I trust that the material in Part Two provided useful information in that regard, first by offering an overview to emphasize commonalities among the techniques used in all fieldwork approaches (Chapter 3), and then by making a close examination of what else ethnography entails "beyond method" (Chapter 4). Following that, the chapters of Part Three reviewed how ethnographers have pursued their work as the locus of their studies has expanded from an early preoccupation with distant and primitive Others to contemporary Others remarkably like themselves. No matter how close to home, ethnographers study culture. If I have made adequate explanation about how ethnographers go about it, then I have answered the question, "How do you study a culture?"

However, in this chapter, and in introducing the analogy to bread making, I have introduced another dimension to the nexus between culture and ethnography. I have suggested that ethnographers not only approach their inquiries from a cultural perspective, they also *write* with one. The concept of culture makes it possible to draw data together into a coherent account, not unlike the way the baker adds liquid(s) in order to form a workable dough. How then do ethnographers write with the concept of culture? I think John's students need to know about that, too, if they are to understand ethnography, even as informed consumers.

In *writing* with culture, using it to combine raw ingredients, the concept enables discrete bits of data to be formed into a cohesive mass. But culture does not impose form or shape; that happens only at the hands of the ethnographer. Thus the culture concept makes it possible for something to happen, but exactly what does happen depends on other factors. As an enabling concept, it is more effective when understated than if allowed to dominate. That may explain why culture today seems to be on everyone else's lips, with "culture this" and "culture that," while some anthropologists avoid the concept completely and occasionally admonish their colleagues to do likewise (see, for example, Brightman 1995).

How does one "write with culture" without letting the concept call attention to itself or overwhelm an account? The advice I offer is to leave the study of capital-C Culture for others, or for another time. Ethnography is not the study of Culture; it is the study of the customary social behaviors of identifiable groups of people. Put forward even more modestly, culture is an account of *particular* social processes as practiced by *particular* people in *particular* settings. Ethnography is particular. As practiced, it can never transcend being a study of microculture(s), in whole or in part. It cannot be directed at studying a macroculture unless the macroculture is treated singularly, i.e., as a national culture or as a microculture. It makes little sense to talk of something like "American culture."

When working with beginning ethnographers, I have on occasion suggested—and with my own students, sometimes insisted—that they write "without culture," that is, write without reference to the term itself. In each instance in which they have used, or might be tempted to use, the word culture, I asked them to substitute another word or phrase to convey more precisely what they had in mind in that instance. Doing this also helps avoid confusion between "society" and "culture," the former referring to people in interactions that can be observed and recorded, the latter referring to patterns of behaving that can only be inferred. Although I may have risked putting student researchers into academic shock with such a request ("How can I write about culture if you won't let me use the word?"), in the long run the result has been salutary.

Clifford Geertz urged many years ago that we attend to "this cutting of the culture concept down to size, therefore actually insuring its continued importance rather than undermining it" (1973b:4). *Culture is never an explanation for behavior.* Like ethnography, culture, too, is *a way of seeing;* it offers *one* perspective for examining social behavior. It is an admittedly preconceived way of examining behavior that seeks out underlying patterns in observed instances.[2] Using words that point more clearly to what is meant in each particular instance has proven an excellent way to prevent the concept from getting out of hand.

Although culture cannot be directly observed, there is plenty to draw upon for making inferences about its influence in the form of custom, or tradition, or prevailing patterns of believing and acting characteristic of a group—at least for anyone willing to think in such terms. For example, in every English sentence employing the word *should* (in the sense of propriety) there is an implicit notion of someone's idea of how things *ought* to be. Such notions of what ought to be reveal culture at work. In our daily lives, we constantly communicate expectations for the behavior of those about us—and for ourselves—in comments about how others should or should not behave. Simply pointing out and tracing the assumptions revealed in those "should" sentences is one way to sensitize others to how culture influences, or guides, human action.

The intellectual challenge for the ethnographer in making culture central to an account is to discern these pervasive patterns in how individuals interact in terms of *what people say*, *what they do*, and the shared, and for the most part inferred, *expectations they hold for the behavior of others* vis-à-vis actions they themselves initiate. In this case, what you see is not what you get, because you cannot see, hear, taste, smell, or feel culture. So the ethnographer can't really "pour in" culture, as a too-literal interpretation of the analogy to bread making might suggest. Rather, we might say that observations are *combined* by a concept that allows data to be *folded* into an account. But I emphasize that culture must be added; it does not rise spontaneously out of the raw materials. If it did, then every social researcher would come up with a cultural focus.

By saying that the ethnographer "combines" data by means of a unifying concept of culture I mean the sense in which Ward Goodenough describes ethnographers as "attributing" culture to a group. The culture concept provides the ethnographer with a particular way of bringing observations together and making sense of them. All data have the *potential* to be formed into a cultural account, but they are not inherently "cultural" any more than every seed of grain is predestined to be served up in a loaf of bread.

Every ethnographer must have a general idea of what other ethnographers have in mind when they refer to culture. Since culture enjoys (perhaps "relishes" is the appropriate term here) its status as a contested concept, the ethnographer needs a grasp of the *consensus* surrounding the concept and some idea of its historical development and the current state of the never-ending critique of it.

That culture cannot be nailed down more precisely is, of course, often cited as a reason for arguing *against* it. I recognize such ambiguity as a serious limitation. But by no means do I find its limitations sufficient for dismissing the concept altogether; all we seem able to accomplish along those lines is to propose alternative terms that point in the same direction. Culture must never be treated as anything more than a mental construct. It is not self-evident. Those hypothetical visitors from Mars may be flabbergasted by the behavior they observe should they come to study us, but unless there has been some prior communication and agreement (perhaps a resolution at an interplanetary congress), it is highly unlikely that they will view social behavior as we do. Most certainly they won't call it by the same set of terms.

Like ethnography, culture offers one way—a conceptual way—to organize disparate observations into a cohesive whole and to convey to others what we have seen. And like ethnography, it is more than a way of looking; it is *a way of seeing*, variously described by others as providing a framework, a grid, a lens, a conceptual scheme, and so forth. Following the bread-making analogy, with "culture" identified (in advance, you understand) as the concept that will hold things together, the ethnographer works up (sifts through?) the data intent on identifying and enhancing their unique properties. Ethnography is not pursued to *prove* that there is something called culture; rather, the concept provides a particular way for those who pursue ethnography to "work up" the material they gather.

And here, alas, I must depart slightly from the analogy, for while the baker may or may not be interested in preserving some of the unique qualities of the ingredients, there is no question that this is what the ethnographer must do. The concept of culture is used to preserve and enhance whatever is unique about the data as well as rendering it in a familiar and palatable form. Sweeping generalizations about "culture" prove ineffective at one extreme; tiny bits of observational data in the form of undigested and indigestible fact are ineffective at the other. The balance is achieved in discerning patterns, cultural patterns perceived in segments of repeated behavior that collectively constitute the abstraction we refer to as culture.

The critical task facing the ethnographer is at once to recognize and to demonstrate the uniqueness in these patterns yet present them in a familiar— and palatable—form. Thus the ethnographer must have not only an ample supply of basic data but, like the baker, must also have a feel for the data, a sense of what the data are and an idea of what can be made of them, both literally and figuratively.

However, getting a feel for *data* isn't exactly the same as getting the feel of a batch of dough. The successful baker usually works with familiar materials to achieve a uniform and relatively standard product that can be reproduced time and again. The ethnographer's success is predicated on recognizing and portraying something unique, with rather limited allowance for variation in form and wide variation acceptable as to content. The very idea of turning out an ethnography identical to one that another ethnographer has produced is unthinkable. The phrase "a model ethnography" appears often in laudatory reviews, but don't believe for a minute that your goal is to replicate exactly some earlier work! The baker can get on with the process of blending; the ethnographer's attention must be given to recognizing and preserving unique qualities in the way the raw materials come together, at the same time giving the whole a pleasing and recognizable shape. Analogy aside, the ethnographer's task is to bring discrete observations together in a way that makes it possible to discern cultural patterning.

Cultural Patterning

Cultural patterning—another elusive idea! Recall Bateson's notion (discussed in Chapter 6) that difference is an *idea*. *Similarity* must be of that order as well, not directly observable except in a "mind's eye" poised to recognize patterning in the repetition of comparable (but never identical) behaviors. Ethnographers look for how people in their ordinary circumstances behave in more or less similar ways, and how they make expected responses, even in unexpected circumstances. Attending to customary behavior does not allow us to predict extraordinary behavior, but it does allow us to predict how people are likely to *react* to behavior, appropriate or inappropriate.

This self-appointed task of recognizing and bundling up something as nebulous as cultural patterns—customary ways of behaving and customary reactions to the behavior of others—is a key step in the effort to make culture explicit. For the title of her 1934 classic, Ruth Benedict called them just that: *Patterns of Culture*. Some years later, Margaret Mead insisted that pattern recognition is so critical for the ethnographer that it should be included in the training of cultural anthropologists (1952:344). More recently, Mike Agar has proposed that ethnographers can override any uncertainty as to what constitutes a pattern by advising them to look for "massively overdetermined" patterns, placed along a scale from "not hardly" to "way overdetermined" (1996:40–42).

Our own cultural pattern of seeking the new in preference to the old may make today's scholars uncomfortable about using a phrase like "patterns of culture" popular more than six decades ago. Nonetheless, identifying patterns, or inferring patterns from what one has observed, is what ethnographers do. Pattern seeking, the identification of regularities, is, in fact, what *all* observers do. Ethnographers accomplish this through positing and examining patterns and changes in patterns as reflected in life cycle events (e.g., birth, puberty, finding a mate), pervasive themes (e.g., the themes of competitiveness or self-reliance associated with mainstream American society), annual cycles of activities, observance of rituals, world view (shared ideas about how members of a society see themselves in relation to everything else), or through cultural patterning revealed in well-contextualized personal life histories. As described in Chapter 5, the traditional approach to examining cultural patterns is to attend to the customary ways that members of a social unit have devised for coping with the problems described through a set of etic categories (e.g., social organization, economic organization) such as those found in introductory texts or standard guides.

There is always too much happening in any setting selected for study; observation presents an impossible task. The observer feels torn between finding patterns everywhere and entertaining serious doubts as to whether there is any systematic patterning at all in what is being observed. From the outset, every observer realizes the need to look at *something* rather than try to attend to everything. It is not so much that ethnographers have settled the question of how to do their looking; they are forever expanding and refining the techniques they draw upon in fieldwork. What they share is a general notion of what they are looking *for* in their efforts to describe and understand behavior. As with viewing through a camera lens, they bring their subjects into sharper and sharper focus, careful to include some peripheral detail as well. Although cognizant that "culture" is reflected in virtually everything they observe, they also realize that there are better and poorer choices the researcher can make for investing the always-limited time available for observation. Such choices are influenced by the purposes of the research, by each researcher's own comfort level with the ambiguities of the culture concept, and by prevailing practice in the culture of researchers themselves.

Pattern seeking is not limited to ethnographers—it is basic to good diagnostic procedure—but it is a behavior characteristic among them, something they do almost out of habit. It need not always be formal, distant, or linked to systematic inquiry. For example, George Marcus (1998) describes what he posits to be a "distinctive pattern in the development of research careers" among anthropologists of his own cohort and younger, a dramatic shift (a "distinct break" in his phrase [p. 233]) between what anthropologists take as the focus for their first project—one that continues to exhibit a preference for a traditionally oriented study—and the focus of whatever major topic is addressed next (the second project). The second project, he continues, necessitates "redesigning the conventions of ethnography for unconventional purposes, sites, and subjects—particularly moving beyond the settled community as site of fieldwork toward dispersed phenomena that defy the way that classic ethnography has been framed and persuades" (p. 234). What better example of the ethnographer at work, in this case recognizing a pattern that offers provocative insight into, or raises provocative questions about, "how ethnographic research is being reshaped in the playing out of careers" (p. 232). His observation feels right. It helps me to think about something going on in a new way and on a grander scale, a discipline-wide pattern that heretofore had seemed only idiosyncratic behavior of cases I knew firsthand. Pattern recognition of this sort is the stuff out of which the study of culture is made.

Culture Revisited

I underscore that culture is never "there," waiting demurely to be unveiled, lest this discussion has suggested that I am about to reveal some surefire way to identify it. Culture—as represented, for example, in an explicit account of how some group of people carry out their activities—does not exist until the observer renders such an account. The *concept* of culture is not essential for carrying on human life, but some basic ideas surrounding the concept are essential to the life of ethnography (and, I hasten to add, to the well-being of cultural anthro-pology). People can and do go about their business without ethnographers; ethnographers cannot go about their business without people. Absolutely no one other than the ethnographically oriented observer ever needs to be so atten-tive to culture itself.

What does an observer make of, or do with, raw observations to trans-form them into studies of culture? The first thing the ethnographer does is something we all do, all too reflexively: we make sense of things in terms of our own cultural frameworks. That isn't much help when trying to make sense of someone else's way of doing things, but it is virtually impossible not to do it anyway. Whether I think of *making* bread, *breaking* it, or *earning* it, the first images that come to mind are drawn from firsthand experience. For the ethnographer, inquiry begins but must not end there.

One example of a softening from the earlier preoccupation with scientific objectivity is the recognition that what we see and subsequently report is indeed of our own making. That notion is succinctly captured with a phrase of great significance in fieldwork, the "social construction" of reality, recogni-tion of the role we ourselves play in the interpretation of the world about us. That same idea is captured another way in a phrase borrowed for the epigraph to Chapter 5 and attributed to E. H. Gombrich: "Artists do not paint what they see, they see what they know how to paint."

Where we once sought to validate claims of observer objectivity and neu-trality, today it is quite in keeping and in vogue to confess to a staggering sub-jectivity. We make no claim that anything is more or less than what we ourselves have made of it, although we can go a long way toward explaining how we have reached our conclusions and what we can offer by way of sup-port. The basic descriptive task remains before us nonetheless; we have not completed our research until we have found a way to make available to oth-ers what we ourselves have experienced, primarily through what we have seen and heard, less confidently through what we have tasted, smelled, perhaps felt emotionally, and what has been reported to us by others.

A deeper professional commitment to cultural interpretation then draws us toward a next step, trying to discern how things more or less make sense *to those in the setting,* as contrasted with the initial task of recognizing—and perhaps reporting—how things more or less make sense to us. That is where some kind of framework—for example, such broad frameworks as cultural orientation, cultural know-how, and cultural beliefs, as suggested in Chapter 4, or traditional etic categories as reviewed in Chapter 5—can help the ethno-grapher to home in on something as amorphous as culture by looking at par-ticular aspects of it. One might try to portray an overarching world view by compiling the set of tacit cultural "rules" that appear to account for the behavior and interactions of members of a group. More realistically, the researcher may wish to focus on explicit questions, such as what one would have to know to participate appropriately in the activities of, or might have to believe in order to be satisfied with, a particular tradition or activity.

A final step in the study of culture goes beyond what can be discerned from the study of only one cultural scene or group. Here one attempts to draw generalizations about the problems and resolutions that life presents for humans everywhere. The central issue now becomes one of identifying pan-human problems and identifying the various ways humans go about confronting them. This task has long been recognized as exceeding the descriptive capabilities of ethnography. Recall a distinction (cited in the epigraph to the first chapter) that Radcliffe-Brown and his British colleagues proposed between *ethnography* as the descriptive account and *comparative study*, the task they assigned to social anthropology.

Social anthropology—or ethnology, as it has been referred to in these pages—uses comparison to achieve a level of generalization about human social life. Anthropologists traditionally have referred to such generalizations as "cultural universals." Not every anthropologist is comfortable working at so abstract a level in which there is always the risk of seeming to reify culture itself. American cultural anthropologists may be found anywhere along this continuum. British anthropology developed along a different tradition, one that distinguished the single-mindedness of the ethnographer (and here is where they prefer the term "ethnologist" in reference to those who engage in fieldwork) from the "social anthropologist" interested in discerning universals or "laws." As with the proper use of the fork or motorway, arguments continue to be heard on both sides of the Atlantic as to whose tradition best serves its intended function. The anthropologies of most other nations are more narrowly confined to ethnic studies that do not invite such wide-ranging considerations. In any case, Robert Lowie observed almost a half century ago, "Whatever differences may divide cultural from social anthropologists, they are hardly greater than those which divide self-styled cultural anthropologists" (Lowie 1953:527).

With interests that range from the study of local behavior patterns (forms of greeting, manner of dress, beliefs about origins or a hereafter) to discovering human universals, it is easy to see how ethnographers can justify intense studies of modest cultural scenes, just as it should be apparent why some anthropologists join other social scientists concerned with macrocultural systems well beyond the purview of the lone ethnographer.

The potential for cultural interpretation is everywhere. How we focus our research efforts depends, as with all of this, on what we seek to accomplish, consistent with local expectations concerning what is "properly" within our domain. But the study of culture is formulated out of the patterned behavior of individuals interacting with other individuals, albeit in ways that they themselves typically perceive as personal and idiosyncratic—to whatever extent they are aware of them at all. The ethnographer looks at such instances in order to discern recurring themes, behavior suggestive of underlying templates for action. So it is to groups that the ethnographer attends, or, if to individuals, to individuals as standing for the group, in some ways like all of its members, in some ways like some of its members, in some ways like no other member.[3] Ethnographic observation begins and ends with individual behavior, yet personality is never the focus of study. Anthropologists prefer phrases like "personality and culture" or "individual and society" to emphasize the contextualized nature of their interest in human behavior.

By simply being at the same place at the same time, people share some behavior characteristics. Macro-level differences are sufficiently noticeable to prompt much of our everyday stereotyping. Consider, for example, the brisk pace of people who live in New York City as noticed by visitors from places farther west, or the leisurely pace of folks out west as noticed by visitors from New York City. Although such differences can be drawn in illustration of "culture," they don't do much to illuminate it. Ethnographers usually home in on smaller, more manageable groups, restricting attention to people in close interaction and leaving the study of crowds or comparable aggregates to others. Identifying a social group significant for and manageable through an ethnographic approach, perhaps narrowing one's focus to only certain individuals or subgroups within a social system, is essential for accomplishing the ethnographic task. Conversely, today's ethnographer must be ready to defend and demonstrate how careful attention to individuals in interaction with each other in everyday lives can contribute to the understanding of problems posed in terms of nation-states and globalization (see, for example, Appaduri 1997).

Like everyone, ethnographers use handy labels to identify manageable units to study: family, neighborhood, congregation, stake, and so forth. This is an accepted and time-saving practice, but the careful observer needs to be chary of accepting even the most common of labels at face value. One must, in a sense, become skeptical about taking *anything* for granted, ever alert for the need to inquire systematically into how people in a setting define themselves and their others. How everyday terms like "family" are used in actual practice warrant careful attention. So, also, do too-ready assumptions we make about the social influences on individual lives. We toss around words like "community" or "peers" as though such terms have clearly identifiable referents, without specifying *precisely* who constitutes an individual's community or peer group. When we try to pin things down, convenient categories like "community" invariably prove to be imagined ones.

Natural settings (a village, the crew on a fishing boat), involuntary settings (internment camps, nursing homes), standard social units (clan, voluntary association), and local usage (summer folk versus year-round residents) are customary ways to identify and locate groups for ethnographic purposes. Any of these can serve as a starting point, at least till the ethnographer finds a more suitable category. No category is likely to be without its exceptions or hard-to-classify cases. Although people are often ready and willing to classify everyone else, they prove highly resistant to the idea of being categorized themselves. Individually, we attribute to ourselves a more fluid status than we recognize in others. We regard ourselves as belonging now in one category, now in another. We cannot resist categorizing others; we strongly resist the efforts of others to categorize us.

I have leaned heavily on the *idea* of culture as the unifying element for rendering ethnographic accounts, something the ethnographer draws upon to make observational data cohesive and malleable. By appropriately appropriating the concept of "culture," one proclaims "Ethnographer at Work." Of course, merely inserting that term into an account doesn't *guarantee* ethnography, but once you have alluded to the concept, the possibility that you might do something with it increases as well. Remember to keep in mind that culture is never an explanation for behavior; whenever you employ the term, be prepared to explain what you mean by it. You may find yourself having to supply your own definition of a term that has defied an agreed-upon definition for decades.

I realize that I may have made you wary of using either the term or the concept of culture, when I intended instead to underscore how useful a concept it is and how central to ethnography. So I remind you again that there are alternatives to consider in addition to simply backing away altogether. They might help you (or John Creswell's students) to move in the *direction* of cultural interpretation without becoming embroiled in controversy about the term itself.

One way to do that is prompted by the idea of ethnographic reconnaissance, for it invites attention to *context,* not only in fieldwork but in the subsequent write-up. It is hard to imagine how *any* effort directed at understanding human behavior could fail to benefit by having researchers take time to look around before zeroing in on some highly focused aspect of it. If John's students—indeed, *any* researchers oriented to the more qualitative approaches—take even that much of an ethnographic nibble, their work ought to benefit by an increased sensitivity to complexity and a corresponding reluctance to be satisfied trying to tease out single causes or offer too-simple explanations. The lesson from ethnography draws attention to the critical importance of *context,* not simply to have researchers make a perfunctory nod in the direction of culture. Without ever using the term "culture," attention to context will be attention to *sociocultural* context. That is a good place to start.

Another alternative phrase for pointing explicitly to "culture" has been proposed by Jean Lave and Etienne Wenger. For groups that otherwise might be described as "culture-sharing" ones, they suggest "communities of practice" (Lave and Wenger 1991:29 ff.; Wenger 1998). The phrase "community of practice" invites attention to a group on the basis of the shared practices and beliefs of its members, at the same time underscoring that we all participate in *multiple* communities. Community in this sense is defined by what people do, not by who belongs. I commend the phrase "communities of practice" to anyone who subscribes to the underlying *idea* of culture but lacks enthusiasm for the term itself.

The idea of a community of practice can also be turned around to examine the assumptions underlying other bases for identifying groups. If the culture concept seems to get in the way or to ignore classificatory schemes essential to the research (e.g., children from broken homes, national origins, religious affiliation, the unemployed), then the orienting concept might better be chosen along other lines and an ethnographic intent defer to some more suitable alternative. Culture in any of its many forms is but *one* framework for examining human social behavior, one way of seeing. That virtually assures that it is also a way of *not* seeing. We simply can't get away from needing a clear idea of what it is we want to accomplish when we set out to do research.

A Piece of Cake?

The analogy pursued here was drawn to help convey the idea that, as in making bread, there are many ingredients ordinarily found in ethnography, yet no single one is critical, save some basic descriptive data and a researcher who understands how to blend and form them into a particular kind of end product. Like the baker, the ethnographer wants to preserve the integrity of the key ingredients, but the analogy stops short of helping to show how to accomplish the critical task of discerning cultural patterns in observed behavior. Perhaps ethnography isn't a piece of cake after all.

What ethnography requires by way of conceptualization is a matter of making considered generalizations about how members of a group tend to speak and act, warranted generalizations appropriate for collectivities of people rather than the usual shoot-from-the-hip stereotyping adequate for allowing us to achieve our individual purposes. What this demands of the ethnographer is keener observations, multiple instances, pervasive skepticism as to whether we have quite got it right, and far more cautious generalizing than we ordinarily tolerate in everyday discourse. And, finally, we must find audiences to whom we can report our observations, as well as to find effective way to communicate with them.

There are many elements that *ordinarily* go into ethnography; one might say that, like human behavior, it, too, is overdetermined. But no single one is critical, not even lingering traditions that insist on the ethnographer's presence or that hint strongly that there really is an absolute minimum length of time one must spend in the field to legitimate a study. Rather than urge the adoption of a rigid set of standards to satisfy, let me suggest that to whatever extent more of the customary conditions are met, the greater the likelihood that ethnography will be achieved. To the extent that the final account implicates culture or explicitly interprets data in terms of a sociocultural framework, that likelihood becomes even greater. The final judgment as to ethnographicness must be made on the basis of what has been accomplished, enhanced but not assured either by appropriate data-gathering techniques or good intentions.

Good intentions do not guarantee ethnography, but ethnography is never accomplished without intent. It is in what ethnographers do with data that transforms ordinarily commonplace observations into ethnography. As the title for one of his several volumes devoted to the history of anthropology, George Stocking chose *The Ethnographer's Magic* (Stocking 1992). In these pages I hope I have dispelled any notion of magic or mystery, but I mention Stocking's title—a phrase he borrowed from Malinowski—to underscore that the ethnographer does indeed do *something* to data to transform them into ethnography.

Notes

1. Ever the empiricist, Creswell not only responded to a request to serve as a developmental reviewer for the manuscript but in turn invited two doctoral students to read and critique it. I am indebted to Chad Buckendahl and Lynn Harter for their suggestions.

2. Recall, for example, Hammersley and Atkinson's critique of the culture concept as reviewed in Chapter 4.

3. Readers may recognize this paraphrase of Kluckhohn and Murray's famous aphorism, "Every man is in certain respects a. like all other men, b. like some other men, c. like no other man" (1948:35).

CHAPTER ELEVEN

Living the Ethnographic Life

Do radical ethnography, one that gets you closer to those you study at the risk of going native and never returning. . . . We have to ask how far we as ethnographers ought to go toward living their lives alongside them and then crafting in textual discourse what we have learned.

—Dan Rose
Living the Ethnographic Life, 1990, p. 12

I borrowed this chapter title, "Living the Ethnographic Life," from Dan Rose's monograph of the same name, and I borrowed a quote for the epigraph. However, I stop short of advocating radical ethnography. I am skeptical that ethnographers make good radicals. They may like to romanticize that they are, and may enjoy recounting their adventures while experiencing different life styles, but those experiences are usually gained under the protective aegis of their self-assigned role. They are safe knowing they can always retreat to whatever more permanent and encompassing role has made ethnography possible as a transitory one.

Dan Rose did not seek that protective aegis. He did not assume—in his phrase, "hide behind"—an ethnographic pose during fieldwork from 1969 to 1971 as a White living and working in a Black area in the inner city. He speaks with personal authority and he labels his inquiries as radical ethnography. To today's reader, he may seem so radical as to be virtually outside the ethical loop; his early research serves as a reminder of how expectations for conducting participant observation research have been changing. In examining his statement quoted below, keep in mind that until recently ethnographers were far more concerned about keeping the research role from getting in the way than with issues like deception. Reflecting on fieldwork in South Philadelphia during 1969–1971 that resulted eventually in his publication *Black American Street Life* (1987), Rose writes:

> Research for that book was covert. At the urging of Erving Goffman I lived
> and worked with welfare- and working-class African-Americans without dis-
> closing my identity as an ethnographer who was documenting their lives. . . .
> Because I did not disclose my identity and reside officially as an anthropolo-
> gist present only to study the people, what occurred was a collapse of the role
> distance between my neighbors and myself. I had no identity, no status to hide
> behind except what I could pick up locally. [Rose 1990:11–13]

I quite agree that being an ethnographer gives the majority of us who do *not* do radical ethnography a status to hide behind, a kind of self-validating identity that allows us to go about "people watching" as though it is our right and duty, not just something we like to do. John Van Maanen almost let the cat out of the bag when he described ethnography as "a wonderful excuse for having an adventurous good time while operating under the pretext of doing serious intellectual work" (1995:2). As he was careful to note, that's how ethnography *was,* not how it is today. "Ethnography is no longer pictured as a relatively simple look, listen and learn procedure," he laments, "but, rather, as something akin to an intense epistemological trial by fire."[1]

That new intensity in ethnography is especially evident in two topics of perennial interest: continued agonizing over ethical issues and concern for—and about—efforts to speed things up. An announcement that crossed my desk describing a forthcoming summer field school illustrates how the latter edges out the former. Traditionally, field schools provided one of few opportunities for students to gain sustained, supervised fieldwork experience prior to embarking on an independent inquiry. But today's field school, if this one is representative, runs for only five-and-a-half weeks, emphasizes rapid appraisal techniques and team approaches to data collecting—neither of which have characterized tradi-tional work—and concludes in time for students to return to the campus for the regular summer session. Not much need for worry about long-term relation-ships of confidence and trust in those circumstances. I now bite my lip when I insist that a little ethnography is better than none at all! I hold fast to that posi-tion, but I must admit that I didn't have quite so little in mind.

Ethnographic Futures and the Future of Ethnography

Following the format used in Ethnographic Futures Research, we might con-template the future for ethnography itself, to ponder a *best* scenario, *worst* sce-nario, and *most probable* scenario. Whither ethnography? I offer only a few comments beyond what I have already said in these pages. For the most part, the answer lies with today's ethnographers, and tomorrow's. Whatever is to become of ethnography is pretty much in their hands—and in yours, if ethnography is what you do or intend to do. As with language, or culture, or even baking a loaf of bread, ethnography, too, is rediscovered and reshaped anew by each individual who engages in it; it is never rediscovered or remade in exactly the same way.

I have assumed that most readers are in the early years of developing careers or are making a career shift in which research is expected to play a significant new role. Those like myself whose early, energetic fieldwork was conducted years ago, and whose more contemplative reflections have pretty much been heard as well, are more likely to cast a backward look than a forward one. If the postmodern era has pretty much run its course, then even that period may have begun to look like the "good old days," compared with the unknown of whatever lies ahead in dour predictions of limited access, diminished funding, uncertain markets, little job security, greater time constraints, and growing resistance to allowing "outsiders" to tell (or sell) stories that insiders feel quite capable of rendering on their own.

First, a reflection on technology, although other than expressing the cautions one expects to hear from an elder, I will not attempt to anticipate the full impact technology is likely to have on ethnography.[2] But it is not the information explosion that impresses me nearly as much as the way technology has facilitated the production and stringing together of words. How did we ever manage to get our writing done prior to the word-processing capabilities of the microcomputer? Still, no gain is without its cost. I find myself once again doing all my own typing after years and years of having been totally dependent on secretarial help. With the requirement to submit a floppy disk along with hard copy, I have become my own typesetter as well. Except for a brief period in the army when I realized that my ability to type could keep me from being sent overseas to fight for peace (?), my typing has always been slow and riddled with errors. In a day when most academics had secretarial help, I was happy to relinquish the typing chore. I realize now that my dependence on others to type and retype my drafts slowed the editing process immeasurably. Whatever success I enjoy as a writer is due to perseverance at editing, not to any natural talent. With my manuscript on the screen in front of me or quickly transformed to hard copy, I now edit continuously, rather than having to wait until someone finishes retyping a corrected draft.

Beyond rather rudimentary word processing, I am not so enamored with all the software programs that have been developed as aids for the qualitative researcher. I concur with John Seidel, the developer of one of the first such programs, labeled, appropriately enough, "The ETHNOGRAPH," about the temptation of computer programs that invite us to substitute breadth for depth (1992:112). The plethora of available software offers false hope to unwary fieldworkers that once their data are "entered," there will be a software program that can do the rest.

Almost everyone returning from the field these days seems to turn immediately to this new data-entering ritual. Ostensibly that task helps to speed them along, but I can't help wondering if it is really an avoidance ritual, one more way to put off the writing. I wish they would confront the writing task more directly by using early drafts to help them assess what data they are actually going to use and in what form they are most likely to need it. Adequate fieldnotes, coupled with the freshness of the experience itself, should provide a sufficient database for preliminary writing. "Cutting through" data is something for a mind to do, not a machine.

Everything about technology that serves to make data collecting easier also tempts us to collect more of it. In the matter of ethnography, more is not necessarily better. (Hmmm, the bread analogy scores again: a thoughtful *selection* among ingredients is the key, not simply pouring in more of everything.) What should concern us is finding ways to be ever more selective and focused as fieldwork proceeds. An ethnographer needs to get at the heart of the matter. The heart of ethnographic matter is not matter, it is "heart," what humans make of the lives of others that helps them to understand those lives and their own. I receive strange inquiries from strangers searching for software programs capable of handling a huge corpus of data, interview data especially. What they desperately hope to find are programs that effortlessly sort out and spit out just what they need. Such software would indeed give a whole new meaning to the idea of the "ethnographer's magic," but there will never be such a day. What we are likely to experience instead are more and more qualitative researchers caught in avalanches of their own making, buried in crumbling mountains of data simply because generating more and more data became an end in itself, so easy to do.

It seemed a continued blessing that students coming to ethnography through enrolling in a class were not likely to know about the computer programs available for qualitative data analysis. I felt they were better off to work with (and *through*) their fieldnotes and interview protocols on hard copy, where the cutting and pasting are literal, rather than be introduced too early to available software. They needed first to understand the problems computer programs are designed to solve, rather than to surrender prematurely to collecting the kinds of data the programs best accommodate. I wanted my students to become informed consumers who understood what kind of help they need that technology can furnish—sorting and searching, for example. As we (as you) become better at that, there should be less concern that computer programmers are changing our data-gathering habits to conform to what is most convenient for the machine.

I don't pretend to offer advice as to which programs are best, but I do recommend following a standard fieldwork strategy to search out individuals with *firsthand* knowledge. That means talking with ethnographers who have found programs useful for handling data similar to what you expect to have, rather than talking to computer buffs who think in terms of computer capacities or to ethnographers attracted to problems of a different magnitude from your own. You don't need a program designed for number crunching if your concern is with text management. If you take firsthand experience with using a computer program for purposes comparable to your own as a criterion for seeking recommendations from others, you may be surprised at the paucity of reliable information.

The use of word processing is a different story. I assume that most everyone processes field-based journal entries with the invaluable assistance of word processing, with the possible exception of someone who prefers to preserve and use fieldnotes as originally recorded in pencil or pen. I have never been able to resolve to my own satisfaction whether to keep fieldnotes in original longhand, or to retype—and, presumably, to expand—brief fieldnotes (jottings) into a computer immediately after returning from a field observation. For those who can afford a laptop computer and are prepared to cope with a new set of problems they introduce (risk of theft, keeping them recharged, working with a tiny keyboard and tiny screen), this is clearly a great place to introduce one, but that entails a thoughtful assessment as to how disruptive it might be in the research setting and how devastating a technological malfunction might be at any time.

I think it advisable to contain all fieldnotes in one place and one format (with adequate provision for a backup safely stored somewhere else, of course), but the final decision as to what seems best depends on very specific circumstances. In studies where my role was essentially that of participant, notes were made later and were typed. In studies in which I was essentially an observer, I took notes in longhand and augmented on-site observations with additional notes made later, also in longhand.

The technology already exists for turning a personal computer into a voice-activated word processor. I have not met anyone who has done fieldwork this way; I can't help wondering whether on-site researchers will begin to sound like on-the-spot newscasters instead. The real threat that technology poses to fieldwork is that everything leads to *faster* ways to record *more* data. What we really need are ways to make better decisions about what warrants recording in the first place. Audio- and videotape recording present the same problem by making it too easy to record too much, too indiscriminately.

As to the future of ethnography, Renato Rosaldo once remarked on how we have theorized ethnography as a book-length enterprise, and his observation helped me realize that it is impossible for me to imagine theorizing it any other way. It does not always have to result in a book; alternative formats have always nibbled at ethnography's heels, but the monograph is standard, and length is a standard problem. Technology hasn't really helped with the problem of being selective about data; instead, it invites us to *put in more* rather than to pick and choose with care. Hear, for example, an enthusiastic argument on behalf of hypertext publication:

> Hypertext . . . allows for ethnographic presentations expanded and embellished by the inclusion of visual images, case studies, complementary texts, and field notes. It also opens the possibility for new forms of expression that can better capture the multilevel referencing and interrelatedness of complex symbolic and behavioral systems. Accordingly, postmodernists might more easily realize their objectives of articulating numerous voices and perspectives without the restraints of linear exposition. [Schwimmer 1996:566]

Most of the discussion of technology has concerned ourselves as ethnographers—how to make our work more efficient, more accurate, and, most often, more detailed. Russ Bernard has proposed a different vision, one that would place technology itself in the hands of our informants:

> Suppose that, *in addition to* (not in replacement of) doing traditional ethnographic fieldwork, every anthropologist were to teach just one native informant to use a microcomputer-based word processor. Suppose further that every anthropologist helped just one native person or group to acquire the technology and the skill to produce a truly native ethnography. Within a matter of a few years, the data base describing the world's extant cultures would double or triple, and a qualitative dimension would be added to the ethnographic record as well. It is clear . . . how much we have learned whenever we have given our informants the opportunity to tell us, in their own words, and in their own narrative style, what their cultures are all about. Their works are monuments both to our ignorance and to the possibilities for understanding the cultural worlds of other peoples. [Bernard 1989:36]

For providing a database—if that is what we need—Bernard's idea is an interesting one. It redefines as *advantage* what I have presented as *threat,* the capacity for handling more and more data. But I repeat a concern expressed in Chapter 6 about confusing narrative for ethnography. In the stark image I have of the native informant at work alone, I miss the reassuring presence of the ethnographer, the interaction, the encouragement, the mentoring to help transform the complexity of a life into something manageable. No, to me this seems to go one step too far. It would be comparable to putting me in front of a piano and encouraging me to write a concerto. I have had enough trouble seated in front of a computer keyboard these past many months writing (and rewriting!) about *ethnography,* and this is a topic I have been working at and thinking about for years. If there is a concerto in me somewhere, even an original tune or two, I think we best leave it where it is.

I am concerned as well that informants may too easily be led to an inflated idea of how the recounting of their life stories will somehow add to their fame and stature. Contributing toward a *database* is like putting grain in the storehouse in preparation for making bread; it is necessary, but it is not sufficient. You see how I remain haunted by Bohannan's observation: "Without an ethnographer, there is no ethnography." Not in the literal sense that *only* an ethnographer can do ethnography, but in the sense that ethnography never "happens" unless someone self-consciously sets out to make it happen.

Ethnography in the Professional Career

So much for technology, recognizing all that it has facilitated in our ability to record and to link data, along with the added burden it places on the ethnographer who can't decide what counts. What about ethnography's own status and role as a mode of inquiry? Some part of that answer lies with the future of anthropology as a discipline. Anthropologists get a lot of mileage out of pondering the question. The following, from a book-jacket review, shows how that perennial concern can be given a positive turn. The commentator is Leonard Plotnicov, writing on behalf of a study by Moshe Shokeid titled *A Gay Synagogue in New York* (Shokeid 1995):

> A clear winner. . . . In the postmodern climate of reflexivity, deconstruction, and cynicism, this volume is much more than an important contribution to gay and lesbian studies and Jewish studies. It is equally valuable for its glimpse of anthropology's future in cultivating the rich soil of contemporary society. Shokeid puts the lie to the notion that ethnography is dead. In his hands, the craft is alive, healthy, and still developing. This book is a model of how to do ethnography in a modern context.

Ethnography requires time and energy, qualities customarily associated with the earlier years of a career. An individual anticipating an academic career in cultural anthropology must make that commitment to attain entry-level credentials. Yet even the anthropologist willing and presumably eager to pursue further fieldwork in far-off places may find it increasingly difficult to do as other urgencies present themselves. Unlike the demands of ethnography, the kinds of problems that compete with it on the home front do not interfere with what a younger anthropologist colleague once referred to derogatorily as "tending the geraniums." It was not too long before he realized that, both literally and figuratively, he had started tending some geraniums of his own.

With its "last on, first off" status among the social sciences, anthropology suffers some abuse as a *relatively* recent invention, its epithet as "the science of leftovers" caricaturizing it as a hodgepodge of loosely coupled topics not already spoken for by one of the disciplines predating it. Anthropologists have turned that to advantage in efforts to develop a unifying social science, not only to incorporate everything within their purview but to nurture links to other disciplines in promoting interests in economic anthropology, linguistic anthropology, political anthropology, psychological anthropology, and so forth. Amidst new academic arrangements and alliances—cognitive sciences to give computer scientists a piece of the action, decision sciences in what we once knew as business administration—anthropology's place, if not its role, may be growing more secure. It has managed to hang in there. If at times its practitioners strain too hard in their efforts to be the integrative, all-consuming "science of man"—with the once-humorous and now politically correct addendum ". . . embracing woman"—*some* discipline must assume that responsibility. Somebody has to try to pull the bits and pieces together: biology, economics, psychology, the arts. Anthropology is well suited to serve that integrative function among the social sciences, between the social and the not-so-social sciences, and between the sciences and the humanities. Incidentally, that also tags it as superbly suited for undergraduate study or the undergraduate major. I firmly believe that any program of studies can be enriched by providing opportunities for students to read ethnographies and to discover culture as a way to think about human social life.

The fact that, like ethnography, anthropology itself is not well defined offers it the (largely unrealized) advantage of flexibility in adapting to the times. It is not so many years ago that applied work was considered beneath most self-respecting anthropologists. Although anthropologists went to war in the 1940s (I think Margaret Mead once commented that during World War II there were some 200 anthropologists in the United States and 196 of them were in some capacity working on behalf of the war effort[3]), they flocked back to academia immediately afterward and stayed there. At one period in the 1970s anthropology even rode the wave of student popularity, a somewhat precarious ride that left departments overstaffed with tenured faculty when the tide turned. Today those applied interests are being carefully nurtured again. Applied Anthropology, and Cultural Resource Management for the more archaeologically inclined, are two areas that hold most promise for employment. One again, ethnography is yielding to pressure to be both practical and efficient, two aspects that old-fashioned academic types have tended to eschew.

Anthropology continues to be poorly understood outside of academia. As Tim Wallace notes, most people still think it "has to do only with archaeological excavation or biological evolution" (Wallace 1996:39). While working with tomato growers in North Carolina on a pest-management program, Wallace also discovered that farmers were less reticent about talking to him than to the sociologist who was co-director of the program. As he explained, "They assumed that anthropology had something to do with insects and that I could help them immediately with insect control advice!" When my own explanations of what ethnographers do that distinguishes them from archaeologists seem to fall on deaf ears, I resort to a line that I have used for years, likening ethnography to "what Margaret Mead used to do." She became a household word; ethnography has not.

Another question in anticipating the future of ethnography has to do with its relationship to and importance within the discipline of anthropology. Ethnography is fundamental to social anthropology. David Jacobson observes, "Since ethnographies are the main product of anthropological inquiry, they constitute the bases for anthropological knowledge" (1991:125). But is the reverse true as well, that anthropology is fundamental to ethnography?

Anthropologists have never seemed terribly covetous about ethnography or insisted that it is theirs and theirs alone. Instead I am occasionally surprised today to hear colleagues make inclusive references to "qualitative research," reflecting their interest in the broadest possible spectrum of fieldwork techniques and perhaps dissociating themselves from being categorized "only" as ethnographers. Yet I remember an incident years ago when an otherwise gentle and gentlemanly anthropologist sharply rebuked a graduate student who included survey research as one of the *anthropological* fieldwork techniques he planned to employ in his dissertation research. In no uncertain terms the student was informed that anthropologists don't do surveys! Even at the time, the statement had more to do with image-building than with fieldwork practice; today's ethnographer would never claim to be "above" conducting a survey.

A more recent illustration of this opening up of what anthropologists include within their research armamentarium can be found in comparing the titles of the two editions of Russ Bernard's authored treatise on method. The first edition was called *Research Methods in Cultural Anthropology* (1988). For the second edition (1994b), the title was transformed into *Research Methods in*

Anthropology, with the important addition of a subtitle, *Qualitative and Quantitative Approaches.* From the table of contents of the second edition, it would appear that yes, today's anthropologists—some of them, at least—do use "Questionnaires and Survey Research" (chapter 12). There are also chapters dealing with "Sampling" (chapter 4), "Scales and Scaling" (chapter 13), "Univariate Statistics" (chapter 18), "Bivariate Statistics" (chapter 19), and "Multivariate Analysis" (chapter 20). Comforting to know, however, that anthropologists—some of them, at least—still do "Participant Observation" (chapter 7) and work closely with "Informants" (chapter 8).

I note once more that not everyone engaged with anthropology is necessarily committed to or even concerned about maintaining a special identity for ethnography. In a 1996 collection, *Ethnography and Human Development,* Richard Jessor, one of the coeditors, writes of a "renewed attention to ethnographic or qualitative approaches" and adds, parenthetically, "the terms are interchangeable as used here" (Jessor 1996:3,5). Further on, he explains, "The terms *ethnography* and *qualitative method* refer to a congeries of approaches and research procedures rather than to any singular, self-contained, unique method" (pp. 5–6). Another of the coeditors, Richard Shweder, is less cavalier in his treatment of the term "ethnography," describing it as "a species of qualitative research" (Shweder 1996:175). Nevertheless, we are 170 pages into the volume before we are privy to that important second opinion. Thus, even among anthropologists who agree on giving ethnography a prominent place in a title, the question of whether or not the term is interchangeable with "qualitative approaches" seems to be moot.

Perhaps I have been too deeply involved and committed to have recognized, as Jessor appears to have done, that ethnography went away for awhile and only recently has enjoyed a revival. Or perhaps it is his time frame that I do not share, when he writes: "This marginalization of qualitative methods in the social science enterprise is precisely what has been changing in the postpositivist climate of epistemological openness and methodological pluralism" (Jessor 1996:5). Whether the change has been gradual or a sharp turnabout, I can agree that Jessor accurately depicts both how things have been and how they are likely to remain. My hunch is that ethnography, alone or in concert with other qualitative approaches, although always apparently making headway, will never quite arrive. If it and other so-called alternative approaches are never quite going to disappear, neither are they likely to attain the status of already well-entrenched quantitative approaches:

> Although long-established in the tool kit of emic anthropology, symbolic interactionist and social constructionist sociology, and phenomenological psy-

chology, ethnographic or qualitative methods have generally been given only limited respect, and they have never been able to attain the scientific status accorded the so-called objective or quantitative methods. [Jessor 1996:5]

There are several embedded arguments here that are typically posed as diametric opposites to keep interest from flagging: scientific versus humanistic, qualitative versus quantitative, subjective versus objective, or a pair that Jessor contrasts elsewhere in the text, the "context of discovery" and the "context of justification." This latter distinction allows that qualitative approaches have a contribution to make in the exploratory phases, but it is to be understood—even when not explicitly stated—that the "real" research doesn't begin until the data crunchers go to work.

I believe we are best served when one or the other of these paired opposites is allowed to run its course at the hands of a competent researcher, major emphasis devoted *either* to the more quantitative aspects, counting and measuring whatever needs to be counted and measured, *or* to qualitative dimensions that examine "what counts?" There are bullies on both sides, but whatever we strive to obtain in balance should be achieved in total programs of research, not in the contribution to be made by each study individually. It is also important to assess "what counts" on the local scene among those who hold power over one's career, whether dissertation committee, present or potential colleagues, immediate supervisors, or an editor or publisher. I do not hold much faith in the power of rhetoric to change people's views on these issues. I have been willing to take time to explain but have never felt it worthwhile to try to convince others of the contribution to be made through qualitative approaches generally, or ethnography in particular, in fields where it has not previously been recognized. Rather than get locked into hopeless argument, I have simply gone about my work and done it as well as I could.

I have endeavored to guide students to make wise choices not only as to their problems and approaches for investigating them but also as to their instructors and, especially, to their choice of dissertation committee members. There is no question that one finds more support for qualitatively or ethnographically oriented studies across the board these days. I perceive such support as new rather than as renewed, but the important point is that it exists. A bit of reconnaissance seems in order to search out supportive individuals on the local scene. Later, that same diligence should be applied to seeking out sympathetic journals, publishers, colleagues, departments, and institutions.

For the *individual* interested in pursuing ethnographic inquiry, I don't think any of this matters except for care in finding an adequate local support group, local in this instance meaning a community of scholars rather than necessarily someone down the hall, although it can be comforting if the proximity is physical as well as intellectual. We need not mope about with dark forebodings about the future of anthropology or the prospects for ethnography in the 21st century. Ethnography seems destined to go on being defined and redefined indefinitely, its applications as much as its practitioners shaping its destiny (see, for example, Marcus 1998). New "quickie" techniques being added to the ethnographer's kit bag are not necessarily squeezing out the old time-consuming ones. New ingredients and speeded-up processes can be added, substituted, or blended with the old. There will always be opportunity to conduct ethnography in the tradition of intimate, long-term acquaintance, but that once sacrosanct tradition no longer defines the full range of uses to which ethnography can be put. Maintaining its reputation for complex thoroughness rests with those who continue to pursue it that way. To the argument (nicely examined in Gupta and Ferguson's discussion, 1997:3) that the world is changing dramatically without a corresponding change in ethnographic practice, perhaps ethnographers ought to be questioning whether human social behavior is changing that much after all. Why do we so often hear the expression, "The more things change, the more they remain the same"?

Ethnography as Occupation and Preoccupation

Ethnography can both occupy and preoccupy, but it is not a career, any more than one might claim to be a "career participant observer" or a "career interviewer." It is something of a paradox that fieldwork—long recognized as the sine qua non of the ethnographer—invariably becomes more and more difficult to pursue even as one establishes a reputation for being successful at it. For anthropologist and nonanthropologist alike, the more engrossed you become with ethnography, the harder it may be to carve out a career that accommodates the opportunity to do more of it. The initial experience through which you establish your reputation may be the only opportunity to do *extended* fieldwork you will ever get. (On the chance this could happen, here is one more reason for making the most of *any* fieldwork opportunity, and especially for thorough note-taking and recordkeeping.)

Other duties that would seem to make ethnography possible in a professional life—with comforting "perks" such as a full-time position and steady income—are likely to become obstacles instead. On the academic side, teaching and writing are what one is expected to do; as Dan Rose observes, academics live "text-dependent" careers (1990:14). By taking priority and precedence, the academic preoccupation with publication is more apt to preempt fieldwork than to enhance it. Ethnographers who might prefer to initiate a new study may find themselves churning old data instead, although they probably regard such behavior as a trait of data-impoverished colleagues in other disciplines, not a problem within their own.

Writing is critical to ethnography and a great asset to an academic career, but fieldwork is neither a prerequisite to writing nor an absolute necessity for a successful anthropological career.[4] On the applied side, reporting, consulting, and preparing proposals for new projects all compete with time and energy available for further fieldwork. The applied anthropologist boasts a field-based approach yet watches available time get whittled away by more immediate demands, the urgencies forever getting an edge on the essentials. Even accepting a position that calls for an experienced ethnographer to serve as curator in a natural history museum may not guarantee opportunity for further fieldwork. About the nearest one can come to being regarded as a more or less full-time ethnographer is to build a reputation as a specialist about some particular people (e.g., the Kwakiutl) or some particular activity amenable to cross-cultural comparison (e.g., schooling, speaking, food gathering and preparation) for which intermittent fieldwork provides a major source of data. At that, the role of ethnographer might seem a bit strange, both in its implication of research forever underway (and thus apparently incapable of completion) and the temptation to lapse into the "my people" syndrome.

To ward off any implied proprietary ownership, one might feel obliged today to wiggle out from under the mantle of ethnographer in exchange for some gentler phrase (e.g., working *with* the Kwakiutl, rather than being an ethnographer of them) or adopt the descriptions, titles, or nicknames suggested by others. I'll admit it would have been nice to be known in anthropological circles as an "expert" on the Kwakiutl, but that might have annoyed the anthropologists who *are* expert and would have amused (or annoyed—see Sewid-Smith 1997) my Kwakiutl acquaintances no end. Instead, for awhile I became "Harry, the ThinkAbout Guy," just as I had earlier survived the nickname "The Shadow" that teachers bestowed upon me during my study of the principal.

About the time one might finally deserve recognition as "the ethnographer" of something or some particular group, other terms may seem better suited. For example, the school principal sometimes introduced me with the explanation, "Harry is doing some research in which I am involved." His earliest introductions had begun on a stronger note, "Harry is doing an anthropological study of me." He changed his tune as he came to realize that his explanation did not produce awe as much as it seemed to raise concerns that for some undisclosed reason this was an administrator who needed to have research done "on" him. Anxious to emphasize the uniqueness of what we were up to, I was not much help when asked if such studies of school princi-pals were customary. My insistence at the time that such a study was unique only succeeded in furthering suspicion that something might be amiss.

If one can neither remain forever in the role of ethnographer nor claim it as an occupation, it is nonetheless quite suitable as a preoccupation, some-thing one "does" if not something one can "be." You can certainly live an ethnographic "life of the mind," drawing upon an ethnographic perspective for viewing the world around you, your personal as well as your professional circumstances. Sociologist Danny Jorgensen is among those who write enthu-siastically of the importance of fieldwork not only to their careers but to their personal identity. Note the importance of his word choice describing his field-work orientation as a *preoccupation* rather than as an *occupation*:

> The methodology of participant observation is for me an abiding preoccu-pation—if not a way of life—and an important component of my social identity. [Jorgensen 1989:8]

I concur wholeheartedly with Jorgensen. Since my focus is on ethnogra-phy, while his is on participant observation, let me paraphrase and add to his words to make the statement my own: *Ethnography is for me an abiding preoccu-pation—if not a way of life—and an important component of my social identity, per-sonally as well as professionally.* In that sense, I have been living the ethnographic life going on four decades.

I am hardly alone in that endeavor, that preoccupation. Many others do so, and do so explicitly, because they employ the conceptual language of ethnography for framing their thoughts. Ethnography is their personal as well as their professional way of seeing. But it is not only its conceptual language that sets ethnography into motion except in the academic setting. Some peo-ple intuitively develop an ethnographer's way of seeing, not because they are natural observers—to some extent we all have to be that—but because they tend to see behavior, *the behavior of those around them as well as their own,* more from a socially oriented perspective than from an individualistic, psychologi-cally oriented one.

Consciously or unconsciously, I suppose I do sometimes try to psyche out others in the course of dealing with them, especially when trying to commu-nicate effectively. But I regard human behavior as eminently social—to a degree to which we ourselves are often unaware, even when we judge it to be otherwise (for example, in describing someone's behavior as anti-social). We act and express ourselves in ways consistent with others in the groups in which we claim or aspire to membership, our "communities of practice."

Whenever I raise an ethnographic perspective to a conscious level, I also become aware of such introspection as an opportunity to test and review notions about culture. The culture concept helps me to think about—to make sense of—my actions and the actions of those with whom I interact. And because I continue to find it helpful as a way to make sense of things, I look for ways to make it more accessible to, more useful to, and better understood by others. I can't work myself up to the point where I want to insist that *everyone* should be an ethnographer (or should learn more about ethnography, which, admittedly, is very good for business), but I do admit to having become a strong advocate, a true believer.

Ethnography offers a thoughtful way to approach the question, "What is going on here?" with some idea of how to go about finding an adequate and adequately informed answer. Elsewhere I have proposed a definition for theory as "a way of asking that is accompanied by a reasonable answer" (HFW 1995:186). In the absence of the ability to predict—or even necessarily to explain—the social behavior of others, the culture concept embodied in the ethnographer's way of seeing offers a path *toward* that understanding. With ethnography to provide both a research strategy and a conceptual framework, I have not been as insistent as some that one cannot initiate research without a theory. Ethnography's central orienting *concept* has served me quite adequately.

A personal vignette, one of those mental snapshots that linger in one's mind for no apparent reason, illustrates my point. The occasion was a morning roughly 20 years ago. I was in a taxi in Kuala Lumpur. I found myself staring at the back of the head of my Malay taxi driver and wondering what was going on inside it. We had negotiated our initial transaction in English, and his driving seemed satisfactory under the always-congested traffic conditions. We had an adequate level of "shared meaning" between us to achieve our mutual purpose in reaching my stated destination. Except for that, however, I had to assume that our sharing ended. My breakfast, lunch, dinner, day's activities, attire, priorities, manner of worship, circle of friends, the language in which each of us was processing both the immediate experience of the drive and more abstract thoughts and concerns about our individual circumstances, even the different type of toilet each of us was most likely to encounter and use during the day—everything was different.

I could easily assume that the driver had a completely different set of worries and delights from mine. I was fairly certain that we did not attribute the same meanings to the days of the week, even if his weekly schedule was somewhat adapted to my Western one in this sprawling "internationalized" Malaysian city. It might make a cute premise for a film, but there was no way in the world he and I could have traded places long enough to get me to my destination, for although I knew where I wanted to go, only he knew how to get there. Once we arrived, his presence served no further purpose, while my presence set other activities in motion. An ethnographic perspective helped me rise above an egocentric one to become preoccupied with what my taxi man might be thinking about me. I rather doubted that he was thinking about me at all, except perhaps as one more faceless foreign fare.

Culture is sometimes likened to a map that we carry in our heads. I referred earlier to Bateson's observation that what gets recorded on a map is difference, but beyond that, the idea of culture as a map has limited appeal. Maps are associated with places, and culture is far more complex than simply moving about in space. Indeed, the taxi man and I shared some general idea of our spatial orientation, for although I did not know exactly how to get where I was going, I would soon enough have been aware had he set off in a wrong direction. No, the map analogy is inadequate. Template may be better, though I'm never sure if the idea of a cultural template isn't too mechanical. Culture as rule book is another, but what size rule book would have been necessary just to get driver and passenger from one intersection to the next? Whatever it was, we had sufficient "sharing" to negotiate a transaction, with virtually nothing left to spare. Not even enough to guide me through the dilemma about whether, and how much, one is expected to tip a taxi driver, especially when traveling abroad. Ah, perhaps we were both thinking about that!

Everybody an Ethnographer?

Would the world be a different (i.e., better) place if everyone developed the kind of ethnographic stance referred to here as "living the ethnographic life"? I doubt it. Further, such an idea would place an almost impossible burden of expectation on ethnography, more likely to crush "enthusiastic untrained people" than to prompt its acceptance among those inclined to be ethnocentric rather than ethnographic. It is probably of more benefit to ethnography to be recognized as akin to behavior in which all humans engage all the time, except that the ethnographer, *acting in the role of ethnographer,* does so more self-consciously, more systematically, and more comparatively, and in professional as well as personal pursuits. Addressing the issue of the role of comparison in the inquiry process, Thomas Weisner makes the case for its centrality in research. One might wonder if the argument cannot be extended to include the role of comparison in *all* human perception:

> All studies have an implicit comparative frame of reference of some sort—a meaning in a context relevant to some cultural place, whether for the pur-

pose of cultural comparison or not. In this sense, all studies have an "ethnographic" component embedded in them, even if ethnography was not done. [Weisner 1996:316]

Dan Rose echoes the idea of ethnography as closely paralleling ordinary social astuteness when he writes, "There is a sense in which we are all ethnographers now" (1990:12). That seems preferable to exalting ethnography by treating it as though it *could* change the world if only more people would study hard and model their behavior on those formally identified as ethnographers. Almost predictably, Rose turns ethnography back on ethnographers to note:

We do not have an adequate understanding of our own culture of ethnographic inquiry—I mean an understanding beyond the confessional, self-observing pieces written in resistance to the hyperscience of 1960s cognitive anthropology. We do not understand ourselves as living within a culture of anthropologists, a subculture within university life. We do not talk about this in profoundly self-critical ways and that is why I would like to comment on the formation of ethnography as a way of living and a way of living differently—as a potent (sub)culture for conducting inquiry into culture. [P. 17]

In spite of the fact that in their own way and for their individual purposes "everybody's doing it," the formal labels "ethnographer" and "ethnography" seem best reserved for those who pursue such endeavors intentionally as a facet of a professional career, those for whom, in the context suggested here, ethnography is not only a way of looking and a way of seeing but a *preferred* way of seeing. Without an ethnographer, there is no ethnography. Bohannan has it right; ethnography does not just happen, there must be intent. But only in the final outcome can each effort be assessed, not so much on an absolute scale as on a relative one. Among the studies presented as ethnographic, some undoubtedly deserve recognition as "more" ethnographic than others. No one who takes the assignment can possibly hope to produce the ultimate one.

Ethnography has sometimes been touted as a means for teaching, and thus for achieving, cultural awareness. Behind such a well-intentioned idea is the hope that to whatever extent we can convey the spirit of ethnography and an appreciation for what ethnographers do, we might someday achieve a society more truly tolerant of and committed to cultural diversity. Restated on a more modest scale, the suggestion is heard that were ethnography to be included in the training of certain professional groups—educators are frequently targeted in illustration—then these practitioners would not only preach tolerance but model it.

Frankly, I think that heralding ethnography as a vehicle for reaching, or teaching, tolerance asks too much. Such an idea might also appear to place anyone who pursues it on a pedestal higher than seems warranted. My experience is that ethnographers are pretty much like folks everywhere. It is not ethnographic prowess that distinguishes the better humans among them, although decent humans must surely be a credit to ethnography. True, during bursts of intense fieldwork researchers often rise to meet role expectations as caring human beings, but neither those expectations nor prolonged experience in the role appear to have had a lasting impact on any ethnographer of my acquaintance. It is essentially a professional status, difficult enough to maintain even for a brief period. It is neither natural nor completely neutral as everyday behavior, for it places the researcher in a more inquisitive role than simply to be empathetic or unusually accepting of difference.

Preoccupied as they can become in their research activities, particularly in participant observation, ethnographers seem unaware that they themselves are often the ones out of place, whether in a setting that is not theirs—some place where they have no function other than to see what others are doing—or a setting where they have assumed a role that no one has asked them to play. As Michael Agar cautions, it is the ethnographer whose behavior doesn't really make sense to anyone (1996:9). That strangeness is reflected in classic fieldwork texts with titles such as Agar's own *Professional Stranger,* Morris Freilich's *Marginal Natives,* or Hortense Powdermaker's *Stranger and Friend.* In spite of the involvement that participant observation is intended to foster, the ethnographer is usually an outsider looking in.

My late colleague Malcolm McFee used to ponder what might happen if anthropologists acted like anthropologists rather than like teachers when they returned to the college classroom. Clearly they don't, although the idea poses an interesting challenge for anthropologists searching for ways to transmit their professional culture other than through lecturing. Based on their fieldwork experiences, anthropologists do feel an obligation to nurture appreciation for other cultures, other ways of doing things, but their message tends to be conveyed more like a moral imperative than as something based on admiration or awe. It may be comforting to entertain high hopes for how ethnography could change the world, but I think it more realistic to reflect on whatever effects the experience seems to have had on past generations of ethnographers than to point to it as the way toward a better tomorrow. Its more immediate benefits are in its potential for broadening perspectives, giving us a way of looking at and trying to understand the lives of others different from ourselves and, as a consequence, gaining some understanding of how we have come to organize our own lives.

Paying a Price for Living the Ethnographic Life

There are personal costs in doing ethnography. Rather than bring this discussion to a close by pushing a canoe off into the sunset, perhaps some reflection on those costs offers an appropriate note on which to conclude.

Readers of early drafts questioned whether I had given sufficient attention to issues of ethics, both in terms of dilemmas facing the ethnographer and the risks and potential problems for those studied. I thought I had done that, sufficiently at least to underscore ideas expressed elsewhere in a piece titled "Fieldwork: The Darker Arts" (HFW 1995, chapter 6). If I seem not to have given adequate explicit attention to the topic, that is consistent with my practice to avoid addressing it in a broad, general way. Of all the topics one can raise in discussing ethnography, ethics is especially tempting for becoming "teachy/preachy."

Raising the topic here does allow me to express dismay at the way research-sponsoring institutions have turned ethics into a whipping boy to make themselves appear superethical vis-à-vis the individual researcher. The burden of ethics has been placed entirely on the individual researcher, with stringent safeguards that continue to pose a threat to the whole ethnographic enterprise. I have no quarrel with holding researchers responsible for their work, but I have been dismayed how, at every level, institutions have managed to place obstacles in the way of researchers when they might instead have tried to assist them to work through the complex issues raised in *any* human research. Watching as rules and regulations ostensibly designed to protect human "subjects" continue to multiply, my recommendation to today's researcher is to comply perfunctorily. Satisfy whatever requirements you must satisfy in the most expedient way possible, without getting bogged down in bureaucratic red tape, or confusing institutional safeguards with your responsibility to those among whom you study.

Ever mindful of both the noble ideals and the thoughtless consequences that originally prompted what has become an outpouring of regulations, my own resolution has been to strive to be as ethical as I can be *all the time,* rather than to fall into the habit of periodically paying ritual homage to ethics. That requires a continual assessment weighing risks against outcomes. In my fieldwork and writing, I have sought to be objective but discrete. As I have noted elsewhere, my discretion necessarily goes unremarked, while questions of possible indiscretion may arise for each reader anew (HFW 1989:138). But I have no Golden Rule to propose. The guideline I try to follow is the Golden Rule restated in negation, to *not* do to others anything I would not want them to do to me. Sometimes that translates simply into *not* saying or *not* telling more than is necessary.

I do not present or defend ethnography as an ethical pursuit. It is, after all, the business of inquiring into other people's business. You can try to be ethical in how you go about doing that, but a basic question remains: Is it *ever* ethical to probe into other people's lives? A telling argument can be made on behalf of the benefits derived *in general* from such efforts, but I cannot claim that such a goal insures that the efforts themselves are necessarily ethical or, in every instance, even beneficial. I regard the underlying issue as one of balancing risks and benefits. My initial premise is that the individual with the most to benefit is *always* the ethnographer, and the individuals with the most to risk are *always* those among whom the ethnographer studies. The risks can be minimized, the benefits or potential benefits maximized, guided by practices of openness and disclosure quite different from those pertaining only a few short years ago, but putting such lofty ideals into practice is always problematic with an approach so open-ended and opportunistic.[5]

Nevertheless, many years and several ethnographies later, I continue to sleep well at night. I feel no uncertainty about, and make no apology for, the realization that I have been the primary beneficiary of my studies. I sleep well because I also believe that the studies reflect an acceptable level of integrity, even as I have watched ethical standards shift and strengthen. I trust that my studies have also made some modest contribution to scholarship in terms of the purposes each study addressed or the way I went about it. Individually and collectively, my contribution to the ethnographic "shelf" is of great personal satisfaction.

At the same time, and without exception, each of those studies has met with resistance of some sort, has caused some anguish, or might seem to have been taken at the expense of someone else. Let me recount these costs in only the briefest way, for I would end on a strange note if I were to belabor what I think properly belongs to the "anthropology of experience" rather than the doing of ethnography. As noted in Chapter 7, these personal dimensions are important to ethnography but they should not be confused for it.

My first study, *A Kwakiutl Village and School*, brought an initial outburst from school officials in the Canadian government worried that the stark picture I painted would make it impossible to recruit teachers to such outposts in the future. Not only did their fears proved unfounded, the monograph was used for years in training programs for teachers headed out for rural or reservation schools (especially in Alaska and Western Canada) so that they were prepared rather than simply "shocked" when confronted by conditions harsher than what they had imagined. On the other hand, the words of a mother of one of the pupils in my village classroom still ring in my ear. Because of offensive language sometimes heard in the village (usually drinking-related) that she felt I had needlessly reported, she had hidden away the copy I had once been so eager to present to her. She informed me that she hoped her children would never have to read those words. That saddened me deeply.

These days, fully three decades since I completed the research, the school administrator who was *The Man in the Principal's Office* has only the kindest remarks to make about that study. He has frequently commended the effort and emphasized how the study helped him to see things he was doing that were not consistent with his own ideal of the kind of principal he wanted to be. Apparently he has forgotten his initial distress and reaction to what he felt was my seeming overattention to things that were going wrong, my inattention to all that was going right. The phrase he used at the time was that he was "disappointed" at the picture of the principalship (and thus of himself) as I had portrayed it.

Had circumstances put me in Zimbabwe's capital city (Salisbury at the time; Harare today) rather than in Bulawayo for my next opportunity for fieldwork, I doubt that I would have been able to do a study of *anything*. I was exceptionally fortunate to link up with Hugh Ashton, an anthropologist turned administrator, who embraced the idea of my proposed study of the African beer gardens. Yet with every sentence I wrote, I worried that some official somewhere within the country might take offense that could, in turn, have severe repercussions for those who had been willing not only to let an uninvited stranger have a look around but to offer their cooperation. There was also the risk, and likelihood, that readers from outside would fail to detect the courage and integrity of certain easily identified administrators during some of that country's dark times.

My study of our own R & D organization's efforts at educational change created unanticipated tension within the organization as I discovered the extent of strife the project was causing in the school system where it was being piloted. Within our organization, the tension was essentially academic, not great for morale but not a threat to job security. Everyone involved seemed self-righteous about defending whatever role had been assigned them, as evidenced by a clear distinction we observed between the designers/implementers of the project and the researchers charged with conducting an independent study of it. In the school district where the pilot study was being conducted, however, those in enthusiastic support were also those in authority, and mounting teacher resistance was viewed with great disfavor. My presence gave the teachers an ear but no voice, for I had the luxury of being able to wait the full course of events before I was expected to spin out my account and interpretation. But neither did I give project developers any satisfaction, since I did not divulge the nature or extent of teacher resistance.

My distress at those circumstances provided a source of energy for following through with a long-term (five-year) study as I came to realize that any such effort to change a social system, whether generated from within or imposed from without, provides an unusual opportunity for learning how that system works. I found it hard to believe how self-serving some key players became, how oblivious to the stress they were causing. Nevertheless, although my published account (HFW 1977) told a story vindicating the teachers, it did not help them. And in spite of writing a solid anthropological monograph (the study in which I employed the analogy to moieties), with some effort on my part to show everyone enacting their roles as they felt they were expected to do, at heart I always felt more like an investigative journalist and crusader than a coolly detached observer. I continue to wonder: Did my moral indignation have a self-serving aspect of its own, giving me the "right" to portray as infamous what might more charitably have been described as persistently poor judgment? Or was this but one more instance in which the ethnographer simply is unable to tell people what they want to hear?

The modest study in community development that I conducted next, during a sabbatical year spent in Malaysia (I did more than just ride around Kuala Lumpur in taxis), found me once again inquiring into a development project, this time at the national and international level. The project raised doubts in my mind as to motives and procedures, but my skeptical nature was no help to a well-intended but floundering project that seemed to do more for project members than for the villagers toward whom it was directed. Intending to be constructive in my criticism, I circulated a first and second draft of impressions and suggestions from my perspective as outside observer, intending that my comments might provoke staff discussion and self-reflection. Apparently my writing provoked the project leaders more literally—to such an extent that they never informed the rest of the staff that they had received my drafts. That effectively cut off the possibility that cooperative junior staff members saw in my work as a way to get higher-ups to listen and to assess project shortcomings. Subsequently the published account (HFW 1983b) was lauded for having provided an instructive lesson for community developers everywhere, but it fell on deaf ears on the local scene, too little, too late. I was dealt with politely but, I think, perceived as an academic with no practical contribution to make other than providing small cash donations or helping with transportation.

A focused ethnographic perspective was specifically sought for the monitoring of instructional television, my next research project, but once again the results were not what anyone wanted to hear. My report and those of the other two ethnographers hired as consultants were simply filed away, a contractual obligation met on our parts and on theirs, no new converts to ethnographic approaches to, or as alternative for, educational evaluation.

The initial research and writing that produced the first article in what was to become the "Brad Trilogy" (HFW 1994, chapters 3, 7, and 11) was based on a life history obtained primarily through taped interviews. Under oath on the witness stand a few years later, Brad's mother stated that Brad had made the whole thing up just to impress me. The events that led to our being in court are tragic and have been recounted elsewhere, but I am amused today (as I was shocked at the time) to have had such a flat-out rejection of the one study in which I felt (and continue to feel) confident I had finally gotten things right. That the account was introduced as evidence in criminal proceedings against Brad himself is as close as I can imagine to an ethnographer's worst nightmare, an informant having his words dutifully recorded for one purpose and subsequently used to build a case against him for another. That I still do not understand all that led up to the events, or am ever likely to understand all that they "mean," is a reminder that we never get the whole story and we are not likely fully to understand whatever part of the story we get.

As issues such as these have arisen about my work, I have taken the occasion to bring them to the public fore rather than hasten to cover them up. I am not adverse to taking certain risks myself, working from what I perceive as the secure and advantaged position of a tenured senior faculty member (bolstered with that familiar air of self-righteousness). I have felt a certain responsibility to take on issues that strike me as being of concern to others who may not "enjoy" (this time I know it is the right word) the same combination of professional obligation coupled with personal security that I feel.

These are new times and new circumstances for the ethnographer. One might say that they come with the territory. The guidelines under which we conduct and report our studies continue to change, whether human behavior is changing all that much or not. Little is to be gained in becoming defensive or apologetic about the past. I did not anticipate the specific problems I have recounted; I would characterize them as predictable but not predicted, reminders that our efforts generate problems of their own. The problems are not insurmountable. In each of these cases, the basic research was solid, the interpretations the best I was able to offer at the time. I trust my studies were served up with enough descriptive detail that readers could judge for themselves the adequacy of my interpretations, as far as I could take them at the time. Interpretation is an ongoing challenge (and responsibility), and I have put forward my own further thoughts and reflections on these inquiries over the years (see especially HFW 1975b, 1989, 1990b, 1994).

As a way of looking, ethnography has shaped my career by presenting me with interesting purposes in challenging places and challenging purposes that made familiar places interesting. As a way of seeing, ethnography has provided a conceptual framework that makes sense to me not only in my academic life but in my personal one. As an approach to research, ethnography has had intuitive appeal with its focus on real behavior in natural settings. In it I find a healthy antidote to my deeply felt skepticism about research on contrived problems studied in contrived settings or to topics reported with imposing levels of statistical significance but lacking significance of a substantive nature.

As ethnography gradually became the focus for much of my teaching, I found it refreshing to be able to bring students to their senses, literally as well as figuratively, in attending to the ordinary behavior of ordinary people and to convey in ordinary language what they had observed and understood. It has been satisfying to have made ethnographers out of a few of them. It has been equally satisfying to have others experience and express appreciation for a sense of personal discovery in their powers of observing, reporting, and interpreting, powers they sometimes felt their academic training had systematically taught them to devalue.

In the foreword to her own *A Way of Seeing*, Margaret Mead wrote in 1961, "It is not the details, as such, that matter but the relationships among them. That is why . . . the life of a small primitive village, studied intensively, so that one comes to know every individual from the newest baby to the oldest grandparents, provides a perfect background for thinking about the problems of our own complicated world" (p. xi). For the most part, that image of the omniscient ethnographer conducting a study in a "small primitive village" is both nostalgic and fictive, but the notion of pursuing research on site and on a manageable scale persists, as does the search for patterns of behavior through studying human social life intensively, intimately, and interactively. Whether your motive in this reading has been to better understand what ethnographers do, to expand your repertoire of fieldwork techniques, or to pursue ethnography in depth in some future inquiry, I hope that in even your most ordinary of everyday social settings you now find yourself asking, "I wonder what an ethnographer would make of all this?"

Notes

1. For examples of radical ethnography or studies conducted in dangerous circumstances, see Philippe Bourgois, *In Search of Respect: Selling Crack in El Barrio* (1995), or a collection edited by Ferrell and Hamm, *Ethnography at the Edge: Crime, Deviance, and Field Research* (1998). See also Lee (1995).

2. James Chadney reports that there are already "thousands of Web pages devoted to anthropology" (1998:5). See, for example, "Ethnographic Studies Resources" at <http://lcweb.loc.gov/folklife/other.html> or "Ethnography and the Internet" (Anthropological Resources on the Internet) at <http://www.aaanet.org/resinet.htm>.

3. The ratio is higher than other estimates and raises an interesting question as to who was considered to be a bona fide anthropologist in a day when that status was not bestowed lightly.

4. Witness Claude Lévi-Strauss's reflection on his own career: "Finally, why not admit it? I realized early on that I was a library man, not a fieldworker. . . . I did enough to learn and to understand what fieldwork is, which is an essential prerequisite for making a sound evaluation and use of the work done by others" (Lévi-Strauss and Eribon 1991:44–45).

5. For a discussion of recent developments on ethical issues in anthropology, including the Code of Ethics of the American Anthropological Association, see Fluehr-Lobban 1998.

References and Select Bibliography

Agar, Michael H.
  1980 The Professional Stranger: An Informal Introduction to Ethnography. New York: Academic Press.
  1994 Language Shock: Understanding the Culture of Conversation. New York: William Morrow and Company.
  1996 The Professional Stranger: An Informal Introduction to Ethnography. 2nd ed. New York: Academic Press.

Anderson, Barbara Gallatin
  1990 First Fieldwork: The Misadventures of an Anthropologist. Prospect Heights, IL: Waveland Press.

Angrosino, Michael V.
  1998 Opportunity House: Ethnographic Stories of Mental Retardation. Walnut Creek, CA: AltaMira Press.

Appaduri, Arjun
  1997 Fieldwork in the Era of Globalization. Anthropology and Humanism 22(1):115–118.

Atkinson, Paul
  1990 The Ethnographic Imagination: Textual Construction of Reality. New York: Routledge.

Atkinson, Paul, and Martyn Hammersley
  1994 Ethnography and Participant Observation. In Handbook of Qualitative Research. Norman K. Denzin and Yvonna S. Lincoln, eds. Pp. 248–261. Thousand Oaks, CA: Sage.

Bandelier, Adolf F.
  1890 The Delight Makers. New York: Dodd, Mead and Co.

Bateson, Gregory
  1972 Steps to an Ecology of Mind. New York: Random House.

Beals, Ralph L.
  1978 Sonoran Fantasy or Coming of Age? American Anthropologist 80(2):355–362.

Becker, Howard S.
  1982 Art Worlds. Berkeley: University of California Press.
  1986 Writing for Social Scientists. Chicago: University of Chicago Press.

Beebe, James
  1995 Basic Concepts and Techniques of Rapid Appraisal. Human Organization 54(1):42–51.

Behar, Ruth
  1996 The Vulnerable Observer: Anthropology That Breaks Your Heart. Boston: Beacon Press.

Bell, Wendell
  1997a Foundations of Future Studies, Volume I: History, Purposes, and Knowledge. New Brunswick, NJ: Transaction Publishers.
  1997b Foundations of Future Studies, Volume II: Values, Objectivity, and the Good Society. New Brunswick, NJ: Transaction Publishers.

Benedict, Ruth
  1934 Patterns of Culture. Boston: Houghton Mifflin.
  1946 The Chrysanthemum and the Sword. Boston: Houghton Mifflin.

Berger, John, and others
  1973 Ways of Seeing. New York: Viking Press. [The booklet was prompted by the TV series *Ways of Seeing*.]

Bernard, H. Russell
  1988 Research Methods in Cultural Anthropology. Newbury Park, CA: Sage.
  1989 Introduction. *In* Native Ethnography. H. Russell Bernard and Jesús Salinas Pedraza. Pp. 11–38. Newbury Park, CA: Sage.
  1994a Methods Belong to All of Us. *In* Assessing Cultural Anthropology. Robert Borofsky, ed. Pp. 168–179. New York: McGraw-Hill.
  1994b Research Methods in Anthropology: Qualitative and Quantitative Approaches. 2nd ed. Thousand Oaks, CA: Sage.
  1996 Language Preservation and Publishing. *In* Indigenous Literacies in the Americas: Language Planning from the Bottom Up. Nancy Hornberger, ed., Pp. 139–156. New York: Mouton de Gruyter.

Bernard, H. Russell, ed.
  1998 Handbook of Methods in Cultural Anthropology. Walnut Creek, CA: AltaMira Press.

Bernard, H. Russell, and M. J. Evans
  1983 New Microcomputer Techniques for Anthropologists. Human Organization 42:182–185.

Bernard, H. Russell, and Jesús Salinas Pedraza
  1989 Native Ethnography: A Mexican Indian Describes His Culture. Newbury Park, CA: Sage.

Berreman, Gerald D.
  1968 Ethnography: Method and Product. *In* Introduction to Cultural
    Anthropology. James A. Clifton, ed. Pp. 336-373. Boston: Houghton Mifflin.

Boas, Franz
  1887 Social Organization and Secret Societies of the Kwakiutl Indians.
    Washington, DC: Government Printing Office.
  1896 The Limitations of the Comparative Method of Anthropology. Science
    4:901–908.

Bock, Philip
  1974 Modern Cultural Anthropology. 2nd ed. New York: Alfred A. Knopf.

Bohannan, Laura [writing as Elenore Smith Bowen]
  1954 Return to Laughter. New York: Harper and Brothers.

Bohannan, Laura, and Paul Bohannan
  1968 Tiv Economy. Evanston, IL: Northwestern University Press.

Bohannan, Paul
  1992 We, The Alien: An Introduction to Cultural Anthropology. Prospect
    Heights, IL: Waveland Press.
  1995 How Culture Works. New York: The Free Press.

Borofsky, Robert, ed.
  1994 Assessing Cultural Anthropology. New York: McGraw-Hill.

Boster, James S.
  1985 "Requiem for the Omniscient Informant": There's Life in the Old Girl Yet.
    In Directions in Cognitive Anthropology. Janet Dougherty, ed. Pp. 177–197.
    Urbana: University of Illinois Press.

Bourgois, Philippe
  1995 In Search of Respect: Selling Crack in El Barrio. New York: Cambridge
    University Press.

Bowen, Elenore Smith (pseudonym). *See* Laura Bohannan.

Bradtmiller, Bruce
  1998 Improving Children's Bike Helmets. Practicing Anthropology 20(2):34–37.

Brettell, Caroline B., ed.
  1993 When They Read What We Write. Westport, CT: Bergin and Garvey.

Brightman, Robert
  1995 Forget Culture: Replacement, Transcendence, Reflexification. Cultural
    Anthropology 10(4):509–546.

British Association for the Advancement of Science
  1912 Notes and Queries on Anthropology. 4th ed. London: Royal
    Anthropological Institute.

Britzman, Deborah P.
  1991 Practice Makes Practice: A Critical Study of Learning to Teach. Albany:
  State University of New York Press.

Brumble, H. David, III
  1981 An Annotated Bibliography of American Indian and Eskimo
  Autobiographies. Lincoln: University of Nebraska Press.
  1988 American Indian Autobiography. Berkeley: University of California Press.

Bruner, Edward M.
  1986 Experience and Its Expressions. *In* The Anthropology of Experience. Victor W.
  Turner and Edward M. Bruner, eds. Pp. 3–30. Urbana: University of Illinois Press.

Buck, P. H.
  1930 Samoan Material Culture. Honolulu: B.P. Bishop Museum Bulletin 75.

Burke, Kenneth
  1935 Permanence and Change. New York: New Republic.

Cassagrande, Joseph B.
  1960 In the Company of Man: Twenty Portraits by Anthropologists. New York:
  Harper and Brothers.

Castaneda, Carlos
  1968 The Teachings of Don Juan: A Yaqui Way of Knowledge. Berkeley:
  University of California Press.
  1971 A Separate Reality: Further Conversations with Don Juan. New York:
  Simon and Schuster.
  1972 Journey to Ixtlan: The Lessons of Don Juan. New York: Simon and
  Schuster.
  1973 Sorcery: A Description of the World. Unpublished doctoral dissertation,
  University of California at Los Angeles.

Cavan, Sheri
  1966 Liquor License: An Ethnography of Bar Behavior. Chicago: Aldine.

Cerroni-Long, E. L., ed.
  1995 Insider Anthropology. National Association for the Practice of
  Anthropology (NAPA) Bulletin #16. Arlington, VA: American
  Anthropological Association.

Chadney, James G.
  1998 Web Sites for Anthropologists. General Anthropology (Bulletin of the
  General Anthropology Division, AAA) 5(1): 1,5–7.

Chambers, Robert
  1987 Shortcut Methods in Social Information Gathering for Rural Development
  Projects. *In* Proceedings of the 1985 International Conference on Rapid Rural

Appraisal. Pp. 33–46. Khon Kaen, Thailand: Rural Systems Research and Farming Systems Research Projects.

1990 Rapid and Participatory Rural Appraisal. Appropriate Technology 16:14–16.

1997 Whose Reality Counts? Putting the First Last. London: Intermediate Technology Publications.

Chapple, Eliot D.

1953 Applied Anthropology in Industry. *In* Anthropology Today. A. L. Kroeber, ed. Pp. 819–831. Chicago: University of Chicago Press.

Clifford, James

1988 The Predicament of Culture. Cambridge, MA: Harvard University Press.

1997 Spatial Practices: Fieldwork, Travel, and the Disciplining of Anthropology. *In* Anthropological Locations. Akhil Gupta and James Ferguson, eds. Pp. 185–222. Berkeley: University of California Press.

Clifford, James, and George E. Marcus

1986 Writing Culture: The Poetics and Politics of Ethnography. Berkeley: University of California Press.

Clifton, James A., and David Levine

1961 Klamath Personalities: Ten Rorschach Case Studies. Department of Anthropology, University of Oregon.

Clough, Patricia Ticineto

1992 The End(s) of Ethnography: From Realism to Social Criticism. Newbury Park, CA: Sage.

1998 The End(s) of Ethnography: Now and Then. Qualitative Inquiry 4(1):3–14.

Codere, Helen, ed.

1966 Kwakiutl Ethnography: Franz Boas. Chicago: University of Chicago Press.

Correll, Shelley

1995 The Ethnography of an Electronic Bar. Journal of Contemporary Ethnography 24(3):270–298.

Crapanzano, Vincent

1977 On the Writing of Ethnography. Dialectical Anthropology 2(1):69–73.

1980 Tuhami: Portrait of a Moroccan. Chicago: University of Chicago Press.

Creswell, John W.

1994 Research Design: Qualitative and Quantitative Approaches. Thousand Oaks, CA: Sage.

1998 Qualitative Inquiry and Research Design: Choosing Among Five Traditions. Thousand Oaks, CA: Sage.

D'Andrade, Roy G.
1987 Modal Responses and Cultural Expertise. American Behavioral Scientist 31:194–202.

Darnell, Regna
1998 Camelot at Yale: The Construction and Dismantling of the Sapirian Synthesis, 1931–1939. American Anthropologist 100(2):361–372.

Deetz, James, and Edwin S. Dethlefsen
1967 Death's Head, Cherub, Urn and Willow. Natural History 76(3):28–37.

deMille, Richard
1978 Castaneda's Journey: The Power and the Allegory. 2nd ed. Santa Barbara, CA: Capra Press. [Originally published 1976.]

deMille, Richard, ed.
1980 The Don Juan Papers: Further Castaneda Controversies. Santa Barbara, CA: Ross-Erikson Publishers.

Denzin, Norman K.
1996 Interpretive Ethnography. Thousand Oaks, CA: Sage.

Denzin, Norman K., and Yvonna S. Lincoln, eds.
1994 Handbook of Qualitative Research. Thousand Oaks, CA: Sage.
2000 Handbook of Qualitative Research. 2nd ed. Thousand Oaks, CA: Sage.

Devereux, George
1968 From Anxiety to Method in the Behavioral Sciences. The Hague: Mouton.

DeWalt, Kathleen M., and Billie R. DeWalt
1998 Participant Observation. In Handbook of Methods in Cultural Anthropology. H. Russell Bernard, ed. Pp. 259–299. Walnut Creek, CA: AltaMira Press.

Dorris, Michael
1989 The Broken Cord. New York: Harper and Row.

Douglas, Mary
1980 The Authenticity of Castaneda. In The Don Juan Papers. Richard deMille, ed. Pp. 25–31. Santa Barbara, CA: Ross-Erikson Publishers. [First published in The Times Higher Education Supplement, London, 15 June 1973 as "Torn Between Two Realities."]

Dozier, Edward P,
1966 Hano: A Tewa Indian Community in Arizona. New York: Holt, Rinehart and Winston.
1967 The Kalinga of Northern Luzon, Philippines. New York: Holt, Rinehart and Winston.

Dumont, Jean-Paul
  1992 The Headman and I: Ambiguity and Ambivalence in the Fieldworking Experience. Prospect Heights, IL: Waveland Press. [First published 1978; reissued 1992 with changes.]

Duneier, Mitchell
  1992 Slim's Table. Chicago: University of Chicago Press.

Eggan, Fred
  1954 Social Anthropology and the Method of Controlled Comparison. American Anthropologist 56(5):743–763.

Eisner, Elliot W.
  1997 The Promise and Perils of Alternative Forms of Data Representation. Educational Researcher 26(6):4–10.

El Guindi, Fadwa, with the collaboration of Abel Hernández Jiménez
  1986 The Myth of Ritual: A Native's Ethnography of Zapotec Life-crisis Rituals. Tucson: University of Arizona Press.

Ellen, Roy. F., ed.
  1984 Ethnographic Research: A Guide to General Conduct. London: Academic Press.

Ellis, Carolyn, and Arthur P. Bochner, eds.
  1996 Composing Ethnography: Alternative Forms of Qualitative Writing. Ethnographic Alternatives Series, Volume 1. Walnut Creek, CA: AltaMira Press.

Ember, Carol
  1994 The Making of a Cross-Cultural Researcher. Research Frontiers Series, Melvin Ember and Carol Ember, eds. Needham Heights, MA: Simon and Schuster Custom Publishing.

Erickson, Frederick
  1984 What Makes School Ethnography "Ethnographic"? Anthropology and Education Quarterly 15(1):51–66.
  1992 Ethnographic Microanalysis of Interaction. *In* Handbook of Qualitative Research in Education. Margaret D. LeCompte, Wendy L. Millroy, and Judith Preissle, eds. Pp. 201–225. San Diego, CA: Academic Press.

Erickson, Ken, and Donald Stull
  1997 Doing Team Ethnography: Warnings and Advice. Thousand Oaks, CA: Sage.

Estroff, Sue E.
  1981 Making It Crazy: An Ethnography of Psychiatric Clients in an American Community. Berkeley: University of California Press. [Reissued in paperback in 1985 with the addition of an Epilogue.]

Evans-Pritchard, E. E.
  1940 The Nuer: A Description of the Modes of Livelihood and Political
    Institutions of a Nilotic People. Oxford, England: Clarendon Press
  1952 Social Anthropology. Glencoe, IL: Free Press.
  1962 Anthropology and History. *In* Social Anthropology and Other Essays. New
    York: Free Press.

Fahim, Hussein, ed.
  1982 Indigenous Anthropology in Non-Western Countries. Durham, NC:
    Carolina Academic Press.

Fei Xiaotong [Fei Hsiao-Tung]
  1939 Peasant Life in China: A Field Study of Country Life in the Yangtze Valley.
    London: Routledge and Kegan Paul.

Ferrell, Jeff, and Mark S. Hamm, eds.
  1998 Ethnography at the Edge: Crime, Deviance, and Field Research. Boston:
    Northeastern University Press.

Fetterman, David M.
  1998 Ethnography Step by Step. 2nd ed. Thousand Oaks, CA: Sage.

Fetterman, David M., ed.
  1984 Ethnography in Educational Evaluation. Beverly Hills, CA: Sage.

Fine, Gary Alan
  1993 Ten Lies of Ethnography. Journal of Contemporary Ethnography
    22(3):267–294.

Fine, Gary Alan, and Kent L. Sandstrom
  1988 Knowing Children: Participant Observation with Minors. Newbury Park,
    CA: Sage.

Firth, Raymond
  1936 We, The Tikopia: A Sociological Analysis of Kinship in Primitive Polynesia.
    London: Allen and Unwin.
  1951 Elements of Social Organization. New York: Philosophical Library.

Fluehr-Lobban, Carolyn
  1998 Ethics. *In* Handbook of Methods in Cultural Anthropology. H. Russell
    Bernard, ed. Pp. 173–202. Walnut Creek, CA: AltaMira Press.

Foley, Douglas E.
  1995 The Heartland Chronicles. Philadelphia: University of Pennsylvania Press.

Fowler, Don D., and Donald L. Hardesty
  1994 Others Knowing Others: Perspectives on Ethnographic Careers.
    Washington, DC: Smithsonian Institution Press.

Fowles, Jib, ed.
1978 Handbook of Futures Research. Westport, CT: Greenwood Press.

Fox, Richard G., ed.
1991 Recapturing Anthropology: Working in the Present. Santa Fe, NM: School of American Research Press.

Frake, Charles O.
1964 A Structural Description of Subanun "Religious Behavior." *In* Explorations in Cultural Anthropology. W. H. Goodenough, ed. Pp. 111–129. New York: McGraw-Hill.
1977 Plying Frames Can Be Dangerous. Quarterly Newsletter of the Institute for Comparative Human Development 1(3):1–7.

Freilich, Morris
1970 Marginal Natives: Anthropologists at Work. New York: Harper and Row.

Fried, Morton H.
1972 The Study of Anthropology. New York: Thomas Y. Crowell Company.

Friedrich, Paul
1991 *Review of* Native Ethnography, by H. Russell Bernard and Jesús Salinas Pedraza. American Anthropologist 93:460.

Garro, Linda
1986 Intracultural Variation in Folk Medical Knowledge: A Comparison Between Groups. American Anthropologist 88:351–370.
1988 Explaining High Blood Pressure: Variation in Knowledge About Illness. American Ethnologist 15:98–119.

Gatewood, John B.
1984 A Short Typology of Ethnographic Genres: Or Ways to Write About Other Peoples. Anthropology and Humanism Quarterly 9(4):5–10.

Geertz, Clifford
1960 The Religion of Java. New York: Free Press.
1963 Agricultural Involution. Berkeley: University of California Press.
1968 Islam Observed: Religious Development in Morocco and Indonesia. Chicago: University of Chicago Press.
1973a The Impact of the Concept of Culture on the Concept of Man. *In* The Interpretation of Cultures. C. Geertz, ed. Pp. 33–54. New York: Basic Books.
1973b Thick Description. *In* The Interpretation of Cultures. C. Geertz, ed. Pp. 3–30. New York: Basic Books.
1983 Local Knowledge. New York: Basic Books.
1988 Works and Lives. Stanford, CA: Stanford University Press.
1995 After the Fact. Cambridge, MA: Harvard University Press.

Gittelsohn, Joel, Pertti J. Pelto, Margaret E. Bentley, Karabi Ghattacharyya, and Joan Jensen
  1998 Rapid Assessment Procedures (RAP): Ethnographic Methods to Investigate Women's Health. Boston: International Nutrition Foundation.

Gold, Raymond L.
  1958 Roles in Sociological Field Observations. Social Forces 36:217–223.
  1997 The Ethnographic Method in Sociology. Qualitative Inquiry 3:388–402.

Goodenough, Ward H.
  1970 Description and Comparison in Cultural Anthropology. Chicago: Aldine.
  1976 Multiculturalism as the Normal Human Experience. Anthropology and Education Quarterly 7(4):4–7.
  1981 Culture, Language, and Society. Menlo Park, CA: Benjamin/Cummings Publishing Company.

Goodwin, J. P.
  1989 More Man than You'll Ever Be: Gay Folklore and Acculturation in Middle America. Bloomington: Indiana University Press.

Gorer, Geoffrey
  1948 The American People. New York: W. W. Norton.

Grandstaff, Terry B.
  1988 Rapid Rural Appraisal Activities at Khon Kaen University: An Overview. *In* Rapid Rural Appraisal in Northeast Thailand. Case Studies. George W. Lovelace, Sukaesinee Subhadhira, and Suchint Simaraks, eds. Pp. 20–25. Khon Kaen University, Thailand. KKU-FORD Rural Systems Research Project.

Grills, Scott
  1998 Doing Ethnographic Research: Fieldwork Settings. Thousand Oaks, CA: Sage.

Gruber, Howard E.
  1981 Darwin on Man: A Psychological Study of Scientific Creativity. 2nd ed. Chicago: University of Chicago Press.

Gupta, Akhil, and James Ferguson, eds.
  1997 Anthropological Locations: Boundaries and Grounds of a Field Science. Berkeley: University of California Press.

HFW (See Wolcott, Harry F.)

Hagan, T.
  1986 Interviewing the Downtrodden. *In* Qualitative Research in Psychology. P. D. Ashworth, A. Giorgi, and A. de Koening, eds. Pp. 332–360. Pittsburgh, PA: Duquesne University Press.

Hammar, Lawrence
  1998 *Review of* The Lost Drum: The Myth of Sexuality in Papua New Guinea and Beyond, by James Weiner. American Anthropologist 100(1):214–215.

Hammersley, Martyn
   1992 What's Wrong with Ethnography? London: Routledge.

Hammersley, Martyn, and Paul Atkinson
   1983 Ethnography: Principles in Practice. London: Tavistock.
   1995 Ethnography: Principles in Practice. 2nd ed. New York: Routledge.

Harris, Kari Jo, Norge W. Jerome, and Stephen B. Fawcett
   1998 Rapid Assessment Procedures: A Review and Critique. Human
       Organization 56(3):375–378.

Harris, Marvin
   1998 Theories of Culture in Postmodern Times. Walnut Creek, CA: AltaMira Press.

Haviland, William A.
   1993 Cultural Anthropology. 7th ed. Fort Worth, TX: Harcourt Brace.

Hayano, David
   1979 Auto-ethnography: Paradigms, Problems, and Prospects. Human
       Organization 38(1):99–104.
   1982 Poker Faces: The Life and Work of Professional Card Players. Berkeley:
       University of California Press.
   1990 Road Through the Rain Forest: Living Anthropology in Highland Papua
       New Guinea. Prospect Heights, IL: Waveland Press.

Heisenberg, Werner
   1958 Physics and Philosophy: The Revolution in Modern Science. New York:
       Harper and Brothers Publishers.

Hennigh, Lawrence
   1981 The Anthropologist as Key Informant: Inside a Rural Oregon Town. *In*
       Anthropologists at Home in North America: Methods and Issue in the Study
       of One's Own Society. Donald A. Messerschmidt, ed. Pp. 121–132.
       Cambridge, MA: Cambridge University Press.

Henry, Jules
   1963 Culture Against Man. New York: Random House.
   1965 Pathways to Madness. New York: Random House.

Henry, Jules, and Melford E. Spiro
   1953 Psychological Techniques: Projective Techniques in Field Work. *In*
       Anthropology Today. Alfred L. Kroeber, ed. Pp. 417–429. Chicago: University
       of Chicago Press.

Herriott, Robert E., and Neal Gross, eds.
   1979 The Dynamics of Planned Educational Change. Berkeley, CA: McCutchan
       Publishing Company.

Herz, Rosanna, and Jonathan B. Imber, eds.
   1995 Studying Elites Using Qualitative Methods. Thousand Oaks, CA: Sage.

Hilger, I.
  1960 Field Guide to the Ethnological Study of Child Life. New Haven, CT:
  Human Relations Area Files.

Hill, Michael R.
  1993 Archival Strategies and Techniques. Newbury Park, CA: Sage.

Honadle, George
  1982 Rapid Reconnaissance for Development Administration: Mapping and
  Moulding Organizational Landscapes. World Development 10(8):623–649.

Howard, Michael C.
  1996 Contemporary Cultural Anthropology. 5th ed. New York: HarperCollins
  College Publishers.

Iwanska, Alicja
  1971 Purgatory and Utopia: A Mazahua Indian Village of Mexico. Cambridge,
  MA: Schenkman Publishing Company.

Jackson, Michael
  1989 Paths Toward a Clearing: Radical Empiricism and Ethnographic Inquiry.
  Bloomington: Indiana University Press.
  1995 At Home in the World. Durham, NC: Duke University Press.
  1996 Introduction. *In* Things as They Are: New Directions in Phenomenological
  Anthropology. Michael Jackson, ed. Pp. 1–50. Bloomington: Indiana
  University Press.

Jacobson, David
  1991 Reading Ethnography. Albany: State University of New York Press.

Jessor, Richard
  1996 Ethnographic Methods in Contemporary Perspective. *In* Ethnography and
  Human Development. Richard Jessor, Anne Colby, and Richard A. Shweder,
  eds. Pp. 3–14. Chicago: University of Chicago Press.

Jorgensen, Danny L.
  1989 Participant Observation. Newbury Park, CA: Sage.

Kaplan, David, and Robert A. Manners
  1972 Culture Theory. Englewood Cliffs, NJ: Prentice Hall. [Reissued 1986 by
  Waveland Press, Prospect Heights, IL.]

Keesing, Felix
  1958 Cultural Anthropology: The Science of Custom. New York: Rinehart and
  Company.

Keesing, Roger M.
  1978 !Elota's Story: The Life and Times of a Solomon Islands Big Man. St. Lucia,
  Queensland: University of Queensland Press.

1976 Cultural Anthropology: A Contemporary Perspective. New York: Holt, Rinehart and Winston.
1981 Cultural Anthropology. New York: Holt, Rinehart and Winston.

Keesing, Roger M., and Felix M. Keesing
1971 New Perspectives in Cultural Anthropology. New York: Holt, Rinehart and Winston.

Kenyatta, Jomo
1938 Facing Mt. Kenya. London: Martin Secker and Warburg.

Ketudat, Sippanondha, with Robert Textor
1990 The Middle Path for the Future of Thailand. Honolulu: East-West Center.

Keyes, Charles F.
1989 Thailand: Buddhist Kingdom as Modern Nation-State. Boulder, CO: Westview Press.

Khon Kaen University
1987 Proceedings of the 1985 International Conference on Rapid Rural Appraisal. Khon Kaen, Thailand: Rural Systems Research and Farming Systems Research Projects.

King, A. Richard
1967 The School at Mopass: A Problem of Identity. New York: Holt, Rinehart and Winston.

Kirk, Jerome, and Marc L. Miller
1986 Reliability and Validity in Qualitative Research. Beverly Hills, CA: Sage.

Kleinman, Arthur
1995 Writing at the Margin: Discourse Between Anthropology and Medicine. Berkeley: University of California Press

Kleinman, Sherryl, and Martha A. Copp
1993 Emotions and Fieldwork. Newbury Park, CA: Sage

Kluckhohn, Clyde
1945 The Personal Document in Anthropological Science. *In* The Use of Personal Documents in History, Anthropology, and Sociology. Louis Gottschalk, Clyde Kluckhohn, and Robert Angell, eds. Pp. 76–173. Social Science Research Council Bulletin 53.
1949 Mirror for Man: The Relation of Anthropology to Modern Life. New York: Whittlesey House, McGraw-Hill.

Kluckhohn, Clyde, and Henry A. Murray, eds.
1948 Personality in Nature, Society, and Culture. New York: Alfred A. Knopf.

Kluckhohn, Florence
  1940 The Participant-Observer Technique in Small Communities. American
  Journal of Sociology 46(3):331–344.

Kondo, Dorinne K.
  1990 Crafting Selves: Power, Gender, and Discourses of Identity in a Japanese
  Workplace. Chicago: University of Chicago Press.

Kridel, Craig, ed.
  1998 Writing Educational Biography: Explorations in Qualitative Research. New
  York: Garland Publishing/Tayor and Francis Group.

Kroeber, Alfred L.
  1922 Introduction. In American Indian Life. Elsie Clews Parsons, ed. Pp. 5–16.
  New York: B. W. Huebsch.

Kuper, Adam
  1996 Anthropology and Anthropologists: The Modern British School. 3rd ed.
  London: Routledge. [First published 1973.]

Kutsche, Paul
  1998 Field Ethnography: A Manual for Doing Cultural Anthropology. Upper
  Saddle River, NJ: Prentice Hall.

Kvale, Steinar
  1996 InterViews: An Introduction to Qualitative Research Interviewing.
  Thousand Oaks, CA: Sage.

LaFarge, Oliver
  1929 Laughing Boy. New York: Literary Guild of America.

Langness, L. L., and Gelya Frank
  1978 Fact, Fiction and the Ethnographic Novel. Anthropology and Humanism
  Quarterly 3(1,2):18–22.
  1981 Lives: An Anthropological Approach to Biography. Novato, CA: Chandler
  and Sharp.

Lave, Jean, and Etienne Wenger
  1991 Situated Learning: Legitimate Peripheral Participation. New York:
  Cambridge University Press.

Leach, Edmund
  1957 The Epistemological Background to Malinowski's Empiricism. In Man and
  Culture: An Evaluation of the Work of Bronislaw Malinowski. Raymond Firth,
  ed. Pp. 119–137. New York: Harper Torchbooks.

LeCompte, Margaret, Wendy L. Millroy, and Judith Preissle, eds.
  1992 Handbook of Qualitative Research in Education. San Diego, CA: Academic
  Press.

Lee, Raymond M.
1995 Dangerous Fieldwork. Thousand Oaks, CA: Sage.

Lévi-Strauss, Claude, and Didier Eribon
1991 Conversations with Claude Lévi-Strauss. [Trans. by Paula Wissing.] Chicago: University of Chicago Press.

Lewin, Kurt
1946 Action Research and Minority Problems. Journal of Social Issues 2:34–46.

Lewis, Oscar
1951 Life in a Mexican Village: Tepoztlán Restudied. Urbana: University of Illinois Press.
1961 The Children of Sánchez: Autobiography of a Mexican Family. New York: Random House.

Lindeman, E. C.
1924 Social Discovery: An Approach to the Study of Functional Groups. New York: Republic.

Lowie, Robert H.
1953 Ethnography, Cultural and Social Anthropology. American Anthropologist 55(4):527–534.

Maiolo, John R., M. Young, E. Glazier, M. Downs, and J. Petterson
1994 Pile Sorts by Phone. Cultural Anthropology Methods 6(1):1–2.

Maitland, Frederick D.
1968 Selected Essays. Freeport, NY: Books for Libraries. [Reprint of a 1936 edition edited by H. D. Hazeltine, published by Lopsley and Winfield.]

Malinowski, Bronislaw
1922 Argonauts of the Western Pacific. London: Routledge.
1967 A Diary in the Strict Sense of the Term. New York: Harcourt, Brace, and World.

Mandelbaum, David G.
1973 The Study of Life History: Gandhi. Current Anthropology 14(3):177–206.

Marchione, Thomas
1981 Ethnographic Study: Phase I. Field Manual. Infant Feeding Practices Study. Population Council/Columbia University/Cornell University. Unpublished technical paper. (Cited in Pelto 1992:265,322.)

Marcus, George E.
1997 The Postmodern Condition and the Teaching of Anthropology. In The Teaching of Anthropology. C. Kottak, Jane White, Richard Furlow, and Patricia Rice, eds. Pp. 103–112. Mountain View, CA: Mayfield Publishing Company.

1998 Sticking with Ethnography through Thick and Thin. *In* Ethnography through Thick and Thin. G. Marcus, ed. Pp. 231–253. Princeton, NJ: Princeton University Press.

Markham, Annette N.
1998 Life Online: Researching Real Experience in Virtual Space. Walnut Creek, CA: AltaMira Press.

Marx, Karl
1974 The German Ideology. New York: International Publishers. [Originally published 1846.]

McCracken, Grant
1988 The Long Interview. Newbury Park, CA: Sage.

McCurdy, David W.
1997 The Ethnographic Approach to Teaching Cultural Anthropology. *In* The Teaching of Anthropology. Conrad Kottak, Jane White, Richard Furlow, and Patricia Rice, eds. Pp. 62–69. Mountain View, CA: Mayfield Publishing Company.

McKeown, C. Timothy
1988 The Future of Science: Young Scientists at the International Institute for Applied Systems Analysis. Unpublished Ph.D. dissertation, Northwestern University.

McLaren, Peter
1993 Schooling as a Ritual Performance: Towards a Political Economy of Educational Symbols and Gestures. 2nd ed. New York: Routledge.

Mead, Margaret
1928 Coming of Age in Samoa: A Psychological Study of Primitive Youth for Western Civilisation. New York: William Morrow.
1942 And Keep Your Powder Dry: An Anthropologist Looks at America. New York: Morrow.
1952 The Training of the Anthropologist. American Anthropologist 54(3):343–346.
1970 The Art and Technology of Fieldwork. *In* Handbook of Method in Cultural Anthropology. Raoul Naroll and Ronald Cohen, eds. Pp. 246–265. Garden City, NY: Natural History Press.

Mead, Margaret, and Rhoda Métraux
1953 The Study of Culture at a Distance. Chicago: University of Chicago Press.
1961 A Way of Seeing. New York: McCall Publishing Company.

Messenger, John
1989 Inis Beag Revisited: The Anthropologist as Observant Participant. Salem, WI: Sheffeld Publishing.

Mintz, Sidney W.
1974 Worker in the Cane: A Puerto Rican Life History. New York: W. W.
Norton. [Originally published 1960 by Yale University Press.]

Moerman, Michael
1988 Talking Culture: Ethnography and Conversation Analysis. Philadelphia:
University of Pennsylvania Press.

Moffatt, Michael
1989 Coming of Age in New Jersey: College and American Culture. New
Brunswick, NJ: Rutgers University Press.

Morgan, David L.
1988 Focus Groups as Qualitative Research. Newbury Park, CA: Sage.

Murdock, George Peter, ed.
1971 Outline of Cultural Materials. 4th ed., 5th printing, with modifications.
New Haven, CT: HRAF Press.

Nabokov, Peter
1967 Two Leggings: The Making of a Crow Warrior. New York: Crowell.

Narayan, Kirin
1993 How Native Is a "Native" Anthropologist? American Anthropologist
95:671–686.

Naroll, Raoul
1962 Data Quality Control. New York: Free Press.

Opler, Morris E.
1969 Apache Odyssey: A Journey Between Two Worlds. New York: Holt,
Rinehart and Winston.

Ortiz, Alfonso
1969 The Tewa World: Space, Time, Being, and Becoming in a Pueblo Society.
Chicago: University of Chicago Press.

Ortner, Sherry B.
1978 Sherpas Through Their Rituals. New York: Cambridge University Press.

Osgood, Cornelius
1940 Ingalik Material Culture. Yale University Publications in Anthropology, No. 22.

Ottenberg, Simon
1990 Thirty Years of Fieldnotes: Changing Relationships to the Text. *In*
Fieldnotes: The Makings of Anthropology. Roger Sanjek, ed. Pp. 139–160.
Ithaca, NY: Cornell University Press.

Otterbein, Keith F.
1994 *Comment on* The Comparative Method in Anthropology. Current
Anthropology 35(5):559–560.

Passaro, Joanne
  1997 "You Can't Take the Subway to the Field!": "Village" Epistemologies in the
    Global Village. *In* Anthropological Locations. Akhil Gupta and James
    Ferguson, eds. Pp. 147–162. Berkeley: University of California Press.

Paul, Benjamin D.
  1953 Interview Techniques and Field Relationships. *In* Anthropology Today. A. L.
    Kroeber, ed. Pp. 430–451. Chicago: University of Chicago Press.

Pelto, Pertti
  1992 Anthropological Research Methods and Applications: Taking Stock. *In*
    Anthropological Research Process and Application. John J. Poggie, Jr., Billie R.
    DeWalt, and William W. Dressler, eds. Pp. 259–270. Albany: State University
    Press of New York.

Pelto, Pertti J., and Gretel H. Pelto
  1978 Anthropological Fieldwork: The Structure of Inquiry. 2nd ed. New York:
    Cambridge University Press.

Plattner, Stuart
  1989 Commentary: Ethnographic Method. Anthropology Newsletter 32:30,21.
    Washington, DC: American Anthropological Association.

Poggie, John J., Jr., Billie R. DeWalt, and William W. Dressler, eds.
  1992 Anthropological Research Process and Application. Albany: State
    University Press of New York.

Powdermaker, Hortense
  1939 After Freedom: A Cultural Study in the Deep South. New York: Viking
    Press.
  1950 Hollywood: The Dream Factory: An Anthropological Look at the Movie-
    makers. Boston: Little, Brown.
  1966 Stranger and Friend: The Way of an Anthropologist. New York: W. W.
    Norton.

Prus, Robert
  1996 Symbolic Interaction and Ethnographic Research: Intersubjectivity and the
    Study of Human Lived Experience. Albany: State University of New York Press.

Quinney, Richard
  1996 Once My Father Traveled West to California. *In* Composing Ethnography:
    Alternative Forms of Qualitative Writing. Carolyn Ellis and Arthur P. Bochner,
    eds. Pp. 357–382. Walnut Creek, CA: AltaMira Press.

Radcliffe-Brown, A. R.
  1951 The Comparative Method in Social Anthropology. Journal of the Royal
    Anthropological Institute of Great Britain and Ireland 81:15–22.
  1952 Historical Note on British Social Anthropology. American Anthropologist
    54(2, part 1):275–277.

Radin, Paul
  1926 Crashing Thunder: The Autobiography of an American Indian. New York: D.
    Appleton and Company. [Reissued 1983 by the University of Nebraska Press.]

Reed-Danahay, Deborah E., ed.
  1997 Auto/Ethnography: Rewriting the Self and the Social. New York: Berg.

Rhoades, Robert E.
  1987 Basic Field Techniques for Rapid Rural Appraisal. *In* Proceedings of the
    1985 International Conference on Rapid Rural Appraisal. Pp. 114–128. Khon
    Kaen, Thailand: Rural Systems Research and Farming Systems Research
    Projects.

Richards, Audrey I.
  1939 The Development of Field Work Methods in Social Anthropology. *In* The
    Study of Society. F. C. Bartlett, M. Ginsberg, E. J. Lindgren, and R. H.
    Thouless, eds. Pp. 272–316. London: Kegan Paul, Trench, Trubner.

Richardson, Miles
  1998 The Poetics of a Resurrection: Re-Seeing 30 Years of Change in a
    Colombian Community and in the Anthropological Enterprise. American
    Anthropologist 100(1):11–40.

Riner, Reed D.
  1991 Anthropology About the Future: Limits and Potentials. Human
    Organization 50(3):297–311.

Rist, Ray C.
  1980 Blitzkrieg Ethnography: On the Transformation of a Method into a
    Movement. Educational Researcher 9(2):8–10.

Roethlisberger, F. J., and William Dickson
  1939 Management and the Worker. New York: Cambridge University Press.

Rohner, Ronald P.
  1964 Ethnography of a Contemporary Kwakiutl Village: Gilford Island Band.
    Unpublished Ph.D. dissertation, Stanford University.
  1968 *Review of* A Kwakiutl Village and School, by Harry F. Wolcott. American
    Anthropologist 70(3):654.

Rohner, Ronald P., ed.
  1969 The Ethnography of Franz Boas. [Trans. by Hedy Parker.] Chicago:
    University of Chicago Press.

Rohner, Ronald P., and Evelyn C. Rohner
  1970 The Kwakiutl: Indians of British Columbia. New York: Holt, Rinehart and
    Winston. [Reissued 1986 by Waveland Press, Prospect Heights, IL.]

Romney, A. Kimball
  1994 Cultural Knowledge and Cognitive Structure. *In* The Making of
  Psychological Anthropology II. M. Suárez-Orozco, G. Spindler, and L. Spindler,
  eds. Pp. 254–283. New York: Harcourt Brace and Company.
  1999 Culture Consensus as a Statistical Model. Current Anthropology
  40(Supplement):S103–S115.

Romney, A. Kimball, and Carmella C. Moore
  1998 Toward a Theory of Culture as Shared Cognitive Structures. Ethos
  26(3):314–337.

Romney, A. K., Susan Weller, and W. H. Batchelder
  1986 Culture as Consensus: A Theory of Culture and Informant Accuracy.
  American Anthropologist 88:313–338.

Rosaldo, Renato
  1989 Culture and Truth: The Remaking of Social Analysis. Boston: Beacon Press.

Rose, Dan
  1987 Black American Street Life: South Philadelphia, 1969–1971. Philadelphia:
  University of Pennsylvania Press.
  1990 Living the Ethnographic Life. Newbury Park, CA: Sage.

Royal Anthropological Institute of Great Britain and Ireland
  1951 Notes and Queries on Anthropology. 6th ed. London: Routledge and
  Kegan Paul. [First edition published 1874; 4th edition is listed above under
  British Association for the Advancement of Science.]

Rubinstein, Robert A., ed.
  1991 Fieldwork: The Correspondence of Robert Redfield and Sol Tax. Boulder,
  CO: Westview Press.

Salinas Pedraza, Jesús
  1996 Saving and Strengthening Indigenous Mexican Languages: The CELIAC
  Experience. *In* Indigenous Literacies in the Americas: Language Planning from
  the Bottom Up. Nancy Hornberger, ed. Pp. 171–187. New York: Mouton de
  Gruyter.

Salinas Pedraza, Jesús, in collaboration with H. Russell Bernard
  1978 Rc Hnychnyu: The Otomí. Volume 1: Geography and Fauna. Albuquerque:
  University of New Mexico Press.

Sands, Kathleen
  1980 Preface. *In* Autobiography of a Yaqui Poet, by R. Savala. Tucson: University
  of Arizona Press.

Sanjek, Roger
  1990 On Ethnographic Validity. *In* Fieldnotes. Roger Sanjek, ed. Pp. 385–418.
  Ithaca, NY: Cornell University Press.

1991 The Ethnographic Present. Man: The Journal of the Royal Anthropological Institute 26:609–628.

Sanjek, Roger, ed.
1990 Fieldnotes: The Makings of Anthropology. Ithaca, NY: Cornell University Press.

Savala, Refugio
1980 Autobiography of a Yaqui Poet. Tucson: University of Arizona Press.

Schensul, Jean J., and Margaret D. LeCompte, series eds.
1999 Ethnographer's Toolkit. [Seven volumes.] Walnut Creek, CA: AltaMira Press.

Schlereth, Thomas J.
1982 Material Culture Studies in America. Nashville, TN: American Association for State and Local History. (Distributed by AltaMira Press, Walnut Creek, CA.)

Schneider, David M.
1984 A Critique of the Study of Kinship. Ann Arbor: University of Michigan Press.

Schwartzman, Helen B.
1989 The Meeting: Gatherings in Organizations and Communities. New York: Plenum Press.

Schwimmer, Brian
1996 Anthropology on the Internet: A Review and Evaluation of Networked Resources. Current Anthropology 37(3):561–568.

Scrimshaw, Susan, and Elena Hurtado
1987 Rapid Assessment Procedures for Nutrition and Primary Health Care. Los Angeles: University of California Latin American Center Publications.

Seidel, John
1992 Method and Madness in the Application of Computer Technology to Qualitative Data Analysis. *In* Using Computers in Qualitative Research. Nigel G. Fielding and Raymond M. Lee, eds. Pp. 107–116. Newbury Park, CA: Sage.

Seidman, I. E.
1991 Interviewing as Qualitative Research: A Guide for Researchers in the Social Sciences. New York: Teachers College Press.

Sewid-Smith, Daisy
1997 The Continuing Reshaping of our Ritual World by Academic Adjuncts. Anthropology and Education Quarterly 28(4):594–605.

Sexton, James D., ed.
1981 Son of Tecún Umán: A Maya Indian Tells His Life Story. Tucson: University of Arizona Press.
1985 Campesino: The Diary of a Guatemalan Indian. Tucson: University of Arizona Press.

Shokeid, Moshe
  1995 A Gay Synagogue in New York. New York: Columbia University Press.

Shore, Bradd
  1996 Culture in Mind: Cognition, Culture, and the Problem of Meaning. New York: Oxford University Press.

Shostak, Marjorie
  1981 Nisa: The Life and Words of a !Kung Woman. Cambridge, MA: Harvard University Press.

Shulman, Martha Rose
  1995 Great Breads. Shelburne, VT: Chapters Publishing Ltd.

Shweder, Richard A.
  1996a *Quanta* and *Qualia:* What Is the "Object" of Ethnographic Method? *In* Ethnography and Human Development. Richard Jessor, Anne Colby, and Richard A. Shweder, eds. Pp. 175–182. Chicago: University of Chicago Press.
  1996b True Ethnography: The Lore, the Law, and the Lure. *In* Ethnography and Human Development. Richard Jessor, Anne Colby, and Richard A. Shweder, eds. Pp. 15–52. Chicago: University of Chicago Press.

Sidky, H.
  1996 Irrigation and State Formation in Hunza: The Anthropology of a Hydraulic Kingdom. Lanham, MD: University Press of America.

Siegel, Bernard
  1996 The Known, Unknown and Unknowable in Anthropology. Anthropology Newsletter 37(7):1,4–6.

Smith, Sheldon, and Philip D. Young
  1998 Cultural Anthropology: Understanding a World in Transition. Boston: Allyn and Bacon.

Smith, Sidonie, and Julia Watson
  1996 Getting a Life: Everyday Uses of Autobiography. Minneapolis: University of Minnesota Press.

Spindler, George
  1955 Education in a Transforming American Culture. Harvard Educational Review 25:145–156.
  1971 Anthropology and Education. Council on Anthropology and Education Newsletter 2(1):1–2.
  1973 An Anthropology of Education? Council on Anthropology and Education Newsletter 4(1):14–16.

Spindler, George, and Louise Spindler
  1965 The Instrumental Activities Inventory: A Technique for the Study of the Psychology of Acculturation. Southwestern Journal of Anthropology 21(1):1–23.

1991 Rorschaching in North America in the Shadow of Hallowell. Psychoanalytic
      Study of Society 16:155–182.

Spradley, James P.
  1967 James Sewid: A Social, Cultural and Psychological Analysis of a Bicultural
        Innovator. Unpublished Ph.D. dissertation, Department of Anthropology,
        University of Washington.
  1970 You Owe Yourself a Drunk: An Ethnography of Urban Nomads. Boston:
        Little, Brown.
  1979 The Ethnographic Interview. New York: Holt, Rinehart and Winston.
  1980 Participant Observation. New York: Holt, Rinehart and Winston.

Spradley, James P., ed.
  1969 Guests Never Leave Hungry: The Autobiography of James Sewid, A
        Kwakiutl Indian. New Haven, CT: Yale University Press.

Spradley, James P., and David W. McCurdy
  1972 The Cultural Experience: Ethnography in Complex Society. Chicago:
        Science Research Associates. [Reissued 1988 by Waveland Press, Prospect
        Heights, IL.]

Stewart, Alex
  1998 The Ethnographer's Method. Thousand Oaks, CA: Sage.

Stocking, George W., Jr.
  1992 The Ethnographer's Magic and Other Essays in the History of
        Anthropology. Madison: University of Wisconsin Press.

Stocking, George W., Jr., general editor
  1983 to present History of Anthropology. Madison: University of Wisconsin
        Press. [Eight volumes to date, each dealing with some particular aspect of
        anthropology. See, for example, Volume I, 1983: Observers Observed: Essays
        on Ethnographic Fieldwork.]

Tedlock, Barbara
  1991 From Participant Observation to the Observation of Participation: The
        Emergence of Narrative Ethnography. Journal of Anthropological Research
        47(1):69–94.
  2000 Ethnography and Ethnographic Representation. *In* Handbook of
        Qualitative Research, 2nd ed. Norman Denzin and Yvonna Lincoln, eds.
        Thousand Oaks, CA: Sage.

Textor, Robert B.
  1990 Methodological Approaches. *In* The Middle Path for the Future of
        Thailand. Sippanondha Ketudat, with Robert B. Textor. Pp. 135–152.
        Honolulu: East-West Center.
  1995 The Ethnographic Futures Research Method: An Application to Thailand.
        Futures 27(4):461–471.

Textor, Robert B., and coauthors
  1985 Anticipatory Anthropology and the Telemicroelectronic Revolution: A
    Preliminary Report from Silicon Valley. Anthropology and Education Quarterly
    16:3–30.

Textor, Robert B., Bhansoon Ladavalya, and Sidthinat Prabudhanitisarn
  1984 Alternative Sociocultural Futures for Thailand: A Pilot Inquiry Among
    Academics. Chiang Mai, Thailand: Faculty of the Social Sciences, Chiang Mai
    University.

Thomas, Jim
  1993 Doing Critical Ethnography. Newbury Park, CA: Sage.

Thomas, W. I., and F. Znaniecki
  1918–1920 The Polish Peasant in America: Monograph of an Immigrant Group.
    5 Vols. Chicago: University of Chicago Press.

Tilley, Christopher
  1996 An Ethnography of the Neolithic: Early Prehistoric Societies in Southern
    Scandinavia. New York: Cambridge University Press.

Turnbull, Colin M.
  1961 The Forest People. New York: Simon and Schuster.
  1965 Wayward Servants. Garden City, NY: Natural History Press.

Turner, Edith
  1985 On the Edge of the Bush: Anthropology as Experience. Tucson: University
    of Arizona Press.

Turner, Victor W., and Edward M. Bruner, eds.
  1986 The Anthropology of Experience. Urbana: University of Illinois Press.

Tylor, Edward B.
  1874 Primitive Cultures. (In two volumes.) New York: Henry Holt and
    Company. [Originally published 1871 in England.]

Uchendu, Victor
  1965 The Igbo of Southeastern Nigeria. New York: Holt, Rinehart and Winston.

Van Maanen, John
  1988 Tales of the Field: On Writing Ethnography. Chicago: University of
    Chicago Press.

Van Maanen, John, ed.
  1995 Representation in Ethnography. Thousand Oaks, CA: Sage.

van Willigen, John, and Billie R. DeWalt
  1985 Reconnaissance Surveys. In Training Manual in Policy Ethnography. John
    van Willigen and Billie R. DeWalt, eds. Pp. 27–35. Washington, DC:
    American Anthropological Association Special Publication #19.

van Willigen, John, and Timothy L. Finan
   1991 Soundings: Rapid and Reliable Research Methods for Practicing
      Anthropologists. NAPA (National Association for the Practice of Anthropology)
      Bulletin #10. Washington, DC: American Anthropological Association.

Veblen, Thorstein
   1899 The Theory of the Leisure Class. New York: Macmillan.

Vidich, Arthur J., and Joseph Bensman
   1958 Small Town in Mass Society. Princeton, NJ: Princeton University Press.

Visweswaran, Kamala
   1997 Histories of Feminist Ethnography. Annual Review of Anthropology
      26:591–621.

Vogt, Evon Z.
   1994 Fieldwork Among the Maya: Reflections on the Harvard Chiapas Project.
      Albuquerque: University of New Mexico Press.

Vogt, Evon Z., and Ethel M. Albert, eds.
   1967 People of Rimrock: A Study of Values in Five Cultures. Cambridge, MA:
      Harvard University Press.

Wallace, A.F.C.
   1965 Driving to Work. *In* Context and Meaning in Cultural Anthropology.
      Melford Spiro, ed. Pp. 277–292. New York: Free Press
   1972 A Day at the Office. *In* Crossing Cultural Boundaries. Solon T. Kimball and
      James B. Watson, eds. Pp. 193–203. San Francisco, CA: Chandler.

Wallace, James M. Tim
   1996 Taking It to the Public: Collaborative Extension Research. Practicing
      Anthropology 18(4):37–39.

Warner, Mildred Hall
   1988 W. Lloyd Warner. New York: Publishing Center for Cultural Resources.

Warner, W. Lloyd
   1937 A Black Civilization: A Social Study of an Australian Tribe. New York:
      Harper and Row.
   1953 American Life: Dream and Reality. Chicago: University of Chicago Press.
   1959 The Living and the Dead: A Study of the Symbolic Life of Americans. New
      Haven, CT: Yale University Press.

Warner, W. Lloyd, series ed.
   1945 The Yankee City Series. 6 Vols. New Haven, CT: Yale University Press.

Watson, Lawrence C., and Maria-Barbara Watson-Franke
   1985 Interpreting Life Histories: An Anthropological Inquiry. New Brunswick,
      NJ: Rutgers University Press.

Wax, Murray L.
1956 The Limitations of Boas's Method in Anthropology. American Anthropologist 58:63–74.

Wax, Rosalie H.
1971 Doing Fieldwork: Warnings and Advice. Chicago: University of Chicago Press.

Weisner, Thomas S.
1996 Why Ethnography Should Be the Most Important Method in the Study of Human Development. *In* Ethnography and Human Development. Richard Jessor, Anne Colby, and Richard A. Shweder, eds. Pp. 305–324. Chicago: University of Chicago Press.

Weller, Susan C., and A. K. Romney
1988 Systematic Data Collection. Newbury Park, CA: Sage.

Wenger, Etienne
1998 Communities of Practice: Learning, Meaning, and Identity. New York: Cambridge University Press.

Werner, Oswald
1998 Short Take 24: Do We Need Standards for Ethnography? Cultural Anthropology Methods Journal 10(1):1–3.

Werner, Oswald, and G. Mark Schoepfle
1987a Systematic Fieldwork. Vol. 1, Foundations of Ethnography and Interviewing. Newbury Park, CA: Sage.
1987b Systematic Fieldwork. Vol. 2, Ethnographic Analysis and Data Management. Newbury Park, CA: Sage.

West, James [pseud. for Carl Withers]
1945 Plainville, U.S.A. New York: Columbia University Press.

Whiting, Beatrice B.
1984 An Alternative Strategy for Studying the Transmission of Culture. Anthropology and Education Quarterly 15(4):334–337.

Whiting, John W. M., and Beatrice B. Whiting
1975 Children of Six Cultures: A Psycho-Cultural Analysis. Cambridge, MA: Harvard University Press.

Wilk, Stan
1977 Castaneda: Coming of Age in Sonora. *Essay review of* Carlos Castaneda's Tales of Power. American Anthropologist 79:84–91.

Wilson, Carter
1966 Crazy February. New York: J. B. Lippincott. [A subtitle, Death and Life in the Mayan Highlands of Mexico, was added in 1974 when the book was reissued by the University of California Press with a new introduction.]
1969 On Firm Ice. New York: Crowell.

1972 A Green Tree and a Dry Tree: A Novel of Chiapas. New York: Macmillan. [Reissued 1995 by the University of New Mexico Press.]

1981 Treasures on Earth: A Novel. New York: Alfred A. Knopf.

Wolcott, Harry F.

1967 A Kwakiutl Village and School. New York: Holt, Rinehart and Winston. [Reissued with a new Afterword in 1989 by Waveland Press.]

1973 The Man in the Principal's Office: An Ethnography. New York: Holt, Rinehart and Winston. [Reissued with a new Preface in 1984 by Waveland Press.]

1974a The African Beer Gardens of Bulawayo: Integrated Drinking in a Segregated Society. New Brunswick, NJ: Rutgers Center of Alcohol Studies. Monograph Number 10.

1974b The Elementary School Principal: Notes from a Field Study. *In* Education and Cultural Process: Toward an Anthropology of Education. George Spindler, ed. Pp. 176–204. New York: Holt, Rinehart and Winston.

1975a Criteria for an Ethnographic Approach to Research in Schools. Human Organization 34(2):111–127.

1975b Feedback Influences on Fieldwork, Or: A Funny Thing Happened on the Way to the Beer Garden. *In* Urban Man in Southern Africa. Clive Kileff and Wade Pendelton, eds. Pp. 99–125. Gwelo, Rhodesia: Mambo Press.

1977 Teachers Versus Technocrats: An Educational Innovation in Anthropological Perspective. Eugene, OR: Center for Educational Policy and Management, University of Oregon.

1981a Confessions of a "Trained" Observer. *In* The Study of Schooling: Field Based Methodologies in Educational Research and Evaluation. Thomas S. Popkewitz and B. Robert Tabachnick, eds. Pp. 247–263. New York: Praeger. [Revised and reprinted 1994 in Transforming Qualitative Data. HFW, ed. Pp. 149–172. Thousand Oaks, CA.]

1981b Home and Away: Personal Contrasts in Ethnographic Style. *In* Anthropologists at Home in North America: Methods and Issues in the Study of One's Own Society. Donald A. Messerschmidt, ed. Pp. 255–265. New York: Cambridge University Press.

1982a A View of Viewers: Observations on the Response to and Classroom Use of *ThinkAbout*. Research on the Introduction, Use, and Impact of the *ThinkAbout* Instructional Television Series, Volume IV. Bloomington, IN: Agency for Instructional Television.

1982b Differing Styles of On-Site Research, Or, "If It Isn't Ethnography, What Is It?" Review Journal of Philosophy and Social Sciences 7(1,2):154–169.

1982c Mirrors, Models, and Monitors: Educator Adaptations of the Ethnographic Innovation. *In* Doing the Ethnography of Schooling. George D. Spindler, ed. Pp. 68–95. New York: Holt, Rinehart and Winston.

1983a Adequate Schools and Inadequate Education: The Life Story of a Sneaky Kid. Anthropology and Education Quarterly 14:3–32. [Also reprinted in HFW 1994.]

1983b A Malay Village That Progress Chose: Sungai Lui and the Institute of Cultural Affairs. Human Organization 42(1):72–81.

1984 Ethnographers sans Ethnography. *In* Ethnography and Educational Evaluation. David M. Fetterman, ed. Pp. 177–210. Beverly Hills, CA: Sage.

1987a Life's Not Working: Cultural Alternatives to Career Alternatives. *In* Schooling in Social Context: Qualitative Studies. G. W. Noblit and W. T. Pink, eds. Pp. 303–325. Norwood, NJ: Ablex. [Also reprinted in HFW 1994.]

1987b On Ethnographic Intent. *In* Interpretive Ethnography of Education: At Home and Abroad. George and Louise Spindler, eds. Pp. 37–57. Hillsdale, NJ: Lawrence Erlbaum Associates.

1988 Ethnographic Research in Education. *In* Complementary Methods for Research in Education. Richard M. Jaeger, ed. Pp. 185–249. Washington, DC: American Educational Research Association. [Also revised and updated for the second edition, 1997.]

1989 Afterword, 1989: A Kwakiutl Village and School, 25 Years Later. [Postscript added to 1st edition of A Kwakiutl Village and School. Prospect Heights, IL: Waveland Press.]

1990a Making a Study More Ethnographic. Journal of Contemporary Ethnography 19(1):44–72.

1990b On Seeking—and Rejecting—Validity in Qualitative Research. *In* Qualitative Inquiry in Education: The Continuing Debate. Elliot W. Eisner and Alan Peshkin, eds. Pp. 121–152. New York: Teachers College. [Also reprinted in HFW 1994.]

1990c Writing Up Qualitative Research. Newbury Park, CA: Sage.

1992–1993 The Right Stuff: Reflections on Qualitative Inquiry in Thailand. Thai Association of Qualitative Researchers Newsletter 5:11–24; 6:35–44.

1994 Transforming Qualitative Data: Description, Analysis, and Interpretation. Thousand Oaks, CA: Sage.

1995 The Art of Fieldwork. Walnut Creek, CA: AltaMira Press.

1996 Peripheral Participation and the Kwakiutl Potlatch. Anthropology and Education Quarterly 27(4):467–492.

Wolf, Eric
1964 Anthropology. Englewood Cliffs, NJ: Prentice-Hall.

Wuthnow, Robert, James D. Hunter, Albert Bergesen, and Edith Kurzweil
1984 Cultural Analysis: The Work of Peter L. Berger, Mary Douglas, Michel Foucault, and Jürgen Habermas. London: Routledge and Kegan Paul.

Young, David E., and Jean-Guy Goulet, eds.
1994 Being Changed: The Anthropology of Extraordinary Experience. Peterborough, Ontario: Broadview Press.

Name Index

Agar, Michael H., 15, 57, 63, 68, 73, 74, 79, 90, 178, 179, 240, 256, 282
Albert, Ethel M., 72
Allen, Mitch, 241
Anderson, Barbara G., 175
Angrosino, Michael V., 192
Appaduri, Arjun, 260
Ashton, Hugh, 23, 285
Atkinson, Paul, 63, 99, 194, 263

Bandelier, Adolf F., 189–190
Barth, Fredrik, 27
Bascom, William, 27
Batchelder, W. H., 100, 218
Bateson, Gregory, 133, 134, 138, 155, 214, 255
Beals, Ralph L., 188
Becker, Howard, 100, 239
Beebe, James, 205, 206, 212, 218
Behar, Ruth, 176
Bell, Henry A., 26, 37, 157
Bell, Wendell, 184
Benedict, Ruth, 55, 93, 147, 256
Bensman, Joseph, 36
Berger, John, 65
Bernard, H. Russell, 15, 42, 63, 106, 129, 130, 148–154, 158, 159, 168, 210, 218, 239, 270, 273–274
Bizarro, Ignacio, 164

Boas, Franz, 10, 24, 25, 54, 85, 110, 144, 146–149, 152, 153, 158, 168, 175
Bochner, Arthur P., 192, 194
Bock, Philip, 121, 122
Bohannan, Laura (pseud. Bowen), 119, 190
Bohannan, Paul J., 119, 123, 124, 131, 141, 249
Boster, James S., 63, 100, 218
Bourgois, Philippe, 109, 111, 288
Bowen, Elenore Smith (See Bohannan, Laura)
Bradtmiller, Bruce, 218
Brettell, Caroline B., 89, 111, 112, 130
Brightman, Robert, 252
Britzman, Deborah P., 182–183
Brumble, H. David, III, 161
Bruner, Edward M., 176, 218
Buck, P. H., 119
Burgess, Anthony, 191
Burke, Kenneth, 70

Cassagrande, Joseph B., 156
Castaneda, Carlos, 186–189, 195
Cavan, Sheri, 37
Cerroni-Long, E. L., 171–172, 173
Chadney, James G., 289
Chambers, Robert, 204, 205, 212
Chapple, Eliot D., 195
Clifford, James, 14, 76, 169, 173, 194

Salinas Pedraza, Jesús, 149–153, 156, 158, 168, 239
Sands, Kathleen, 159
Sandstrom, Kent L., 64
Sanjek, Roger, 15, 25, 28
Santayana, George, 87
Sapir, Edward, 157
Savage, Bill, 127
Savala, Refugio, 159
Schapera, Isaac, 27
Schensul, Jean J., 130
Schlereth, Thomas J., 119
Schneider, David M., 128, 131
Schoepfle, G. Mark, 218
Schwartzman, Helen B., 171
Schwimmer, Brian, 270
Scrimshaw, Susan, 203
Seidel, John, 267–268
Seidman, I. E., 64
Sewid, James, 37, 157
Sewid-Smith, Daisy, 277
Sexton, James D., 164
Shokeid, Moshe, 271
Shore, Bradd, 132
Shostak, Marjorie, 133, 160
Shulman, Martha Rose, 251
Shweder, Richard A., 75, 191, 274
Sidky, H., 31
Siegel, Bernard, 94
Simonds, Ann, 40, 57
Smith, Sheldon, 124
Smith, Sidonie, 171
Spindler, George, 21, 36, 53, 82, 100, 113, 119
Spindler, Louise, 21, 53, 100
Spiro, Melford E., 53
Spradley, James P., 34–38, 40, 64, 130, 157, 163
Stewart, Alex, 126, 167, 194

Stocking, George W., Jr., 11, 128, 131, 263
Stull, Donald, 72

Taso (See also Mintz, Sidney), 157
Tax, Sol, 218
Tedlock, Barbara, 45, 63, 72, 190, 194, 195, 240
Textor, Robert, 183–185
Thomas, Jim, 181–183
Thomas, W. I., 59
Tilley, Christopher, 190
Tuhami (See also Crapanzano, Vincent), 154
Tukey, John, 167
Turnbull, Colin M., 143
Turner, Edith, 176
Turner, Victor, 176
Two Leggings (See also Nabokov, Peter), 133, 159
Tylor, Edward B., 127

Uchendu, Victor, 155

Van Maanen, John, 170, 266
van Willigen, John, 205, 206, 208, 217, 218
Vidich, Arthur, 36
Visweswaran, Kamala, 182
Vogt, Evon Z., 72
Vonnegut, Kurt, 189, 195

Wallace, A. F. C., 171, 173
Wallace, James M. Tim, 273
Warner, Mildred Hall, 19
Warner, W. Lloyd, 19, 26, 36, 59
Watson, Julia, 171
Watson, Lawrence C., 168
Watson-Franke, Maria-Barbara, 168
Wax, Murray, 146

Subject Index

acquisition of culture. *See* cultural acquisition

advocacy, 178, 183

American Anthropologist, 9, 10, 117, 153, 189, 192

analogies
in ethnography, 88, 194, 244–245
in this text: to designing a house, 101–127; to hunting, 90–91; to making bread, 244–251, 255, 262; to moieties, 225, 286; to N-P-K formula, 51; to ripples on a pond, 16, 132, 169, 194n

analysis of data, 50–51, 81, 215, 255–263

annual cycle of activities, 84–85, 116, 256

anthropological life history, 146–154, 159–167, 168n, 184, 287

anthropology
cultural. *See* cultural anthropology
and education, 20, 39, 82, 83, 225, 229
of experience, 174–178, 193–194, 284
social. *See* social anthropology
status of, 271–276
subfields, 221, 272, 273

anthropometry, 216, 218n

anticipatory anthropology. *See* ethnographic futures research

applied anthropology, 180, 185, 195n, 202, 209, 211, 216, 218n, 221, 272–273

archival research, 46–47, 58–61, 211, 214, 218n

Art of Fieldwork, 47, 100n, 283

autobiography, 149, 159, 172, 175, 194

autoethnography, 170–174

backyard ethnography, 92, 171

belief, cultural. *See* cultural beliefs

bias, 61, 175

Brad trilogy, 92, 102, 162, 287

British social anthropology. *See* social anthropology

change, directed change, 100n, 180–181, 217, 235–236, 238, 285–286

Chicago School sociology, 26, 40n

collaborative research, 51, 90, 146–159, 204

community of practice, 224, 262, 275, 278, 281
finding one's "way in" to, 224, 240n

comparative method/study, 82–88, 132–135, 193, 244–245, 259, 280

Acknowledgments

In *Writing for Social Scientists,* Howard S. Becker reminds us that the only version of a manuscript that matters is the last one (1986:12). Thank goodness! When I started this project I felt I had plenty to say about ethnography. I had no idea how much I have yet to learn. Part of that discovery came about as a result of searching published materials, and I must note my indebtedness for the resources of the University of Oregon Library and the incredible institution in Portland called Powell's City of Books.

The most critical contribution, literally as well as figuratively, came from colleagues invited to read parts or all of the manuscript. Those who read the entire manuscript at some stage in its development were John W. Creswell, Kathleen M. DeWalt, David C. Eisler, Rachel Fudge, Letty C. Lincoln, Geoff E. Mills, Thomas H. Schram, and Philip D. Young. Several people mentioned in the text read or advised on specific topics or sections, with particular help in that regard from Norman Delue and Ronald P. Rohner. Three reviewers, Mitch Allen, Terri L. McCarty, and Mark Wohl, were patient enough to read and critique the entire manuscript twice, and I am especially grateful to them.

Collectively my reviewers came up with suggestions about parts to cut (though with little agreement as to which ones) and parts that needed more development (though with little agreement on that, either). No one agreed with everything I had to say, although they all seemed to agree that I seemed to be trying to say everything. This final version has benefited greatly by their careful review. They also spared me some incredible gaffes and prompted some rewriting to emphasize differences that did not need to reach the level of disagreement. My thanks to all. Special appreciation to Phil Young, who has cast his keen reader's eyes over all my more anthropologically oriented writing for the past 25 years. Of course I knew that the Inuit didn't build igloos with blocks of *ice,* Phil. I just put that in to try to catch you!

About the Author/About the Book

Harry F. Wolcott is professor emeritus in the Department of Anthropology at the University of Oregon. He has been at the university since completing a Ph.D. at Stanford in 1964 and has served on the faculties of the College of Education and the Department of Anthropology. His long tenure afforded opportunities for sponsored research, for working with students and faculty from several disciplines, for sabbatical leaves overseas, and for brief teaching assignments at other institutions. His research studies illustrate how place and serendipity play important roles in the way ethnographic opportunities present themselves. In addition to monographs reporting ethnographic research, he has written extensively on topics in qualitative inquiry, culminating in three recent books each devoted to a particular aspect of it: *The Art of Fieldwork,* on the topic of data gathering; *Transforming Qualitative Data,* discussing ways to organize and analyze that information, and *Writing Up Qualitative Research* to insure that what gets studied also gets reported.

In *Ethnography: A Way of Seeing,* the author takes a different tack from his previous writing. Here the focus is exclusively on ethnography, from its disciplinary origins to some of its adaptations as interest has grown beyond studies once associated only with anthropology and sociology. Although the book may be of interest to experienced ethnographers, who no doubt have anecdotes and advice of their own to pass along, it is intended primarily for those unfamiliar with ethnography or familiar (through prior reading) but not yet experienced in it. That audience now includes not only students in anthropology but researchers in many professional fields who want to understand what is distinctive about ethnography and what it means to conduct an inquiry in the ethnographic tradition. Fieldwork techniques are part of it. Ethnography is more than fieldwork techniques, however, and much of the book is devoted to tracking down its other, more elusive qualities. The critique of ethnography is left for others; here an enthusiastic proponent lays out some of the ways ethnographers go about their work. Whether you intend to join in that effort or merely want a better grasp of what ethnographers are up to, this book should help you understand their special way of seeing.

FAWLTY

the complete

TOWERS